To my mother, whose love of music set the stage
for what was to come

To my father, who inspired me with his hard work
and devotion to his loved ones

To Jacquelyne, who with love has brought
us together as family

And to Maharishi, for giving me the tools to develop
the inner strength that is the basis of all success in life.

GOOD VIBRATIONS

MY LIFE AS A BEACH BOY

MIKE LOVE

WITH JAMES S. HIRSCH

First published in the UK in 2016 by
Faber & Faber Limited
Bloomsbury House, 74–77 Great Russell Street
London WC1B 3DA

This paperback edition published in 2017

Published by arrangement with Blue Rider Press, an imprint
of The Penguin Publishing Group, a division of
Penguin Random House, LLC

Printed and bound in the UK by CPI Group (UK) Ltd, Croydon, CR0 4YY

A CIP record for this book
is available from the British Library

ISBN 978-0-571-32469-9

FSC
www.fsc.org
MIX
Paper from
responsible sources
FSC® C020471

2 4 6 8 10 9 7 5 3 1

CONTENTS

CHAPTER 1

CALIFORNIA IS
THE ULTIMATE

Growing up in Southern California, I loved watching the sun descend across the calm waters of the Pacific. I infused its disappearance with something cosmic and mystical. Darkness fell. The earth spun. And then dawn broke, bringing light and renewal to all.

I've tried to maintain that attitude in all aspects of life—to recall the warmth of the sun even on the coldest of nights. My approach toward music bore that out. As a member of the Beach Boys, I was the one most apt to find the positives, the silver lining, even in moments of despair. My parents were responsible for that. They gave me every reason to be hopeful.

My mom's side of the family came from the dry prairies of Kansas, while my dad's forebears arrived from the cotton fields of Louisiana. All my ancestors, poor and desperate, were lured westward by the promise of a better life: flowers in bloom, lush farmland, green mountains, clean beaches, warm sunshine, jobs in oil, agriculture, and construction—Southern California in the first quarter of the twentieth century. This image rightfully endured for the next fifty years, hallowed in *The Grapes of Wrath*, memorialized on film, promoted on radio and in popular music. That image lingers to this day. Southern California was and still is a land where the American dream can become a reality. Yes, those words are a cliché, and it's easy to ridicule the "California myth": from the Spanish settlers to the gold hunters to the Okies, all migrating to what was once known as the mañana country, the country of tomorrow. But to me it wasn't a myth—I saw how much could be achieved in one generation. The big house. The fancy cars. The nice vacations. All of it, plus newfound respect.

Make no mistake, I wasn't raised at Disneyland. I also saw hard times and understood how ephemeral, how random, success could be, and those experiences shaped my life as well. I knew that the streets of California were not paved with gold, but I've gone through my life believing that if you had the imagination, the ability, and the work ethic, you might find the beaches sprinkled with some gold dust.

It was a fine omen that my mother's first residence in California was a beach.

Born in Hutchinson, Kansas, in 1919, Emily Wilson was named after her mother's favorite sister. But as the story goes, on the night she was born, her mother attended an opera featuring Glee Starr, so she gave her newborn the middle name Glee. That story must have been true, as it prefigured her lifelong devotion to the opera, and Glee became the name by which she was known.

My mom's father, Coral "Buddy" Wilson, was a plumber, volatile and restless, who traveled far beyond his Kansas roots seeking work at Army camps in the Southwest while also visiting California in search of his own fortune. My mom's mother, Edith, was Swedish (I take pride in knowing that I come from a long line of Swedish pacifists). She was born on a farm and had to quit school to help her family plant potatoes. Marriage didn't rescue her from poverty, however. With her husband often gone, Edith was left in Hutchinson to take care of her young family, and Glee, her fourth child, and her older brother, Murry, were briefly sent to live with their second cousins. Then in 1924, Buddy sent Edith a telegram, $200, and instructions to take a train to California. Glee was too young to remember the trip, but her mom later told her how kind the other passengers were—they pitied her, traveling with five children, and they would bring food for all of them. The Wilsons settled in an oceanside hamlet called Cardiff-by-the-Sea, but unable to find a landlord who would rent them a room, they pitched a tent on a windswept beach and lived there for nine weeks. That sounds harsh, but the complete novelty of the ocean provided its own variety of excitement. The family finally rented an apartment in Pasadena and eventually a small house in Inglewood, southwest of downtown Los Angeles.

Buddy and Edith had nine children, though one died in infancy. Buddy eked out a living working in the Huntington Beach oil fields and later as a freelance plumber. Suffering chronic allergies and sinus problems, he sought relief by traveling to the desert, which further isolated him from his family. (When I was a boy, my grandfather joined us for dinner and used an empty Campbell's soup can as a spittoon.) His temper often got the better of him, as did the alcohol. He never did strike it rich in California and, betrayed by his own illusions, became abusive, lashing out at his wife but saving his severest whippings for his four sons. One of them, Charles, was once beaten so relentlessly that his older brother, Murry, had to yank Buddy off the boy and temporarily lock the enraged patriarch outside his own house. Murry frequently came to blows with his father, at times to protect his siblings. But Murry also inherited his father's paranoid, combustible wrath, which he carried into the parenting of his own three sons: Brian, Dennis, and Carl. My mom despised her father for his savage treatment of his own family and his derelictions as provider and protector, and her childhood left her with feelings of insecurity, anxiety, and even abandonment. She battled these fears for the rest of her life. She did, however, have a sturdy role model in her own mother. In addition to raising eight children, Edith brought in extra income by taking in washing and eventually worked as a presser for a garment manufacturer. She lived with us when I was in junior high school, a heavyset woman who was tender but tough and baked killer cinnamon rolls and butterscotch pies. After she was diagnosed with breast cancer, she prepared for surgery by taking long swims every morning in the Pacific, the same body of water that served as the adventuresome gateway for her homeless young family upon reaching California. After her mastectomy, she showed me the gruesome scar as a badge of survival.

Don't complain, was her message. Life on the frontier has always been tough.

I don't recall ever seeing my maternal grandparents together. I just assumed that at some point, my grandfather left and never returned. When Grandma Wilson died in 1963, my mother blamed my grandfather for driving her to an early grave, and my mom wanted no part of him either. Edith Wilson had indeed died young—she was sixty-six—but her legacy was significant. She had dreams of her own of being a concert pianist. Though that never happened, she passed her appreciation of the arts to her children, including my mom. Edith sang to little Glee in the kitchen while preparing meals, and Glee would fall asleep listening to her mom play the piano while her aunts and uncles harmonized.

Glee Wilson had many talents. Lean and athletic, she danced ballet and tap, and she was a star pitcher on her Washington High School softball team. She could walk upstairs on her hands, a skill she learned from an eccentric uncle. She later took up tennis and water-skiing as well as golf; her instructors encouraged her to go pro, but she opted for music, her greatest love. She sang alto in a high school chorus and was part of a trio that sang *Madama Butterfly* and performed on KFWB in Los Angeles; she was always proud that a high school teacher gave up her lunch hour to coach them. My mom had the ability as well as the desire to pursue a singing career, but she was also bound by the conventions of her time. In high school, she met the man of her dreams, a rawboned football player of English Scottish lineage, and her life took a more traditional path.

My father's side of the family also looked to California as their Eden. My paternal grandfather, Edward Felton Love, born in 1894, grew up in Plain Dealing, Louisiana, a speck of a town between Shreveport and the Arkansas border that once served as a trading post for antebellum cotton plantations. After the Civil War, our family sawmill provided the lumber to rebuild what had been destroyed by the Union Army. The Reconstruction Era—and the liberation of the slaves—did not come easily to these parts. The sawmill provided the wooden planks for the building that hosted the Knights of the White Camellia, a white supremacist group.

Edward's mom died when he was a baby, and not much is known about his childhood, except the poverty. He often didn't have shoes, forcing him to drag the logs to the mill barefoot. He moved to Los Angeles in 1909 and found work at a sheet metal shop. Though he had only a fifth-grade education, he soon started his own business, Love Sheet Metal Company, which initially served restaurants but expanded to Army camps and recruitment centers in need of large-scale kitchen facilities and custom appliances. In 1916, Edward married a neighbor, seventeen-year-old Edith Clardy (she was born on an orange ranch), and their son, Milton, was born the following year. They lived in a new house so remote that Milt was awakened on Sunday mornings by rifle shots of locals hunting rabbits.

While the Great Depression ravaged many businesses, Love Sheet Metal survived on its government contracts with the Army and with public universities, and this gave Milt a stable childhood. He tooled around town in a Ford Model A, hanging out at Chili Bowl outlets while earning extra money picking beans in fields that would become the runways of Los Angeles International Airport. He also discovered the virtues of government work with the Civilian Conservation Corps in a fire-suppression crew near Pasadena.

Milt found love early at Washington High School in the slim figure of Glee Wilson, who at fifteen was two years his junior. They were a striking couple—he six-foot-three, red hair, princely and athletic; she five-foot-seven, blond hair and high cheekbones, a Nordic beauty. They dated for four years, often dancing to Benny Goodman at the Palomar Ballroom, and in 1938 they wanted to marry. But the families were opposed—the first of many rifts between the Loves and the Wilsons—and their poverty complicated matters. Even a small wedding would have been a financial stretch. Glee's parents couldn't afford a traditional dress, though my mom later noted, pointedly, that she was entitled to wear white. So the couple eloped, a move both daring and romantic, my mom's only regret being that she always wondered what she would have looked like in a wedding gown.

The timing of the marriage could not have been better, as Love Sheet Metal—for which Milt as well as his brother Stan now worked, with their father still in charge—was about to take off.

During World War II, the company manufactured galley equipment for Navy ships while experiencing greater demand for their kitchen hardware. In the mid-1940s, my grandfather moved the company south of downtown Los Angeles to 3301 East Fourteenth Street, employed more than a hundred skilled laborers, and added a paint and wood shop. Even after the war ended, demand for the company's products was strong as California became the destination for growing numbers of Americans. Between 1940 and 1960, the state's population surged by 128 percent, to 15.7 million people. I don't recall anyone talking about smog in my youth. It was a time when new highways connected pristine subdivisions, mass production created millionaires, and a building boom of schools, hospitals, and restaurants as well as homes rippled across the Los Angeles region. Love Sheet Metal could barely keep up: a massive kitchen for the UCLA

Medical Center, custom laboratory tables for junior colleges, impeccable sinks for tony restaurants in Hollywood.

All of a sudden, after so many bleak years, the Loves were rich. It was almost too much to fathom, but it affirmed Grandpa Love's faith in his decision to come to this state of vineyards, citrus, and endless shorelines. As he used to tell me, "California is the ultimate."

After my parents married, they bought a two-bedroom home in Inglewood for $7,500. (They borrowed $1,000 from my grandfather, who later waived the debt.) I was their first child, born March 15, 1941, with my sister Maureen born two years later—our mom subsequently noted that she was in her "Irish phase," giving her first two children *M* names. Stephen was born four years later. Our house was too small, so with cash on hand, my parents looked for a residence befitting their new station in life.

They visited no fewer than thirty homes until they found one in Baldwin Hills in West Los Angeles. The hills themselves are a low mountain range with active oil wells and a grand Spanish heritage. One neighborhood of winding roads is called the *Dons*, with such street names as Don Luis and Don Felipe, and I attended Dorsey High School, whose teams were known as the Dons.

In slick promotional brochures or glossy travel magazines, the California dream was often expressed through the glory of one's home, and my parents found a residence that qualified. It was on the corner of Mount Vernon and Fairway, purchased in 1948 for $40,000. With doctors and dentists up and down the streets, the neighborhood was nicknamed "Pill Hill," but I don't think any of the other houses had quite the history, or worldly touches, as ours. It was built by a USC professor and his wealthy wife who wanted accoutrements from around the globe. So off they went on a three-month journey, sending back dark red tile from Italy, a stained glass window from

Jerusalem, and magnificent stones from God knows where for five different fireplaces. The house had three floors, fourteen rooms, five bathrooms, and amenities of all kinds. The plush red carpet caressed your feet. The chandelier cast a soft glow over the living room. The swimming pool beckoned. We had a winding staircase, a subterranean garage, and a rear sun deck, from which I would watch the Fourth of July fireworks set off from the Los Angeles Coliseum or get a clear view of the snow-covered San Gabriel Mountains. My parents never took it for granted—a graceful, Mediterranean-style palace that reflected the aspirations of an entire region.

We needed every square inch of the house because our family continued to grow. After Stephen came Stanley and then Stephanie—my mom was now in her sibilant phase, with Stephanie having the added benefit, according to my mom, of sounding kind of French. Portraits of all the kids soon hung along the staircase. With our blond or reddish hair, blue eyes, and rangy frames, we fit right in as homegrown California WASPs. My dad, the stoic provider, woke up at five each morning and frequently worked the weekends making boat trailers. I made the connection between his sacrifices and our current bounty. Love Sheet Metal was so strong that each year my grandfather bought two Cadillacs, with their wraparound windshields and wire wheels, and he gave one to my dad and one to my uncle. For a while in the 1950s, we drove a different luxury car every year.

Much to our embarrassment, my mom dressed us in identical denim clothes or matching sailor outfits, including the captain hats, and she took us to Fosters Freeze (whose mascot was an ice cream cone wearing a chef's hat) or, for special occasions, Joe Petrelli's Famous Steakhouse (sirloins $3.65). Parts of my childhood came right out of a 1950s tableau. One Sunday afternoon, my parents took us to Clyde's Corner, a hamburger place in Inglewood, and we saw Pat Boone, who was already a singing star and who—to my mom's delight—stopped to talk to us. He and his wife, he told us, had just come back from church.

My parents bought a trailer that slept seven and had a shower, and we once drove north to Banff National Park in Canada and stayed at Chateau Lake Louise. We'd eat dinner in an elegant dining room and then go to another room for a recital given by a soloist or ensemble. The kids preferred the room service, chocolate malts for all. Our parents also wanted us to appreciate nature's beauty—the powder-blue color of the lake, the Oregon coast on a cold, overcast day. Those impressions indeed stayed with me. We also made frequent trips to Estero Beach, south of the Mexican border, and spent long weekends wading into the clear surf, catching dorado and yellowtail and preparing them ourselves. One time on the beach, a young *soldado* with his guitar came along on his horse and sang for a few cigarettes. He had a beautiful voice, sounding very much like the Mexican-American baritone Andy Russell, whose bilingual style had become all the rage. I was interested in the cute Mexican girls but also in the different language and culture, an early sign of my fascination with ethnicity of any kind. When a shabbily dressed Mexican trio with guitars sang for tips in a restaurant, I added an extra part to their harmonies.

I was closer to my paternal grandparents than to my own mom and dad, and I often stayed at their home in nearby Arcadia. Grandma Love was classy, educated, and keenly interested in astrology, an interest that she passed on to me. Grandpa Love was the taciturn patriarch whose tough, powerful hands testified to a lifetime of hauling logs and bending metal. His great passion was gambling. Each day at lunchtime at Love Sheet Metal, he converted a worktable for craps. He also had a gambling room in his own home—with roulette, craps, poker, even a slot machine—and he taught me to be a croupier.

I've always been competitive, a reflection of the home in which I was raised. My siblings and I often battled one another, never in a mean-spirited way, though one time my mom started to call the police to break up a fight between Stephen and Stan. (They stopped as soon as they heard her voice on the phone.) We were all athletes, including my sisters. Maureen excelled at tetherball, Ping-Pong, and tennis, while Stephanie—perhaps the most combative in the group—broke her leg sliding into second base. Stephanie also had a beautiful soprano, which reminded my mom of her own mother's voice. Stephen was a football star in high school but was also the most academically driven, his sharp mind evident early on. When he was four years old, I taught him the different car models, and he would sit on our front stoop and yell them out as each car drove by: "Chevy!" "Cadillac!" "Dodge!"

We loved pulling pranks on one another, particularly the brothers. Stan, for example, was two years younger than Stephen, but his height, even at a young age, made him stand out. When he was five years old, Stephen and I told Stan that he was tall because he was adopted, and he believed us. (We tried to enlist Maureen in our scheme, but she wasn't devious enough.) Stan ran out onto the front steps and started crying. Stephen and I followed.

"Don't worry, Stan," Stephen said. "I'll help you look for your parents."

"No way," I said. "They're long gone by now."

My mom later recalled that we convinced Stan of his adopted state for two years. I don't believe it was that long, but I don't think Stan ever forgave us.

Regardless, Stan grew to be six-foot-eight and put his height to good use, starring in basketball at the University of Oregon and then playing in the NBA.

My mom encouraged all of us to play sports, but she believed her primary parental mission was to instill the arts into all of her children, my dad her partner in this task. They required my siblings and me to take lessons in music and oil painting; and Maureen, who felt the greatest connection to her faith, painted a large portrait of Jesus when she was in high school. My dad had a darkroom in the basement, took thousands of pictures, and taught us photography. Stan became his most avid protégé and took countless Beach Boy photos over the years. My dad was an artist as well. Driving into the countryside, he would set up an easel and paint barns or landscapes.

My mom liked to say, "I feel so sorry for people who don't enjoy music," and even as adults, my parents wanted to grow musically, with my dad taking cello lessons and my mom, piano. But it was my mom's passion that ran deepest. She sang in a professional chorus, which performed for church groups and women's clubs, but she savored opera the most. It had voice, drama, orchestration, and occasionally ballet. A member of the Opera Reading Club of Hollywood, she would go to the famous Grauman's Chinese Theatre on Hollywood Boulevard and hear an opera sung in English, though she much preferred to hear it at the Met in its proper Italian. Her four years of Latin in high school helped her read the librettos. My mom did housework to symphonies, concertos, and operas, which she spun on the hi-fi. To wake us in the morning, she rattled the chandelier with Enrico Caruso's rendition of "Vesti la giubba," Giuseppe Verdi's *Requiem*, Maria Callas, and the Mozart *Requiem Mass* sung by the Roger Wagner Chorale.

One day, a neighbor walked up the hill to our house and said a dying woman a block away could hear the music and asked if my mom would turn it down. My mom thought that was the perfect way to go.

I was ten years old when my mother used the house for her first musical, inviting over about a hundred people for a sing-along. Nowadays, inviting such a number is no big deal, with email and evites, but back then it required calling each person on the phone, and my mom allocated three weeks to the task. She bought sheet music for the participants, who were grouped by tenors, sopranos, altos, and basses, and the woman who led their high school music department was recruited to conduct them. They sang "Some Enchanted Evening" and "Bali Hai" while using our Hammond organ and Steinway grand piano to play classical numbers and boogie-woogie. It was the first of many home musicals, with the kids confined to the second floor but able to hear every note. My mom also invited the ladies over for fund raisers and tea parties, in which she would tap-dance, and the attendees became part of my mom's "glee club."

Musically, it was inevitable that my siblings and I would be influenced by what we saw and heard; the only question was how.

At one recital my parents hired a harpist, which enchanted Maureen. She loved the instrument's physical beauty and its delicate, mellow tone, and her fascination deepened when she attended a harp recital. That Christmas, my parents bought her a $7,000 Lyon & Healy harp, which would be more than $61,000 today. On Maureen's first day she figured out the right hand to "Silent Night." She was nine years old. My dad carried that harp to so many of Maureen's practices and concerts that my mom joked he lost an inch in height.

As for me, I didn't really love my parents' music, but the atmosphere made a lasting impression. I had a very clear idea that the music was not just about the music. It was about entertainment. It was about bringing together friends to sing and to laugh and to set aside the problems of the outside world.

The first number I ever sang was "That Old Black Magic," when I was two years old. According to my mom, she taught it to me while I was being potty trained, which was an odd bit of multitasking, but I can't argue with any of the results. I apparently sang this Glenn Miller standard, with considerable aplomb, for adults who stopped by the house. In time, I also played some clarinet and sang in a glee club, but my most important music lessons came from nature.

I went to 54th Street Elementary School, and on my way home I walked along a small wooded ravine, where chickens roamed, and I flustered them by crowing like a rooster. I listened to the birds—mockingbirds, starlings, redwing blackbirds—and tried to mimic their song. The melodious whistles and harsh rasps. The warbling harmonies and abrupt trills. The scolding *chak chak chaks*. They were all singing to one another, just like humans, flirting and preening and boasting, and I tried to fit my voice right into theirs.

Environmentalism, I think, was just part of the community. I attended Audubon Junior High School, which included a field trip to the Audubon Society. A grade school teacher had a stack of *National Geographic* magazines, which I devoured for stories about the wildlife, the oceans, the planet. Another teacher wrote a book called *Gifts of the Forest*, which she shared with us. Insects intrigued me, none more than the monarch butterfly. With its black-and-gold wings that resembled stained glass windows, it is considered the most beautiful of all butterflies, and they flew around the eucalyptus trees in our backyard. I had a good friend, Thomas Emmel, who shared my passion for this delicate creature, and we spent afternoons chasing the graceful monarchs with a net, catching them when possible, and setting them free. We read about their remarkable life cycles: how they would lay their eggs on the leaves, hatch into larvae, go into the cocoon stage, and emerge as butterflies. And then it was all over. The adult monarchs live only a few weeks, giving us a bracing lesson on the fragility of life.

My sensitivity to the rhythms of the earth never left me and would influence some of my future music, but Tom Emmel turned his interest in butterflies into a distinguished career as an educator, author, and conservationist. Our paths would cross again, much later in life, as he would reconnect me to the miracle of the monarch.

I've always been a dedicated reader and loved literature and languages. As a kid, I bought a newspaper called *Elijah Speaks*, about Elijah Muhammad, because I was curious about Black Muslims. In junior high school, my friend Craig Owens and I did a "buddy report" on Adolf Hitler, which required us to read *Mein Kampf* as well as other books on the Nazis. We did extensive research, and it had a major impact on me. It was the first time I had ever thought seriously about man's inhumanity to man, and I had some sense that our conventional institutions—political, religious, social—were no match against our most violent instincts. These were troublesome and powerful thoughts in the mind of an eighth grader, but in one form or the other they would stay with me for many years to come.

We received an A+ on the project, and I knew that I was one of the best-read students in my class—my mom once received a call from my sixth-grade teacher reprimanding me for reading when I should have been doing some other assignment. I got good grades in literature, history, and social studies but didn't apply myself in science and math. I also had a rebel streak and gave some of my teachers fits. At Dorsey High School, one of my instructors spoke with an affected air, and one day when he was blathering on about his trip to the Netherlands, I helpfully suggested to my classmates that he had visited a whorehouse. The remark landed me in the vice principal's office, for neither the first nor last time.

Dorsey, in the late 1950s, retained the defined sexual roles of the era: the boys fielded most of the sports teams while the girls populated the clubs for "Welfare," "Hospitality," and "Hostess." But in a highly segregated region, state, and country, Dorsey was a racially mixed stew that I found appealing. The school had African-Americans, Jews, and Japanese, as well as Protestants and Catholics (we were Lutheran), and I enjoyed the mix of languages and cultures. To show my solidarity with my Jewish friends, I skipped school on Rosh Hashanah and

Yom Kippur. I learned to speak some Spanish, Japanese, and Yiddish. The Japanese kids taught me their alphabet and clever wordplays. For example, *ku* means nine, *ichi* means one, and *ju* is ten: *ku* + *ichi* = *ju*. So the Japanese students referred to the Jewish kids as *ku-ichi*.

By high school, I was six feet tall and had long legs, well suited for long distances, so I ran track and cross-country and was captain of the latter team, which was part of the Southern League of the Los Angeles City School System. Craig Owens would come to my house early in the morning, and we'd run five miles before school. I never had the kind of athletic talent that my brother Stan had, but when it came to a meet, I don't recall anyone on my high school cross-country team beating me.

Running track meant that I spent a lot of time with the black kids, and that had a profound musical influence. A couple of my track teammates, Paul Denkins and Frank Mayfield, sang R&B in the shower. With the backbeat of pounding water and the steam swirling above, they belted out some of the funkiest blues I'd ever heard, like Jimmy Reed's "Baby What You Want Me to Do," and "Sick and Tired" (by Dave Bartholomew, Christopher Kenner, and Fats Domino), in which the early-to-rise narrator is "sick and tired of foolin' around" with his layabout lover.

It was soul-stirring, primordial shit, something that transcended racial or ethnic groups. I loved it, and it further opened my eyes and ears to a very different world.

I grew up in a conventionally bigoted household, but bigoted nonetheless. My parents didn't want me to hang out with Catholics or Jews or Asians, let alone blacks, and my father didn't even want to see blacks on TV. I defied those edicts, not to strike a blow for social justice but because the off-limit groups were too cool to ignore. Most of the black kids had moved here from the Deep South, bringing with them their own style, vernacular, and prejudices. I learned that dark-skinned blacks were looked down upon by their lighter-skinned counterparts, and straight hair was more coveted than kinky.

But it was the language that captivated me. Even their caustic profanities had a lyrical quality. One guy would mockingly say, "I'm gonna *do you in*." Their emphasis on *do you in* found its way into the first two lines of "Help Me, Rhonda":

> *Well since she put me down*
> *I've been out doin' in my head.*

I got along with the black kids, in part because I was good at sports but also because I spoke their own windy slang and could trade verbal or actual blows. One time at lunch, several black guys started complaining rather heatedly that Elvis, Pat Boone, and Jerry Lee Lewis had become famous by playing music that wasn't really theirs.

"The white man stole the black man's music!" one guy yelled at me.

He had a point, but I wasn't about to give in.

"Hey, man," I said. "Ain't no nigger ever invented no guitar!"

They laughed. I could use that language because they knew I had some appreciation—indeed, affection—for who they were and what they were all about. Some of my teachers also recognized that I could cross these racial boundaries. In my junior year, a Filipino student was shot and killed as a bystander in a gang-related incident. Our English class was allowed to send one student to the funeral, and our teacher asked me to be its representative. In a more positive example, Dorsey High School played host to a visit by President Sukarno of Indonesia. Dorsey was chosen as a fine example of America's melting pot, and I was asked to escort the president's son around for the day. I think I've always known how to get along with different people from different backgrounds, and my parents were proud of these honors as evidence of the manners they had taught me.

Though my childhood was touched by the California ideal, I didn't live in a bubble. Mine was also a gritty, discordant youth, which shaped my life in equally important ways. I didn't have a lot of close friends or maybe just didn't let many people get close to me. I was more comfortable as a renegade, sometimes expressed through harmless sibling high jinks, but a few pranks were more serious. I liked to play with matches and once lit one of our mattresses on fire. Smoke filled the bedroom, and a fire engine was summoned. (Notwithstanding a charred mattress, no harm came to property or person.)

I took risks outside the home as well. I mixed together my own gunpowder, constructed a small cannon, and shot it in the backyard. I once took small explosive caps, wrapped them around the tracks used by streetcars, and then stepped back and watched the show as the passing cars triggered the explosives. No one got hurt, but it got people's attention. I liked to flaunt a tough-guy image, so at Dorsey I played the "penny stomp," in which the bigger kids threw coins to the ground and dared others to pick them up without getting their hands stomped. I got scuffed and bloodied but never backed down. Some kids threw down dimes to get more bodies colliding with one another, a quarter drawing even heavier blows. One rich kid would toss in a fifty-cent piece just to trigger a near riot.

To stay eligible for sports, I took summer classes at Manual Arts High School in South Los Angeles. It was a mostly black school, and visiting white students were not particularly welcome, some having been taken away in ambulances after encounters with hoodlums. They drove lowriding cars and were plain frightening. The National Guard in Arkansas had recently protected black students who integrated Central High School in Little Rock, and I was thinking, Where is my National Guard?

I hung out with some black guys from our football team who were taking classes for the same reason I was, and they provided protection. But I also kept in my pocket a stiletto and brass knuckles as well as some half-pint liquor bottles. Once in chemistry, I sold shots of tequila for a nickel, and on another day in American literature, a kid next to me pulled out his switchblade to trim his nails, and I asked him where he got it.

"Pawnshop," he said.

I pulled out the lean handle of my stiletto, pressed a button on the side, and out shot the gleaming, straight blade. I started working on my nails.

"Hey," he said, "where'd you get that?"

"Mexico."

"Okay. Cool."

One day in chemistry, a guy told me, "Best not go down to the head today."

"Why not?"

"Because there are some bad dudes there smoking pot."

I promptly asked to go to the bathroom, and when I got there, I saw the black guys in bandannas smoking joints. I went into a stall, took out three cherry bombs, lit them, and ran like hell, with the three guys hightailing right behind. I was in my seat when the bombs exploded.

"Hey, Love, what'd you do?" the guy asked me.

"Blew up the head, man."

I sent the message: Don't mess with Love. He appears to be crazy.

Well, I wasn't crazy, but I had these two different people inside me. I was the guy who loved to mimic the songbirds in a pleasant voice, and I was the guy who loved to rattle the hoods with cherry bombs. I was a peacenik and a badass. A butterfly and a switchblade.

Tensions rose at home as well. My mom was overprotective, and I bore the brunt of her insecurities. She wouldn't let me join the Boy Scouts because she feared I'd fall off a cliff, and she tried to deter me from running cross-country because she thought I'd collapse. Upon seeing me complete a race, she told my dad, "My God, he looks forty." I was seventeen. In the mid-1970s, my mom wrote an unpublished memoir, which is sprinkled with near-disaster stories—one child almost dies in a lake, another nearly falls out a window, another almost loses an eye in a baseball accident. She lived in the shadow of her own chaotic youth, with a tyrannical father and eight kids running wild, and she wanted something very different for her children.

"When I was young," she wrote, "I thought I would put all my energies into raising children who were going to be perfect. I had given up all the things I personally wanted to do and would be the *best* mother in the world."

She was forty years old when her last child, Marjorie, was born in 1960—a nineteen-year age difference between her oldest (me) and her youngest. She now had three sons and three daughters, three children whose first name began with an *S*, and three with an *M*. Marjorie was indeed a gift, a sweet, wholesome girl who also developed a passion for the harp. When she was a teenager, my two brothers and I bought her a station wagon so she could carry the instrument around. One time when Maureen couldn't perform at a wedding, she asked Marjorie to fill in for her. Because it was an outdoor wedding, overlooking the ocean, my mom feared that the strings would stretch in the dampness, but the harp emerged unscathed.

Those kinds of doubts, of premonitions, unnerved my mom, and the stress of raising six "perfect" children could overwhelm her. She sometimes got into the cooking sherry and suffered fits of depression and melodrama. "I'm dying," she would tell us. "I'm dying." She was emotive but, at least for me, not always emotionally available, and the distance between us grew with the birth of each child. Part of that distance was inevitable, as she had to tend to her growing brood, but I don't believe either of us knew how to navigate a household that had experienced so much change and disruption.

Pressures also mounted on my dad. Unknown to any of us, Love Sheet Metal began to struggle in the late 1950s, when the big contracts dwindled, the economy fell into a recession, and the fading Eisenhower administration was unable to revive it. Clients were unhappy. There were suits and countersuits. We had spent beyond our means. My dad, always grimly determined about his work, never shared the difficulties with us, but he also wanted no grief when he got home. One night he lost his temper and threw the hi-fi against the wall, making a dent. Other times he used his belt, though never to hurt us. Hell, sometimes we deserved to be smacked, and it did get our attention. He preferred sarcasm, a bonding rite among the males in the family. My father, brothers, and I sat at the dinner table and had "chop sessions," in which the goal was to use humor to mock or belittle. We thought ourselves smart and funny, and I'll always appreciate the clever insult or the stinging retort. But I now know that my mom and sisters often found our chop sessions hurtful and divisive.

Our name was Love, but the word itself, spoken between parents and children, was mostly absent in our house. Nor were my parents natural huggers. My dad viewed the open display of any emotion as a sign of weakness. He once fell down our circular staircase, tumbling to the bottom. Fearing the worst, Maureen ran over and asked him if he was okay. "Yes" was all he said. He wasn't okay, but he wouldn't acknowledge otherwise. He had to be strong for the children.

CHAPTER 2

TEENAGE GROOVE

I was closer to my cousin Brian than to my siblings. Whether it was double dating together or cruising in our cars or going to high school football games, we shared typical teenage pursuits. We loved hanging out at Scrivner's drive-in on Sunset Boulevard, which served burgers and Cokes and played a lot of R&B. At my mom's parties, when the kids weren't allowed, we hovered on the second floor with a fishing pole, dropped down a line, and reeled up steak tips. Our senior class in high school took a field trip to Catalina Island, and we were allowed to bring one friend. I took Brian.

We were pranksters at heart. His car had a broken speedometer that spun around like crazy, and we developed this whole Dean Martin and Jerry Lewis routine around it. Our personalities just blended together for a lot of laughs.

Our families, however, did not always blend so well. Brian lived on 119th Street in Hawthorne, about ten miles south of us, a short distance by car but a significant divide socially.

Hawthorne is often cited as the "home" of the Beach Boys. Founded as a land development in 1905, it was promoted as the community "Between City and Sea"—specifically, about three miles from the Los Angeles city limits and five miles inland. Regardless of location, Hawthorne was a struggling enclave that did not have elec-

tricity until 1910 and that saw nearly half of its population go on relief during the Great Depression. It was revived during the war years
when Northrop Aircraft built a plant that provided 20,000 jobs, but
it remained a flat town of tract homes without sidewalks and streets
with no trees bordering them. Perhaps its most endearing trait was
its lack of pretension. Its motto, adopted in 1961: "City of Good
Neighbors."

But Hawthorne was a step up for Uncle Murry and Aunt Audree
when in 1945 they moved there from their apartment in Inglewood.
Their second son, Dennis, had recently been born, and Brian turned
three that year; Carl was born in 1946. When my aunt and uncle
came into a bit of money in the 1950s, they remodeled the kitchen,
adding an island. That was big back then. So were the two pianos
and the jukebox. But the house itself had only two bedrooms, with
the three boys sharing one of them. The brothers had all the accesso-
ries of a typical California childhood—the bicycles, the go-carts, the
tree house—and they were close. At night after the lights went out,
they harmonized to "Ivory Tower." Other nights, Brian sat up in the
bed and tried to make Dennis and Carl laugh until their mom came
in to warn them or their dad entered to threaten them, or worse. You
did not want to mess with Uncle Murry.

He was a blunt, brusque, pipe-smoking bull of a man who was
quite the athlete in his youth—a fast quarterback at Washington
High School, a high diver who could do three and a half turns off the
board, and a graceful dancer as well. After high school, he held various administrative and industrial jobs, including one at Goodyear
Tire & Rubber. There in 1945, he was on the factory floor when an
errant pole harpooned him in his left eye, shattering his glasses and
toppling him to the ground. Twenty-five years old at the time, he
lived the rest of his life with a glass eye and an unclaimed grievance.
He later worked as a foreman for an aeronautics company and then
opened his own leasing firm, A.B.L.E. Machinery Company (Always

Better Lasting Equipment), mostly lathes and other hardware, which his sons were conscripted to clean.

But to Uncle Murry, these businesses were mere diversions from his true calling. He had a burning desire for music, but unlike my mom, who curtailed her own ambitions for her family, my uncle had no such constraints. He saw himself as a gifted songwriter who just needed that one break, so he wrote songs and had my aunt Audree copy them by hand and take them to a professional copyist, who wrote out the instrumental parts of each arrangement. My uncle then hand delivered the sheet music to a publisher.

But the breakthrough never came, and as the rejections mounted, my mom tried to help. She once rented a hall, hired three musicians, and invited 150 people for food, dance, and music—Uncle Murry's music. All her brother needed, she believed, was exposure. Helping out too were Brian and I. At age nine, I wrote my first song, about a casualty from World War II, called "The Old Soldier," and I gave it to Brian to sing at the recital. Uncle Murry apparently tinkered with it, and Brian, wearing a suit that his parents bought him with borrowed money, sang both versions. His father said he "brought down the house," and I don't doubt it. The first time I saw Brian perform, he was sitting on Grandma Wilson's lap and singing "Danny Boy." I can still see him *and* hear him: he sang like an angel.

My uncle never gave up on his dream, though in time he would have to channel it through his sons. But his personal failures worsened his baser instincts, his penchant for intimidation accompanied by a theatrical flair. One of his more ghastly tactics was removing his fake eye and forcing his boys to look at the empty socket. With kids in the neighborhood, he liked to apply the "Vulcan nerve pinch," as it later became known, until the kids were on their knees, pleading, "Mr. Wilson! Stop! Stop!" My uncle laughed. He never truly hurt anyone, but he inspired plenty of fear.

Uncle Murry was also capable of acts of kindness—giving money, for example, to a family member in need. And musically, he was devoted to his boys. But what is often missed in the Wilson family history is that my aunt Audree was the true musical talent in that marriage.

Born in Minneapolis, Audree Korthof moved to downtown Los Angeles as a child. Her father owned a bakery, but the family business didn't hold much appeal to her. She had a sweet singing voice and deft piano skills—she began at age five, and boogie-woogie was her favorite—and her world centered on music. She was also pretty, all of which made her a natural partner for Uncle Murry, whom she met at Washington High School. But unlike my raging uncle, Aunt Audree was wise and warm and eager to connect, with this habit of leaning forward, looking you in the eye, and trying to see inside you. She was no shrinking violet and could curse with the rest of the men, but she also summoned these pleasant phrases. "I love to be *enveloped* in the music," she would say. That was certainly true when she was on the piano. You could sing any song in any key, and even if my aunt hadn't heard it before, she could pick it up and accompany you all by ear. My mom, who had spent her entire life around the arts, said Aunt Audree was the finest musician she had ever known.

Many of Brian's talents can easily be traced to his mother, including that of his musical (left) ear. Brian lost his hearing in his right ear as a boy, though the cause is unclear. (Aunt Audree has variously attributed the hearing loss to a congenital defect and to Murry striking the boy with an iron while the youngster was asleep.) My aunt sang nursery rhymes to all her sons and brought them to Grandma Korthof's house, where Brian first heard Glenn Miller's 1943 rendition of George Gershwin's "Rhapsody in Blue," which Brian has often described as one of his favorites.

My aunt enlarged Brian's music world, taking him to record shops that allowed patrons to listen to individual songs in "demonstration booths." It was there that Brian first heard the Four Freshmen, the jazz-influenced pop quartet with innovative four-note chordal harmonies. As he later recounted in a documentary: "Something magic happened in my head. I instantly transcended. It was unbelievable. It gave me so much spiritual strength. It came out of me. You know how you like to sit in a sauna bath and your pores open up, and all the sweat will come out. That's what that whole experience in the record store did to me. I purged all kinds of bullshit and picked up the Four Freshmen. It was magic. Total magic."

The "bullshit" that poured out of him was his father's abuse, and the examples are many. One time when Brian was fourteen, he went to a church meeting at night and stayed late to listen to music at the parish house with the minister's son. But he lost track of time, and his parents drove the neighborhood in a hopeless search. According to Audree, by the time Brian did come home, Murry was so livid that he walloped him. As Brian described the abuse in general, "The way I had it, my dad would double over his belt, and he'd have us take our pants over our shoes, and lean over the bathtub, and it's like you can imagine a spanking—*whap whap whap*—very, very hard . . . Pretty tough business."

There was one refuge. "Because my father was so cruel to me," Brian said, "I turned to music. It was my only friend."

Brian's lanky athletic build served him well in playing baseball as well as football at Hawthorne High School—he could chuck a ball fifty yards—but even when he was involved in sports, his musical instincts were difficult to repress. He preferred center field so the other players couldn't hear him sing, and while he was in the football huddle, he would sometimes hear the cheerleaders and break out in song. For his sixteenth birthday, his parents gave him a Wollensak tape recorder, on which he made his first four-part harmony recordings. As a high school senior, he flunked a music assignment because instead of handing in the required sonata, he delivered a melody that later became a surf song.

If Brian was the musical dreamer, Dennis was the furious rebel, whose brawn and belligerence most closely resembled those attributes in his father. He once came to actual blows with his dad, a scuffle in the garage that had to be broken up by a neighbor. That was noteworthy because he was the one son who actually fought back. Yet Dennis was the boy who most craved his father's approval. On family outings, he was always first in line, ready to go, trying to please Murry. But he never could, so the cycle of disobedience and punishment continued throughout his childhood. Dennis once left his house in the middle of the night, snuck into an open window of a mortuary, and pushed in the nose of a dead man. Why? Because he could. He loved speed, driving fast cars even before he was allowed to drive, and he craved anything that might be dangerous. He used to dive by himself at night off Palos Verdes Peninsula in Los Angeles, searching for abalone. At Hawthorne Municipal Airport he once talked a guy into giving him a ride on his light aircraft, and as an adult, while flying on a commuter plane into New York, Dennis told the pilot to fly between the Twin Towers—he thought it'd be fun to buzz them—or else he'd be fired. (The pilot refused and kept his job.)

Some of Dennis's teenage stunts were more serious, such as using a BB gun to shatter windows from passing cars, lighting a neighborhood brush fire with alcohol from a chemistry set, or throwing a screwdriver at the head of a fellow student. He was kicked out of school at least once, and a deep scar under his chin was evidence of his brawling, frenetic youth. He had plenty of friends and a generous spirit, and attracted girls in droves, but even as a young teen he raged against the world.

Carl, the youngest, was closest to his mother and most like her in temperament. He spent much of his childhood keeping his head down so that he was not collateral damage in the family wars. He tried to get along. With handsome, talented, athletic older brothers, Carl was teased for being chubby, but he found his niche. Like Brian, he gravitated to music at an early age. When he was three, he watched a TV show starring Spade Cooley, a cowboy artist, and little Carl would put his foot on a stool and pretend to play the violin. Strings were in his future. He began playing guitar at age ten and in high school took lessons from John Maus (who—as John Walker—was a lead singer and the lead guitarist for the Walker Brothers). He was always the most protected of the three brothers, sweet and obedient, but also the most reliable, practical, and businesslike.

My mom and her brother Murry always got along. She pitied his financial struggles and physical misfortunes, and remembered his protective efforts in their youth. And Murry had no reason to resent his sister. But the hostilities were rife between my uncle and my dad. They played on the same high school football team and, as far as I know, got along fine in their youth, when everyone was struggling to make ends meet. But it was different when they became adults. Murry begrudged my dad's success, perhaps seeing him as a lucky inheritor of a family business, and our well-appointed home was a painful reminder that the spoils of the free market had not fallen evenly on the transplanted siblings from Kansas. My dad, meanwhile, saw Uncle Murry for what he was—a violent blowhard—and despised him right back, their mutual contempt erupting in heated arguments. My mom tried to play peacemaker, her weapon of choice holiday cheer.

Of all the social events at our house, my mom's holiday parties were her most lavish, none more than Christmas. We drove to Hollywood in search of the biggest tree and then put it in the entrance hall, the highest branches grazing the second-story ceiling. At least fifty people came over on Christmas Eve. My father brought a truck home from Love Sheet Metal, and the adults piled in while the kids walked alongside. We sang "Silent Night," "Deck the Halls," "Joy to the World," and other carols in the neighborhood (though skipping the Colemans, our Jewish neighbors, whose son, Michael, I often played chess with). After caroling we returned to the house, where the Ping-Pong table was laden with turkey, ham, and cakes as well as potato salad whose recipe my mom got from her mom (the vinegar was key). The local newspaper actually came and wrote stories about the party, including photographs of Maureen on the harp, Stephen at the piano, and me at the organ.

The Wilsons were always there, and we sat around the piano and sang. The adults favored the 1940s standards, while the kids preferred the likes of "Speedoo" by the Cadillacs and "(Baby) Hully Gully" by the Olympics. Brian sang the high parts, Carl the middle, and I the bass. Maureen or Aunt Audree sang the fourth part. Sometimes my mom or Uncle Murry or Stan or others joined in. Among the adults, the music was always a respite from any ill will between the two families, a saving grace. The cousins, by comparison, always got along, and sometimes we retreated to the kitchen, where Brian and I figured out different parts from still more songs, and we staged our own little concert.

This wasn't unusual. In high school, Maureen, Brian, and I performed on Wednesday youth nights at the Angeles Mesa Presbyterian Church, about a mile from our house. During the walk home, Brian turned two-part hits from the country-influenced Everly Brothers— "Wake Up Little Susie," "Bird Dog," "Devoted to You"—into three parts, distributing them on the fly. Once we reached our house, he dashed to the piano and tried new chords, pounding the keys as loudly as he could. He often spent the night, and sometimes we stayed up late and played the hi-fi so loud ("Rock Around the Clock," "See You Later Alligator") that my father, yelling that he had to wake up at dawn, pushed us out of the house. We settled into Brian's Nash Rambler, turned on Johnny Otis's R&B show on KFOX or Huggy Boy's rock and roll show on KGFJ, reclined the seats, and stayed up singing.

Most of the time we slept in my room, in the trim knotty pine bunks built into the wall, the glowing fireplace nearby. Transistor radios, invented only in the late 1940s, were everywhere back then, kind of like smartphones today, and I had my transistor under my pillow so we could listen to music late into the night. We talked about girls and our parents as well as music. While Elvis was popular, he played a more hillbilly southern rock, which wasn't our thing. For his part, Brian was playing and studying a lot of Ricky Nelson, the Four Preps, and the Hi-Lo's, often in his garage, which his father had turned into a music room. But Brian's interest in the Four Freshmen, specifically the arrangements of Dick Reynolds and Pete Rugolo—how they made four voices converge on the same note and then diverge to four notes—had become obsessive. (Brian later said that "Dick Reynolds was practically a god to me.")

I appreciated the harmonies, but my true love was doo-wop and R&B. I thought that Little Richard had a mind-blowing band, and I loved the Coasters, the Olympics, and the Robins. But my favorite was Chuck Berry: the clever vignettes, the syncopation, the alliteration in such classics as "Johnny B. Goode" and "Maybellene." I can't tell you how many times I listened to "Nadine."

As I got on a city bus and found a vacant seat.
I thought I saw my future bride walkin' up the street.
I shouted to the driver, "Hey, conductor, you must slow down.
I think I see her, please let me off this bus."

I saw her from the corner when she turned and doubled back.
And started walking toward a coffee-colored Cadillac.
I was pushin' through the crowd to get where she's at.
And I was campaign shouting like a southern diplomat.

"Campaign shouting like a southern diplomat!" That just floored me. The words had a descriptive, even poetic beauty. Many of these

R&B guys could tell these everyday stories in a way that was raw and vital but also lyrical, and they hit me on a whole other level.

I also saw my first concert in high school—the Kingston Trio, a Bay Area group that had a No. 1 song in 1958 ("Tom Dooley"). The Trio played at the Shrine Auditorium in Los Angeles. Folk music really wasn't my thing, but after watching my first live performance, I bought an acoustic guitar. The communal setting seemed to elevate every song. It was no longer about me and my experiences but about us and our world. I loved the gentle banter between the performers (Dave Guard, Bob Shane, and Nick Reynolds) and the audience, and I realized that the response of the latter was as much a part of the show as the musicianship of the former.

Brian and I had something else in common. We were both loners: I played sports but didn't join any of the clubs, and Brian was focused on his music, using his Wollensak recorder to tape voice and piano renditions of his favorite pop songs. I admired my father's work ethic and my mom's love of music and culture, but I can't say I felt close to them. Brian's home life bordered on toxic. We both had other friends and we both had girlfriends, but I don't know that either of us had a better friend.

I knew that Brian was a prodigy. We all knew that. But we never talked about creating a band, as we had no role models for such a thing. Music was just about having fun with family and friends. It was to no one's surprise that after Brian graduated from high school in 1960, he enrolled at El Camino Community College to study psychology.

I graduated from high school in the winter of 1959 and attended Los Angeles City College for two semesters, running track and posting a 4:30 mile. But structure didn't suit me. So I went to work, holding down a night job in the "oil and gas business." That sounded better than saying I had the graveyard shift at the Standard Oil station in a gang-ridden section of Los Angeles on the corner of South

La Brea Avenue and West Washington. I stood on the dimly lit island between the pumps, and one night at around three A.M., a guy walked up to me, pulled out a gun, and stuck it in my side, saying, "Give me all your money." His hand was shaking, which made me even more frightened. I took all the cash and gave it to him, and could breathe again only after he fled into the night.

My day job was as a sheet metal apprentice at our family business, whose boom days were gone though the operation was still viable. As my father saw it, Love Sheet Metal had provided well for his family, and it survived even during the Depression. While the company had a paint and wood shop, its main business remained bending and rounding sheet metal for tables and counters. My grandfather still ran the place, and he was a perfectionist—nothing could go out the doors unless it was exactly as designed. It was hard, relentless work. The top of welded hinges often had slag, or coarse residue, and my job was to buff and grind it out. I also sanded cabinets, bent the metal, mixed the paints. What I enjoyed most was learning to speak Spanish, starting where everyone else started—the curse words.

Of course I wasn't all work and no play.

For much of my youth, I was shy around girls, though that doesn't mean I didn't like them. My family called me "girl crazy," which probably overstates it. I was selective in the girls I was crazy about, attracted to those who were intelligent as well as pretty. I experienced plenty of heartbreak—or, more accurately, had my heart broken easily. In middle school, a girl named Sally asked me to my first dance. I wore a new suit, with a handkerchief in the pocket, and bought Sally a corsage, but once we got to the dance, she ignored me most of the night. When I got home, I threw myself onto my bunk and began to cry, cursing the money that I had squandered on the flower.

In high school, I started dating a beautiful girl named Nelda whose father was a Baptist minister and whose mother was Mexican— he had met her doing mission work in Mexico. Nelda had actually enthralled me since grade school. I walked her home from school, or maybe just followed her, and while she was recovering from an appendectomy, I stood outside her house, unable to leave, until her mom shooed me away. Her ethnicity and spirituality fascinated me, and by high school, I was overwhelmed with operatic affections. As I told Maureen, "I just hope you can feel this deep love someday." Nelda, unfortunately, did not feel the same love, and the relationship soon ended.

You were supposed to have a nice car if you were going to have any luck picking up girls. My car fell a little bit short. As a senior in high school I drove a 1949 green Chevy, whose wear and tear had earned it the nickname "Gangrene." Nonetheless, one day I was driving up Homeland Drive when I saw this cute girl walking in her cheerleader uniform, the *D* emblazoned across her chest. I pulled over and asked if she needed a ride. She did indeed.

Francis Emily St. Martin had dark hair, hazel eyes, and a beautiful figure; she was a former Brownie and Girl Scout who cared about the people around her. She was already friends with Maureen and had even been to our house to swim in our pool. She lived nearby in Leimert Park. We double-dated with Brian, I sang her ballads, and she became my first serious romance. We started sleeping together, which was no small thing in those days. I sneaked in through her bedroom window in the dead of night and left with her parents unaware; or we drove to the oil fields and, with the car door open for extra room, consummated our affections, even if they were visible to the guys on a derrick a hundred yards away. We tried being careful—I used a condom—but it didn't work, and Frannie got pregnant. We thought we were in no position to become parents. Frannie would be enrolling in UCLA, and I was working at the family business and pumping gas. So I went with Frannie to an abortion clinic in East Los Angeles. Abortion was illegal at the time, and it was a traumatic experience for both of us.

We continued dating after Frannie began college. We again used protection, but Frannie got pregnant a second time. We again decided to end the pregnancy, but it was even more complicated, as the pregnancy was further along. We drove to Tijuana but didn't go through with the procedure and came back home. There was one thing we could do: get married and have the child.

My parents were traditionalists, and my mom in particular had a strict moral code: You did not have sex before you got married. Those who did sacrificed their honor and respect, and pregnancy before marriage brought shame to the entire family. My mom had had hard pregnancies, but that didn't prevent her from having six children. In her mind, that was the noble lot of every woman, and for any man or woman to short-circuit the process (be it through premarital sex, birth control, or abortion) was an offense to the natural order.

So I can't say that I was surprised by my mother's reaction when I told her that Frannie was pregnant and that we were going to get married. She flipped out. She gathered my shirts, my typewriter, and my green-and-white letterman jacket and threw them to the lawn two stories below. I was kicked out of the house. I didn't argue with her or make a chaotic scene even more of a spectacle. The men in our family were taught to stay strong in the face of adversity, to suppress their emotions. If anything, the eviction may have had a greater impact on my younger siblings, who realized they could be next.

My father wouldn't have thrown me out—we continued to see each other every day at the factory—but I understood that my mom did what she had to do. Her vision of the family was having all of her children singing in perfect harmony on the front steps, and in that quest of being the perfect mother with the perfect family, she could not accept a child who obliterated those expectations. Her sacrifices had been too great. I gathered my belongings and drove off.

Frannie and I married at Los Angeles City Hall (absent my parents), and we lived in a small cottage in need of paint and tile on property owned by her folks. When our daughter, Melinda, was born on July 15, 1961, the birth certificate included a line for *father's occupation*. Mine read: "gas station attendant."

My path, like that of many twenty-year-olds, was unclear. But I could turn a phrase and knew what made a good lyric. I also believed that the Love and Wilson families had all kinds of artistic gifts, none more than music. My cousins understood that as well. We were just a bunch of blue-collar kids whose ancestors had come from the sticks, but there was magic in that gene pool. We just had to set it free.

CHAPTER 3

SURFING THE CULTURAL WAVES

As teenagers, Dennis and I would wake up early and go fishing on the Redondo Beach breakwater, passing the day talking about girls, our parents, the indignity of adolescence, and sex. I was only three years older than Dennis, but that's about thirty in teenage years, so I tried to give him some pointers and was the first to tell him about cunnilingus. It piqued his interest.

Dennis knew Redondo Beach better than I did because he surfed there regularly. It was, for him, the perfect sport, requiring athleticism and daring in an ocean that was open and untroubled. For someone who balked at every constraint and convention, Dennis found freedom in the hollow of a turbulent wave. Even better, surfing immersed him in a beach culture that indulged his appetites, sex and booze chief among them. How fine it was—the sinuous beauties in their bikinis who mixed with the buffed renegades and wave-top zealots while drinking jugs of vodka and orange juice.

I certainly knew about beaches. When I was a kid, our family pitched umbrellas on Manhattan Beach and El Segundo Beach, where we roasted hot dogs and marshmallows in the fire pits. Though never an avid surfer, by high school I knew how to ride a wave, and my friends and I listened to "surf reports" on the radio. If these were promising, we cut class in the afternoon and headed for the ocean. My friend Bill Jackson had a Ford convertible, which was ideal for loading surfboards; and on weekends, we went to San Onofre or Malibu or even south of the border to Ensenada and enjoyed the hedonistic pleasures of those sandy locales.

Southern California had all kinds of microethnic groups or subcultures, such as the greasers, the jocks, and the beaners (Mexicans). But the surfers stood out. With their blond-streaked hair and their distinctive dress (Pendleton shirts sporting two flap pockets, worn over T-shirts and khakis) and lingo (*kook* for beginner, *ho-daddy* for wise guy, and *bitchin'* for, well, bitchin'), they had a rugged mystique. I had a sense of the sport's exotic history. It came to California from Hawaii and featured legends with cool names like Duke Kahanamoku. Surf bands, meanwhile, were big in Southern California, Dick Dale and the Del-Tones being the most popular, drawing big numbers at the Rendezvous Ballroom in Balboa. With crowd pleasers like "Surf Beat," "Misirlou," and "Let's Go Trippin'," Dale played the Fender Stratocaster in a rapid-picking style that imitated the curling waves. He didn't sing. None of the surf songs had vocals. They were just high-volume instrumentals, but the kids loved them. The connection between surfing and romance, or between the sport and America's burgeoning youth culture, was given a full ride in the popular 1959 movie *Gidget*, starring Sandra Dee in a dopey teenage romance with a young surfer named Moondoggie.

I was aware of these cultural eddies, but what I mainly knew was how the surfers themselves made up this freewheeling clique in which Dennis was a sometime member. During one of our fishing trips in July of 1961, we started talking about the whole surfing craze and why it made sense to do a real surf song, not just one with instrumentals. I knew our families had singing talent, and I had seen how a teenage duo from Southern California, Jan and Dean, had turned a pop song like "Baby Talk" into a hit. If they could do it, why couldn't we?

At the time, Dennis was not as musically driven as his brothers, but he saw the possibility, so he went home all fired up and told Brian about it. Brian didn't surf and knew little about it, but the idea intrigued him immediately.

Things were moving fast that summer. Brian, attending El Camino Community College, bumped into a friend, Alan Jardine, with whom he had attended Hawthorne High School. They were teammates on the football team, and Al, playing running back, broke his leg on a botched play by the quarterback, Brian, who carried some guilt about the misstep. But it didn't undermine their friendship, which was based on a shared passion for vocal harmonies.

Like the rest of us, Al grew up in a household of music, and like the Loves and Wilsons, the Jardines came to California from a far distant strip of the American heartland.

Al's parents, Don and Virginia, met at the University of Toledo during orchestra practice—he played clarinet; she, violin—and they both sang in church choirs. Don in particular had a strong voice, which he used to sing the "Hallelujah Chorus" from Handel's *Messiah*. After college, the couple moved to Lima, Ohio, where Don worked as the photographer at the Lima Locomotive Works. Al was born in 1942, the second of two boys, and he grew up listening to symphonies on the Magnavox and to hits on the radio. He also played clarinet in grade school. By the end of the decade, the family had moved to upstate New York and then in 1952 relocated all the way to San Francisco, where Don accepted a position at a blueprinting and lithograph company. He was reassigned to Los Angeles in 1955, and the family settled in Hawthorne, two streets away from the Wilsons. Al had blue eyes and short brown hair, and was a wiry five-foot-four.

He also had a smooth tenor voice and his own folk group—his favorite artists were the Kingston Trio—and by the time he entered college, he was looking to break into the business.

The specific details on the origins of the Beach Boys—who played what, when, where, and how—have been recounted in many, and at times contradictory, ways over the past fifty-five years. I can only offer my best memory about what happened.

What I know for certain is that not many people in Hawthorne knew much about the music industry, but my Uncle Murry did, so Al sought him out after he graduated high school. My uncle introduced Al and his folk group to Hite and Dorinda Morgan, a husband-and-wife team with a small music publishing business and recording studio on Melrose Avenue in Hollywood. The Morgans' no-frills studio gave aspiring artists a chance to record demos, which could then be sold to record labels. Some years back, Uncle Murry himself tried to use the Morgans for his songs, with a teenage Brian singing in their studio. The Morgans passed. Al and his group hoped to have better luck, but the couple was not impressed, with Dorinda supposedly noting, "They were imitators, not originators."

Al was not deterred. When he saw Brian at El Camino in that summer of 1961, they talked about doing some songs together, and maybe they could even start a group. Brian said his cousin Mike and brother Carl should be part of it. He did not envision, nor did I, that Dennis should be part of the group, as Dennis didn't play any instruments or seem that interested. But Aunt Audree insisted that he be included—she was so upset that she cried. Regardless, it wasn't as if we had some big meeting and decided to create a band. It was more of a natural evolution, as we had been singing together as a family for years while also performing and practicing with others. Now with Al on board, we just coalesced, singing in the Wilsons' music room, sometimes with my sister Maureen. We sang R&B tunes from the

Coasters and some Four Freshmen arrangements (one of which, "Their Hearts Were Full of Spring," the Beach Boys perform to this day). At the end of August, we decided to try our songs for the Morgans, as they were the only ones we knew with a studio. Our group was made up of Brian, Dennis, Carl, Al, and me, and with fashion in mind, we called ourselves the Pendletones. If we hit it big, maybe the company would send us some free shirts.

Brian spoke first when we entered the studio. "Mrs. Morgan, I bet you don't remember me," he said. She didn't. Brian reminded her that he had accompanied his father several years ago to audition a song.

This tryout didn't go any better. Whatever we sang, they didn't like it, and Mrs. Morgan didn't believe we had even chosen the right genre.

"Do you have any folk songs?" she asked.

Her instincts weren't terrible. Peter, Paul and Mary would have their first album out the following year. So would Bob Dylan. But we preferred R&B and rock and roll, and I knew we weren't folksingers.

Dennis spoke up, asking the Morgans if they listened to the surf reports and knew about the surf craze. "It's bigger than you might think!" After the Morgans said they were unaware, Dennis volunteered that we were working on a surfing song and maybe we could come back and sing it.

True enough. Brian and I had been working on a surfing song, so we returned to his house and sat down at the piano to finish it.

Our collaborations were usually interactive. Either one of us might come up with the concept—what's this song about? Brian started with a melody, which he played for me; my specialty was finding the hook, or phrase, that drew people in. I typically wrote the bulk of the words, while Brian structured the harmonies to fit our voices. I weighed in on the arrangements as well, in particular the bass parts.

Our first song wasn't about surfing as a sport, because I wasn't into it as a sport. Surfing was really about a way of life.

Surfin' is the only life.
The only way for me.
Now surf, surf with me.

That was the intro and the hook. Then the verse reflected my own experiences.

I got up this mornin' turned on the radio.
I was checkin' on the surfin' scene
To see if I would go.
And when the DJ tells me that the surfin' is fine.
That's when I know my baby and I will have a good time . . .

Those were my first real lyrics. Were they any good? I had no idea, but they had the Chuck Berry–style rhyme, alliteration, and vignettes. Brian included the "Surfin' . . . Surfin' . . ." in the chorus, and I came up with the doo-wop-inspired *bom bom dit dit dip*s. And we had our first song.

Uncle Murry and Aunt Audree took a trip with another couple to Mexico, leaving behind a hundred dollars or so for food. We wanted to use the money to rent some instruments but were still short of cash, so we went to Al's house and asked his mom for a few more dollars. To demonstrate our worthiness, we sang "Their Hearts Were Full of Spring." It's deceptive—most Four Freshmen arrangements are—with bewildering chord changes in each of the parts. We sang it a cappella, I on the bottom, Carl right above me, Al in the middle range, Brian on top.

Even at that young age and even without any formal music train-ing, our voices lay gently atop one another. For the harmonies to work, the voices cannot have too much individual character or too much vibrato. Ours was a seamless genetic blend, a pureness of tone. That was the secret to our vocals. They became more refined as we gained experience, but the polished harmonies for which we became known were evident long before we had recorded a single song. When we used to sing at our Christmas parties, the challenge was finding the fourth voice in our four-part harmonies. Dennis was often doing his own thing, and his voice, like his father's, had a hoarser quality. Brian sometimes used his mom or Maureen for that fourth part, but it was really Al who gave us the last piece.

I can't claim that our rendition of "Their Hearts Were Full of Spring" was flawless, but it sufficiently impressed Mrs. Jardine, who gave us additional money for our rentals: some carbon microphones, guitars, drums, amplifiers, a stand-up bass for Al. We then played endless variations of "Surfin'" for the next three days, with Dennis learning the drums. We thought we had a catchy tune, but when Uncle Murry and Aunt Audree returned home, Murry was livid that we had squandered food money on instruments. Brian had made a tape recording of "Surfin'" and just asked his parents to listen. The *bom bom dit dit dips* filled the room as we anxiously awaited judgment. Aunt Audree spoke first, complimenting our efforts (but later acknowledging that she didn't think anything would come of it). Uncle Murry stopped seething and admitted that the song had potential.

A few weeks later, we returned to the Morgans' home studio to record a demo of "Surfin'," with our finger snaps acting as a snare drum, and with passing traffic audible from the street. I sang the lead, we all pitched in on the harmonies, and the Morgans liked it. We also sang two ballads, "Luau" and "Lavender," written by Morgan family members. In early November, the Morgans booked us in World Pacific Studio in Los Angeles to create a quality master. Uncle Murry and Aunt Audree were with us, and an argument broke out between Murry and Dennis about the latter's drumming, causing Dennis to stalk off briefly, though he returned for the vocals. Brian took off his shirt, laid it across the snare to dampen the sound, and beat it with one hand, while Carl played his acoustic guitar and Al the stand-up bass. It took seven takes, but we recorded "Surfin'," and we did "Luau" on the flip side. The Morgans sent the master to Candix Records, a tiny label that had been founded by a couple of brothers a year earlier. Frankly, I think the company was run out of their station wagon. Candix released the single in either late November or early December, and it was a shock when we opened the record and saw our name: the Beach Boys.

I guess someone at Candix didn't like the Pendletones, and one of its distributors—Russ Regan, who would have a distinguished executive career in the record industry—gave us our new name. I thought it fit us pretty well. The Morgans sent the record to a couple of local stations, and our break came from a contest sponsored by KDAY; it played several songs, and whichever received the most call-in votes would be added to the playlist. "Surfin'" squared off against "Duke of Earl," among others, and all the Loves and Wilsons called in repeatedly, changing our voices when necessary, to push "Surfin'" to victory.

The song entered the local KFWB Top 40 Survey at No. 33 and reached 75 on the national *Billboard* chart.*

I was the oldest at twenty, Carl the youngest at fourteen; but we were now a real band, and that meant playing in front of live audiences. Mrs. Morgan booked us for the Rendezvous Ballroom on a Saturday night, December 23, during the intermission of a Dick Dale set. We wore gold jackets, which I think cost us about $30 apiece. We looked lousy, but everyone wore uniforms back then, so that's what

---

* Unless otherwise indicated, all chart rankings are derived from *Billboard*.

we did. Jittery, and not very well rehearsed (I still had a day job), we stumbled through our songs, and the crowd ignored us.

Our third performance, booked by a local radio station, was on New Year's Eve at the Municipal Auditorium in Long Beach. The event was a tribute for Ritchie Valens, the young Latino singer from the San Fernando Valley who in 1959 was killed in the plane crash that also claimed the lives of Buddy Holly and J. P. Richardson ("The Big Bopper"). The party exposed us to some different lifestyles, with Carl seeing a member of the Rivingtons, a doo-wop group, shooting up heroin in the bathroom. There were about ten acts, including Frankie Avalon and Della Reese, but we followed Ike Turner and the Kings of Rhythm, and their backup vocalists, the Ikettes. Performing "I'm Blue (The Gong-Gong Song)," they were sexy and charismatic and had complete command of the audience. We were in awe and had to follow them, and I was petrified. But we took the stage and sounded better than before. Uncle Murry had bought Brian an amplifier and a bass; Carl had been playing an electric guitar for a while and now Al bought one as well.

We made it through "Surfin'," "Johnny B. Goode," and one other song, and definitely improved from our first showing. Afterward, I made the decision that I would never be anxious onstage again. It was just negative energy, and I would not let nerves drag me down. We were also paid $300. There were five of us, and we went to the box office and collected $60 each. That was amazing to me. I had to work eight hours a day at a sheet metal factory to make anything close to $60. Now I got that for singing three songs.

The payout, combined with the surprising playtime for "Surfin'," confirmed in my mind that we had a chance to be successful, a chance to transform a family avocation into a career. Part of that may have been wishful thinking, as I couldn't envision myself working in sheet metal for the next four decades. But I knew we could sing.

What I didn't know was how much good luck we were about to have. How we were in the right place with the right sound at the right time. It was like a single rolling wave that catches a magical wind and becomes a tsunami.

On September 1, 1961, *Life* magazine published a cover photograph of a beatific Jacqueline Kennedy, in a two-piece white ensemble, standing against a white guardrail, with the Washington Monument in the background. The headline: "She tells her plans for the White House." A new era had arrived. Glamour and fashion had come to the nation's capital. And inside the magazine was a seven-page spread on surfing, with photos of supple young men and women riding the Pacific waves and running the Malibu beach and driving cars with boards sticking out the side. The title described it as "A Way of Life."

As the story read, "Surfing, just beginning to catch on around the rest of the United States, has become an established craze in California . . . The addicts are mostly teenagers for whom the sport, besides being healthy and immensely exhilarating, has become a cult."

Life was one of America's cultural weather vanes, and its introduction of surfing to many of its readers—at the very time we recorded "Surfin'" and employed the very same California lifestyle themes—was indeed a gift. We had no idea what the national media were doing. In our songs, we were just singing about what we knew—the beach, cars, girls. Yet our timing was perfect.

The surfing obsession continued in films, as the success of *Gidget* led to two sequels and a television series (the latter with Sally Field, canceled after one year). It also paved the way for the popular "beach party" musical films, *Beach Blanket Bingo* being the most successful, starring wholesome Frankie Avalon and virginal Annette Funicello but mainly featuring bikinis and beach balls and happy endings. From 1963 to 1967, a dozen of these movies were produced, evoking the same images from our songs.

That we were a California group also served us well. Given its size, beauty, and resources, California had always had a mythic quality, but the exaltation of the state was about to reach its zenith. In 1962, California surpassed New York as the largest state in the union (17.3 million people), symbolizing a shift of power and prestige from east to west. The news hook was irresistible. California was big (158,693 square miles), rich (personal income of $45 billion, second only to New York), and breathtakingly diverse (it was "five states rolled into one," according to *Newsweek*). *National Geographic* called California "The Golden Magnet," and that it was: in 1962, an estimated 1,000 Americans moved to California each day. We were fertile as well. Accounting for births and deaths, California was adding 1,600 new people a day, and who could blame them? *Better Homes and Gardens* ran a piece titled "What It's Really Like to Move to California," quoting one transplant: "We left Milwaukee's rigorous winters and humid summers so we could be outdoors all year long."

In October, *Life* published a special issue devoted entirely to California, the cover featuring a thin cascade of fire streaking Yosemite at dusk. The issue was a paean to the state's climate, industry, sports, and fashions; a florid tribute to its history and its role in America's future. "It is now time to wish California Godspeed, and to note that its only limitations rest within the power contained in the burning sun, the moisture untapped in the 1,200-mile salt-water shore, the brain power of its mass-educated millions and the spirit of its ever-blooming harvest of modern pioneers." (I don't believe *Life* or its advertisers made it to Dorsey High School. In 143 pages and hundreds of photographs, the only black person to appear was Dizzy Gillespie. Asians and Hispanics were equally absent.)

There were great music groups before us and after us who were associated with California, but by dint of our lyrics, distinctive harmonies, and timing, it was the Beach Boys who represented the "California sound."

In the moment itself, we weren't thinking about any of these larger issues. We had much more basic concerns. We needed songs.

For a first effort, "Surfin'" rated a success, but any hope for instant riches was quickly dashed. Candix sent us a royalty check—all of $990, on which Uncle Murry added $10, so the five Beach Boys could walk away with $200 apiece. In the early months of 1962, we performed underwhelming gigs in Southern California: high school auditoriums, department stores, women's clubs, roller rinks, rec centers. Sometimes a surfboard was given out as a door prize; other times we were paired with teen fashion shows. Some nights we received $500; other shows we did for free. We played our one original song, did some covers, and filled out the set with instrumentals. I could play the sax, but it was really more of a prop that allowed me to bounce around the stage and "bop" at opportune times. Our gold sports jackets got plenty of use.

In February of 1962, Brian and I returned to the Wilsons' music room, sat at the piano, and hashed out another beach song. This time, however, I wasn't just thinking about the reality of our experiences but a kind of (as advertisers called it) "heightened reality." Why go surfing when you could go on a "surfin' safari"? Thus was born one of our most famous introductory hooks:

Let's go surfin' now.
Everybody's learning how.
Come on a safari with me.

I used a travelogue for the first time, citing the popular surfing spots of Huntington, Malibu, Rincon, and beyond.

They're anglin' in Laguna and Cerro Azul.
They're kicking out in Doheny too.
I tell you surfin's goin' wild.
It's getting bigger every day.
From Hawaii to the shores of Peru.

I came up with the words and the melody and sang the lead, while Brian moved away from the standard three-chord structure, pounded out the vocal arrangements on the piano, and gave the electric guitars more prominence (Uncle Murry had bought a white Fender Jaguar for Carl). This gave our music more of a Chuck Berry resonance.

We returned to World Pacific Studio, with Hite Morgan booking the time for us, to record a master of "Surfin' Safari," along with three other songs. But we couldn't get it played or sold. We were still trying to figure out what to do when we faced our first real crisis.

Al announced that he was quitting and returning to college, intent on being a dentist. We were all disappointed, Brian in particular. They were friends, and Al's departure left a hole. But given that Al's true love was folk music, I couldn't blame him. There were all kinds of bands who recorded a few songs, maybe even had a hit or two, and then vanished. In early 1962, the Beach Boys were literally a garage band—the Wilsons' music room was a converted garage. And Al, as the group's one non–family member, may have thought he wouldn't get a fair shake from Murry, who was our manager.

Fortunately, we didn't have to look far to find a replacement, as he lived across the street from the Wilsons. David Marks was seven years old when his parents, Elmer and Jo Ann, packed up their Mercury Monterey and moved the family from New Castle, Pennsylvania, to

Southern California—better weather, a better life. They eventually settled in Hawthorne, Elmer Marks finding a job at Douglas Aircraft. David, born in 1948, was closest in age to Carl (who was two years older), but the new kid on the block initially befriended Dennis, serving as his confederate on juvenile escapades, gladly allowing Dennis to serve as his protector in neighborhood scraps, but also falling victim to Dennis's pranks. Dennis once showed up at David's house with a jar of ashes and tears in his eyes, jabbering that Brian had died in a house fire and the ashes were all that remained. David believed him until Dennis burst into laughter.

At age nine, David received a trumpet from his grandmother, and he wanted to be the next Harry James, whom he saw on *The Tonight Show*. David knew about the reputation of Dennis's older brother, and he would sneak into the Wilson house and spy on Brian playing the piano. David soon got his first guitar and began taking lessons from John Maus, who, as noted, was Carl's teacher as well. David, in fact, introduced Carl to John. Sharing the same mentor, David and Carl began practicing guitar together on a daily basis, jam sessions beneath the haze of smoke from their mutual interest in cigarettes.

Leading up to "Surfin'," David sometimes practiced with us and thought he'd be included in the band. But at thirteen, he was too young. I didn't know him well, but for all his precocious music skills, he was considered immature (not that any of us were paragons of responsibility). Nonetheless, when Al jumped ship, David was the natural replacement. He was only an average singer at the time, so he could not replace Al's voice, but he was much more of a rock and roller, and the chemistry he had already established with Carl would fortify our electric guitar sound.

David was watching *Bonanza* on the night that Uncle Murry and Brian came to his house and made the offer. He was ecstatic. His parents had reservations—David had not yet turned fourteen—but they agreed, and we had our five-piece band back.

Around this time, Brian met Gary Usher, a bank teller in his early twenties who had recorded a couple of songs. Brian and Gary developed a quick friendship, and they collaborated on the lyrics for some of our early classics on heartbreak and solitude—"Lonely Sea" and "In My Room," both released in 1963. Gary was immensely talented, and he helped Brian transform his feelings of melancholy and despair into moving ballads. Gary also liked cars, his favorite being the 409 Chevrolet, so named because of its massive 409-cubic-inch engine. So Gary and Brian started working on a song about that particular model, and they wanted the real sound.

One night around two A.M., I joined them outside Brian's front lawn in Hawthorne. Brian turned on his tape recorder, and Gary started dragging down the street, peeling rubber in his Chevy. A neighbor stepped out and told us to shut up, but they got the sound. It was actually a 326 engine, and it led off the track.

As lyrical subjects go, hot rods made sense. They were a national passion, certainly among teenagers, who conferred names to their cars and related to them much more closely than teens do today. I know I did. I saved $500 for my '49 Chevy and then kept adding to it—this week a new radiator, next week a muffler. My friends did the same thing, and we felt as though we nurtured these cars, scrap by scrap, into existence.

But I wasn't a gearhead and didn't know enough of the technical aspects to write car lyrics. I understood hooks, however, and I also understood how the music industry had completely changed in just a few short years. The first 45 rpm record was introduced in 1949, which allowed record companies to ply radio stations with 45s instead of clunky 78 rpm records. For teenagers, 45s were less expensive and could be spun on portable record players, away from their parents. At the same time, the widespread use of transistors and car stereos gave record companies direct access to a young, diverse, and very big audience.

This group was now a major force in the market, but if you wanted a hit, you needed a song that your ear could immediately latch onto, that did well over the airwaves—that jumped right out of your transistor or car stereo—and had great hooks.

All the great R&B songs had them—think of Little Richard's "Good Golly, Miss Molly," Chuck Berry's "Maybellene," the Supremes' "Stop! In the Name of Love," James Brown's "I Feel Good." The music connected with the audience directly, viscerally, and I wanted that same R&B influence in our work. That approach didn't work in Brian's slower, more introspective arrangements, but I thought it was possible in our fast-tempo songs.

When I first heard "409," I told Brian that I thought the lyrics were really good (*Well, I saved my pennies and I saved my dimes/For I knew there would be a time*), but the song lacked an opening hook.

So I wrote:

She's real fine, my 409.
She's real fine, my 409
My four-oh-nine.

I also wrote the *"Giddyap, giddyap, giddyap, 409,"* as a loping bass part that runs through the song.

Still seeking to make our next record, we recorded "Surfin' Safari" and "409" in April at Western Recorders in Hollywood. First we did the instrumental tracks, then Brian, Carl, and I laid down the vocals.

In May, Candix folded, leaving us short of cash and in search of a record label. By now Uncle Murry had also soured on the Morgans, even though they owned the publishing rights for the new masters. My uncle just ignored the Morgans and the contract we were under. With the new demos in hand, he began visiting other record labels but was supposedly turned down by Dot, Decca, and Liberty Records. In May, he landed a meeting with Capitol Records, which had a distinguished history as the first West Coast record label (1942). The Capitol Records Tower, on Vine Street in Hollywood, was itself a musical icon, shaped like a stack of white records. Over the years its artists included Nat "King" Cole, Frank Sinatra, and the Four Freshmen. But by 1960 its most successful act was the Kingston Trio, so it probably recognized that it needed some new blood to appeal to a younger market.

Murry met with Nik Venet, a twenty-two-year-old producer with styled jet-black hair and French cuffs who liked to boast that he was responsible for tens of millions of dollars in record sales in a single year. Venet was technically an A&R (artists and repertoire) man, responsible for listening to demos or records and finding the next great talent. Venet loved the job, even though he acknowledged he had a hard time spelling "repertoire." The youngest A&R guy at Capitol, he was charged specifically with finding songs that would reach teenagers.

As Venet later recounted, he listened to "Surfin' Safari" with Murry in his office, and he knew he had a hit "before the second eight bars were finished." We had a different sound than Elvis—who, as Venet put it, played "black blues for white people"—but like Elvis, we could reach young people. Venet went down the hall and played the song for Capitol's vice president, Voyle Gilmore, who was in his fifties but agreed with Venet's assessment. Venet returned to his office and told my uncle he wanted to sign us.

"What do you want, Mr. Wilson?"

Uncle Murry opened his wallet, showed it was empty, and said, "I just paid the boys my last thousand dollars. I need three hundred dollars."

"Is that all you want?" Venet asked.

"Three hundred dollars," he said.

Venet later said he had the authority to sign us for $50,000, so he got us pretty cheap.

Capitol released the "Surfin' Safari"/"409" single on June 4 (and later settled a lawsuit with the Morgans for use of the songs). Capitol had planned to put "409" on the A side on the theory that the car theme had greater national appeal, and in promoting the record to radio stations, that idea worked in some places. A DJ in Memphis urged his listeners who had a 409 Chevy to cruise Poplar Street, and when they did, the DJ played "409" for an hour nonstop. But across much of the nation, the song received little airplay, so Capitol began promoting "Surfin' Safari," which proved to have more appeal (and became the A side). The record gradually climbed the charts, selling about 900,000 units and reaching No. 14. What was most unexpected was the record's strength in places like Phoenix and Buffalo and Minneapolis/St. Paul, far removed from any beach. (The single was also our first to be released in the United Kingdom.)

Maybe we shouldn't have been surprised by the broad appeal. A good beat is a good beat, and the remoteness of surfing was part of the fantasy. You don't need to be an astronaut to love "Fly Me to the Moon."

Capitol was impressed. We returned to the Tower on July 16, 1962, and signed a seven-year contract, spelling out how many songs we were required to record each year. We were thrilled, believing for the first time that we could actually do this for a living. Brian quit college. Dennis, suspended from high school, never returned. Carl remained in high school, though he transferred to Hollywood Professional School for his senior year. David Marks transferred there as well.

I reached a crossroads. I was missing days at Love Sheet Metal because I was spending more time with the Beach Boys. For my dad, who rarely missed a day, that didn't go over well, and now that I had my first taste of music success, the factory was that much more unappealing. It was time to move on. So one day after work, I told my dad that I wanted to leave and devote all my time to the band. Part of him, I believe, was relieved. Though a family business, Love Sheet

Metal didn't hold much sentimental value. He knew it was a grueling, volatile enterprise, and he also knew that I loved music and so did my cousins. What he didn't know was whether we could make a living.

"What if you fail?" he asked me.

"Well," I said, "if it doesn't work out, I guess I'll be back here scraping shit off metal."

I regret the comment now. I also had no idea how serious Love Sheet Metal's financial condition was. Just as my father and grandfather rarely discussed their feelings or emotions, they were equally silent about the company business. Maureen knew something was amiss. Around this time, my dad asked her if he could borrow money from her piggy bank. Even a thriving economy could not keep Love Sheet Metal afloat. Within months of my leaving, it filed for bankruptcy and soon had to shut its doors.

My dad eventually found work at Chulich Sheet Metal, but it wasn't enough. My parents had to sell their home on Mount Vernon and Fairway and move south about seven miles into a 1,800-square-foot house in a rough section of Inglewood, in the flight path for Los Angeles International Airport. One night after my mom washed her hair and was letting it dry on the patio, someone from the street shot a BB that whizzed right by her. My youngest sister, Marjorie, was two when they moved, and she grew up hearing about "the big house" in which they once lived.

Meanwhile, Grandpa Love retired, and he and my grandma had to sell their house as well. I doubt the gambling room was ever used again.

CHAPTER 4

OUR OWN WALL
OF SOUND

These family setbacks left their mark on me. I would have been a hard worker under any circumstance, and as the only Beach Boy who was a husband and father when the group began, I had responsibilities that the others didn't. But it was more than that. Professionally, I never took anything for granted. No matter how much success I achieved individually or as part of a band, I knew it could be gone tomorrow. That was particularly true in the music business, in which performers are at the mercy of public opinion or shifts in the cultural winds. The only way to combat that uncertainty—your only defense against premature demise—is to work and learn, to find ways to market and promote, and to reinvent yourself.

None of that, of course, was necessary in the early 1960s. An ascendant California needed a voice to convey the appeal of this "promised land" (*Life*), and that group was the Beach Boys. Our most popular songs reinforced this utopian narrative and even served as a recruiting tool. I can't tell you how many people over the years have told me that they moved to California from Nebraska or Vermont or wherever because of the Beach Boys.

At the same time, our music merged with the idealism of the early

1960s, embodied by President Kennedy—his youth and eloquence, not to mention his glamorous wife, were impossible to ignore. His was the language of possibility. As he said in his inaugural, "If a free society cannot help the many who are poor, it cannot save the few who are rich." What followed, with both Presidents Kennedy and Johnson, were policies or pledges to reduce poverty, improve education, grant civil rights, protect the environment, engage the world, and send men to the moon. Along the way, there would be failure and disappointment, and I'll let the historians sort out what worked and what didn't. What I do know is that our music provided the soundtrack to a special time in American history, a time that would later be canonized for its lofty goals and willful innocence. But we weren't part of some screenwriter's nostalgic story line. We lived in that moment, and in the years to come, as I traveled the world and met others from all walks of life (soldiers, humanitarians, spiritual leaders), I gained a much deeper appreciation of how our music helped define the era.

W hatever idealism I had about the music industry disappeared in the next few years when I learned the details about our contract with Capitol. At the time, the record companies took advantage of virtually all artists who played rock, R&B, or pop music. For the most part, we were young, we lacked savvy, and our desperation to have our music heard made us easy prey. In our case, we were represented by my uncle Murry, but he wasn't a lawyer, and even if he was, it wouldn't have made a difference. The record companies had all the leverage.

Our contract with Capitol was typical. The publisher, who owned and administered the copyrights, received 5 percent of a record's retail price, which was then split with the songwriter. (It took me years to know who the Beach Boys' publisher was or even what the publisher did.) The artist, or singer, received 5 percent of the remaining 95 percent—in our case, because we had five performers, we each received 20 percent of the 5 percent of the 95 percent. Albums back then sold for about $3, which meant the publisher received 15 cents for each unit sold, and each Beach Boy received about 3 cents an album. By its own estimates, Capitol, after expenses, netted $1.80 for each album. That's a pretty big disparity between what the artist made and what the label made, but the terms were even worse than that. Capitol also deducted the cost of the recording sessions from artist payments, so if an album cost, say, $10,000 to record, the artist wouldn't see a nickel until that ten grand was paid back.

I had a general sense that this wasn't a good deal for us. I mean, we did virtually all the work and got a tiny fraction of the money. How could that be considered fair? But I didn't complain. None of us did. We were just grateful that Capitol was going to record and sell our music. I was a songwriter, so I assumed I would at least see additional money for that. I didn't know anything about songwriter agreements or copyrights, but I figured I didn't have to. Uncle Murry, as our manager, was in charge of all our business dealings and copyright filings. Remarkably, I was considered the one adult in the band. Brian, Dennis, and Carl as well as David were all minors and had to go to court with their parents to approve the contract.

Capitol, for its part, wasn't waiting around. After "Surfin' Safari," it rushed us into its own studio, where we spent three days recording our first album by that name. The studio was much bigger than what we were used to, designed for orchestras. Brian complained about the acoustics, but that was the least of his problems.

Venet was technically our producer, but he kept hurrying us, claiming that he had to get to New York to record Bobby Darin. Uncle Murry was also in the studio, trying to impose his will on the proceedings and claim his share of the producer's credit. Then there was Brian, working with a sound engineer and still learning his way around the studio and trying to establish his credentials as a producer. Arguments soon broke out between father and son—Brian adjusted the settings on the control board, only to have his dad change them, sending Brian into a fit.

Aunt Audree would also join us in the studio, and the contrast with her husband couldn't have been starker. She would sit patiently for hours, always with words of encouragement, while Uncle Murry ridiculed all of us, claiming it was for our own good. As he later told a reporter, "Sometimes they were so exhausted I had to make them mad at me to get the best out of them. So I'd insult their musical integrity. I'd say, 'That's lousy. You guys can do better than that!' I'd make them so damn mad that they'd be hitting me over the head, practically. But then they'd give that extra burst of energy and do it beautifully. When they were exhausted, I drove them harder because they asked for it."

Actually I think Murry feared his son's musical prowess and was determined to undermine his confidence so that Brian, nineteen at the time, would allow him to remain as producer. But Brian knew that his dad didn't understand rock and roll, or as he put it, his father "couldn't ramrod." The two could not coexist in the same studio for long.

In addition to "Surfin'," "Surfin' Safari," and "409," we recorded six new songs, known, if at all, for their youth-oriented, even corny themes: Brian and Gary Usher's "Ten Little Indians," "Cuckoo Clock," and "County Fair," for example, or "Chug-A-Lug," which I cowrote, about drinking mugs of root beer. (Venet feared people would think we were talking about actual beer.)

Rock groups, up to that point, rarely did albums, Elvis being the one exception. The thinking was that teenagers would pay for hit singles but not bulky LPs. Capitol, however, believed that one hit song—"Surfin' Safari"—would carry our first album's commercial load, and our label played the surf idea to the hilt. For the album's cover, Venet rented a yellow Ford Model A for $50 from a bearded guy known as Calypso Joe. We drove the truck to Paradise Cove in Malibu, parked it in the sand, and, wearing our white chinos and blue Pendleton shirts, were photographed holding a surfboard and peering into the ocean.

Released on October 1, the LP reached No. 32, a respectable showing for a debut album that was rushed out the door and whose production was fairly primitive. Nonetheless, we learned that while "Surfin' Safari" was a good single, it wasn't strong enough to move the LP. Big hits moved albums.

Even as Uncle Murry drove us mad in the studio, he succeeded in booking concerts, all of which were in California in our first full year. Promotion became easier over time, but in the beginning my uncle begged to get us onstage. Our performing skills were raw, we played covers just to fill out sets, and though we technically didn't play "surf music," that's how we were promoted ("Let's Go Surfin'" would appear on tickets). The approach triggered a backlash, as real surfers resented that a bunch of interlopers were profiting off their sport. We received some threats but avoided any real altercations.

We slowly raised our profile. In July, at the Diaper Derby in Oxnard (babies crawled across the rug while parents cheered them on), our appearance was broadcast on a local radio station, and we rated a few references in the *Los Angeles Times*. In September, we performed at the Pandora's Box on Sunset Strip, a small club that attracted young hipsters, and we received invitations to return. In October, we were invited to join a group of established singers and actors (Bobby Vee, Billy Vaughn, Chuck Connors, Soupy Sales) to perform at the famous Hollywood Bowl in Los Angeles, as part of a YMCA event that attracted 15,000 people. In December, the DJ and TV host Bob Eubanks asked us to open his new nightclub, Cinnamon Cinder, in Long Beach.

Though our music was geared to the *American Bandstand* crowd (the show made its debut in 1957), Uncle Murry wanted us to project an image that evoked Lawrence Welk or the Lennon Sisters. We had short hair and wore white dress shirts and could not use profanity onstage, a single curse word resulting in a $50 fine, assessed by my uncle. Drugs and alcohol were forbidden. His controlling style bred resentments, but we also knew that he was a canny salesman.

He understood that the radio was the gateway to success. Once the kids heard your music, they'd buy your record and see you perform. So Uncle Murry got in his car, toured the radio stations, and set up meetings with the DJs. He asked them about their families, offered some perfume for the wife back home, and followed up with thank-you notes. Aunt Audree, meanwhile, was answering phone calls for us, filling out paperwork, and depositing checks.

Paying DJs to play songs was against the law—recent payola investigations had shaken the industry—but Uncle Murry could finesse his way around the strictures. He would arrange with a DJ to throw a dance party or sock hop featuring the Beach Boys; he called it the "forty freebies," implying the length of our set list and including mostly covers. Tickets were sold. Sometimes the proceeds were split between the DJ and us, but the DJ usually kept all of it, putting several hundred dollars in his pocket. Throughout the Los Angeles area, we played dances on playgrounds and rooftops, in gyms and shopping malls, and we made it as far north as Bakersfield, about a hundred miles away. The DJ was the star, the impresario. It was *his* show. And he was grateful to Uncle Murry, reciprocating the goodwill by playing both sides of our single on the air.

Though no one used the phrase back then, we were the first boy band, meaning a group of young guys who played pop songs for teenagers. But the act that most closely resembled us was probably Jan and Dean, or Jan Berry and Dean Torrence, who in some ways paved the way for our success. In the late 1950s, as high school students in Los Angeles, Jan and Dean began singing doo-wop together. At the time, most of the teen idol singers were dark Italian guys on the East Coast. Jan and Dean were tall, tan, blond, and handsome, practically oozing California from every pore. Their break came in 1959 when they performed "Baby Talk" on *American Bandstand*, giving them an instant hit, placing them on the covers of fan magazines, and launching the whole California ideal of music, beaches, and young love.

But their celebrity didn't deliver them any lucrative record contracts. Jan and Dean both attended college with nonmusic careers in mind—Jan was premed at UCLA, Dean majored in architecture at USC. But they continued to perform on weekends.

When we were asked to open for them on Valentine's Day in February of 1963—one month after they released their next big single, "Linda"—we gladly accepted, and both groups performed together onstage. Jan was so taken by the sound that he called us a few days later and asked if they could record "Surfin'" and "Surfin' Safari" for their next album, whose title would be changed to *Jan and Dean Take Linda Surfin'*. We said of course and also provided some backup vocals. After the recording, Brian was having some fun on the piano and wanted Jan and Dean to listen to a song we'd been working on. He started pounding the keys and belted out the first line:

If everybody had an ocean

Jan immediately recognized the melody: Chuck Berry's "Sweet Little Sixteen."

"That's a really great song," Jan told him, "but you do realize that that's Chuck Berry's melody, and you can't just take someone's song and change the words and have it be yours."

Brian shrugged.

Jan offered to help. "We know Chuck. We can reach him in person, so why don't you give the song to us and maybe we can all do it together."

"My dad said it was okay," Brian said.

"Your dad works in a machine shop. He doesn't exactly know the business."

"I'll think about it," Brian said. "But I have another surf song that I'm not going to finish. Do you want to hear it?"

Two girls for every boy!

Brian sang a couple of verses of "Surf City" and repeated his offer.

"That's a pretty good song," Dean said. "But if you want our advice, you should finish 'Surf City' and you should give us 'Surfin' USA.' We'll contact Chuck Berry."

Brian wouldn't budge, so Jan and Dean accepted "Surf City," which they finished and released in May. Two months later, it became the first No. 1 surf song in history. Uncle Murry fumed, calling Jan and Dean "pirates," but there was enough surf glory to go around. "Surfin' USA" was indeed the better song, even if it did emulate "Sweet Little Sixteen." That song was about a teenage girl who wants to see rock and roll *in Philadelphia, PA . . . deep in the heart of Texas . . . 'round the Frisco Bay . . . All over St. Louis . . . way down in New Orleans*. Brian thought that surfing had that same appeal, if only everyone had an ocean.

A friend gave Brian the names of surfing spots in California and beyond, which he gave to me, and I modeled the lyrics to the melody, keeping the words in sync with the galloping track.

If everybody had an ocean.
Across the USA.
Then everybody'd be surfin',

Like Californi-a.
You'd see 'em wearing their baggies.
Huarache sandals too.
A bushy bushy blond hairdo.
Surfin' USA.

Carl and David devised a fierce opening guitar riff while Brian had us sing the vocals twice, the second time exactly on top of the first, perfectly synchronized, giving the lyrics—as Brian later described them—"a rather shrill and magical, much brighter, more gutsy and spectacular sound."

"Surfin' USA" was one of my favorite lead vocals. The truth is, I've never considered myself a particularly good singer. For one thing, I have a relatively soft voice, due in part to a bad case of whooping cough I had as a child. In the studio, the other guys shared a microphone, but—for maximum volume—I had my own. I saw myself as an earnest singer who employed different-sounding voices for different effects. I have a bass voice that I use for our harmonies, and then I have a louder lead voice that some people say has a "nasal" quality. Others call it "chesty." To me, it's just a voice that stands out in a way that's both distinctive and commercial. The vocals in "Surfin' USA" appealed to me if only because so many people have told me that the "Mike Love voice" was more evident on that track than any other.

We were now working with the William Morris Agency, and I would drive to its offices in Beverly Hills a couple times a week to talk about touring strategies. The offices also had the latest edition of *Billboard* or *Cashbox*, the most important weekly industry publications that charted record sales. Sometimes we'd get calls from Capitol or William Morris about how our records were doing, but I liked seeing the actual charts in print. "Surfin' USA," which was released on March 4, was only our fourth single, and we hadn't had a Top 10 hit yet. So each week I'd go to our agency, pick up *Billboard*, and watch "Surfin' USA" climb the chart, and then even higher, until it peaked at No. 3 on June 1.

Wow. The first hit is a big moment for any rock group, and "Surfin' USA" catapulted us from a regional garage band to a national force. I had considered ourselves a California group; "Surfin' USA," however, made me feel like we represented the United States, and I was proud of that. That sense of patriotism was heightened when I saw "Surfin' USA" race up the foreign charts as well, also listed in *Billboard*. The song charted in the United Kingdom, France, Sweden, Australia, and Japan. (The B side, "Shut Down," about a drag race involving a fuel-injected Stingray, was translated by the French as "Attention Accident.")

The superb arrangement of "Surfin' USA" would work in any country, but the aspirational message was also universal.

If everybody had an ocean, how good life would be.

Alas, Chuck Berry's lawyers heard the song as well. As predicted, Berry's publisher, ARC Music, immediately accused the Beach Boys of copyright infringement. The case was settled, with Berry receiving credit as a writer of "Surfin' USA."

I doubt Berry knew much about it at the time, as he was incarcerated in federal prison in Missouri, on trumped-up charges that he had had sex with a fourteen-year-old waitress whom he transported over state lines. Years later, I met Berry on a plane ride, and he told me, "I like what you did with 'Sixteen,'" which I took as a compliment.

"Shut Down" was cowritten by Brian and Roger Christian, a prominent DJ at KFWB in Los Angeles who was also an expert on cars. Uncle Murry didn't like Gary Usher, for no other reason, in my opinion, than my uncle didn't like anyone who got too close to Brian who was outside the family. He wanted Brian to find another writer who knew hot rods, so he introduced him to Roger. Though in his late thirties, Roger knew the youth culture, and he and Brian collaborated on some of our biggest car hits, including "Little Deuce Coupe" and "Don't Worry Baby."

I thought that Roger was gifted, and he was more than a gearhead. He cowrote with Brian one of my absolute favorite Beach Boy songs, "The Ballad of Ole' Betsy," about a 1932 jalopy; the lyrics captured how many of us felt about our first cars.

She had a classic beauty that everyone could see.
I was the last to meet her, but she gave her life to me.
She may be rusted iron, but to me she's solid gold.
And I just can't hold the tears back 'cause Betsy's growing old.

Three weeks after Capitol released "Surfin' USA," it distributed our next album, titled . . . *Surfin' USA*. We had become America's most popular band, closely associated with a particular theme, and Capitol assumed that fans couldn't get enough of it. The album, which had nine original Beach Boy songs, reached No. 2, eventually certified by the Recording Industry Association of America as gold (more than 500,000 units sold). Not every song was memorable, but we tried to keep things fun. Brian and I wrote about a "noble surfer" who was "dedicated to the mighty sea," but I would sing it like "no bull surfer," as in "no bullshit," he's a great surfer. The album included Carl's first song, "Surf's Jam," which he composed as an instrumental solo. Though other groups had recorded surf instrumentals (this album had five), we probably made them the most popular. Even the ballads about pain and loneliness had an oceanic theme. "Lonely Sea," written by Brian and Gary Usher (*This pain in my heart/These tears in my eyes/Please tell the truth/You're like the lonely sea*), deftly captured another side of Brian.

Capitol credited Nik Venet as the producer for the *Surfin' USA*

LP, even though Brian was the actual producer. Brian told Capitol that he would no longer work with Nik and would no longer record in the Capitol Tower. He wanted total control, a bold demand for any artist, let alone someone who was only twenty-one. But the Beach Boys had become a huge money-maker, so Capitol acceded. Brian knew he could get better sound at other studios, and he knew the people who could help him make it.

If Brian was generous in giving Jan and Dean a No. 1 song, they more than repaid the favor by opening up new musical doors for Brian. Jan was keenly interested in studio technology, liked trying out different recording equipment and playing with different studio musicians, including a young guitarist named Glen Campbell. Jan introduced Brian to these studio guys, or session players, and told him they were professionals, costing about $200 an hour. It made a lot more sense, Jan said, to work on the instrumental tracks with the session players and have the other Beach Boys sing the vocals later.

The idea appealed to Brian, and though he would not use the session players in full until 1965, a fundamental shift in the structure of the band had begun. Brian would stay in the studio, creating musical tracks, while the rest of us were on the road touring. Brian was never comfortable onstage, while he felt much more confident, secure, and productive in the studio.

Brian had other incentives for staying close to home. While performing at the Pandora's Box, he had met two teenage sisters, Diane and Marilyn Rovell, who along with their cousin Ginger Blake had a singing group. An instant connection was made, and Brian began writing music for them. He also spent time at the Rovells' house in the Fairfax section of Los Angeles, the historic center of the city's Jewish community. Brian became close with the parents, Irv and

Mae, who welcomed all of the Beach Boys to their home. Mrs. Rovell cooked for us and allowed us to hang out, play their piano, work on songs, and even crash on their sofa.

Mr. Rovell, an airplane machinist, was a stern figure who lightened up when we were around, and it was easy to see why Brian found a second home here. Mae possessed the nurturing qualities of his mother, while Irv had Murry's domineering personality without the penchant for abuse. The Rovells actually had three daughters, all attractive in their own way, and I wasn't sure which of the three Brian was most interested in or which of the three was most interested in him. What I knew was that Brian enjoyed the entire family's support and hospitality.

In 1963, Brian began missing some of our live performances, sometimes due to sickness or exhaustion, and he told us that he wanted to limit his time on the road. I don't recall any of us panicking. We assumed Brian would be back onstage soon enough. But the timing was difficult, as we had our first tours of the Midwest lined up for April and July. So Brian reached out to Al Jardine and asked that he fill in for him, playing bass and singing his parts. Al, recognizing our success and tiring of college life, agreed to come back. Everyone was relieved, except for Uncle Murry. In his mind, this was a family band, and Al, though helping to create it, wasn't part of the family. He treated Al with contempt while telling Brian that he was a quitter and that the fans expected him to be onstage, but there was nothing Murry could do about it.

Even though I was the oldest in the group, I don't believe I was better prepared for handling our success. One day you're sweating in a hot sheet metal factory, learning Spanish curse words, and the next day, you're singing before a thousand girls screaming at the top of their lungs. Dennis said the first time he heard the girls screaming, he thought there was a fire. It felt good to be a rock star, I can't deny that. In interviews, I said I was single—a complete lie, but I thought that was the image we were supposed to have. Frannie heard one of those interviews, and it hurt her. She was pregnant at the time, with our second child. When Frannie was near delivery, I drove her to the hospital and dropped her off, without ever entering. Our beautiful daughter Teresa was born on December 2, 1962; the first time I saw her was when I picked her up from the hospital with her mom.

There were obviously different expectations for men at the time, but even so, I was not prepared to be a father or a husband. I suddenly had this new life, the life of a young rock star, and for me that meant yielding to every sexual impulse and sleeping with as many women as possible. I didn't have many girlfriends in high school and can't say that girls beat the fence down trying to meet me. But now, suddenly, everything was different. I was like a kid in a candy store, and there was a lot of candy.

I know that Frannie was proud of the Beach Boys, delighted when she came to a concert at the Rendezvous Ballroom and from the mezzanine watched everyone on the floor doing the surfer's stomp in sync with our music. Our lifestyle improved gradually, as we moved into a small home in the Highland Park area of Northeast Los Angeles, and I upgraded from a Volkswagen to a blue Jaguar for $4,000. But I traveled. I stayed out late. I wasn't faithful. I also had a temper, and we argued, sometimes—in my case—far more heatedly than I should have. Trying to make sense out of it all, Frannie spoke to a psychologist, who told her, "You're married to a perennial adolescent, and he's not going to grow up."

I believe Frannie and I were both too young, but I could see where the psychologist was coming from. Frannie and I divorced in 1963. Because of the children, we always stayed in touch. Frannie earned her master's degree in nutrition, married a man who was worthy of her kindness, and she and I are better friends now than when we were married—a bad marriage with a good outcome, if there is such a thing.

After we split up, I rented a four-room unit on Hermosa Beach at 1727 Hermosa Avenue, for a while sharing it with Dennis, who was not yet twenty but had left his own house. Dennis and I had our battles over the years, often about women and later about his drug use and lifestyle. But no one ever said Dennis didn't have fun, and we had our share as roommates. We were both drinking a lot then, and the apartment was a nonstop party pad—I'd come home sometimes and not recognize half of the people there. I'm not sure Dennis recognized them either.

If the home front was a sexual wonderland, the opportunities multiplied once we started traveling around the country and then the world. It was a crazy time. The pill was approved in 1960, the country was moving toward a revolution in sexual and social mores, and rock music was an aphrodisiac. And for me, no matter how many flings or how many girlfriends, I was never satisfied.

As Frannie once said, women were my drug of choice.

On one of my weekend jaunts to Hawaii, I stayed at the Biltmore, where I met a beautiful young Japanese woman who sold real estate. She liked to wine and dine her clients, and though I wasn't looking for property, she invited me to her apartment for the night. The next day, I met an equally gorgeous Filipina woman. At lunch, the maître d' told us that her boyfriend was looking for her, so we escaped through the kitchen and spent the rest of the afternoon in my hotel room. That evening I happened to bump into an attractive young woman whom I knew from Dallas, and well, you know the rest. I was drinking mai tais, rum and Coke, and vodka and orange juice, and this delirious circuit, of three girls and copious booze, went on for a couple of days. Then I noticed—how shall I put it?—some leakage, and I feared the worst. So I went to a clinic and was examined by a Chinese doctor.

His diagnosis: nonspecific urethritis.

"Mr. Love," he said, "you're going to have to give up either women or drinking."

"Doc," I said, "I'm no longer thirsty."

For all of our recording success, we were still a party band, in every sense of the word. We were hired in January of 1963 by the ZBT House at the University of Arizona, our first trip outside of California. Elmer Marks agreed to come with us, and with his massive forearms and a barrel chest, he certainly looked the part of a road manager. But even he couldn't keep us in line. When we were playing in the frat house, I kept my saxophone case at the back of the stage and had a bottle of vodka in it. Unknown to me, David was taking swigs while we were playing our sets. After the performance, he staggered down a corridor of the house when his father approached him.

"Have you been drinking?" he demanded.

David shook his head.

"Have you been drinking?"

David again shook his head.

"Let me smell your breath."

David stepped forward and blew intoxicated air through pursed lips right into his father's face. Mr. Marks was not happy about it, but we stayed for three days.

Recognizing that we were not to be trusted, Mr. Marks agreed to be our road manager for our first midwestern tour in April of 1963. We flew to Chicago, rented a station wagon and a U-Haul trailer, and were off. At the William Morris Agency, we had been assigned to a junior agent, Marshall Berle, the nephew of Milton. Marshall did his best to find us gigs, even if it meant bouncing around the Midwest like a pinball. Our first show was 330 miles due west to Des Moines, where we drew 1,870 people at the Val Air Ballroom, a 1930s jazz club. The next night, we returned to Illinois, to the town of Rockville, one hour south of Chicago, and played at a teen club ($1.25 for members, $2.00 for guests). Then it was back to Iowa, this time at a ballroom in Cedar Rapids, the ticket announcing "The Phenomenal Beach Boys." The very next night, we drove 160 miles north to Austin, Minnesota, where we performed at the Terp Ballroom—or, according to the promotional ad, "The Famous Terp." Patrons, the ticket said, played "the exciting bell game for cash." I don't know how much cash, but we got $500. We next drove 200 miles west to Sioux City, South Dakota, where Al requested a $10 advance for new pants. Then we rambled a long 500 miles south to play at a dusty roller rink in Wichita.

For a bunch of California kids, this was a strange, exciting, bewildering time. One foggy night on a road in Iowa, we almost hit a cow. Another time we pulled over in a field and ate corn right out of the shucks. The Everly Brothers, whom we tried to emulate growing up, had recently toured many of the same cities; they apparently had damaged some motel rooms and—in David Marks's words—"devirginized" some of the local girls. The motel managers told us we had to behave or get tossed. To pass the time, we played ridiculous games, including eating huge meals to see who could produce the largest bowel movement.

But traveling itself, lugging our instruments and hauling our bags, was hard work as well as humbling. The sound was terrible in most of these places, the payouts were modest, the motels cheap. But the crowds, even the small ones, were always into it, the girls always shrieking. There were autographs. There were trysts. But more than anything, there was love for the music. It's quite a feeling to be driving through some cornfield and someone turns on the radio and you hear that you have the hottest record in America—"Surfin' USA!"— and then you hear yourself singing through multiple speakers.

After the roller rink in Wichita, we drove back north, more than

600 grueling miles, to Excelsior Park, Minnesota, southwest of the Twin Cities. We performed at Big Reggie's Danceland, a cavernous wooden structure that stood across from an amusement park and next to Lake Minnetonka. It held 2,000 people. Driving there, we heard on the radio "409" and "Surfin' Safari" as well as "Surfin' USA," and the DJs hyperventilating—"The Beach Boys are coming!"

At Big Reggie's, we stood on the wide stage, which had huge beams and a rafter overhead, and we played to a sold-out crowd. But the radio stations kept promoting us, and the people kept coming. They wouldn't sell any more tickets, so some fans came through a broken window in the bathroom. We played four forty-five-minute sets, and between sets, Dennis and I stepped outside and saw headlights stacked up a mile down the road.

"Wow," I said. "This must have been how Elvis started."

We finished the tour in Iowa and were scheduled to fly out of Des Moines. We had been on the road for only two weeks, but maybe it was too many cities in too few days, because at the airport, all hell broke loose between Dennis and me. We had water pistols and liked to goof around with them on the road, but today Dennis went to the bathroom, filled it with urine, and fired it at me and others in the airport lounge. I told him to cut that shit out, we got into an argument, and we decided to take it outside. We'd had plenty of arguments over the years but had never come to serious blows. It's not that Dennis and I were like oil and water. We were like burning oil and burning oil. Now we stood face-to-face on a grassy knoll . . . and then just mauled each other.

I was several inches taller and could handle myself pretty well, but he was strong and relentless. I jump-kicked him right in the chest and knocked him over, but he had barely hit the ground when he was right back on the attack. We pummeled each for a minute or so until Dennis tackled me and got me in a headlock. Lacking options, I opened my mouth, wrapped my teeth around his wrist, and bit as hard as I could. He yelled as I broke the skin, leaving him a scar. We lunged at each other again and rolled on the ground, with Dennis eventually standing over me. He was preparing to smash me with his fist but realized that his legs were spread and I was ready to drive my heel into his groin. "You motherfucker!" I said. "You hit me and you'll never have kids!" We stopped. We looked each other in the eye. We came to our senses. And we realized that we were still cousins, still bandmates, still booked to do our next show in a couple of nights. We walked back to the airport lounge.

Curiously, our hostilities served us well onstage, as the rest of the guys were usually static. Brian was in his own world. Carl was shy. David, young. Al, impassive. But Dennis and I hammed it up. We were, to be sure, competing for the attention of women, but it was also about putting on a great show. I pranced around, waving my arms, swinging my sax, banging a tambourine, trying to make eye contact with the prettiest girls. When we did "Monster Mash," they shined a green light on me, and I prowled the stage with a campish glare. Dennis, however, sitting on the riser, was nearly impossible to upstage. He held his drumsticks in an unconventional manner and was sometimes described as a "clubber," but he was riveting, pounding so hard that welts formed on the drumhead, rocking to the beat, sweat dripping from his brow, hair flopped across his forehead, sometimes standing at the end of a roll, his fist pumped to the sky. When he sang the lead on "Do You Wanna Dance?"—flailing the snare, smashing the cymbals, bellowing every word with that husky voice— girls literally wept. As one woman told me years later, "Dennis could just move his head, and women's zippers would drop."

By the time Jan Berry introduced Brian to the group of session players, Brian had become obsessed with Phil Spector, the wunderkind who had used some of those same musicians to become the most celebrated rock and roll producer in America. Like others in the field, Spector channeled boyhood anger and angst into fame and fortune. Born in the Bronx in 1939, he was only nine when his beloved father committed suicide. His mother, seeking to create a new life, moved the family to Los Angeles, but that only deepened the awkward youth's own feelings as an outcast. At thirteen, however, Phil got his first guitar, found refuge playing it alone in his bedroom, and dedicated himself to music. He had his first No. 1 single at nineteen, "To Know Him Is to Love Him," inspired by words from his father's tombstone. Spector was an accomplished producer by twenty-one, crowned the "Tycoon of Teen."

Brian discovered Spector in 1962 when he heard "He's Sure the Boy I Love" by Darlene Love and the Crystals, who the following year sang the Spector hits "Da Doo Ron Ron" and "Then He Kissed Me." But what really entranced Brian was "Be My Baby" by the Ronettes, which was to him pop perfection. When we'd go to Brian's house, he would play that song over and over again, comparing it to Einstein's theory of relativity.

Spector was one of the first to realize the difference between a great song and a great record, his goal being to create an ecstatic aural experience in the studio through the unconventional blending of instruments. He started with guitars. Then pianos. Horns. Drums. Saxes. Then maracas, tambourines, chimes, bells, castanets, doubling or tripling a single part. He liked Gold Star's Studio A because its low ceilings and tight configuration allowed for little separation among the ricocheting notes, coming at you as if in a wave, or a wall. Thus was born the Wall of Sound, played by the musicians who came to be known as the "Wrecking Crew." (The drummer Hal Blaine coined the name because older, more conservative musicians kept saying these young session players were going to "wreck the business.")

Brian was invited to Gold Star to watch Spector, a five-foot-seven ball of rage who bullied his singers relentlessly. Brian thought Spector was scary—he'd play things back at deafening levels—but he also held him in awe, a manic egotist who had redefined the producer's role: the producer, not the singer or the lyricist, was the star. Carl said that Spector put Brian "under a spell almost." Brian's competitive streak was always a mile wide. Now he saw in Spector not just the producer he wanted to emulate but the maestro he wanted to surpass.

It didn't take long to see Brian's own evolution as a producer.

On June 12, 1963, barely ten weeks after the *Surfin' USA* album was released, we began recording our next single as well as our next album. Nik Venet had left Capitol, but Brian didn't have complete control as producer because his father was still around. Brian, however, had gained more confidence and would no longer tolerate Murray's meddling. When his dad showed up at the studio, Brian told him to leave.

"Look, you don't understand rock and roll," he said. "I'm at the helm here. I'm producing these records."

He told his dad he was fired as producer.

"If I don't produce these records, you're going out of business," Murry said. "That's all there is to it."

"I know how to produce! I've been around."

"You guys are going down the tubes in six months!"

Brian prevailed, sort of. Uncle Murry remained in the studio and still voiced his opinions (he also remained our manager), but Brian was now the sole producer. The following month, Capitol released the single "Surfer Girl"/"Little Deuce Coupe," which hit No. 7 and removed all doubts about Brian's studio skills. It also ensured Capitol's blessing to allow Brian to produce our next album.

"Little Deuce Coupe," written by Brian and Roger Christian, had a shuffle beat and a memorable opening hook. While we were recording it, I thought it'd be fun to introduce the song in a way that lifted the veil on how a record was made, and I incorporated it into our live performances.

I'd tell the audience, "Some of you have asked how we go about making a record. We start with Denny Wilson on the drums!" (*Ba-da-dum!*) "Followed by David Marks on rhythm guitar!" (He and Dennis would play.) "Helped out by Carl 'Lead Guitar' Wilson." (All three would play.) "And filled out by our leader, Brian Wilson, on the bass." (They'd all play.) "And when we're ready to sing, we step up to the microphone, and it comes out something like this":

> *Little Deuce Coupe!*
> *You don't know what I got.*

The success of "Surfer Girl" paved the way for our next LP, titled—what else?—*Surfer Girl*. The album included both "In My Room" and "Catch a Wave," on which Brian wanted to use a harp, so he contacted the best harpist he knew—my sister Maureen. She was living in San Jose, and Brian called at ten A.M. and asked if she could be there that night. With her harp.

Maureen said she could, but he'd have to rent a harp locally, which he did. The recording session was supposed to last two or three hours. It took about seven, which wasn't unusual for Brian but meant Maureen didn't finish until around three A.M. It was well worth it, as her harp provided a magnificent glissando for both songs.

Not everything turned out exactly as expected on *Surfer Girl*. When I opened the album and looked at the record, I noticed that I hadn't been credited on two songs I had cowritten with Brian, "Catch a Wave" and "Hawaii." Only Brian's name was listed. I wasn't credited on "Surfin' USA" either, but I don't recall saying anything about that, because it was involved in threatened litigation as soon as it was released. But I couldn't understand how my name was omitted again.

I asked Brian, and he said he forgot to tell his dad, who was responsible for filing the songwriter agreements and copyright applications. Brian said his father would get it done.

In October, Capitol Records released the *Little Deuce Coupe* album—distributed just three weeks after our last LP and marking the third Beach Boy album in only seven months. Capitol pushed the breakneck pace, assuming the window of opportunity for any musical group—particularly one that appealed to teenagers—was small. With higher price points, wider profit margins, and loyal fans, our LPs were also a boon to retailers, none more than Tower Records, whose first store opened in Sacramento in 1960. Our surf and car albums created a frenzy among young buyers and affirmed the viability of a music megastore, which Tower pioneered across California, the United States, and overseas.

Led by Brian, we kept churning out new songs. *Little Deuce Coupe* was composed of mostly hot rod numbers (seven cowritten by Roger Christian), with Capitol sending DJs and record stores a book of car-racing terms to get everyone in the right frame of mind.

The album charted at No. 4, giving us three Top 10 LPs for the year, and it included an unlikely breakout song in "Be True to Your School"—that is, an album cut that was turned into a single.

When we recorded "Be True to Your School" for the album, Brian had the title and instrumental tracks but not the lyrics. So I wrote them on the fly—a breezy ode to our high school days, with references to a letterman's sweater, Friday-night football games, and cheerleaders. I took great care in every word. The first line, for example, was:

When some loud braggart tries to put me down,

"Braggart," to my ears, is more formal than "bragger," so I thought our more erudite fans would appreciate the subtlety.

When some loud braggart tries to put me down,
And says his school is great,
I tell him right away,
"Now what's the matter, buddy,
Ain't you heard of my school?
It's number one in the state."
So be true to your school.

The album cut was fine, but we thought it had more potential; so we re-recorded it as a single, including marching drums and cheerleaders. Released three weeks after the album, it reached No. 6 (and also hit No. 6 in Sweden). The B side, "In My Room," rose to No. 23.

I was pleased, except once again neither the album cut nor the single of "Be True to Your School" credited me as a cowriter. Only Brian's name was listed. When I asked Brian about it, he shrugged, said, "My dad fucked up," and dismissed it. I was disappointed that he didn't take it more seriously. The next time I saw my uncle, I asked him about it, and he told me he would take care of it. No big deal. I asked him several times over the next year or so, and each time he told me the same thing.

I had no reason to worry. The previous year, my uncle and Brian had established the Sea of Tunes, a music publishing company that would hold the copyrights of our songs, and Brian told me that the Sea of Tunes allowed him to control the numbers while his father handled the paperwork. I didn't understand the logistics but figured I didn't have to. I trusted Brian and assumed that his father would take care of the details and my name would eventually appear on the records. This was, after all, a family business.

CHAPTER 5

WHAT GOOD
IS THE DAWN

David Marks did not finish the year 1963 with the Beach Boys. Uncle Murry drove him out.

On another tour of the Midwest in July, my uncle hired a road manager to look over us, but the manager let us do what we wanted, even buying us beer and whiskey. When Uncle Murry discovered that we were having too much fun, he joined the tour in Chicago, fired the road manager, and drove us to our last concert in Brooklyn. (I had opted out of the crowded Chevy and was driving a separate car, my Jaguar.) In the car, a nasty argument erupted after Dennis told his father that some of them had contracted VD. Uncle Murry berated all of them but then narrowed in on David for his poor attitude. David yelled right back. "We're making you rich!"

Uncle Murry barked that if he didn't like the rules, he was welcomed to leave.

"Okay," David said. "I quit!"

My uncle confirmed it. "Well, all right, man. Does everybody hear that?"

By the time the guys told me what happened, no one believed David had actually quit. It was just an argument, and we argued all the time. David performed with us at the Fox Theatre in Brooklyn, and I assumed the issues with David would blow over. He played with us for our first national TV appearance on September 24 on *The Red Skelton Show.* (We lip-synched "Surfin' USA" while wearing sailor outfits.)

But David's problems were deeper than one argument. As he has long acknowledged, he was immature and cocky. After the blowup in the car, he'd sometimes distort the lyrics onstage—singing *"She's real fine, my 69,"* or *"Little Douche Kit!"* David had also begun rehearsing with his own band on the side. But the real issue was that Uncle Murry wanted him out of the group. On one of our famous photographs of the Beach Boys carrying a surfboard, David stood at the far right, and my uncle would take a scissors, cut him out, and then hand the picture to him, or on other promotional pictures, he put Carl's face over David's so there were two Carls.

Why the resentment? David's parents were pressuring my uncle about their son's compensation. Lacking any trust in Murry, Elmer and Jo Ann Marks wanted to be part of the management team. Uncle Murry refused. As far as he was concerned, David served at his pleasure. The tensions reached a head in October when David and his parents met with my uncle at his house. When no compromise could be reached, Mrs. Marks announced that David was out of the Beach Boys.

"Go ahead," my uncle said. "He'll be nothing."

Al Jardine returned on a permanent basis, and the group rolled on. But David's contributions have often been overlooked. He played his electric Fender Stratocaster, with panache and swagger, on our first four LPs and on some of our biggest songs, including "Surfin' USA," "Little Deuce Coupe," and "409"—all before he was old enough to drive. But as his parents feared, my uncle exploited him. When David left the Beach Boys, he signed an agreement that he was no longer a member as of August 30, 1963. That seemingly nullified the contract with Capitol that he had signed a year earlier, but that contract—approved by the Los Angeles Superior Court—stipulated that the court had to approve any changes in his status. The court, however, was never informed of David's departure and therefore did not approve it, which meant the terms of the original contract remained in force until 1969. In other words, David was denied artist royalties that he was owed for six years. His share was absorbed by the rest of the band. David's parents, a blue-collar worker and a homemaker, didn't realize what they were doing, and David didn't discover the betrayal until more than forty years later—too late to recover the millions of dollars that he had lost.

Capitol continued to pressure us for hits, so in November of 1963, Brian and I set aside some time to write a new song. Brian had recently rented a house for himself, which gave him the space to create his music. There was a keyboard and a bass guitar in the living room, a couple of mattresses in the bedroom, a lamp or two. If there was any food in the place, you ate it at your own risk. There was no TV. When I opened the door, Brian was immersed in his own world, at the keyboard in the evening light, working out a haunting melody, and I sat next to him with my yellow pad in hand.

I'm a Pisces, and Brian, a Gemini; and it is said that a Pisces writes out of inspiration while a Gemini writes out of desperation. I think that was true of Brian and me. Brian could be moody, disenchanted, traits that were evident in "In My Room" or "Lonely Sea," while I was naturally drawn to more upbeat melodies that lent themselves to feel-good verses. But as I now listened to these tones—with Brian leaning into the keyboard, finding the chords to complement the melody that had come to him—I felt a profound sadness wash over both of us.

This song was obviously no place for cheerleaders or beaches. Instead, I remembered a girl named Georgia.

I had met her earlier that year, on a long weekend in Hawaii, where you could fly round trip on Western Airlines for $200.04. Georgia was blond and radiant, the daughter of a musician, and I was smitten. When I returned to Los Angeles, I was eager to see her again. Until I got the letter. She wrote that she didn't feel the same toward me as I toward her. It was over before it began.

Georgia wasn't the love of my life. I barely knew her. But in writing these lyrics, I drew on that feeling of lost love. We all know that feeling. Maybe it was your first love and she broke your heart, or it was a deep love that faded before you were ready to let it go, or it was the infatuation with a woman you had just met over a long weekend.

Lost love lingers, in a positive way, because the experience itself has value. That's how I saw it. Though Georgia did not reciprocate my feelings, what she had made me feel still lived on. Now in working with Brian, I needed a phrase or image to capture that feeling, conveying that things have changed, that the love is no longer there, but the memory of it lingers like . . . *the warmth of the sun.*

Brian had written the opening, which could have been scored for strings but instead would use the finest instruments we owned—our voices. We then worked on the verse and the chorus, batting around ideas and words. I write fast, and this poem took us about thirty minutes.

What good is the dawn that grows into day.
The sunset at night, or living this way.
For I have the warmth of the sun within me at night.

The love of my life, she left me one day.
I cried when she said, "I don't feel the same way."
Still I have the warmth of the sun within me tonight.

I'll dream of her arms and though they're not real.
Just like she's still there's the way that I feel.
My love's like the warmth of the sun, it won't ever die.

I sang it for Brian as he continued to play those exquisite chords. It felt like a song that could stir the soul, and it was one of the most emotional, even mystical experiences that we had ever had together. Exhausted, we crashed on his mattresses at around two A.M.

In the morning, we woke up and turned on the radio. It was November 22, 1963, and the broadcaster said, "President Kennedy was taken to Parkland Memorial Hospital in Dallas . . ."

My response was typical of that of most Americans. Total shock. Complete disbelief. I wasn't terribly political, but this had nothing to do with politics. Something had been lost—call it innocence if you wish—and for a group of guys who had spent much of their time exalting sunny California pastimes, it defied all explanation.

The Beach Boys were scheduled to play that night—it was a Friday—in Marysville, California, about forty miles north of Sacramento. Our promoter, Fred Vail, who himself was only a nineteen-year-old college student, called city officials in Marysville to see if we should still perform. He was told yes—everyone was still looking forward to seeing us. So we flew up there, paid tribute to President Kennedy with a moment of silence, and fulfilled our commitment. (Our show the following night, in Sacramento, was rescheduled.)

I don't recall much about the concert, but I do know that Brian and I were even more motivated to refine our new song. The country had changed, and we somehow understood that this piece of music had assumed a different meaning. On January 1, we recorded "The Warmth of the Sun" in Western Recorders Studio 3, and Brian's arrangement elevated the song to a whole other level. The wordless melody that began the song unfurled our voices, with Brian on top. The lyrics, as originally written and never changed, were about the loss of any loved one, but when we recorded the track, we were all thinking about the loss of President Kennedy. He may be gone, but his idealism, like any lost love, would linger forever. The studio was absolutely charged, and the vocals were filled with a depth of emotion rarely experienced in the life of any band.

"The Warmth of the Sun," released on *Shut Down Volume 2* in March and then as a single in October, was embraced by music fans around the country and the world as an anthem to the slain president. To me and others of my generation, it continues to evoke memories of JFK and all that he represented. The song was also a reminder that while pop music is often marginalized as that which is simply popular at a given moment, a mere confection for the masses, the best pop music endures far beyond the moment; it can comfort and soothe and touch you deep in your heart, and it can even play a small role in the healing of a nation.

Unintentionally, our final single of 1963 also fit the mood of the country.

In August, during one of Brian's studio visits with Phil Spector, he watched Spector produce songs for a Christmas album, which would feature mostly secular tunes, such as "White Christmas" and "Frosty the Snowman." Spector's was not the first Christmas album, but he redefined the genre with his tour de force production. For one song, he invited Brian to play the piano, which Brian declined. Nonetheless, Brian was inspired to create his own Christmas song—"Little Saint Nick," which included sleigh bells, a triangle, and a glockenspiel (a percussion instrument similar to a xylophone). Brian composed it while he was driving in his car, his head bobbing, his fingers thrumming the wheel, remembering every note until he could put it down on paper. In rhythm and structure "Little Saint Nick" was similar to "Little Deuce Coupe," except the lyrics (most of which I wrote) were about a bobsled instead of a car.

The single was released on December 9 and became a revered holiday classic. But I was far more impressed with the B side—an a cappella rendition of Albert Hay Malotte's musical adaptation of "The Lord's Prayer." The prayer itself, taught by Jesus to his disciples (*Thy Kingdom come/Thy will be done*), is one of the most venerated in Christianity.

Brian, sitting at the piano, worked out four interlocking harmonies, somehow tracking each in his head, and then he hummed each one to us. I sang the bass part, which moved all over the place. It was all I could do to learn it. How Brian mastered all four, I have no idea, but each voice wrapped exquisitely around the other. We sang it over and over again in search of perfection.

The intricate harmonies were similar to those in other songs we did that year, including "Surfer Girl" and "In My Room." Over the decades, critics have suggested that the Beach Boys' early music was facile or "poppy"—easy listening but lacking in depth or sophistication. But Brian's arrangements had complex layers that were so seamless they were not appreciated or recognized. It was, I believe, one of the secrets to his genius: simplicity camouflaging complexity.

We spent many hours on "The Lord's Prayer." It wasn't about ego or money or fame or any expectation that a solemn blessing was going to be commercial. It was about using vocals to elevate sacred words into something deeper and more spiritual.

When we finally got it right, we played the recording back to the session players, and they were overwhelmed by its power and beauty. I do believe it was Brian's greatest vocal arrangement. As Beach Boys' historian James B. Murphy wrote, it was "perhaps the purest two minutes of vocal harmony every recorded."

———

The Beach Boys closed out 1963 sitting on a comfortable perch as the nation's No. 1 band, with four singles during the year, all Top 10 hits, and three Top 10 LPs. Even "Little St. Nick" reached No. 3. In January of 1964, we embarked on our first international tour to Australia and New Zealand, performing to the throngs in Brisbane and Sydney and Melbourne. It was somewhere in the Pacific that we heard the Beatles were coming to America.

CHAPTER 6

KEEPING UP WITH
THE BEATLES

certainly knew about the Beatles, who had already released two albums and four singles in the United Kingdom, breaking sales records in the process. "She Loves You" sold 750,000 records in a month. Though Beatlemania had swept the United Kingdom, none of us in America—neither the Beach Boys nor most anyone else in the recording industry—recognized how the Fab Four would transform American rock and roll. British rock groups simply hadn't had much success here. I know our label didn't see the Beatles as a revolutionary force. Capitol's parent company in the United Kingdom, EMI Records, signed the Beatles in early 1962, but Capitol refused to pick up their option for more than a year. Capitol did not release a Beatles' single in the United States ("I Want to Hold Your Hand"/"I Saw Her Standing There") until the last week of 1963, and only then under pressure from its British parent. It didn't take long for Capitol to realize what it had been missing. By February 1, "I Want to Hold Your Hand" was No. 1.

We knew the Beatles had a good sound, and any uncertainty about their appeal—could four "mop-tops" from Liverpool make it in America?—quickly vanished. When they flew in to New York on

February 7, they were met by an estimated 3,000 fans at John F. Kennedy Airport, and then two nights later were watched by nearly 74 million on *The Ed Sullivan Show*, appearing there again the following week. Ed Sullivan had yet to invite us. To varying degrees, all of us in the Beach Boys were rattled, but most of all Brian, who saw the Beatles as a challenge to his emerging position as a leader in pop music. It didn't help any of us that Capitol launched a huge promotional campaign for the Brits ("The Beatles Are Coming!"), including newspaper ads that touted albums from the Beatles but not the Beach Boys.

Personally, I loved the Beatles' music and saw, at least in the early days, similar themes between them and us in our boisterous songs about teenage life. Whether you wanted to twist and shout or load up your woody, you were living in the same carefree world. Neither band was about a single performer but about an entire group and the countries they represented. Though I knew the Beatles had changed the competitive landscape, I never felt threatened or resentful. I thought they would make us better.

What is often overlooked about the Beatles is how smart they were in their marketing, merchandising, and publicity, and in that regard, they ran circles around us for the next several years. I'm not suggesting their music wasn't superb—it was—but they also knew how to exploit its commercial value. They understood film in ways that we did not: *A Hard Day's Night*, starring the Beatles and released in 1964, at the height of Beatlemania, became one of the most influential music films of all time. On the other hand, the Beach Boys in 1965 played backup to Annette Funicello in *The Monkey's Uncle*, a Disney film about college kids and a chimpanzee. The Beatles had the long hair, the dark suits, the boots, the glamorous publicity shots, the creative album covers, all of which evolved with the times. The Beach Boys, in 1964, began wearing candy-striped shirts. (In interviews, we said, "We accidently picked up the Kingston Trio's dry cleaning.")

The Beatles knew how to merchandise, not just with T-shirts, stickers, and posters but with lampshades and lunch boxes and pinball machines. The Beach Boys? Uncle Murry made buttons that read "I Know Brian's Dad." On Ringo's Ludwig Oyster Black Pearl drums, the Beatles had their name, with the drop *T*, emblazed boldly across the bass drumhead—a suave modern logo. Our bass drumhead was just a bass drumhead.

We lacked management. We had no one who could do for us what Brian Epstein did for our counterparts, nor could we compete with their irreverence, charisma, or wit. In November of 1963, when the Beatles played at the Royal Variety Performance in London—attended by Queen Elizabeth, among other luminaries—John Lennon said, "For our last number, I'd like to ask your help. Would the people in the cheaper seats clap their hands? And the rest of you, if you'll just rattle your jewelry."

We could not rival that. But musically, that was a different story.

Our two-week tour to Australia and New Zealand confirmed that our act traveled to other countries. That shouldn't have been surprising, as the cultural overlap between these Pacific nations and America (including surfing) is significant. Our tour's headliner, Roy Orbison, the shades-wearing country-pop singer who was at the peak of his career, had one of the finest voices I've ever heard; I was spellbound when he sang "Crying." After three shows in Sydney, we flew to Melbourne and were met midday at the airport by 3,000 teenagers. We did four shows in Melbourne, four in Tasmania (an island off the coast of Australia), and then sixteen in New Zealand, including five in two days in Auckland. Packed houses were the norm.

January was the summer in these countries, which allowed us to spend plenty of time on the beach, though that was just one of many diversions. We had an opening act called the Joy Boys, a popular Australian surf band whose members were a bit older than we. They had a rapturous effect on young women and liked to invite their most attractive groupies to something called a Shalomanakee. The same invitation was extended to us (including our backup singers, roadies, and managers). At a hotel suite in Sydney, we entered a dim, smoky room, with sheets covering table lamps. Music played softly in the background and the Australian beer poured freely. Shalomanakee implied an exotic ritual or even something spiritual. But there were the Joy Boys and their lady friends, all in various stages of undress. We had walked into our first Australian orgy. I personally had no interest in group sex (neither did Carl), but it must be said, the Joy Boys were true performers. A naked Joy Boy rolled up a newspaper into a funnel, lit the big end on fire, and stuck the other end in his buttocks. Then he started waltzing around the room—they called this "the dance of the flames." The other Joy Boys did this as well and even some of the groupies. They were fearless. You just don't see buck-naked men and women romping around a darkened room with flames shooting out of their asses all that often. I thought it was a miracle.

Well, Dennis and I absolutely had to bring the dance of the flames to America, and we believed that the Hawaiian Islands were the perfect locale for such an original import. So along with others in our group, and with the help of a mai tai or two, we did our own interpretation of this unique jig, though not without a fire extinguisher nearby. A few lamps were knocked over, but no one got burned.

Brian sat out most of these escapades. While we were in Australia, he spent much of his free time in his hotel room talking on the phone to Marilyn. We knew he didn't like being on the road, but his loneliness and discomfort became even more evident on our first trip abroad. He would talk to Marilyn in his hotel room before our concert began; then he would go to the arena and perform onstage; then he would return to his hotel room; and Marilyn would still be on the phone!

The trip was noteworthy for one other reason: Uncle Murry accompanied us. He was still upset by some of our high jinks from the last midwestern tour, and he may have been concerned that as we became more successful, we had more to lose. Whatever it was, he hovered over us with moralistic zeal, prowling the corridors of our hotels in his largely hopeless efforts to ensure that we hadn't broken curfew or were not with a date. He fined us up to $200 if we used profanity near reporters or fans. Given that cursing came pretty easily to all of us, that seemed unreasonable. I later found out that he tried to get Nik Venet to fire me because I swore within earshot of some fans. Well, fuck him. That's how I talked.

Brian actually had it worse, his father still trying to exert control over the music at the very time that Brian's skills were blossoming. Uncle Murry walked right onstage in Sydney and turned down Brian's bass—Brian liked the low-end distortion, while his father didn't. At other times, my uncle stood side stage and made a *T* signal for "treble up," or more highs on the bass. Brian resisted.

Murry had bullied Brian for years, but he increasingly called into question his manhood.

"If you were a man, you would tell Mike to stand closer to the microphone."

"If you were a man, you would tell Carl and Dennis to brush up on their harmonies."

"If you were a man . . ."

"If you were a man . . ."

Man came up all the time, which probably influenced Brian's idea behind our 1964 song, "When I Grow Up (To Be a Man)." (I cowrote the number and most of the lyrics.) Murry's focus on what it meant to be a man, or masculinity, also hinted at one of his great fears for his sons. "I don't want any of my boys," he would say, "to end up being one of those Hollywood fags."

Enough was enough. After we got back from Australia, Brian and I got the guys together, and we took a vote on whether Murry should remain as our manager. Even Carl, who might have been most reluctant to fire his father, knew it had to be done. It was five-zero to dismiss. Brian and I drove to his parents' house, and Brian told him straight out: "Look, we can't deal with you anymore. We've got to get a new manager."

His dad was shocked. How could he be fired? This was *his* band!

Some nasty words were exchanged between father and son, and then we left. My uncle was only forty-six years old, but the episode sent his life into a spiral. He already had an ulcer, and he had sold his leasing company to devote all his energies to the Beach Boys. Aunt Audree later said that his dismissal "destroyed" him—he stayed in bed for weeks. A couple of months later, in April of 1964, he appeared at a studio session, inflamed and inebriated, and approached Brian, who was at the control board.

"Get out of the way," Murry huffed. "Get out of my way for a minute."

Brian had a hard time standing up to his father, but this time he did. "No! You get out of my way!" Then he shoved his dad, who went sprawling backward. That was the only time I ever saw Brian defy him physically, and Murry, defeated, left the studio.

That summer, Audree and Murry sold their house in Hawthorne and moved about twenty-five miles east to Whittier, a town founded by Quakers but mostly known, in years to come, as the childhood home of Richard Nixon. Though his role with the Beach Boys had diminished, my uncle still managed the Sea of Tunes catalog, still controlled our song credits, and could still influence the future of the band. He was also entering a period in which his grievances only deepened. A letter he wrote on August 7, 1964, surfaced years later on the Internet. Titled "Last Will and Testament," it spelled out his bill of particulars against Audree.

Regarding their sons, he wrote, she was "too lax, too indulgent, too soft," which undermined his authority. "The result of this is that I am a very unhappy and broken hearted man." It got worse. "When [Audree] told me on this date, August 7, 1964, that she did not enjoy intercourse with me anymore, although she would pretend to be my wife and even sleep in the same bed with me, this proved to my satisfaction that she did not love me any more." Murry preferred the appearance of a marriage and laid down this threat: "If Audree Wilson, my wife, is not legally married to me at the time of my death, I ask the court handling my estate to see that she receives only one half of any said monies."

The letter showed, beyond resentment and self-pity, my uncle's desire to impose financial hardship on his wife in case she ended the marriage. Vindictiveness came naturally to him. I'd find that out personally soon enough.

On February 3, 1964, even as the Beatles were sweeping America, we released a new single, conceived in rather spontaneous fashion. The previous September, Brian and I were in a taxi in Salt Lake City, Utah, heading from a Holiday Inn to the airport. I told Brian that I thought we should write a song about that teenage experience of getting your driver's license, borrowing your parents' car, and then driving to see and be seen. It was a rite of passage. But instead of a teenage boy doing it, I had this image of a great-looking girl in a hot car, and she tells her father one thing to borrow the car but then does something else. We unspooled the idea further. We thought it should be up-tempo, with a

Chuck Berry opening guitar riff (like that in "Johnny B. Goode"), and because we were in Southern California, the girl should not be taking her "father's car" but her "daddy's car." Brian wrote the music, and I wrote most of the lyrics.

> Well she got her daddy's car and she cruised through the
>   hamburger stand now.
> Seems she forgot all about the library like she told her old
>   man now.
> And with the radio blasting,
> Goes cruising just as fast as she can now.
> And she'll have fun, fun, fun,
> Till her daddy takes the T-bird away.

Showcasing Brian's falsetto, "Fun, Fun, Fun" reached No. 5. I always felt that any time you had a Top 10 song—a hit—you've done well. But we didn't get any higher because the Beatles occupied the top three slots ("She Loves You," "I Want to Hold Your Hand," and "Please Please Me") while the Four Seasons held No. 4 ("Dawn [Go Away]").

Capitol wanted our next album out immediately, so on March 2 it released the oddly titled *Shut Down Volume 2*. The previous year, the label released an album called *Shut Down*, a hot rod compilation of various artists that included the Beach Boys' "Shut Down" and "409." In *Shut Down 2*, however, fewer than half of the songs mentioned cars. Though it included some of our finest originals ("Fun, Fun, Fun," "Don't Worry Baby," "The Warmth of the Sun"), plus some quality covers ("Why Do Fools Fall in Love"), the whole thing was rushed to keep up with the Beatles. It also included one of our more unusual collective efforts: "Cassius Love vs. Sonny Wilson." Cassius Clay and Sonny Liston were to square off in a title match days before the release of the album. Our song was a mock fight between Brian and me, with the guys joining. It was all in fun, but it captured part of my relationship with Brian: We showed our respect and love for each other through sarcastic gibes and clever put-downs.

In the song, I tell Brian, "When I'm singing, it doesn't sound like Mickey Mouse with a sore throat."

He later responds, "Man, at least I don't sound like my nose is on the critical list."

He got me on that one.

After three consecutive Top 10 albums, *Shut Down Volume 2* stalled at 13, which was disappointing. We didn't want to fall further behind the Brits, and our next record ensured that we didn't. In April, Brian invited us to his office on 9000 Sunset in Hollywood and played us some new tracks, which revealed how much he was progressing as a composer. He employed unusual chord progressions to create "fake modulations," when you think a song is moving into a different key but it stays in the same key. Brian also combined chords that do not occur naturally in the same key, which was rarely done in pop music, yet they fit together beautifully.

The lyrics, I thought, needed some work. I was never shy in expressing my views about the wording, and Brian was not reluctant to tell me when my vocals had fallen short. These exchanges— sometimes tense, at times crude, but never disrespectful—usually produced a good outcome. In this case, Brian had written lines about a guy looking for a new place to hang out. The opening was:

Well there's a million little girls just waitin' around.
But there's only so much to do in a little town.
I get around from town to town.

I thought it meandered, without a strong beat.

"Those are pussy lyrics," I said. "I went to Dorsey High, and I'm not going to sing them."

I had another idea. "Why don't we do it like this? Remember 'Barbara Ann'"—performed by the Regents and released in 1961. "It goes, 'Ba ba ba ba Barbara Ann.' How about, 'Round, round. Get around. I get around.'"

"Whoa," Brian said. "Terrific."

I didn't know that we would cover "Barbara Ann" the following year. It was just a song that I really liked, particularly the hook.

I also tinkered with Brian's first verse, which was about this bored kid driving around but was really about our own experiences: how we had this instant fame, some fortune, had traveled all over the country, but did any of that bring us happiness? Maybe we needed to find a different kind of place.

I'm getting bugged driving up and down the same old strip.
I gotta find a new place where the kids are hip.
My buddies and me are getting real well known.
Yeah, the bad guys know us and they leave us alone.

Brian rearranged the vocals and had us sing the opening a cappella, which we did again in the latter third of the song. The opening hook became the recurring chorus, some handclaps were added; so were bongos and an organ and specific guitar parts instead of just chords; and Brian's falsetto soared across the top of the melody.

It was an unbelievable arrangement; the song just jumped out of the radio. "I Get Around," released on May 11, became the Beach Boys' first No. 1 single; it also reached No. 7 in the United Kingdom, making it our first Top 10 hit there, and hit No. 38 in Germany. The B side was "Don't Worry Baby," which was modeled after the Ronettes' "Be My Baby." It was one of Brian's strongest vocals and had a great vocal counterpoint: Brian sang *Everything will be all right,* and Al, Dennis, and Carl backed him up with *Don't worry, baby,* while I sang a moving bass part *Now don't you worry, baby.*

To have two classics—"I Get Around" and "Don't Worry Baby"—on one single was pretty good, but we discovered what all pop artists discovered. As exciting as it is to see a record climb the charts, it inevitably falls, sometimes quickly. "I Get Around" remained No. 1 for two weeks. So it was all about the next new song, recording it, getting it on the radio, getting it charted, keeping the ball rolling.

Our next album, *All Summer Long*, was released in July, with "I Get Around" as the lead, and it reached No. 4. Capitol wanted a "live LP," so we obliged with *Beach Boys Concert*, which drew from our live performances and was released in October. Led by "Fun, Fun, Fun" and including covers of "Little Old Lady from Pasadena" and "Papa-Oom-Mow-Mow," that album was our first to reach No. 1. October also saw the release of our first Christmas album, which charted at No. 6. We released three other singles as well, including "When I Grow Up (To Be a Man)" and "Dance, Dance, Dance," which Carl and I cowrote with Brian, reaching No. 8.

Five singles and four albums—by any measure, an extraordinary year. It did nothing to slow down the Beatles, who had nine Top 10 singles and six albums that charted either 1 or 2, but both commercially and artistically, we were doing our best to hold our own.

After Uncle Murry was fired, I became more involved in touring strategy. It was something that fascinated me. How do we maximize our time on the road? What's the best itinerary to reach the most fans in the fewest number of days? I wasn't satisfied with getting telephone updates from the William Morris Agency; instead I visited the office a couple of times a week and tried to figure out this part of the business. What I learned was that it wasn't a very good business for the artists. The big cities were controlled by individual promoters, who would take a significant percentage of the take in exchange for securing a venue and handling the security and the publicity. The promoters were local power brokers, and if circumvented, they could block artists' access to the best sites or deter radio stations from playing their music. The artists themselves had little recourse.

My response: We'll capitulate when we have to, but let's also play in secondary or tertiary markets. For a gig in Philadelphia, we followed it with concerts in Harrisburg and Hershey. If we were booked in Seattle, let's also play in Hoquiam and Spokane. And why settle for only one performance a day? We once played two concerts in Canton and two in Akron on the same day.

To pull this off, we hired our own promoter, Irving Granz, whose older brother, Norman, was perhaps America's most famous jazz producer. Irv also had an impressive client list, including Peter, Paul and Mary, the Righteous Brothers, and the Kingston Trio, not to mention a fast-rising black comedian named Bill Cosby. In our arrangement with Irv, we covered his costs for finding the concert venue, publicity, and security, and then he took 10 percent of the gross. It was a great deal for Irv; one of his assistants later wrote a book on the Beach Boys, which included a chapter, "How to Make a Buck on Someone Else's Dime."

But we wanted to perform as much as possible, and I've always liked playing in smaller markets. It's not that fans in New York or Los Angeles don't enjoy good concerts, but I think that fans in, say, Wichita or Tulsa, who are often ignored by top acts, appreciate you even more. In July of 1964, we embarked on a thirty-three-day tour across America, playing forty-two concerts. We weren't a hit everywhere—support was a bit tepid in Amarillo—but we were mostly well received, regardless of market size. Our concert in Davenport, Iowa, according to news reports, almost started a riot. In Worcester, Massachusetts, we did have a riot. We performed at Memorial Auditorium on the night before Halloween, a Friday, so maybe that contributed to the mayhem. We were on for less than fifteen minutes, and right at the beginning of "Fun, Fun, Fun," a bunch of girls climbed onto the stage and began to mob us. The cops were there but couldn't stem the tide. We tried playing one more time, but when the stage was about to be stormed again, the curtain fell, and the concert was canceled. Meanwhile, outside the auditorium, kids without tickets had gone on a rampage. A newspaper reported a roving gang of two to three hundred boys was breaking windows and doors to try to enter the building, and the police had to use clubs to keep them outside. It was one of our most memorable nights, for all the wrong reasons.

For the most part, I believe, we always delivered what the crowd came to see, and we kept up this touring pace for several years. For me, it was never a hardship. I much preferred being onstage over being in a studio, which I thought was cramped and claustrophobic. I also liked being the front man and seeing the response of the audience. That part of the job never gets old. How could it? I loved as well many of our opening acts. One of the most flamboyant was Sam the Sham and the Pharaohs, who hit it big with "Wooly Bully"; their lead singer was Mexican American, even though the group itself was Egyptian-themed (they wore turbans and drove a hearse with velvet curtains). We had opening acts with colorful names: the Tulu Babies, the Peanut Butter Conspiracy, the Strawberry Alarm Clock (whose big hit was "Incense and Peppermints"). We had opening acts that were either already stars or nearing stardom: Buffalo Springfield, the Byrds, Paul Revere and the Raiders, Neil Diamond, the Righteous Brothers, Sonny and Cher, the Kinks, Billy Joel, and Dino, Desi, and Billy, just to name a few.

In October of 1964, we played at the T.A.M.I. Show (Teenage Music International) in Santa Monica. The event, which was filmed for a documentary, included Chuck Berry, James Brown, the Supremes, and Smokey Robinson, among other amazing performers. The Beach Boys played four songs, but hell, it was just an honor to be onstage with some of my heroes. I met Marvin Gaye there.

Though Marvin was still early in his career—he would have two No. 1 R&B songs the following year and would record "I Heard It Through the Grapevine" (No. 1) in 1968—he was one of my favorite singers. We struck up a conversation, ended up smoking a joint outside during rehearsal, and maintained a friendship, sometimes seeing each other on tour and even sharing in a few harmless pranks. We were once staying at the same hotel in London, in which the guests set their shoes outside their doors at night to be polished. So we moved the shoes to different doors. It was silly, but so were we, and we're sure that all the wing tips and pumps made it back to their well-heeled owners.

Marvin established himself as a Motown star, singing the timeless classic "What's Going On" in 1971 and becoming a crossover sensation. But his chaotic personal life, caused mostly by drug addiction, tore him apart. Depression, divorces, and financial loss were all part of the mix; at one point he spent a year in Europe to avoid the IRS. But in the early 1980s, some promoters were going to help Marvin get his career back on track. They invited me to come to a meeting, at the Circle Star Theatre in San Carlos, California. That night, Barry Manilow was performing, and one of Marvin's promoters asked Barry if he would acknowledge that Marvin Gaye and Mike Love were in the audience.

The word soon came back. "Barry feels this is his night," the promoter said. "He doesn't want to really bring attention to you guys being here."

I didn't think that was too generous of him, but then I thought about it. "Marvin," I said, "that's all right. I don't think we really want people to know we're here anyway, do we?"

After the meeting, Marvin and I went out to the limo and caught up.

"Hey, Love. I got a song to tell you about."

"What's that?"

"It's a song about a lady, and it's called 'Sanctified Pussy.'"

I howled. "Whew, Marvin. That's one of the greatest titles I've ever heard!"

Marvin's comeback succeeded, as he won Grammys for his 1982 releases of "Sexual Healing" and the album *Midnight Love*. But he couldn't beat the heroin. In 1984, I saw him in his dressing room before a concert in Orlando, and it was obvious he had just shot up. He was leaning back in his chair and seemed nearly out of it. "Oh, Mike, I am so sick," he said.

Incredibly, he went onstage about forty minutes later and did his set, and I don't think the fans even knew how wasted he was. This was billed as the Sexual Healing Tour, but there wasn't nearly enough healing.

Within a month or so, I got the news that Marvin, one day shy of his forty-fifth birthday, was dead. His father, after an argument, had shot him twice at point-blank range, once in the heart. Marvin Senior, diagnosed with a brain tumor, pleaded no contest to voluntary manslaughter. Marvin Junior's autopsy revealed cocaine in his body. So much soul, so many demons. His ashes were scattered in the Pacific Ocean.

And what about the "sanctified" song? It was renamed "Sanctified Lady" and released posthumously, though I'm sure Marvin would be glad to know that if you listen to it closely, when the chorus chants "sanctified lady," you can hear him murmur "sanctified pussy."

A lso at the T.A.M.I. Show were the Rolling Stones, whose first tour of the United States was in June of 1964 and, combined with the Beatles, represented the first salvo of the British Invasion. I wasn't as enamored of the Stones as I was of the Beatles. They wanted to be white blues players. Call me a homer, but I preferred the actual blues players—the guys I had seen, like Bo Diddley and Bobby "Blue"

Bland as well as James Brown and Marvin Gaye. The difference was clear to anyone who saw James Brown at the T.A.M.I.—the hurling frenetic dynamo who "died" onstage, only to be revived by a cape that was placed over his body. The Stones followed that performance, and Keith Richards supposedly said that following James Brown was the biggest mistake the group ever made.

The only other time we performed with the Stones was on May 7, 1965, at Legion Field in Birmingham, Alabama. The event drew 15,000 fans and included some other top-drawer acts, but the Beach Boys and the Stones were the headliners. There was tension in the dressing area. Their egos. Our egos. We thought they were interlopers. The good state of Alabama wasn't exactly Beach Boys' territory either, but I had some connections to it. Grandma Love once showed me a Bible from one of Grandpa Love's ancestors, who had been a sheriff in Alabama before the Civil War.

The Rolling Stones preceded us at the concert, and I can't deny it—they played well and did all they could to bury us. Then we came on, and I stepped to the mic. "Hey, that was fun, that was nice. But it's about time we stand up for Alabama!"

The crowd went berserk.

If the British bands were given a hero's welcome in the United States, it was gratifying that the Beach Boys were also embraced in England. On our first European tour in 1964 (with Brian), we landed in London on November 1 and were met at the airport by hundreds of teenagers. We spent eight days in England, mostly doing television and radio promotions while also taping several performances. Our first TV appearance was on *Ready Steady Go!*, a popular rock show, and above the din of screaming girls, we sang "I Get Around" and "When I Grow Up (To Be a Man)." When the host Keith Fordyce introduced us between songs, he called Dennis "Ringo" and asked Brian and me some questions, but our answers were mostly drowned out by the cheers.

For the Beach Boys, it was the beginning of a long and beautiful friendship with England, and on this trip, we bonded with the Brits in some unusual ways.

Late one night, Brian and I walked into a café looking for something to eat, and after we sat down, a young woman with auburn hair approached us. She asked if either of us would like a date. She was tall, slender, and attractive, but I didn't engage in such activities— why pay for something that was abundant and free?—and neither did Brian. He was simply shy. Though no business was transacted, the woman was friendly and asked us where we were from and what we did. We told her we were from America and played in a band called the Beach Boys. A fan of American music, she asked us who our favorites were. At some point Brian mentioned the Four Freshmen and—wouldn't you know it—she *loved* the Four Freshmen. We discussed their harmonies and lyrics, and one thing led to the next, and soon we were singing "It's a Blue World" with a prostitute in London at an all-night café. And we sounded pretty good.

We also visited Paris, where I was mesmerized by the nightlife along the Champs-Élysées—the theaters, the cafés, the gardens, the artists, not to mention the ladies of the night. We were tourists more than anything else. We had one concert, at Olympia Hall, and I had this image of Parisians as aloof and sophisticated and not the ideal audience for our music. But the response in Paris was no different from that in London. As a reviewer in *Melody Maker* wrote, "It was the first time that I have heard Beatles-type shrieks at the famous Paris Theater. And though the sons and daughters of Paris's large American colony were there in force, it was clear from the chants of *'une autre, une autre'* ["another, another"] that the Beach Boys have a big following among French teenagers. Before they were halfway through their act, the kids were dancing wildly in the aisles and rushing the stage for autographs."

We also went to Berlin and Rome and Copenhagen and Stockholm, and we tried to see the sights, but we also couldn't help notice—or at least I couldn't help notice—that no matter where we were, we saw beautiful women. That may not seem like a revelation, but it was on my mind the following year when I wrote the lyrics to a certain song about California girls.

My desire for those women, as well as my temper, almost got the better of me in Munich. I walked into a bar one night, and a pretty hostess invited me to buy her champagne, implying that she would come back to my hotel. When we finished the bottle, I left the bar and waited for her on a median outside. A Mercedes drove up, and the very same hostess jumped in. I assumed the driver was her boyfriend, and I'd been conned out of the champagne. The car stopped near where I was standing, and maybe they didn't see me, as I was dressed in a black overcoat, black pants, black hat, and black gloves. Angry, I walked over to the car, made a fist with my gloved hand, and smashed in the driver's window. That didn't go over too well. The guy behind the wheel pulled out a Luger, pointed it at me, and said, "Son of a bitch, you're not in Texas anymore."

The switchblade . . . and the butterfly.

I thought it might have been over for me right then, but he flagged down a cop. I spent a few hours in a German jail, was bailed out by our road manager, and had to pay for the broken window, but that was better than leaving in a coffin.

Trying to keep pace with the Beatles, trying to satisfy the label, trying to become a global band, we were all under a lot of pressure, but Brian felt it the most. He usually looked comfortable onstage and was meticulous in his physical appearance. But unknown to us, an internal storm was brewing. We already knew that he didn't like the road, and his ongoing battles with his father took an emotional toll. And there were other concerns.

Earlier in the year, during one of our swings through Texas, I stopped by Brian's hotel room. He was gone, but I saw a red light in his toiletry kit as well as a syringe and other drug paraphernalia. Exactly what drugs, I can't recall, or maybe I wasn't even sure at the time. But it wasn't marijuana, which was prevalent on the road. Weed could screw you up; so could hash, which I had also tried. But we'd been touring for almost three years now, and those drugs were tame compared to the other stuff I had seen. LSD, for one. Heroin as well. Saw plenty of guys in clubs, dressing rooms, and hotel rooms who thought they were being cool and then just began freaking out. Didn't need to read any of the literature (though in time I did). Didn't need to hear any of the dangerous-drug lectures. In 1964, I was pretty naive about the emerging psychedelic movement and how that would influence the music world. All I knew was what I had seen, and what I had seen was quite straightforward: this shit fucked people up.

I didn't know what kind of drugs Brian had, nor did I confront him. While I had a temper, my first impulse with other people was usually to avoid conflict for as long as possible. With Brian I might also have been in denial, as he was the last person I imagined getting involved in drugs. When we were in high school, he didn't drink or smoke and disapproved of any girlfriend who did smoke. But Brian's drug abuse would soon be evident to all of us. Eventually, it was also known that in Brian's circle of new friends, a talent agent named Loren Schwartz introduced him to psychedelics. In 2012, Schwartz posted a blog in which he took credit for giving Brian his first hit of LSD in 1964. Schwartz wrote that he gave Brian "a clean, pure, and correct dose from the best source known," and blamed Brian's later descent on "food, tobacco, cocaine, speed, downers, more LSD, as well as many other drugs . . . as Brian related to me."

If the immaculate purity and sourcing of Loren Schwartz's LSD allowed him to maintain a clear conscience, more power to him. As noted, I had seen indications of Brian's drug use in 1964, but I don't believe any of his family or long-term friends knew that he had taken hallucinogens in that year. What we did know was that Brian's travels abroad had heightened his longing for Marilyn and the stability that she brought to his life. Within two weeks after we returned from Europe—on December 7—Brian and Marilyn were married. He was twenty-two and she was sixteen.

Sixteen days later, on a flight from Los Angeles to Houston, where the Beach Boys had a concert, Brian had an extreme panic attack. I was in a different part of the plane and didn't see it but was later told what happened. Brian began screaming and crying, then grabbed his pillow and yelled, "I just can't take it! I just can't take it!" Carl and Al tried to comfort him, and Brian soon regained his breathing and was able to relax. He performed with us that night in Houston but decided to return home the next day. His meltdown on the plane has often been described as a nervous breakdown, though I don't believe it was a coincidence that it occurred within months of his taking drugs, including, evidently, LSD.

Curiously, Brian later said that the episode was triggered by his belief that Marilyn had her eyes on me, which wasn't true but was revealing in its own way. I've never been competitive with Brian, but he grew up listening to his father rail against my family, with our sumptuous home and fashionable cars and fine vacations. Perhaps Brian still saw me in that privileged light, and that's why he feared he was going to lose his bride to his cousin.

Regardless, when Brian flew back home to Los Angeles, he requested that he be picked up at the airport by the person whom he trusted most—his mom.

CHAPTER 7

A SONIC OASIS

We were in the studio, in January of 1965, halfway through recording a new album, when Brian told us he had something important to say. He was done with touring, done with live performances. He later told a journalist that he was boiling with resentment for both Phil Spector and the Beatles ("I was real fucked up and jealous"), and to compete with them, he wanted to sit at the piano and write songs while we played and promoted them across the country. We knew that Brian didn't like to travel, but we were still stunned. For the last couple of years, he had taken breaks from the tour so he could stay home to compose and arrange. This wasn't a break, however, but something permanent.

Brian later said that I got teary eyed when he delivered the news. I don't recall that but don't doubt it either. (He also said Dennis picked up an ashtray and told everyone to leave or else he'd brain 'em.) Brian's decision left a void on the stage. Who else could sing like Brian Wilson? The answer was nobody. His piercing falsetto had no equals. Brian's physical appearance was also important. We were five guys, but Brian was a commanding, meticulous anchor. He still had an athlete's build; his thick, layered pompadour was always perfectly groomed; he even had his nails manicured. But the performing consideration was only part of it. Brian and I had been singing together since we were kids. He was my cousin, and I'd miss him on the road.

I wasn't angry (unlike his father, who accused Brian of abandoning his responsibilities). I understood—we all did, I think. So we continued touring without him under the agreement that Brian would receive tour revenue with the expectation that he would continue writing music. The Beach Boys were effectively two entities: one group, led by Brian, created and recorded the music; the other group, led by me, performed and promoted it on the road. After two years, when Brian pulled back from recording, the development of the music was more broadly shared among the rest of us. The touring group, meanwhile, went through various personnel changes—through the years and indeed through the decades—but Brian himself, with the exception of one stretch between 1977 and 1982, never returned as a regular member. Throughout most of our history, however, Brian has continued to receive tour revenues from the Beach Boys.

Fortunately, the band had options on finding a replacement. When Brian left us in Houston at the end of 1964, Carl and I called the session guitarist Glen Campbell, who had already played for us on "Be True to Your School," "I Get Around," and "Dance, Dance, Dance." The twenty-eight-year-old golden-haired musician also had plenty of experience performing live onstage; clean-cut and handsome, with a dulcet tenor voice and a falsetto to reach the high notes, he seemed a good choice to replace Brian.

When we asked him to join us, he thought we were asking him to be our opening act. I clarified. "Do you want to play the bass part and sing Brian's part?"

"You gotta be kidding me," he said.

Glen may have been hesitant because he did not exactly come from the land of surf, hot rods, and pop music. Born and raised in Pike County, Arkansas, one of ten children, he grew up in a rickety shack, picking cotton for his father amid the chicken snakes, rats, and mice skittering across the fields. With little interest in school, he learned to play the guitar by age ten (all by ear) and left home at thirteen; he had one goal in mind—to become the world's greatest guitar player. He made it to Los Angeles and soon became one of Phil Spector's favorite session players.

For his first performance as a Beach Boy, Glen flew to Dallas, and Brian's pants had to be hemmed so they'd fit. We played before 10,000 screaming fans at Memorial Auditorium, which was new to Glen. Petrified, he couldn't hear himself sing and could barely hear the music. Without any rehearsal, he made all kinds of mistakes, but it was so damn loud, no one knew. He also wasn't prepared, after the concert, for our mad rush to the cars. Some of our female fans jumped him, ripped his shirt, and even took his watch.

Glen learned the music soon enough, and we had a good time on the road—he called me "the world's oldest living teenager." But the Beach Boys weren't the right fit for him. He preferred country music and wanted to be a solo artist, so after five months, he embarked on his own career.

He had the most important attribute to be a star, the work ethic: by the time he joined us, his guitar or vocals had appeared on more than 600 recorded tracks, including Elvis Presley's songs for the soundtrack of *Viva Las Vegas*. He also had a quiet charisma that played brilliantly on television, which launched him as our first country-pop crossover artist. I know of no one else who can make an audience swoon over the plight of a Wichita lineman. As a solo performer, with such megahits as "By the Time I Get to Phoenix" and "Rhinestone Cowboy," he sold 45 million records and won five Grammys, and I couldn't have been happier for him. He also never forgot his time with us. In his later shows, he often did a Beach Boys medley, and when he appeared on *The Tonight Show* in the 1970s, he told Johnny Carson that touring with the Beach Boys was the happiest year of his life.

"The Beach Boys' music will never die," Glen said.

"Everyone has to die," Carson said. "Even the Beach Boys have to die sometime."

Glen didn't leave us until May of 1965, but in April he had to cancel a couple of nights before a concert in New Orleans. Once again we were in the lurch, so I called Bruce Johnston, a twenty-two-year-old producer whom I had known for several years, and I asked Bruce if he could find someone who could take Glen's place for a few weekend concerts.

Bruce was well connected, part of a constellation of young Californians (including the Beach Boys) who'd had early success in the music business and aspired for more. His background could not have been more different than Glen Campbell's. Bruce grew up in Beverly Hills, the son of a wealthy executive, a connoisseur of fine wine, and a fan of impressionistic art. He was a singer, writer, and piano player who released his first record in 1959 while also recording with Phil Spector and Jan and Dean. He was driving to one of his favorite surf spots when he heard "Surfin'" on the radio. *Damn! They've written a song about my sport!* Duly inspired, he wrote and recorded "Do the Surfer Stomp," which became a regional hit, and he did a surfer album as well. He began recording with Terry Melcher, the son of Doris Day, while producing with Terry as well, including covers of Beach Boy songs. They had a good feel for both the artistic and commercial end of the business—at Columbia Records, they produced the Rip Chords' "Hey Little Cobra," one of the most popular hot rod songs of all time.

Bruce and I were always crossing paths, and I trusted his judgment on recommending a fill-in Beach Boy. When he called me back, he said he'd been unable to find a replacement, but he had a suggestion—himself. He had never played before a live crowd and didn't play the bass, but he knew the music, could play the piano, and could sing the high parts. And he actually surfed. So he joined us on April 9 in New Orleans and was able to squeeze into an extra pair of Al Jardine's white pants. Carl asked him how much money he wanted. At the time, Bruce was making $87 a week, after taxes, from Columbia, so he told Carl, "I want $250."

He figured, two weeks, $500, that's good money, and then he'd go back to his other life.

Several weeks passed, and Bruce played in more shows than anticipated. He then received his first check—for almost $3,000. Carl thought Bruce was asking for $250 *a show*, so that's what he paid him. The Beach Boys, it should be noted, were never that careful about money, and Carl, even at age eighteen, was probably the most responsible among us but not one to negotiate favorable agreements. Bruce, for his part, figured that this gig might be pretty good long-term, and when Glen did leave us for good, he slid right in, and with the exception of one hiatus in the 1970s, has been with the band ever since.

Musically, we were in such a groove in 1965 that even the songs we didn't anticipate being hits ended up being just that.

That's what we discovered with *The Beach Boys Today!* album, released in March, which had something of a split personality. The A side featured upbeat songs such as "Dance, Dance, Dance" and "Do You Wanna Dance," while the B side included melancholy ballads like "Kiss Me, Baby," "She Knows Me Too Well," and "In the Back of My Mind." I cowrote all three and thought that "Kiss Me, Baby" was one of Brian's finest arrangements. The song had a wistful bass line, which led to my lyrics about a guy who has a disagreement with his girlfriend, even though they can't even remember what they fought about, leaving them both brokenhearted. But the chorus, which had a subtle doo-wop feel (*Kiss me, baby/[whoa baby] Love to hold you*), offered a redemptive second chance. The track was similar to "The Warmth of the Sun," capturing a sad moment that is universal (a broken heart) while still offering a ray of hope.

The album charted at No. 4 and was released in the United Kingdom the following year. "Kiss Me, Baby" was issued on the B side of a single in April, which I was glad to see. What I didn't anticipate was the breakout hit of the single's A side—"Help Me, Rhonda."

It was originally "Help Me, Ronda," on *The Beach Boys Today!*, cowritten by Brian and me, even though neither of us knew a girl named Rhonda (or Ronda). It was just a name that fit the track. In the original version, Brian had written a chorus that also served as a nice hook (*Help me, Ronda/Help, help me, Ronda*), and he had drafted some of the lyrics. Then I worked on them, summoning my experiences from Dorsey High to craft a gritty opening: *Well, since she put me down/I've been out doin' in my head*—the last four words could mean anything from "I'm suicidal" to "I'm just all messed up." The song itself, which had a harmonica solo, was a meandering romp about a man whose fiancée dumped him for another guy. Al Jardine sang the lead (one of his first), and I thought that was perfect.

But then Brian heard that Terry Melcher wanted to release his own version of "Ronda" for the Rip Chords. Brian asked Terry to wait because he wanted to take another crack at it, so he decided to re-record it (and changed the spelling to "Rhonda"). This time the tempo was much faster, with more instrumental and vocal hooks, including my "bow bow bow" counterpoint in the harmony. The harmonica break gave way to a boogie-woogie piano riff and a bracing guitar solo, and Carol Kaye added a jaunty bass line. I also changed the last line of the second verse, from *And it ruined our plan*, to something with assonance: *And it shattered our plan*. It's only one word, but you get very few words in any given song or poem, so each one counts.

The re-recording included another disastrous visit from Uncle Murry, whose drunken rambling was preserved on tape, eventually finding its way onto the Internet.

Murry: "When you guys get so big that you can't sing from your hearts, you're going downhill."

Brian: "Downhill?"

Murry: "Downhill . . . Son, I'm sorry. I've protected you for twenty-two years, but I can't go on if you're not going to listen to an intelligent man."

Fortunately, Brian didn't listen.

Released on April 5, "Help Me, Rhonda" became the Beach Boys' second No. 1 song, replacing the Beatles' "Ticket to Ride." It also reached No. 27 in the United Kingdom, and we even slapped it onto our next album, *Summer Days (And Summer Nights!)*.

If "Help Me, Rhonda"'s success came as a surprise, then "Barbara Ann" was even more stunning. In October, even though we had already released two albums for the year, Capitol demanded a third, and I had the idea to do a quick "party album": Gather all the guys in the studio and do a bunch of covers. Anything to get Capitol off our back. So we did the Beatles ("I Should Have Known Better"), Bob Dylan ("The Times They Are A-Changin'"), and Phil Spector ("There's No Other [Like My Baby]"). We did some of the songs we enjoyed before we became the Beach Boys ("Hully Gully" and "Alley Oop"), and we re-recorded some of our old stuff. Almost as an afterthought, we decided to do "Barbara Ann," the Regents' original that influenced the opening of "I Get Around." I don't recall if the song was my idea or someone else's, but I would have supported it, as it was one of my favorites.

We did this in Western Recorders Studio 2, and our old friends Jan and Dean happened to be recording in the next studio. Dean ambled in just as we were about to start "Barbara Ann," so we asked him to join us. Dean's label, Liberty Records, saw the Beach Boys as a competitor and had forbidden him from recording with us, but he figured they would never know. Dean took the high falsetto lead along with Brian. We didn't rehearse the song, and it required maybe ten minutes, all fun and spontaneous. Brian later added some percussion, handclaps, and a few other "sweeteners," and onto the album it went. At the end of the recording, someone blurted out "Thanks, Dean," which should have blown his cover. But it didn't. As Dean later said, "the suits" don't actually listen to the records. Then we invited our wives or girlfriends and other friends, brought in some beer and chips, cracked some jokes, and recorded a party overdub on top of the already completed music.

For such an ad hoc recording, *Beach Boys' Party!* did surprisingly well, released in early November and charting at No. 6 in the United States and No. 3 in the United Kingdom. To sell, an album typically needs at least one hit, and damn if we didn't have one in "Barbara Ann." But it didn't become a sensation by itself. It got some help from a Capitol Records promotion man named Al Coury.

A Lebanese American with a keen sense of pop culture, Coury was also a strident advocate for his artists. Across a long career he would represent everyone from Nat King Cole to Guns N' Roses. He badgered the DJs for more airtime. He lobbied *Billboard* and *Cashbox* for higher placement on their charts. He bullied his own employees. The author Fredric Dannen described Coury as "the greatest promotion man of all time." In 1965, he was responsible for promoting songs in New England, and he latched on to our cut of "Barbara Ann," persuading radio stations, starting in his hometown of Worcester, Massachusetts, to play it . . . and play it . . . and play it again. With the song's opening hook and the smooth vocals, people started calling to request it. Other stations picked it up in Boston and then it just caught fire. Capitol noticed, and without telling us issued "Barbara Ann" as a single (pared down from 2:53 to 2:05); it reached No. 2 in the United States, 2 in Canada, 3 in the United Kingdom, 2 in Germany, and 7 in France.

That's what happens when you have something that plays really well on radio and someone pushing it relentlessly. (Contrast that to "The Little Girl I Once Knew," released three weeks before "Barbara Ann"; it included the complete stops, or silent breaks, that alienated radio programmers, and the song only reached No. 20.) I also believe that Coury heard something that even we took for granted. Our arrangement of the song was not much different from that of the original. What was different was our vocals. For all of our growth and development with instruments, we were first and foremost a vocal group (in this case, with Dean Torrence as well). Brian once said that each band member's voice made a "righteous contribution," and that virtuous blend made all the difference in songs like "Barbara Ann." It is so closely identified with us, most people nowadays believe we wrote it. It's been a concert favorite for five decades, and to this day parents tell me that they named their daughter Barbara because of it.

There was nothing accidental about our other big single in 1965. It represented one of Brian's most exquisitely produced numbers and, in my view, a turning point in his musical growth.

In April, while the rest of us were beginning a sixteen-day tour, Brian began producing the instrumental tracks for a song that did not yet have a title (thus given the working title of "We Don't Know"). From Western Recorders Studio 3, he wanted to create a new kind of introduction—not snappy or catchy but classical. Having already expanded his instrumental repertoire, he wanted to exploit those sounds further. He brought together his favorite session musicians—as Jules Siegel, using stereotypes of the day, described them, "In sports shirts and slacks, they looked like insurance salesmen and used car dealers, except for one blonde female who might have been stamped out by a special machine that supplied plastic mannequin housewives for detergent commercials."

But the veneer of ordinariness didn't conceal their talents to anyone who ever heard them play: Hal Blaine (drums), Russell Bridges (piano), Frank Capp (vibraphone), Roy Caton (trumpet), Jerry Cole and Howard Roberts (guitar), Al De Lory (organ), Steve Douglas, Jay Migliori, and Jack Nimitz (saxophone), Carol Kaye (bass), Lyle Ritz (stand-up bass), Leon Russell (piano), and Billy Strange (tambourine). For his part, Brian became more specific about what he wanted each person to do and took greater control of the arrangement. This is known in part because the introduction alone, the first eight to twelve bars, required more than forty takes. The song opened with Carl playing his twelve-string electric guitar, supported with the tumbling bass—Carol Kaye kept her Fender bass strings extra tight to get a big, punchy bottom sound. That was followed by light cymbals and then mellow horns and saxophones. It was radically different from the drum-bass-guitar-and-piano rhythm tracks that usually accompanied our voices. What emerged was something so delicate, it was like a twenty-five-second prelude to heaven.

When Brian and I began collaborating on songs, we often sat down at the piano together. But once Brian began writing the music full-time, he would often give me an acetate of the instrumental tracks, and I would take it home and play it twenty, fifty, even a hundred times, to try to figure out what words conformed to their rhythm and feel.

But this song was different. This time I was in the recording booth at the studio, and I listened to the session players and heard the tracks. Then I stepped into the hallway with a yellow pad and a pen. The song's working title had evolved to "I Dig the Girls," and Brian had written one line of the chorus: *I wish they all could be California girls.*

I wanted the song to be a tribute to girls everywhere—not just in the United States, let alone California, but everywhere in the world. My goal was to put words on paper that reflected what I had seen with my own eyes while also fitting Brian's melody.

Okay, I thought, so we're going to travel around the world, where does such a trip begin? New York, I figured, America's mecca. And what is New York known for? Fashion. Style. The models who stroll the city. But New York itself is too narrow a locale. It's Boston. It's the Ivy League. It's the whole East Coast.

So I wrote, "The East Coast girls are cool." No.

"The East Coast girls are sharp." Not quite.

Then:

Well, East Coast girls are hip,
I really dig those styles they wear.

And then I wanted to pay homage to the girls down South, and who isn't charmed by the drawl of a southern belle?

And the southern girls,
With the way they talk.
They knock me out
When I'm down there.

It was all sequential, so next I moved to the Midwest and tapped into every man's fantasy.

The Midwest farmer's daughters really make you feel all right.

And after you've hung out with the down-to-earth girls of the Midwest, you realize the winter's setting in, and the girls up in Minnesota and Wisconsin know how to keep you warm.

And the northern girls,
With the way they kiss,
They keep their boyfriends warm at night.

After the chorus, I wanted to affirm the primacy of California girls while expanding the geography of our affections.

The West Coast has the sunshine,
And the girls all get so tanned.
I dig a French bikini on Hawaii Island,
Dolls by a palm tree in the sand.

I thought juxtaposing those two seductive images, "French bikini" and "Hawaii Island," was damn economical, and then I unfurled a final globe-trotting salute:

I been all around this great big world,
And I seen all kinds of girls.
Yeah, but I couldn't wait to get back to the states,
Back to the cutest girls in the world.

I spent less than an hour on the lyrics, and then we all convened at Columbia Studio in early June to sing the vocals. Columbia had a rare eight-track tape machine, instead of the more common three or four, giving Brian more flexibility to improvise and innovate. I sang the lead. Brian was always exacting on how everything should sound, and on this song, he adjusted the melody to conform to what he wanted to hear and what I could sing. The harmonies, meanwhile, had an unusual chord progression, cycling through different keys, and my line—"I wish they all could be California"—was sung as the counterpoint to the same line by the other guys, giving it a choral effect.

The title, of course, became "California Girls," and between that and the memorable chorus, the song was never viewed as the global celebration that I had originally intended. It just further cemented our connection to our home state while enhancing the mystique of our female residents. Brian has often said that "California Girls" is his favorite Beach Boy song, and it was one of our biggest international hits, from Sweden to Rhodesia, from South Africa to Australia. In 2010, it was inducted into the Grammy Hall of Fame.

Brian has also said that one of his biggest professional disappointments is that the song did not reach No. 1—released on July 12, it stalled at No. 3. I share his disappointment, as I too thought it was one of our best numbers. And it was all the more reason why I was upset when my name wasn't on the label; I once again was not given credit for writing the song. As I had done in the past, I approached Brian and asked him straight out. "Why am I not accredited on the label here?"

It seemed to unsettle him. "My dad screwed up," he said.

"Well, what are you going to do about it?"

"I'll tell my dad. We'll work it out. We'll fix it."

This repeated what Brian had been telling me for three years now. I was frustrated but not panicked. I knew I was losing out on songwriter royalties but figured that would be made up eventually. I just wanted my name on the label. It never occurred to me to seek help from my own parents, neither of whom knew anything about the music business. I could have asked my mom to speak to her brother, but I assumed that as long as the music stayed in the family, I was protected.

The year 1965 also marked a pivot in what was happening in the country. So much of the Beach Boys' early success was tied to the optimism of the era, a feeling of goodwill that survived even after President Kennedy's assassination. "These are the most hopeful times since Christ was born in Bethlehem," President Lyndon Johnson declared when lighting the White House Christmas tree in December of 1964. The president, in his State of Union Address the following month, laid out his vision for a Great Society: Restore American cities. Attack diseases. Improve the environment. Enhance voting rights. Offer preschool to poor children. Nurture the arts.

Progress was seen on many of those fronts, with the Voting Rights Act, Medicare, and Medicaid all established in the coming months. The economy was booming. The first American walked in space. Why not a Great Society, or at least a continuation of what we had going? But in those same months, President Johnson introduced combat troops into Vietnam. The first antiwar arrests were made. Acid Test parties and psychedelic dances foreshadowed the enthrallment of LSD as a counterculture movement. Protest songs by the Turtles and the Animals were bubbling up. The Beatles and the Rolling Stones weren't far behind. The backlash was coming.

Less than one month after the release of "California Girls," a California motorist had a disagreement with a California Highway Patrol officer, and the eruption riveted the nation. Watts was on fire.

I grew up near Watts and was familiar with the area. So when the riots broke out on August 11, filmed by news cameras from helicopters and lasting six days, I watched the news footage: the flames stretching to the power lines, the black smoke rolling across the rooftops, the upturned cars along sidewalks and the streets littered with debris, and all the helmeted cops in their black leather jackets and the soldiers with rifles and the bare-chested rioters breaking into stores and dancing on smashed vehicles. Thirty-four dead. More than 3,000 arrested. Some $40 million in property damage. Total fucking chaos.

I wish they all could be Californi-a, gir-r-rls!

Obviously, we weren't singing about the urban experience, but it's also true that the most famous song in history with "California" in its title was released just as this one community in California was self-destructing. I found it impossible not to think about who we were and what we were singing about. Would we be doing a greater good in writing social protest songs? There was plenty to protest, and in the years ahead, we did some of that, particularly about protecting the environment. Many artists in the 1960s and beyond built their careers around those kinds of songs, and I applaud those efforts. The more voices, the better.

But I had a different goal for our music. I never saw it as a catalyst for leading movements or changing policies. It was, instead, a way to lift spirits, to bring people together, to offer them an escape. I wanted our concerts to be a sonic oasis—Aunt Audree called them a dreamland. And I believe they were, and our message and our music were still timely in 1965. But Watts was also a harbinger. As the country's divisions intensified in the next few years, in searing conflicts over the war, race relations, police tactics, and drugs, our "sonic oasis" turned into a besieged refuge.

Not yet, however, not by a long shot. The cultural waves were changing, but we were still riding the crest.

CHAPTER 8

A BLOSSOM WORLD

first saw her at the recording session for the *Beach Boys' Party!* album, in September of 1965. She had dark hair with bangs, full lips, large brown eyes, and olive skin. Physically toned and strikingly beautiful, Suzanne Belcher was the sexiest girl I had ever seen. She was there with a friend, and I walked over, introduced myself, and asked her out. She said she had a boyfriend in the military, but she agreed to meet me. It didn't take long to appreciate that she was creative and artistic, and, in an era of miniskirts, wore one that put all others to shame.

I had been divorced for two years and had been living the life of a rock star. I had a girlfriend in every city, except in those cities in which I had two. Or three. But Suzanne rocked my world. I was still young—twenty-four—and Suzanne was only nineteen, living at home. I knew that I didn't want to lose her. I was more into serial relationships than serious ones, but the way I was brought up, if you were serious, you made a commitment. So after dating for about two weeks, Suzanne and I flew to Las Vegas and were married.

It was impulsive, but I knew the life that I had wasn't the one I wanted, and I thought I would find it with Suzanne.

All the Beach Boys were tying the knot. Both Brian and Al got married in 1964, Al to his girlfriend, Lynda. In August of 1965, Dennis, now twenty, married Carole Freedman, an eighteen-year-old raven-haired beauty who had been divorced and had an infant son, Scott. Around that time Carl met Annie Hinsche, a doe-eyed brunette who was born in the Philippines and raised in Beverly Hills. Carl was already friends with Annie's younger brother, Billy, who had opened for the Beach Boys with the rock group Dino, Desi, and Billy (Dino was Dean Martin's son; Desi was the son of Desi Arnaz and Lucille Ball). Carl had given Annie an engagement ring within months of meeting her. Annie, a student at a Catholic high school, was told by the head nun that she had to either return the ring or leave school. She left. Carl was nineteen and Annie sixteen when they married in February of 1966. The union had another benefit for the family, as Dennis, who was always gravitating toward father figures, loved to hang out with Annie's father. Otto "Pop" Hinsche survived the Bataan Death March, used to run a casino in the Philippines, and loved to watch the boxing matches. He was Dennis's kind of guy.

Getting married young was pretty common back then, and hasty courtships weren't all that unusual. But it was still something that Brian, Dennis, and Carl were all married within fourteen months (and all by the same judge), while all five original Beach Boys were married within two years. Brian and Marilyn bought a home on Laurel Way in Beverly Hills. Dennis and Carole acquired a house on several acres in the Benedict Canyon area of Los Angeles, plenty of room for their two horses and a Shetland pony as well as two Ferraris and a ski boat. Carl and Annie moved into a home in Beverly Hills that Carl had recently purchased, and Suzanne and I became homeowners as well—she saw a For Sale sign on a property at 1215 Coldwater Canyon in Beverly Hills. She said it was her favorite, so I bought it.

We were all looking for stability. Because of the Beach Boys' success, Dennis and Carl (as well as David Marks) had their childhoods stunted. Brian, Al, and I were all out of high school, but we were no more prepared than they were. I'm not complaining, but it was not a natural life. Fairly sheltered growing up, we were suddenly traveling from city to city, country to country; climbing onto stages; standing in front of cameras; seeing our names in print, in lights, on the charts; and reveling in all the fringe benefits. It may have felt good in the moment, but it was never comfortable, never secure. I believe we each hoped that settling down would give us more of an anchor and would reconnect us to the lives that we once knew.

In Brian's case, we saw signs that something was amiss. In July 1965, after a concert in San Jose, he was driving with Bruce Johnston and Steve Korthof, Brian's cousin on his mother's side. It was dark, and Brian pulled into a gas station and began ramming his car into a 7-Up machine, laughing all the while. Brian loved pranks, but this was more bizarre than funny, and out of character. He wheeled out of the station before anyone gave him any trouble.

Other signs of change were also visible. Brian began wearing black-rimmed glasses. His hair, normally perfectly combed, fell past his ears and onto his shoulders. He gained some weight. By January of 1966, not yet twenty-four years old, he was no longer a wunderkind but an established star, and the Beach Boys had been challenged once again.

We had listened to the U.S. version of the Beatles' *Rubber Soul* album, which discarded past conventions—one or two hit songs, the rest filler—and presented a unified musical narrative; or as Brian said, "A whole album with all good stuff." When the Beatles did something that surpassed anything we had done, it made us all the more determined. And it wasn't just the Beatles. The entire recording industry was changing, integrating new studio technology and introducing novel sounds. Brian figured there was only one way to respond—record the greatest rock album of all time. He and Carl had occasional prayer sessions, and they had one before Brian began his new undertaking. As he later said, "We intertwined prayer with a competitive spirit."

On January 5, after Capitol gave us three gold records for our LPs that topped the $1 million mark (*Surfer Girl*, *Surfin' USA*, and *The Beach Boys Today!*), Dennis, Carl, Al, Bruce, and I left on tour: fourteen shows in sixteen nights in Japan, plus one in Hawaii, made it one of the most exhausting trips of our career.

Even before we left, Brian was at Western Recorders one morning, working by himself in the near-empty studios. He was standing in a hallway when a young man in a dress shirt and tie, searching for the coffee machine, walked by. He recognized Brian.

"Hey. How you doing?"

Brian didn't know who the guy was. "I'm just laying down some tunes that I've written," he said. "Just a little demo stuff."

The man introduced himself as Tony Asher, an advertising copywriter who was there to record one of his jingles; he wrote the lyrics and then hired jazz players to record them. Brian invited Tony into a studio to listen to some tracks. Tony knew his way around a piano. He took lessons as a kid and wanted to play professionally, but he soon realized that Los Angeles alone had at least five hundred players better than him. So he went to UCLA and continued to write and play music while also studying journalism. After college he landed a job at Carson/Roberts, one of the city's largest ad agencies, and he developed a niche writing catchy songs for his corporate clients. The biggest challenge was putting the product name in the jingle. For Mattel, he wrote:

> *Hot Wheels! Look at 'em go now! Wouldn't you know they're . . .*
> *Hot Wheels!*

Fram Oil Filters were even more difficult.

Tony was understandably surprised, though delighted, when Brian asked him to sit down with him in the studio. Though he didn't have any Beach Boy records, Tony loved our music. Brian, for his part, enjoyed soliciting opinions from as many people as possible—even the occasional deliveryman who would drop off something at Brian's house. Brian would invite him in, play something, and ask, "What'd you think?"

Now playing the piano for Tony, Brian asked him his opinion of this new track. Tony offered some ideas, and then he sat at the piano and played a couple of riffs. The back-and-forth continued until someone came in and told Tony that his client had arrived. The session ended, Tony left, and he assumed that was the last time he'd ever see Brian Wilson. When he told his colleagues what had happened—*a jam session with Brian Wilson*—not many believed him.

A couple of weeks later, Tony received a call from some guy saying he was Brian Wilson. Tony assumed he was playing a joke.

"Maybe we can get together?" the voice on the other end said.

"Who the hell is this?" Tony demanded. "Is this Dave?"

He finally realized it was indeed Brian, who apparently got his number from Loren Schwartz (Tony and Loren went to college together).

Brian explained that the Beach Boys were in Japan, and he was in the studio trying to do something completely different musically. He had gotten bogged down, however, and he needed help with some lyrics for the album that would later be named *Pet Sounds*. He asked Tony if he could chip in, and Tony agreed. He knew he was a good wordsmith, and this improbable opportunity was a dream come true. After receiving a three-week leave from his job, he began writing with Brian.

Brian would call us in Japan and play some of the tracks over the phone, but we had other concerns. We were used to punishing schedules, but this was our first trip to Asia, and very few Western rock bands had ever performed in Japan—we beat the Beatles by five months. We had no idea how our music would be accepted. The trip, for me, was an introduction to the history and culture of the Orient, which would later dovetail with my interest in Eastern spirituality. In Tokyo, we visited some of the shrines and walked the temple gardens, and for a magazine article, we dressed in samurai costumes and engaged in mock sword fights. (We were all getting along, so no blood was drawn.) At the hotel, I loved the delicate designs of the shoji doors, with rice paper panels framed in wood, and I slept comfortably on the tatami mats, which were rolled up each morning.

The Japanese themselves couldn't have been nicer and more gracious—almost to a fault. They were the most polite audiences we had ever encountered, but by the end of each show, the girls were screaming in the aisles just as they had in the United States, Europe, and Australia.

Perhaps the most jarring surprise centered on the food. The Japanese like to serve some of their seafood with the head still attached, and I don't like to eat anything that is still looking at me.

Meanwhile, Tony learned Brian's idiosyncrasies early. On his first day, he arrived at Brian's house in the morning and had to wait two hours before Brian woke up and came downstairs. This happened a few times before Tony realized he was no longer in corporate America. On most days, according to Tony, he and Brian would spend an hour or so talking, usually about girls, past and present (Tony was still a bachelor). Brian was disarmingly honest, one time telling Tony that he had just returned from his in-laws' house, where he found Marilyn's sister, Diane, so appealing. That triggered broader discussions about their complex feelings toward women and relationships— about seeking love, finding love, falling out of love, and having your heart broken. They smoked weed and once ate hash brownies and developed a comfortable rapport.

In a couple of songs, Brian had the tracks mostly completed, and Tony took them home to draft the lyrics. He did that for "You Still

Believe in Me," in which the narrator laments falling short of his own expectations. In other cases, they sat at the piano and talked through the subject. Brian, for example, wanted to write a song about a girl who changes as she matures, with her loss of innocence breaking her boyfriend's heart; that became "Caroline, No." They talked about the difficulties in dating and all the nonverbal cues that occur between couples: that was the lyrical basis of "Don't Talk (Put Your Head on My Shoulder)." They discussed not being part of the in-crowd in high school, which led to the lyrics of "I Just Wasn't Made for These Times."

At the studio, the album sessions began in earnest in the latter half of January, a time when Brian was at his height as a producer, demanding, improvising, driven to excel. He typically didn't have music written out on sheets. He just came in, played it on the piano, and someone wrote it out. On one song alone, "I Just Wasn't Made for These Times," he used a harpsichord, an electric bass, flutes, guitars, a piano, four saxophones, a bongo, timpani, and Latin percussion. In search of unique sounds, for "Caroline, No" he had Hal Blaine hit the bottom of an empty plastic water bottle; other times, he used tape to mute the strings on a small grand piano.

No sound was too precious, as the trumpet player Roy Caton learned when Brian told him to use a Harmon mute for one note—a G, at the end of bar twenty-four. That's all Roy played for the whole session, and with his muted horn, you could hardly hear him. But it was what Brian wanted. Indifferent about costs, Brian had players sit around for hours before doing anything. He also drove them without mercy—Carol Kaye's fingers once bled during a grueling session.

If Brian was relentless, he could also be generous. One Sunday afternoon, he called guitarist Billy Strange and told him he needed to get to Western Recorders now. Billy went but didn't bring any instruments. When he arrived, Brian played him the track and said, "I want you to do a solo right here."

"I don't have my guitar," Billy said.

Brian asked what would sound good, and Billy suggested an electric twelve-string and told him he'd bring one tomorrow.

Brian said he needed one now, so he got on the phone and found a music-store owner to send a Fender twelve-string and an amp.

They waited around a couple of hours. The instrument came. Billy played his eight-bar solo, went home, and collected his $500. Brian also gave him the guitar and the amp.

Brian knew the songs were a significant departure from what we had done in the past, and he openly fretted (around Tony) over how we would respond. His fears were overblown. When we returned from the Japan tour, Brian played us the tracks. The music was indeed different, not like anything you'd hear on a typical pop record. While I had issues with the lyrics on one of the songs, I thought the richly layered tracks were beautiful. So did the other guys. Now Brian needed the vocals. We were exhausted from the trip, doing double duty touring and promoting the music as well as recording it, but Brian was going to extend us like never before.

He was a stickler about mics, as we were reminded when we did the vocals for "Wouldn't It Be Nice." The song itself is about the idealism of young love, and Brian listened with his ear close to the main studio speaker and barked out steady instructions—closer to the mic, farther away from the mic, softer, louder, slower, quicker. About the twentieth take, frustrated, I demanded, "Who's gonna hear that? You've got the ears of a dog!"

I said it with respect, even awe. They say that dogs can hear sounds that humans cannot, and I believe that Brian was reaching for something, some aural effect, that was imperceptible to all but him. That was never truer than on "God Only Knows," originally titled "Fred Only Knows," as Brian was skittish about invoking the divine. The ballad itself, with harmonic counterpoints and an angular melody—steep jumps—became one of the album's most celebrated numbers. Carl sang the lead, his dulcet voice heightening its spiritual dimensions while also signaling that he wasn't just the little brother who tagged along but was a musical force in his own right.

It was during these sessions that I named Brian "the Stalin of the studio." Bruce Johnston, opting for a less inflammatory historical figure, called him "General Patton." As Al Jardine later recalled, Brian "would not be satisfied. 'Wouldn't It Be Nice' in particular . . . It was painful beyond belief for all of us."

In truth, you needed a benign dictator in the studio, particularly back in the 1960s, before multitrack tape recorders allowed you to delay critical decisions such as how much bass you want in the mix or how much echo you want in the snare. Brian had to make those calls on the spot, had to improvise when things went wrong, and that gave our records an organic, spontaneous feel. In "You Still Believe in Me," Brian used a backing track that included a bicycle bell and a horn, which were remnants from a previous version of that song. When he combined that track with a new one, he couldn't purge the bell and horn. They just became part of the song. Those imperfections, however—compared to the flawless recordings of today—are what made our songs human and nearly impossible to replicate.

Brian saw our voices as another set of instruments, which he adjusted with unerring, autocratic whim, pushing us to achieve the closest thing possible to perfection. Did we succeed? Well, if you ever have a chance to listen to the *Pet Sounds* box set CD with just the vocals, I would say that we got as close as humanly possible.

When I first heard the musical tracks for *Pet Sounds*, I was concerned about how all this orchestral music would be performed onstage, when we had only four guys playing instruments, and some of our concerts would be criticized for not reproducing the same sounds that were heard on the records. I also had one disagreement. Brian and one of our road managers, Terry Sachen, wrote a song called "Hang On to Your Ego." The language was right out of the LSD experience—the notion that taking the drug could lead to a higher consciousness and offer a gleam of "transcendental reality," as its proponents claimed; but that could happen only if an acid trip killed your ego.

The drug culture was upon us. I knew that psychedelic records were being cut ("Eight Miles High" by the Byrds was released in March), that Hollywood was in its own hallucinogenic throes (Peter Fonda, Jack Nicholson, Dennis Hopper), and that the likes of Allen Ginsberg were urging everyone over fourteen to try LSD at least once.

I thought otherwise, and the last thing I wanted was for the Beach Boys to have any association with this drug or any drug. I told that to Brian. By early 1966, I knew he had begun to experiment with psychedelics—he had asked me to join him, and I said no. Other people had already told Brian about the risks. In 1965, he had gone to the offices of Bill Wagner, a manager for the Four Freshmen, and asked him about LSD. Wagner set up a meeting for Brian with a psychiatric resident in the Department of Psychology at UCLA. Afterward the resident told Wagner, "I don't know if he is savable. He gives me the impression he's been on it for a while, and he's entirely enamored of it."

There was little that I or anyone in the band could do about Brian's personal life. We were usually on the road, and Brian was now married and surrounding himself with other people. But I could at least edit the title of a song. Brian agreed to change "Hang On to Your Ego" to "I Know There's an Answer," and I rewrote some of the lyrics. What had been:

Now how can I say it.
And how can I come on when I know I'm guilty.

Became more hopeful:

Now how can I come on.
And tell them the way that they live could be better.

And what had been the chorus:

Hang on to your ego.
Hang on, but I know that you're going to lose the fight.

Became less funereal:

I know there's an answer.
I know now, but I had to find it myself.

Not until we had almost finished the vocals did we think of the album's title. One day we were milling around just outside Studio 3 at Western Recorders, and from the speakers we heard the sound of a train passing into the distance. That's how the album ended—the train passing, the clanging of a bell at a railroad crossing, and two dogs barking. (They were Brian's: Banana, a purebred beagle, and Louie, a dark-chocolate Weimaraner.) With the sound of the dogs echoing in my ears, I said, "What about *Pet Sounds?*"

That seemed an appropriate double entendre, and I guess it worked for Capitol, whose working title for the album had been *Our Freaky Friends.* To illustrate that cover, Capitol had sent us to the San Diego petting zoo to photograph us with our new "freaky friends," the animals. When the LP was renamed *Pet Sounds,* Capitol reviewed the pictures from that same photo shoot and selected an image of us feeding a bunch of hungry goats. Not exactly inspired artwork, but indicative of Capitol's creative efforts.

On March 7, Capitol released "Caroline, No" as a Brian Wilson single and an early test for *Pet Sounds,* which would be released in two months. To promote the single, we all taped individual radio spots. Some were funny. Mine was pretty straightforward. "Hi, this is Mike Love of the Beach Boys. I'd like to thank all the guys at KUNZ for playing and making my cousin Brian's record 'Caroline, No,' a hit in Houston!" But our efforts didn't help much. The song, which had gorgeous melodies but was unremittingly sad, didn't catch on with Beach Boy fans, and it reached a disappointing No. 32, our least popular single since 1962.

Capitol thought it had to respond somehow, so on March 21, it released our cover of "Sloop John B," which we had recorded in December. The song is about a seafaring misadventure, featuring drunken fistfights and a cook who got the "fits." A relatively well-known folk song, it was recorded by the Kingston Trio and Johnny Cash, among others, and was even part of a Carl Sandburg songbook from the 1920s. Al Jardine passed it along to Brian, and he worked with Brian to give it a completely different arrangement, including a memorable flute introduction, six-part harmonies, and a moment in which the instruments fell completely silent. Using my "lead voice," I sang the bridge (*The first mate he got drunk/And broke in the captain's trunk . . .*).

"Sloop John B" bolted to No. 3 in the United States and No. 2 in the United Kingdom. From Capitol's point of view, it sounded more like a traditional Beach Boy song and was received accordingly.

That was the backdrop of the meeting with Karl Engemann, Capitol's A&R guy for the Beach Boys. Brian and I met Karl to play him all of *Pet Sounds*. Karl himself was one of the nicest guys in the industry, but he couldn't hide his concern. "This is great, guys," he said, "but couldn't you do something more like 'California Girls' or 'I Get Around.'" In an interview years later, Engemann said he knew *Pet Sounds* was different, though he was still excited about it. "But then it was played at a sales meeting, and the marketing guys were really disappointed and down about the record, because it wasn't the normal 'Surfin' USA,' 'Help Me, Rhonda,' 'Barbara Ann' kinda production."

Brian shoehorned "Sloop John B" onto the album, even though it didn't connect thematically with the rest of the record but may have appeased Capitol's concerns. There was not much chance of that, and Capitol's tepid feelings about the album hurt it. Music needs to be promoted, and that was even truer for *Pet Sounds*, which was more artistic than commercial. But Capitol did little to market it. The album was released on May 16, and on July 2 peaked at No. 10. It might have gone higher, except by then Capitol was promoting its July 5 release of *Best of the Beach Boys*, which promptly outsold *Pet Sounds*. Our best-of album peaked at No. 8 and stayed on the charts for seventy-eight weeks.

Brian was devastated by the public's response and took it personally. Tony Asher was disappointed but not stunned by the commercial reception. He loved the album—his favorite song was "You Still Believe in Me"—but knew the introspective lyrics were not as accessible as those in typical Beach Boy hits. Tony returned to the ad business but continued to collaborate with other songwriters, including Roger Nichols and Paul Williams. He never worked with Brian again.

I was disappointed for Brian. I also would have liked to have had a greater hand in some of the songs and been able to incorporate more often my "lead voice," which we'd had so much success with (I recall thinking that while using that voice for the bridge in "Wouldn't It Be Nice"). I had great respect for Tony Asher, and we've been friends for fifty years, but my history with Brian spoke for itself. The conventional wisdom on *Pet Sounds* is that Brian needed a different lyricist who could connect with his feelings of longing and disillusionment. I did that with "The Warmth of the Sun" and "Kiss Me, Baby" and believe I could have done that for some of the tracks on *Pet Sounds*, maintaining Brian's artistic vision while broadening its appeal. If you're a singer-songwriter and don't believe you can do that, then you shouldn't be in the business in the first place.

Everything worked out eventually, for both Brian and *Pet Sounds*.

Bruce Johnston took the album to London and, with the help of our publicist, set up a meeting with Keith Moon in Bruce's hotel suite. The Who's drummer heard the record and was so impressed that he contacted Lennon and McCartney, who swung by and said they wanted to hear it as well. They listened to it several times and left inspired, later saying that *Pet Sounds* influenced *Sgt. Pepper's Lonely Hearts Club Band.* British fans loved *Pet Sounds* immediately, sending it to No. 2 on their charts, and McCartney has praised "God Only Knows" as one of the greatest rock songs in history.

Capitol finally realized what it had in *Pet Sounds*, commercially and artistically, and in July released a single with "Wouldn't It Be Nice" on the A side and "God Only Knows" on the B side; it charted at No. 8. The same 45 was released in other parts of the world, except with the sides flipped, and it reached the top 25 in Canada, Australia, France, Norway, Germany, and the Netherlands, while it hit No. 2 in the United Kingdom.

Americans eventually embraced *Pet Sounds*, which in 2000 reached platinum level, or one million copies sold.* It has also won numerous accolades, including the greatest rock album of all time by *New Musical Express*, a British magazine.

E ven while we were working on *Pet Sounds*, Brian was developing another track that was more adventuresome than anything he had done to date. I heard it piecemeal when I stopped by the studio— saxophones, tambourines, flutes. Brian had begun working on it in February, continued in May and June, but then set it aside. With all the traveling, touring, promoting, and recording, and with all the

---

* The Recording Industry Association of America introduced the platinum certification in 1976 for the sale of one million units. The RIAA had previously defined a gold record as one that generated more than $1 million in retail sales, but after 1976, gold was redefined as a record with at least 500,000 units sold.

My grandfather, Edward Love, second from right,
founded Love Sheet Metal as a young man.

I was close to my paternal grandparents,
Edward and Edith Love.

My mom, fifth from left,
moved to California as a
young child. Here with her
seven siblings, Murry is
standing behind her with
their parents on the far right.

My parents, a striking couple, faced opposition from both the Wilson and Love families, so they eloped.

My childhood was defined by a protective mom as well
as a love of nature and a passion for music.

(top) My parents bought a trailer for family trips. I'm the oldest, third from left, followed by Maureen, Stephen, Stanley, and Stephanie.

(left) Maureen's harp was a magnificent addition to our family recitals.

(below) A prankster even as a kid, here I'm with my siblings, running away with the ice cream.

Whether writing alone or with Brian, crafting lyrics came naturally for me.

Brian, Dennis, and I burying Carl as part of an album photo shoot.

Brian and I goofing around, as we often did.

Carl, Brian, Dennis, Al, and I projected a wholesome image of America in the early 1960s.

Capitol Records sent the Beach Boys to the San Diego petting zoo for a photo shoot of *Freaky Friends*, which I renamed *Pet Sounds*. Capitol put a goat on the album cover.

By 1966, we tried to present ourselves with a bit more style. Bruce Johnston is far right.

Dennis, Carl, myself, and Al all practiced Transcendental Meditation.
So did Brian. But only Al and I stuck with it.

angst over *Pet Sounds*, I didn't know what this song was about, though at one point he was going to abandon it completely and give it to a friend. Then on August 11, when we were performing in Fargo, North Dakota, Brian called Carl from a studio back home. He had started working on the track again, and he played it on the phone. Carl thought to himself, How bizarre, how exciting, how strange and new.

The title of the track was "Good Vibrations."

It was a song and a title that fit the spirit of the times.

By 1966, the whole flower-power movement was well on its way. Haight-Ashbury had not yet emerged as its epicenter, but its ideals—peace, love, and liberation from authority, often fueled by psychedelics—had been defined. Hippies. Mystics. Longhairs. A new youth culture was rising, and rock and roll was its liturgy, its soundtrack, speaking to the aspirations and discontent of young Americans, as well as their search for spirituality and truth. The Beatles captured some of those themes in *Revolver*, while the Mamas and the Papas, Buffalo Springfield, Donovan, Dylan, and Janis Joplin, among many others, were all appealing to the same restive audience.

The timing of "Good Vibrations" wasn't an accident. It reflected Brian's own interest in mysticism and spirituality as well as his growing use of drugs. The title itself came from a conversation he had as a boy with his mom, who said that a dog could pick up "vibrations" from humans. The word itself, *vibrations*, scared Brian. How could a dog feel something invisible? But it also appealed to him—the possibility of communicating on a nonverbal plane.

Brian wanted to push the recording boundaries even beyond what he had done for *Pet Sounds*. Still seeking the perfect tonality, he used four different studios—Western, Sunset Sounds, Gold Star, and Columbia—to maximize each one's unique acoustics. To create contrasting moods and movements, he continued to exploit different instruments, including a Jew's harp, sleigh bells, a tack piano, and wind chimes. Like a painter mixing oils, Brian used disparate sounds to create treasured blends. Most notably, he used an Electro-Theremin, which emits an eerie, high-pitched scream that was typically used in horror films. (Alfred Hitchcock used it in *Spellbound*.) At Carl's recommendation, a cello was added, which Brian believed was a first for a rock song.

But what was truly radical was that Brian recorded the song in a modular format. Instead of creating a single instrumental backing track at one session, he produced short, seemingly unrelated snatches of music and then pieced them together. It was like working with a vast jigsaw puzzle—record tiny fragments; then re-record some of those; then add a bridge or new section; then re-record that section; then make trial mixes; then re-record new sections; and then try to assemble it all.

Only Brian would even attempt such a feat, though it wasn't clear that even he knew what he was doing. On some days the musicians would play for an hour; other days, ten minutes; and sometimes, all day. "We had no idea what the finished piece was going to sound like," Hal Blaine later said. "I think we were working on the song for six months, and this was the same bunch of musicians that cut 'MacArthur Park' in two takes."

At some point, Brian gave me an acetate of the track and asked me to write the lyrics. (I was later told that Tony Asher had taken a crack at the words, but Brian wasn't satisfied.) I didn't have much time, as Brian kept making changes on the track until he gave it to me. I also tend to procrastinate. As a result, I hadn't written anything until the day that we were supposed to record the vocals.

On that day, August 24, Suzanne and I were at her parents' condo in the San Fernando Valley. We got into our yellow Jaguar XKE, which had a built-in turntable for 45s. I put on the acetate and began listening to the track as I pulled onto the road. I thought it had a cool bass line with an R&B feel, something that James Brown and the Famous Flames would play. The melody was lush but also different and esoteric. I listened to it twice. Suzanne, who was pregnant, sat next to me with a notepad, and I told her, "Take this down."

Maybe I write best when I'm under pressure, but I began writing the lyrics to "Good Vibrations" while en route to Highway 101. I needed words that conformed to the tempo as well as the concept of "vibrations," and I thought they needed to be something that our fans could connect to, and what's easier to connect to than boy-girl?

So I wrote, or actually recited, the poem.

I—I love the colorful clothes she wears.
And the way the sunlight plays upon her hair.
I hear the sound of a gentle word.
On the wind that lifts her perfume through the air.

I wrote the chorus, which also served as the song's hook.

I'm picking up good vibrations.
She's giving me ex-ci-tations.

I'll be the first to acknowledge that *excitations* is not really a word, but it rhymed.

We were somewhere on the Hollywood Freeway when I recited the next verse.

Close my eyes, she's somehow closer now.
Softly smile, I know she must be kind.
When I look in her eyes,
She goes with me to a blossom world we find.

The poem was finished by the time we reached Columbia Studios on 6121 Sunset Boulevard. The ride took about twenty minutes. Suzanne gave me the notepad, which I handed to Brian. Carl later said that the session was delayed because I got there late.

In the vocal sessions, Brian demanded not only the right note but the right timbre, until all four parts blended together. Seeking extra texture, we did twenty-five to thirty overdubs for one section that was no longer than five seconds long. "There's a 'phase' in your voice," Carl later noted, "and even if you try to sing it exactly the same way, it's not exactly the same, and more overtones and harmonics come out. It has a choral sound, a choir effect. When I first heard [the vocal track], it was a much rougher sound; it had more whomp to it. Instead of making it bigger, bulgier, and more raucous as [Phil Spector] might have, Brian refined it and got it more even sounding."

"Good Vibrations" required twenty-two sessions, and the cost has been estimated at $10,000 to $50,000 ($74,000 to $369,000 in 2016 dollars). I doubt Brian had any idea about the cost, nor did he care, but at the time it was certainly the most expensive single ever produced. Brian recorded at least a dozen versions until settling on one. My only surprise was that in the last line of the second verse, Brian cut the final words, *we find*, eliminating the rhyme and ending the sentence with *blossom world*. I preferred the rhyme, but I can't argue with ending on "blossom world"—evoking the peace movement that was gaining steam while suggesting the euphoria of being in love.

The song was also three minutes and thirty seconds, unheard of for a pop song then. That was risky, but as Brian later said, the song came together "very divinely."

"Good Vibrations" was released on October 10. Cousin Brucie, the leading DJ in New York, told me that he didn't like it initially, but it grew on him. Otherwise, the holdouts were few. It sold more than 100,000 copies each day of its first week and passed one million in unit sales after one month. It hit No. 1 on December 10 while reaching No. 1 in the United Kingdom as well. A headline in the London *Sunday Express* proclaimed: "They Found a New Sound at Last!" Our one disappointment was that "Good Vibrations" did not win the Grammy Award for best rock song (losing to "Winchester Cathedral," which wasn't even a rock song). But its status has grown over the years. In a 1997 *Mojo* list, artists, producers, and industry personalities voted "Good Vibrations" as the greatest single of all time, and in 2010 *Rolling Stone* ranked it as the sixth best song of all time.

Brian has been rightfully hailed for producing a track that in length, construction, and complexity defied all expectations of how a rock song could be written and performed. After *Pet Sounds*, it also reestablished my partnership with Brian and served as another example of our unique collaboration—the tour de force studio work, the lyrical messaging, a triumph of both art and commerce. But more than anything, "Good Vibrations" indicated that we could evolve with the times. The Beach Boys were never just a "surf band," as the stereotype would have it. By 1966, we had recorded all kinds of music, but what had been successful in the past wouldn't necessarily succeed in the future. The question was, could we develop a new sound that retained the idealistic ethos of our early music while staying in sync with an era of tumult and protest—music that was avant-garde and edgy, with a spiritual sheen? "Good Vibrations" said we could.

I n late October we flew to Paris for a twenty-two-day tour of Western Europe. It had been only two years since we had last been there, but our image was slowly changing. Onstage we still wore white pants and either striped or checkered shirts. But offstage was different. We were all practically adults now (Carl turned twenty in a few months), and as we walked through London or Munich, we tried to look it. Dennis wore suede boots, a tie, and a double-breasted jacket. Carl remained casual, with his Levi's and Pendleton shirt but adding a scarf. Al favored a double-breasted coat, a scarf, slacks, and Hush Puppies. Bruce—white boots and a turtleneck. And me? I probably had the greatest change. I grew a beard, which was full but closely cropped. I wore a suede coat, turtleneck, and Levi's. I bought a pipe and used it as a humorous air of distinction. Meanwhile, my hair had begun to thin, and in such circumstances, some men (particularly in show business) opt for hairpieces; others just let it be and go natural. I started wearing caps. For one thing, the visors shield my eyes from the glare of the lights onstage. But I also thought that hats were stylish and fun, and I've worn all kinds over the years, from "Sherlock Holmes" deerstalkers to turbans to baseball caps with logos. By now the hats have become my trademark, and if I ever went onstage without one, the audience would think it was watching an impostor.

However we were dressed in Europe, our trip from Hamburg to Vienna, from Stockholm to Leicester, felt like one extended victory lap. These were tough markets for outsiders. France had a quota on how many foreign records could be played on national radio, but we somehow broke through that. Germany was also difficult for most English-speaking groups, the language difference being the most obvious handicap. The Beatles were one exception, but the Germans loved the Beach Boys as well. The last time I had been there, I ended up in jail, but this time when we landed in West Berlin, we were met by 300 police officers—there to escort us instead of to arrest me. As I told a reporter, "We just walked into the lobby, threw up our hands, and surrendered. The people were real nice."

We performed our first concerts in Germany, in Essen, drawing 9,000 fans, some of whom forced their way onstage for autographs. I don't know how many in the crowd understood English, but there was something about the beat, the rhythm, the fact that we were from America—it all transcended the music. When we played in

Vienna, the Wiener Stadthalle (or town hall) was sold out, and some of them wore biker helmets, others were lighting firecrackers, and when we performed "Help Me, Rhonda," everyone stamped to the beat in perfect unity. It was impressive, in an unnerving, Teutonic sort of way. The security officers wore three-quarter-length trench coats, and they reminded me of Gestapo characters in the movies.

Perhaps the tour's highlight was our landing in London, where we were met by a mob at Heathrow that was compared to Beatlemania. It felt good to get that kind of reception in the Beatles' own backyard. We drove in cars with placards reading "This Car Is Fitted with Good Vibrations." (The song was charting at 15.) A twenty-minute documentary was made of our visit, excerpts of which were played on the BBC's *Top of the Pops*. According to the narrator (singer Marianne Faithfull), "London on a gray, rainy morning became bright as a California surf when America's top group the Beach Boys flew into London's airport to be welcomed by thousands of their fans, many of whom had probably never ever seen their idols in person before."

Lulu, the Scottish singer, opened for us throughout England. This was right before "To Sir with Love" made her a star in the United States, but she was a teenage phenomenon in the United Kingdom, adding that much more excitement to our shows. The craziest it got, at least for me, was in Manchester, when I was late getting to the Odeon, and the promoters had to put me in a newsboy's cap and earmuffs to smuggle me through the mob.

We always spent money freely, but now we had more of it. So before we left London, Dennis, Carl, and I walked into a Rolls-Royce showroom and bought four $32,000 Phantom limousines, one for each of us and one for Brian. The cars had to be shipped, so in the interim, Brian bought a $20,000 Rolls-Royce from the producer Lou Adler; the car had once belonged to John Lennon.

The year's capstone occurred in December when *New Musical Express* announced that the Beach Boys had been selected by its readers as the world's No. 1 vocal group, defeating the Beatles (who had won the last three years) and the Rolling Stones. Press reports noted that the Beatles had not released a 45 since early August and that their concerts had lagged. At their concert at Candlestick Park in August, 25,000 tickets were sold—a dramatic decline from their concert at Shea Stadium one year earlier in August, which drew 55,600 fans.

Meanwhile, December of 1966 also saw the *Best of the Beach Boys* album knock the soundtrack to the film *The Sound of Music* from the top of the LP charts.

Time has a way of blurring memories. It is now assumed that the Beatles came to America in 1964, conquered the country, and left the Beach Boys in their dust. Not exactly. We could never match the Beatles song for song, album for album, but our records continued to chart, our tours continued to sell out, and in 1966 we proved we were just as good as they were, just as innovative, and, according to the Brits, even more popular. As one London newspaper wrote, "The sensational success of the Beach Boys . . . is being taken as a portent that the popularity of the top British groups of the last three years is past its peak." Or as an American publication said, "The number one group in the world is right here in the United States."

A blossom world indeed.

CHAPTER 9

THE UNRAVELING

If we were neck and neck with the Beatles, it made perfect sense for us to hire Derek Taylor as our new publicist. Born in Liverpool, Derek began his career as a journalist, and in 1963 he covered a Beatles show at the Manchester Odeon. His review so impressed the Beatles' manager, Brian Epstein, that he hired Derek as a publicist. Derek accompanied the group on its first tour in the United States and helped craft some of the story lines that were fed to the press and contributed to the band's renown. Derek left the Beatles after a few years and settled in Los Angeles, where his connections to fan magazines helped him promote the Byrds as well as Terry Melcher and Bruce Johnston. Bruce in turn introduced him to Brian, and the two became fast friends. We were all impressed with his Beatles' pedigree, and the Beach Boys hired Derek in March of 1966 to be our publicist.

We'd never really had a publicist. Our music fit the early 1960s so seamlessly, no one needed to "package us." That era, however, was over. Derek himself was a quick study, and his connections paid off immediately. When Bruce took *Pet Sounds* to London, it was Derek who lined up interviews for him. When we toured in Europe in October and November, it was Derek who made sure that the British music magazines had plenty of stories about us. But his most ambitious effort focused on Brian, who felt his music skills were underappreciated and was bothered that some rock critics dismissed our music, particularly our hits, as unsophisticated. How could they be taken seriously if they're about surfing, girls, and hot rods?

These critics were never my biggest concern. If our songs were so simple, why didn't everyone do them? (The answer is, the songs weren't simple, the harmonies far too complex for most artists to even attempt.) I always thought this critique of the Beach Boys was elitism at its worst: because so many people loved our music, there must be something wrong with it.

I cared about what our peers thought, but mostly I cared about what our fans thought—were we reaching them or weren't we? That concerned all of us. Brian and I both craved hits, but he also seemed to need the approval of the critics, of the illuminati, and it was Derek's job to spread the word, create the buzz, and make sure he got it. He just needed the right story line, and he found one.

Brian's a genius.

A genius, Derek pointed out, who could be compared to Lennon, McCartney, and Dylan, but even these comparisons understated Brian's virtuosity. Profiles on Brian would compare him to Bach, Mozart, Beethoven. The campaign began in August of 1966, and it was definitely a change. Compared to the Beatles, who were known on a first-name basis, the Beach Boys had been more famous as a group, in part because we had a revolving cast of performers. Now Brian was the star. As far as I was concerned, Brian *was* a genius, deserving of that recognition. But the rest of us were seen as nameless components in Brian's music machine—or, as the British publication *Melody Maker* asked, "Are the five touring Beach Boys just puppets for sound genius Brian Wilson?"

This frustrated all of us but infuriated Carl, who after Brian was the most musically gifted of the group. As he told the press in London: "No, we are not just Brian's puppets . . . Brian plays the major creative role in the production of our music, but everyone in the group contributes something to the finished product. It's not like an orchestra translating the wishes of the conductor. We all have a part to play in the production of the records."

Carl as well as Dennis felt this challenge acutely. How do you emerge from the shadow of a "genius" who is also your oldest brother? How do you forge your own musical identity? My challenge was even more complicated: How do I, as the cowriter of our most successful songs, receive recognition when I had not even been given credit for most of those songs? How do I even demand credit when we were all just "Brian's puppets"? We all wanted Brian to get his due, but it was also true that Dennis, Carl, Al, Bruce, and I were the ones on the road, at the airports, on the buses, playing three or four shows in two or three nights, generating the tour revenue, showcasing the music so that the DJs would play it and the people would buy it and the royalty checks would keep coming in . . . and then returning home, jet-lagged, and spending long nights in the studio trying to lay down the vocals for the next record. It didn't feel to us as if we were just riding on Brian's coattails. We thought we were all working pretty hard to keep the operation going.

But if the "genius" campaign gave the other Beach Boys short shrift, the real damage was to Brian himself. It put even greater pressure on him. It made him even more driven and caused him to fear failure all the more. It was hard enough to match the Beatles, but now he had to keep up with Mozart? Years later, one of Brian's psychiatrists, Dr. Garrett O'Connor, disclosed what Brian once told him: "I love being a genius," he said, "but I hate the responsibility."

Or as Brian told one of our fan magazines (*Beach Boy Freaks United*) in 1985, "I was thrilled to see some of the stuff that happened to us. It was great . . . [but] it was a little disturbing on the central nervous system . . . You go through a shock, and if you fail at something, it hurts ten times worse . . . And then you fall down and you are just a human being, like everyone else. It's like, that's the hard part. Playing the two roles. The legend and the person."

Derek Taylor wasn't the only newcomer in Brian's life. Once he stopped touring, Brian expanded his circle of friends and collaborators who thought they could help him ascend to new heights musically. Brian wanted the approval of the "hip intelligentsia," as they were called, or leaders of the emerging counterculture. That role was played most notably by David Anderle, an artist, record producer, and manager who had met Brian years ago through a family connection. Described as the "mayor of hip," Anderle became the Beach Boys' would-be business partner, persuading us to establish a record company (called Brother Records) while also pressing a lawsuit against Capitol to renegotiate our contract. With his contacts in the media, he may have been most responsible for the mystique surrounding an ambitious new album that would be known as *Smile*. Brian saw it as our follow-up to *Pet Sounds* and "Good Vibrations" and envisioned it as a "teenage symphony to God."

The music writer Jules Siegel, sent by *The Saturday Evening Post*, visited Brian to document the *Smile* effort as well as to determine if Brian was a "genius, Genius, or GENIUS." Richard Goldstein, the first rock critic for *The Village Voice*, also arrived at Brian's doorstep and, as he later recounted in his memoir, ended up getting stoned with Brian in the California desert, with Marilyn shouting at her husband, "Pick up your pants!" Other visiting journalists included Paul Williams of *Crawdaddy!*, which was founded in 1966 to write critically about rock and roll, and Lawrence Dietz of the more mainstream *New York* magazine. Then there was the film crew from CBS News, shooting scenes for a rock and roll documentary produced and narrated by David Oppenheim. A classical musician himself, Oppenheim had worked with such highbrow figures as the Russian composer Igor Stravinsky, the Spanish cellist Pablo Casals, and Leonard

Bernstein (who would appear in the documentary). Oppenheim thought that Brian was their equal.

Still others came into Brian's orbit, whom I'll call the hipsters. There was Anderle's friend Michael Vosse, who was put on the payroll to scout out TV opportunities. There was Danny Hutton, a young musician who was managed by Anderle and who became one of the lead vocalists for Three Dog Night. Then there was Van Dyke Parks, an erudite young songwriter also managed by Anderle who became Brian's lyricist for the *Smile* tracks.

We were on the road touring, but when we stopped by the house, we knew things were getting weird. Brian had a tent—red and maroon with a heavy gold brocade—built in the den, with huge pillows on the inside and hookahs for the marijuana. Brian had removed the dining room table and chairs and had a carpenter build an eighteen-inch-high sandbox around the grand piano. A truck poured in eight tons of sand, allowing Brian to feel as if he were writing music at the beach, which was strange, because Brian didn't like the beach. Meanwhile, he removed the furniture from his living room and put down workout mats, which were good in theory if not in practice—Brian's weight continued to balloon. According to Marilyn, when Brian was writing the song "Love to Say Dada," he asked her to buy him a baby bottle and fill it with chocolate milk, which he would drink as he wrote.

Brian's increasingly erratic behavior was chronicled by Siegel (whose article was rejected by the *Saturday Evening Post* but published in the premier issue of *Cheetah*). The most notorious incident centered on the so-called "Fire" track, in which Brian tried to record a song, at Gold Star, that evoked the sound and fury of a blaze. It was titled "Mrs. O'Leary's Cow," after the cow that started Chicago's deadly fire in 1871. To get the musicians in the mood, Brian had them play their instruments wearing red fire hats (I wore one also), and he burned wood in buckets so everyone smelled smoke. Musically, Brian got what he wanted. According to Siegel: "A gigantic fire howled out of the massive studio speakers in a pounding crush of pictorial music that summoned up visions of roaring, windstorm flames, falling timbers, mournful sirens and sweating firemen, building into a peak and crackling off into fading embers as a single drum turned into a collapsing wall and the fire-engine cellos dissolved and disappeared."

A few days later, a building across the street from the studio caught fire and burned down, and Brian panicked. He investigated fires across the region, determined the area had experienced an unusually high number, and concluded that his recording had caused the outbreak. As Brian later told *Rolling Stone*, "We thought maybe it was witchcraft or something. We didn't know what we were into. So we decided not to finish [the song]. I got into drugs, and I began doing things that were over my head."

Siegel described Brian's growing paranoia. Brian wanted to see the science-fiction movie *Seconds*, but when he walked into the theater, he said, "The first thing that happened was a voice from the screen said, 'Hello, Mr. Wilson.' It completely blew my mind . . . That's not all. Then the whole thing was there. I mean, my whole life. Birth and death and rebirth. Even the beach was in it." He theorized that "mind gangsters" were involved, and he identified Phil Spector as the possible outlaw. "He could be involved, couldn't he? He's going into films." At another point, one of Brian's friends came by the studio but was not allowed to enter. "It's not you," Michael Vosse told him. "It's your chick. Brian says she's a witch, and she's messing with his brain so bad by ESP that he can't work."

The problem, of course, was the drugs, and the people who persuaded Brian to use them. As Brian told Mike Douglas in 1976, "Well, a lot of people—a lot of hippies in the sixties said, well, the great Messiah is supposed to come in the sixties, and it came in the form of drugs. Which I agree, there's a certain amount to be said for that. But in my personal story, I have to tell, it really didn't work out so well, so positively."

Marilyn saw the repercussions, not just from the LSD, but from the large amounts of marijuana and hashish as well as the amphetamines. As she later told the BBC's Radio 1, "I think the drugs he was taking had started to confuse him. He had met a lot of strange people who had encouraged drugs and told him that they would expand his mind. I think he was caught up in experimenting and finding out who he was as a person." She was frightened too. "I slept with one eye open because I never knew what he was going to do," she later said. "He was like a wild man."

To be sure, many of us were taking drugs. At the time, I was smoking weed and drinking as well, but my work wasn't affected. That was also true of Dennis and Carl. Though I didn't know it, Dennis later said he was taking acid during the *Smile* sessions. But we all saw how the drugs were affecting Brian, and I don't think any of us knew what to do. I became painfully aware, however, that addiction affects not only the addicted but those close to them, and I felt that I was losing my best friend.

When the Beach Boys returned from Europe in late November of 1966, Brian had recorded the instrumental tracks for a number of *Smile* songs, including "Wind Chimes," "Wonderful," "Our Prayer," and "Cabin Essence." They were unlike anything we'd ever heard—bizarre, yes, but also beautiful. It was obvious that Brian had taken what he'd done with *Pet Sounds* and "Good Vibrations" but added more layers and complexity. The problem, for me anyway, was the lyrics. I didn't understand many of them and thought they had been influenced by the drugs. I called them "acid alliteration," or something that had been taken out of a Lewis Carroll poem. They were often clever and subtle but virtually inscrutable in a rock song.

There was, in "Surf's Up," *Columnated ruins domino!* Or in

"Cabin Essence," *Over and over, the crow cries uncover the cornfield/ Over and over, the thresher and hover the wheat field.* Or in "Heroes and Villains," the double entendre *dude'll* do—for "dude will do" as well as "doodle doo," but who would catch those nuances in a galloping rock song?

The lyricist Van Dyke Parks, born in Mississippi, worked as a child actor and studied music at Carnegie Mellon before moving to California and immersing himself among the beatniks. Brian ran into Van Dyke at Terry Melcher's house and was impressed with his literary sensibilities, but that wasn't his only appeal as a collaborator. As Van Dyke told *Crawdaddy!* in 1976, "Brian sought me out . . . At that time, people who experimented with psychedelics—no matter who they were—were viewed as 'enlightened people,' and Brian sought out the enlightened people."

I've always admired Van Dyke's intellect and like him personally as well. But we had different views about drugs, and we disagreed about lyrics.

I once asked Van Dyke, "What do these lyrics mean?"

He said, "I haven't a clue, Mike."

Well, if he doesn't know, how would our fans know? He was like a painter whose individual brushstrokes were masterly, but the picture itself was an abstraction. That's great if your audience is relatively narrow, but what if you're trying to appeal to the masses?

I always thought that our lyrics should connect with the largest number of people possible. I used to think, How will our fans in Peoria react to this song? My position as the front man informed my views. Every performance was like convening a very large focus group—I knew which songs resonated. I acknowledge that I have always been the most business-minded member of the Beach Boys, but I would call that being the most practical. The question facing any rock band is, How do you survive? You survive by creating and performing music that people want to hear. That's tough to do. Most rock bands flame out after a few years. Many don't even make it out of the garage. For the Beach Boys or any other band, there will always be tension between art and commerce. I believe you can straddle both worlds, but I *know* you can't have art without commerce.

I had never hesitated in telling Brian what I thought about the words to a particular song or about anything else; but he was acting so strange, I couldn't have any conversation with him. My concerns about the lyrics, however, offended the hipsters, who saw the Beach Boys as a bunch of hopelessly square yahoos in striped shirts and white pants, removed from the youth revolution brewing in the streets.

Accordingly, my complaints were ignored. The lyrics didn't change. So our next job was to provide the vocals, and while the songs were difficult enough, Brian asked us to do bizarre things. In the studio, he had us lie on our backs, with a microphone above us, and make strange guttural sounds. He drained his swimming pool, put a mic at the bottom, and had us sing while on our backs. For "Heroes and Villains," we sang through our noses, in four parts. These are not pleasant memories for any of us. In 1995, Bruce told *Mojo* magazine, "The music was cool, but it's always tinged with the reality of making it. Brian degraded us, made us lie down for hours and make barnyard noises, demoralized us, freaked us out. I can't tell you a lot of it, it's really fucked up. He was stoned and laughing . . . [but] we didn't really know what was happening to him."

We all had questions, but we did what Brian wanted, and we worked harder on those vocals than on any others in the history of the band.

Brian had originally promised Capitol that the album would be done by Christmas. Cover art was created, and Brian gave Capitol the list of songs in the middle of December. But he began to burn out. He brought together an entire orchestra, did one take, then sent everyone home. Sessions were canceled. Brian stopped working on all the songs except "Heroes and Villains." At one point, Carl said to me, "Brian's not well."

As the New Year rolled in, we had other things to worry about beyond the new album. We filed a $2 million lawsuit against Capitol, which meant that whatever records we might have completed might not even be released. Eventually, however, we did reach an agreement with the label: the Beach Boys would record on our own Brother Records label in the United States, while Capitol would press and distribute our work.

A more urgent problem confronted Carl. On January 3, he was ordered to report for induction into the Army, but he refused. Carl wasn't political and was not opposed to the Vietnam War per se. But he wouldn't touch a gun under any circumstance. He was opposed to all wars, all killing, driven by a deep spirituality that infused his music as well. On April 5, he was indicted by a federal grand jury, and he planned to fight the charge as a conscientious objector. But on April 26, prior to an evening show on Long Island, FBI agents arrested Carl for evading the draft. It was just a publicity stunt by the feds, and they got the news coverage they wanted. Carl posted bond in time to play the concert.

In four days we flew to Dublin to begin a European tour, but Carl had to appear in federal court in Los Angeles. I was pissed. If the conscientious objector status applied to anyone, it was Carl. But if convicted, he faced up to five years in prison as well as a $10,000 fine. Our immediate concern was reuniting Carl with the band. At a press conference in Dublin, I said, "For our part, we are hoping that the big, strong U.S. will find it in their hearts to let him come." In Los Angeles, Carl pleaded not guilty. A federal judge ordered Carl to return on June 20 for his trial but allowed him to leave the country, after posting a $25,000 bond.

On May 2, we had two shows at the Adelphi in Dublin and hoped

Carl would arrive in time. Except he was 5,200 miles away. He and his wife, Annie, flew to Chicago, where they chartered a ten-seat Learjet for $5,000. They were the only passengers, bound for Dublin, but when a cap fell off one of the fuel tanks, they had to make an unscheduled stop in Newfoundland. Carl loved to fly, but I don't think he loved it that much. By the time we were supposed to take the stage, Carl hadn't arrived, we hadn't heard from him, and we had no idea what had happened. Fearing the worst, we began the concert and did our usual songs, but the crowd was chanting, "We want Carl! We want Carl!"

Hell, so did we!

Bruce sang Carl's lead on "God Only Knows" but forgot some of the words. "Sloop John B" drew boos. Others shouted for their money back. We finished the show but did not give any interviews or allow our picture to be taken. We thought about canceling the second show.

Twenty minutes before that performance, we were told that Carl's tiny jet was crossing the Irish coastline. He and Annie were safe. He still hadn't arrived by the time the show was to begin, so we trudged back onstage. But at some point in the first set, Carl's taxi pulled up to the stage door. Disheveled and unshaven, having traveled for about twenty hours nonstop, Carl walked right on the stage, grabbed his guitar, and started playing. We were just grateful he was alive. And when he gave a flawless rendition of "God Only Knows," it must be said that truer words were never sung.

Carl's opposition to the draft took courage—he was willing to go to prison rather than go to war. I didn't have to make that decision because, as a father, I was deferred. But if I had been drafted, I would have returned to the land of my forefathers and would now be fluent in Swedish. Bruce, meanwhile, did receive his draft card. He too strongly opposed the war, though he took a more creative path to avoid service. He had a slender surfer's body, and he bought a pair of jeans, washed and dried them several times so they were extremely tight, and wore them when he went to his draft board for induction. He also borrowed a girlfriend's blouse, applied a touch of makeup, and found opportune times to bat his eyes and shake his hips. The draft board disqualified Bruce as a homosexual—or, in the vernacular of the day, he "fagged out."

In Carl's case, his trial occurred in June in Los Angeles, and at one point he told the judge, "We were put here to live—killing is very evil and destructive and results in human suffering. I love my country very much, but I won't take part in the destruction of people." Judge A. Andrew Hauk ruled in favor of Carl, though he was acquitted on a technicality over how the draft board handled Carl's induction papers. The judge asked Carl if he would consent to a noncombatant role, such as working in a hospital, and Carl said, "Most definitely—I just want to do something good." Carl still wasn't out of the woods. Because he had won on a procedural issue—not because he was a conscientious objector—his draft board could still induct him. The threat hung over Carl for years.

Brian's troubles with *Smile* continued. In February of 1967, Van Dyke left the project, forcing Brian to continue without his collaborator. More deadlines were missed. In April, Derek Taylor, in a press release, tried to put a positive spin on the delay but just created more confusion. "Wilson's only concern is that when the music is ready, it is also good. And the very power which enables them to take time is based on a greatness of their past product. So there is a logic in this situation. So much logic that one goes in a circle. But not a vicious circle. Rather a commercial/artistic infinite curve in which fine music makes great money in good time."

Well, okay then.

Brian and Marilyn needed to start over. They sold their house on Laurel Way and moved into a Spanish-style mansion on Bellagio Road in Bel Air, taking with them little else besides the grand piano.

They built a high brick wall with an electronically controlled gate around the property. The Beach Boys installed a studio in the house so that Brian would have fewer distractions. Most of the hipsters were gone or would soon be gone. The journalists had left.

On April 17, CBS aired *Inside Pop: The Rock Revolution*, in which Leonard Bernstein, in his silver mane, expressed his amazement for the "strange and compelling scene called pop music." It was the first time that a network had investigated rock as a cultural phenomenon. Interviews with Frank Zappa, Graham Nash, Tim Buckley, and others described how the music was creating a more loving, peaceful America. Janis Ian even sang "Society's Child," about the then-taboo subject of interracial romance. But the show's highlight, filmed in December, was Brian's haunting performance of "Surf's Up." He played it at his piano, the lights dim, a candelabra in the foreground, his falsetto reaching every note.

"There is a new song," David Oppenheim told his viewers, speaking solemnly over the chords, "too complex to get all of the first time around. It could come only from the ferment that characterizes today's pop music scene. Brian Wilson, leader of the famous Beach Boys and one of today's most important pop musicians, sings his own 'Surf's Up' . . . Poetic, beautiful even in its obscurity, 'Surf's Up' is one aspect of new things happening in pop music today. As such, it is a symbol of the change many of these young musicians see in our future."

Whatever Brian was looking for—validation from both the mainstream media and the alternative press, recognition that he was in the cultural vanguard, separation between himself and the Beach Boys—he now had it. He was at the pinnacle. All he had to do was finish *Smile* and bask in the glory.

Then it all collapsed. Just two weeks after the CBS documentary, Derek Taylor announced that *Smile* had been scrapped. "As an average fan of the Beach Boys," he said, "I think it is bitterly disappointing."

Smile didn't vanish entirely. "Heroes and Villains," the centerpiece of the album, was released as a single. Also released was the album *Smiley Smile*, which included reworked, stripped-down versions of the original songs. Future albums included versions of "Our Prayer," "Cabin Essence," and "Surf's Up," the latter also distributed as a single. But for years to come, *Smile* would become legend as the greatest album never released. In February 2002, a reporter for *Mojo*, lamenting that all he could listen to were the album's fragmentary "sound files," wrote: "We're left to ponder what kind of world it would have been if *Smile* had actually made it to the record stores."

Others of us were more concerned about Brian. Every great artist, I believe, straddles a fine line between confidence and fear—confident that he can do something that no one else can do, but fearful of rejection, of being laughed at, of not being understood. If those fears are properly channeled, they can be motivating. But if not, they can be debilitating. Something like that happened to my cousin. His standards were so high, even he couldn't attain them, and the genius campaign made the expectations that much higher. The drugs, meanwhile, offered deliverance, tempering his fears while making him believe that he could reach new creative peaks. And strictly speaking they did just that, at least for a while.

Industry-wide, there was a pre- and post-psychedelic era—from "I Want to Hold Your Hand" to "Lucy in the Sky with Diamonds." The years 1965 and '66 were more or less the dividing line, with the Beatles the most conspicuous agents of that transition. Paul McCartney told *Life* magazine in June 1967: "After I took [LSD], it opened my eyes. We only use one-tenth of our brain. Just think what we could accomplish if we could only tap that hidden part. It would mean a whole new world."

Brian has spoken often about his drug use as well. In a legal deposition in 1993, he said that by 1965 he was smoking three or four marijuana cigarettes a day and taking one LSD pill a day. In a *Mojo* article in January of 2007, he said, "For *Pet Sounds*, it was definitely LSD. That's what led to 'California Girls,' 'Good Vibrations,' and *Pet Sounds*." Asked if he would have written those songs anyway, Brian said, "No, LSD definitely helped me out a little bit. It helped me keep on top of that particular music." In 2003, during a video interview at Capitol Records to promote the release of our *Sounds of Summer* compilation, Brian was asked what led him to write more introspective songs in the mid-1960s. Brian responded flatly: "I started taking drugs, marijuana and amphetamines." Those drugs, he added, "opened up my soul," and "the feelings came out in the music."

But what served as creative ballast ultimately became sticks of dynamite, until Brian's confidence waned, the paranoia set in, and the unraveling began. Musically, it was a defining trade-off. If Brian hadn't taken the drugs, we might have had ten "Good Vibrations." But if he hadn't taken the drugs, we might not have had one "Good Vibrations."

Whatever the artistic consequences, it took decades for my cousin to get his life back on track, and he was never truly the same. As Van Dyke Parks said of Brian's drug use in the documentary *Brian Wilson: I Just Wasn't Made for These Times* (1995): "You go to places where you don't want to go. You discover the dark side of the moon. You're lucky if you get back and don't burn up on reentry."

Doctors would diagnose Brian with a variety of mental illnesses, including depression, paranoid schizophrenia, auditory hallucinations, and organic personality disorder. Which diagnoses were accurate, I couldn't say, and the causal relationship between Brian's drug use and his mental illness is hard to document. What I know is that Brian was healthy before he took the drugs, and then he wasn't healthy. And according to Brian himself, in an interview with the health magazine *Ability* in 2006, after he took his first LSD trip, "I knew right from the start something was wrong. I'd take some psychedelic drugs, and then about a week after that I started hearing voices . . . All day every day, and I can't get them out. Every few minutes, the voices say something derogatory to me . . . But I have to be strong enough to say to them, 'Hey, would you quit stalking me? Fuck off! Don't talk to me—leave me alone!' I have to say these types of things all day long . . . I believe they are picking on me because they are jealous."

All of this had obvious implications for the Beach Boys. Brian could still create wonderful music, and he did, but not like before. Brian was twenty-four when he composed "Good Vibrations," and that was his last No. 1 hit. Excluding one cover, he never had another Top 10 hit either. Something was missing. He lost that drive, that magic, that desire for immortality. After our banner year in 1966, it was not preordained that the Beatles would have four or five more years of commercial and critical success while we would drift off the charts. But Brian was our quarterback, and once he was out of the game, we could never keep up.

From my perspective, I didn't know if or when Brian would pick up the *Smile* tracks again. Our focus, beyond Brian's health, was on recording, performing, and keeping the band viable in what would be some lean years. But reporters kept asking us about the lost album, so we knew there was interest. Then in 1978, the publication of a book, *The Beach Boys and the California Myth*, laid out a narrative about *Smile*, Brian, and the Beach Boys that would take hold.

The author, David Leaf, described himself in a 1995 essay as a "Brian Wilson fanatic" who had listened to "Surf's Up" in 1971 and believed that "the death of *Smile* was the public tombstone for the artistic repression of Brian." Leaf said that Brian had been "submerged by insensitivity and greed . . . interrupted while traveling a brand-new path of popular music, and that was clearly a cultural crime."

Brian's *Smile* experience had been called many things, but this was the first time it had been called a "crime." Every crime needs a culprit. So whodunit?

It was me.

Well, it wasn't me alone. Brian's brothers were also implicated. And his wife. And Al and Bruce. And Capitol Records. My uncle Murry was incriminated as well. Leaf's theory, as described in the first paragraph of his book, was that "Brian created the California myth through his music. Ultimately, he became one of the myth's most tragic victims." A lot of us were responsible, but according to Leaf, I had emerged "as a villain."

My villainy was alleged by the hipsters, most notably from the mayor of hip himself, David Anderle. (He was quoted by name. Others spoke bravely behind the veil of anonymity.) Anderle was our business partner for less than a year, but that was long enough for him to conclude that those of us who'd been with Brian his entire life were conspiring to sabotage his career. He made the charge as early as November of 1967, when he told *Crawdaddy!* that starting with *Pet Sounds*, Brian's "major problem" has been "the Beach Boys always being negative towards Brian's experimentation . . . Brian would come in, and he would want to do different things, and [the Beach Boys] would balk." Anderle contended that "a great wall had been put down on [Brian's] creativity . . . [and] a great reason why *Smile* wasn't finished, the way Brian wanted it, [was] because of [the Beach Boys'] resistance in the studio."

Anderle was there to save Brian. "I think had myself and a few other people really gotten behind him, and been on his side against whoever he had to fight, [*Smile*] would have happened a year and a half ago."

Anderle reprised his critique in a lengthy two-part profile of Brian in *Rolling Stone* in 1971. Brian was in terrible shape—he had begun taking cocaine in 1969 and had become increasingly reclusive—but his well-being didn't seem to concern anyone in the article. A large part dwelled on *Smile*, and, according to the reporter Tom Nolan, "David [Anderle] really holds Mike Love responsible for the collapse. Mike wanted the bread."

The profile inspired Leaf's book, which explicitly cast Brian as a victim. His drug use is acknowledged, but, Leaf wrote, "If Brian sought refuge within drugs, in reaction to all the pressure, then everybody must share the blame—the record company, the family, the Beach Boys, and Brian's entourage."

Even Marilyn, who took care of Brian, ran the house, and raised their two daughters by herself, was thrown under the bus. Brian's friends, quoted anonymously, depicted her as an ungrateful, profligate nag: "If Brian wanted to buy some musical equipment for one of his friends, that caused a big stink, but it was okay if Marilyn bought matching fur coats for herself and her friends. After all, it was Brian who made the money . . . She digs being Mrs. Brian Wilson and the money and the status that goes with that."

The attacks weren't surprising. Marilyn had called Brian's new friends "users" because she saw how they exploited Brian for their own careers while bringing the drugs into her house. I was even more outspoken about the drugs and my contempt for these same opportunists, so I took the brunt of their scorn.

What was noteworthy about Leaf's book was that readers never heard from Brian about *Smile*. It's not as if his thoughts were secret. In the 1971 *Rolling Stone* article, Brian was asked why the album didn't come out. "The lyrics," he said, "were so poetic and symbolic they were abstract, we couldn't . . . Oh, no, wait. It was, no, really, I remember, this is it, this is why. It didn't come out because I'd bought a lot of hashish. It was a really large purchase, I mean perhaps $2,000 worth. We didn't realize, but the music was getting so influenced by it. The music had a really drugged feeling. I mean, we had to lie on the floor with the microphones next to our mouths to do the vocals. We didn't have any energy."

In *Crawdaddy!* in July of 1976, the reporter Timothy White asked Brian why he didn't finish *Smile*.

"Because a lot of that shit just bothered me—but half of the shit we didn't finish anyway. Van Dyke Parks did a lot of it; we used a lot of fuzz tone. It was inspiring, 'cause Van Dyke had a lot of energy and a lot of fresh ideas, so that energy has helped me. But a lot of the stuff was what I call little 'segments' of songs, and it was a period when I was getting stoned, and so we never really got an album; we never finished anything!"

White again asked why.

Brian: "Why? Because we got off on bags that just fucking didn't have any value for vocals. A lot of tracks just weren't made for vocals, so the group couldn't do it! We really got stoned! We were too fucking high, you know, to complete the stuff. We were stoned! You know, stoned on hash 'n' shit!"

Even under oath Brian gave the same account. After Brian wrote his memoir in 1991, he and his publisher, HarperCollins, were sued for defamation in separate actions by Brother Records Incorporated, Carl, and me. Brian acknowledged that he had little to do with the writing of the book and disavowed much of its content. He did, however, grant interviews to a writer named Todd Gold, and those transcripts were used in Brian's depositions. Asked by Gold about *Smile*, Brian said it was "an experiment with grass and hashish. I was smoking it. I got freaked out inside my head and started writing freakier songs. I was heavily influenced by marijuana and hashish. It was fun. It was a good trip." Asked specifically why he junked the album, Brian said the "Fire" sequence so frightened him that he stopped taking drugs for a couple of weeks. "And I said hash and marijuana are fucking me up. I don't think I'm going to make this, and I junked this album. I don't like where I'm at on drugs."

In a 1998 deposition of Brian regarding his memoir, Brian was asked if my opposition to some of the lyrics caused him to stop working on the album. Brian said, "No. There weren't as many lyrics as there was just—see, *Smile* wasn't a lyrical thing."

I t's understandable that Anderle and the other hipsters would not want Brian's own account to be the accepted history of *Smile*. If it should be, then those who gave Brian the drugs, sold him the drugs, took the drugs with him—who convinced Brian that the Messiah was coming—then they would be complicit in Brian's unraveling. And it wasn't temporary. According to Brian, LSD "shattered my mind" (*The Mike Douglas Show*, 1976), and it "killed me. It ruined me. It put my mind away . . . [It caused] permanent damage" (*Charlie Rose*, 2005). And in a 1991 deposition, Brian said: "I was a rich person who could afford to buy a lot of drugs over the years, and the drugs have literally fouled up my head . . . No doctor in the world could cure me of the damage that I got, brain damage."

Brian's *Smile*-era friends didn't want that responsibility. Much better to blame me and the other Beach Boys as the mercenaries who snuffed out Brian's creative light. And for Brian's awestruck biographers (Leaf was only the first), the morality tale of the tormented genius who was undone by his own family—putting commerce ahead of art—that tale was too great to resist.

Anderle crystallized this theme, in the 1971 *Rolling Stone* article, by claiming that I told Brian, "Don't fuck with the formula." By the time Leaf's book was published, Anderle told Leaf that my quote "was taken slightly out of context." It was still used. Actually, the quote had no context, because it was never spoken. When Brian, whose memoir invoked the same line, was asked under oath in 1998 if I ever said, "Don't fuck with the formula," Brian responded, "No. No. Absolutely not."

The line was absurd on its face. We've recorded hundreds of songs across virtually all genres. We have no formula. In 1967 alone, the year I supposedly made the comment, we recorded *Wild Honey*, an R&B album that was entirely different from anything we'd ever done, and I cowrote ten songs and sang three leads.*

All that didn't matter. "Don't fuck with the formula" has been repeated in book after book, in articles and on websites and on blogs. It's the most famous thing I've ever said, even though I never said it. But the myth was too strong to be inconvenienced by the truth. And the need for absolution, among those who caused the hero's downfall, trumped the facts.

Over the years, I've tried not to let the personal attacks bother me, as I learned long ago that if you're going to be in the spotlight, either you develop a thick skin or you find another job. I also had faith that the truth about the Beach Boys' role in the *Smile* era would come out, and it did.

Specifically, the claim that the Beach Boys torpedoed *Smile* was finally put to rest when the album was released as a box set in 2011. Brian had revisited the recordings in 2004, finished the songs, and released *Brian Wilson Presents Smile* with his own band. Until then, there was no album, just song fragments. But using the sequencing of *BWPS*, sound engineer Mark Linett and Beach Boy archivist Alan Boyd dove into the master tapes and slowly pieced them together. Brian, it turns out, had tried to take the modular format that he used for "Good Vibrations" and apply it to an entire album, creating a nearly infinite number of ways that it could be assembled. Everything was interchangeable with everything else—except Brian was using a razor blade to splice analog tape. Brian liked to push all musical boundaries, but as Linett noted, "*Smile* was a proj-

---

* We recorded in Brian's home studio, and my lyrics for the title track were inspired by my spotting the label of a jar of wild honey when I went to the kitchen to make a cup of tea.

ect that was begun decades before the necessary technology was invented."

Linett and Boyd transferred seventy analog 4-track and 8-track session tapes to high-resolution digital tapes, and the final masters were ultimately encoded for HDCD on compact discs. They spent thousands of hours editing and mixing the sessions. I'm grateful for their efforts, as they exposed the lie that had long been told about Dennis, Carl, Al, Bruce, and me. Just listen to those CDs. Vocally, the Beach Boys were still at their peak, and the vocals were absolutely fantastic. Whatever reservations we had about *Smile*—and yes, I had them—we put them aside and did everything we could to help Brian realize his dream. It was no different from what we did for "Good Vibrations" or for *Pet Sounds*, no different from what we always did for Brian, going all the way back to my mom's Christmas parties, when he gave us our parts, and we sang them our best.

I've long since abandoned trying to track the commentary about *Smile*. I know Brian is proud of his work, as he should be, but it speaks to the self-absorption of Brian's hagiographers and sycophants who view *Smile* only as a musical event. Not me. The album is a reminder of a painful time in the history of our band and our family. I cannot separate the music from the man, and I cannot separate the man from the physical and emotional turmoil that befell him. Alan Boyd, asked about his experience in reconstructing the tracks, said it well:

"Putting *Smile* together was an intense process, and not a happy experience. I think it's a brilliant piece musically, but it comes from a very dark place. There are parts that, to me, present a beautiful yet chilling portrait of a mind coming unhinged. Listen closely to 'Cabin Essence' and tell me that's not severely bipolar in its extreme musical mood swings. Listen closely to 'Fire' and tell me that isn't an expression of pure rage. Listen to the modularity and fragmentation of the whole album and tell me that isn't the product of an artist whose psyche isn't itself seriously fractured. It's beautiful, it's an amazing work of art, and it's also disturbing. It's like looking at Van Gogh's later work. I will admit it got to me . . . and listening to every last bit of the session tapes was a trip down a rabbit hole I'd never want to take again."

CHAPTER 10

HOLY GROUNDS ON THE GANGES

I n Ernest Hemingway's *The Sun Also Rises*, a character is asked how he went bankrupt. "Two ways," he said. "Gradually and then suddenly."

The Beach Boys' fall from the top happened in a similar fashion. When we left for Dublin in late April of 1967, we knew we had problems—Carl's arrest, Brian's delay with *Smile*—but our European tours had always been successful, and we assumed this one would be as well. But it was bad from the start. EMI, which owned Capitol, was unhappy that we didn't have a new single, so without asking us, it released "Then I Kissed Her," a 1965 track that was nice but in no way representative of our current music. In London, we picked up our *New Musical Express* award for best vocal group, but our label was selling a record that seemed to be taking us backward. Meanwhile, the British musicians' union forbade us from using the four extra musicians we had brought from the states, so we couldn't re-create the studio sounds onstage. Reviews described us as "amateurish" and "floundering." Then when we were in Birmingham, Derek Taylor announced that *Smile* had been scrapped, reinforcing the view that we were adrift. Bad luck followed us across the continent, as we had to cancel concerts in Paris and Holland because we failed to get work permits. In Amsterdam, a reporter asked us why we wore outdated striped shirts onstage. We didn't really have an answer beyond that's what we wore.

Less than two weeks after we returned to the states came the release of *Sgt. Pepper's Lonely Hearts Club Band*, which spent fifteen weeks at the top of the charts in the United States and twenty-seven weeks in the United Kingdom. Groundbreaking musically, beloved by critics and fans alike, it was in sync with the drug culture (no odes to teen romance) and firmly reestablished the Beatles as the world's No. 1 rock band.

Just a few weeks after *Sgt. Pepper's,* on June 17, we were scheduled to perform at the Monterey Pop Festival. No one knew exactly how important this three-day event would be, but it was organized by a group whose board of directors were the pop elite, including Paul McCartney, Smokey Robinson, and Paul Simon. Brian was also on the board, and the Beach Boys were to be the headliner on Saturday night—a prime-time slot for California's favorite sons.

But shortly before the festival, we were at Brian's house, in his backyard, and we decided to cancel. Several factors were at play. Carl was to appear in federal court the Tuesday after the concert, but for all we knew, they were going to arrest him again if he performed onstage. In addition, Brian was despondent over *Smile*, and due to whatever he was taking, he was not feeling or looking all that great. I don't know all the drugs Dennis and Carl were doing at that point, but I know I was smoking pot and drinking my share of alcohol. None of us was afraid to perform at Monterey, but we just weren't unified as a band. Even though we had already sent our PA system to the festival (and it would be used by the other acts), our decision to cancel was unanimous.

It turned out that Monterey would be seen as a countercultural milestone that inaugurated the whole tradition of rock festivals. Janis Joplin, in her first event before a large audience, wailed "Ball and Chain." Pete Townshend, during "My Generation," threw his guitar into the amps and Keith Moon kicked over his drums while the rest of the band was enveloped in smoke. Jefferson Airplane, the Grateful Dead, and Moby Grape, all psychedelic bands from San Francisco, signaled geographic and cultural shifts in the music world. And Jimi Hendrix doused his Stratocaster in lighter fluid, set it aflame, and threw it offstage. He also said, from "Third Stone from the Sun," *You'll never hear surf music again.*

Perhaps nothing illustrated how quickly the tides had turned against us than Brian's effort to release "Heroes and Villains." Compared to what we had worked on in the *Smile* sessions, much of the track had been redone, including new vocals. Brian himself, having become increasingly interested in astrology, decided that the stars were aligned at the end of July. One night after midnight, he called our friend Terry Melcher and a couple of executives at Capitol, and he told them that they had to release "Heroes and Villains" right now.

They arrived at Brian's house by 1:45 A.M. and drove to KHJ, a Top 40 station. Whenever Brian finished a song, he felt an urgency to hear it on the radio, a sign of validation, but in this case, the gates were locked. Terry got out of the car, found the security guard, and somehow convinced him to let in the group. Once in the studio, Brian approached the DJ with his new song.

"Here is the follow-up to 'Good Vibrations,'" he said.

"Well, I can't play that. It isn't on the playlist."

Terry pulled the DJ into the control room. "Look, get the program director on the phone right now!"

"I can't wake him up," the DJ said.

"You better wake his ass up," Terry said, "or this is the last minute you're in the record business."

The DJ called the program director—Bill Drake—and handed the phone to Terry. "Bill, I'm down here with Brian and Capitol," Terry said. "He wants to give you the exclusive for 'Heroes and Villains.' Tell him to put the fucking record on right now, please. Thank you very much."

The record was played, but from where Brian was just a few months ago—heralded on national television as the apostle of pop—to where he was now, literally begging to have his song played in the dead of night, the drop-off was dismaying. The single did reasonably well, reaching No. 12, but for a track that Brian envisioned as the successor to "Good Vibrations," it was another disappointment. That same month, July, Capitol released *Best of Beach Boys Volume 2*, and even though it was packed with our hits ("California Girls," "Help Me, Rhonda," etc.), it fizzled at No. 50.

Our downward spiral accelerated with the September release of the *Smiley Smile* album.

To create elaborate productions, Brian had been using the top session musicians in the city's best studios; but for *Smiley Smile*, he opted for the studio that we had put in his new house. Gone were all those superior musicians. Brian instead used a rented tape deck, and the backing tracks that were so intricate were now minimalist in the extreme, mainly Brian playing a white Baldwin organ. Some of the songs we recorded could barely be called songs. They were chants, spacey fragments, weird sound effects. Every group produces at least one bad album, but for our fans, who had such high expectations after *Pet Sounds* and "Good Vibrations" and who had been swept up in the *Smile* hype, *Smiley Smile* was a baffling departure from everything we'd ever done, and we pretty much alienated our entire market. It was also our first album officially labeled "Produced by the Beach Boys" instead of "Produced by Brian Wilson," reflecting his reduced role. (It was also our first album for Brother Records.) I don't think Brian wanted to be associated with it either. Ironically, the music's ethereal nature was deemed helpful for those trying to get off drugs, and the album became a favorite in drug rehab centers.

Despite the professional downturn, I could still help buy a new home for my parents in Cypress, Orange Country. There were no lingering resentments between them and me over how I was thrown out of the house. They came to some of my concerts, and my mom was thrilled that her effort to instill in me a love of music had paid off so handsomely. But we were all caught up in our own lives—they were still raising their own kids and really didn't have time for mine, and I wasn't one to reach out on my own. We kept a loving distance.

I spoke more often to Grandma Love than to either of my parents, and I was able to acquire a small home for her and Grandpa in Monrovia. When she told me that Grandpa was having heart pains and needed an operation, I sent him to Dr. Theodore Batchelder, a pioneering cardiovascular surgeon in Jacksonville, Florida. The doctor told me that he would have to chisel Grandpa's sternum to open the chest cavity, which was difficult on any surgeon's hands. A new medical tool, however, was now available—an electronic sternum saw that could zip open a patient easily. So I donated one to Dr. Batchelder and his practice, and it was successfully used on my grandfather.

He soon fell ill, however, and the last time I saw him, in the hospital in 1971, I held his hands. The decades of cutting metal and hauling wood had left them callused and gnarled, and I understood that if I had stayed in the family business, those hands would have been mine. Time had not softened Grandpa's temperament either. He was seventy-seven, a delightful curmudgeon. He didn't want sympathy or pity and didn't care about himself at all. He just asked me to look after Grandma.

I told him I would.

———

Meanwhile, Suzanne and I were living comfortably on Coldwater Canyon in our 4,700-square-foot home, which included a large master bedroom with walk-in dressing rooms, a bedroom for the maid, and a spacious living room with a canary-yellow carpet and matching sofas. We also had a swimming pool and pool house amid lemon and tangerine trees, and a small fleet of British cars: our yellow Jaguar XKE, a 1939 Rolls-Royce, a 1948 MG TC, and a Jaguar sedan. The good life included some drug use. We smoked marijuana on occasion and twice did mescaline, which, I am told, has similar effects to LSD. The first time was intense, everything magnified. Suzanne had acquired the drug the second time, so maybe it was a different kind; but I remember opening the refrigerator and seeing all these colors explode. The orange juice. The apples. The butter. A cannonade of hues. Then I walked into our bedroom, glanced at the mirror, and saw myself but with hair all over my face. I looked like a werewolf.

Way too intense, and it was the last time I ever did mescaline.

Our daughter, Hayleigh, was born on December 27, 1966, while our son, Christian, would be born on May 23, 1968. All of that should have been enough for me—the gorgeous wife, the adorable children, the lavish home. We had also accomplished so much professionally. But something was missing. I think I was looking for ways to understand it all, or maybe just for ways to cope—something beyond the material world. My Lutheran faith offered one option, but by my middle twenties, I was more focused on the fallibility of man than on faith in God. People talked about their lofty religious principles— Christian, Jewish, Islamic—and then committed atrocities. Hypocrisy seemed to unite all faith traditions. I was done with dogma, but not with spirituality.

I had always been interested in literature and philosophy, and those interests encompassed unconventional ways of understanding the world. I devoured Edmond Bordeaux Szekely's *The Essene Gospel of Peace*, transcribed from Aramaic scriptures, which present an unknown gospel of Jesus. In addition to explorations of temptation and sin, faith and love, Szekely claimed that Jesus taught natural health practices, including fasting and vegetarianism, as ways to purify the body.

This struck a chord at a time when I had seen so many people poisoning their own bodies. I was also taken by the author's invocation of nature as a pathway to heaven, to bliss. I was someone who had always loved the outdoors, so those words spoke a deeper truth that I knew and felt.

> Seek the fresh air of the forest and of the fields, and there in the midst of them shall you find the angel of air. Put off your shoes and your clothing and suffer the angel of air to embrace all your body. Then breathe long and deeply, that the angel of air may be brought within you . . . Truly, all must be born again by air and by truth, for your body breathes the air of the Earthly Mother, and your spirit breathes the truth of the Heavenly Father.

I included these ideas in some of our music, as I wrote "Country Air," with Brian, which drew explicitly on this search for purification through nature (the song appeared on *Wild Honey*). This organic approach to life also seemed to capture something that was going on in parts of the country.

In the fall of 1967, I heard that Jerry Jarvis would be giving a lecture at the Santa Monica Civic Auditorium. Jarvis, the director of the Students International Meditation Society, had been working closely with Maharishi Mahesh Yogi since the early 1960s to bring Transcendental Meditation to the states. Maharishi was in the headlines as the new spiritual guru for the Beatles. I didn't know anything about Transcendental Meditation or any kind of meditation, but wanted to learn more, so Suzanne and I drove to Jarvis's lecture in Santa Monica.

Afterward, we went to the Students International Meditation Center in Westwood, but upon arriving we were told that the place was only for students, though we could attend another meeting in another part of town for adults. On our way, Suzanne and I got into an argument, so I just blew it off. I knew a better time would come. Then within a few days, the Beach Boys were invited to perform at a UNICEF gala in Paris, at the Palais de Chaillot.

The event, on December 15, was going to feature a cast of stars, including Marlon Brando, Elizabeth Taylor, and Richard Burton. But when we arrived for rehearsal, we saw an unexpected figure— Maharishi, who was watching us from one of the seats. The organizers had considered allowing him to speak during the gala, but then thought better of it. It was a "variety" show, but not that much variety. Maharishi was a small, brown-skinned man with a high voice and a beard and long hair streaked with gray. We introduced ourselves and asked him a few questions, including if Transcendental Meditation was similar to astrology. He said no, but we didn't have time to discuss matters.

The show was broadcast all over Europe, and we watched like everyone else: Marlon Brando dancing barefoot to a Polynesian jig, with his Tahitian wife whom he met while filming *Mutiny on the Bounty*; Ravi Shankar playing an Indian raga on the sitar; and Richard Burton crooning "How to Handle a Woman" while Elizabeth Taylor paraded across the stage. Before we did our set, I had a rare moment of stage fright. Most everyone in the audience was in a tux or a gown, all to see so many marquee names. With an orchestra behind us, we walked onstage and started singing "Barbara Ann," and then I saw Maharishi sitting in the front row, with George Harrison and John Lennon on either side.

After the gala, we were all invited to a party at some embassy, and Brando was there with his wife. For whatever reason, at around one A.M., Brando, with whom I'd been speaking, turned to me and asked, "Do you want to get some breakfast?"

Me? Breakfast? Brando was forty-three, still in his physical prime, an international star whose performances in *A Streetcar Named Desire*, *On the Waterfront*, and *Viva Zapata!* had amazed me.

"Sure," I said. "What's open?"

We left the party, and even though it was a chilly December night in Paris, Brando and his Tahitian entourage jumped into a Cadillac convertible. A group of us—Al Jardine and Carl and their wives, plus Suzanne and me—followed them in a couple of taxis and ended up at Maxim's de Paris. We walked through the entrance and, following Brando, reached a private room, where we saw Elizabeth Taylor and Richard Burton getting sloshed, the Danish comedian Victor Borge at the piano, and others in fancy gowns and jewels who appeared to be royalty. As we were about to enter, a woman spread her arms across the door and said, "I'm terribly sorry. This is a private party."

Without missing a beat, Brando looked at her and said, "Oh, man, I'm sorry, but in Tahiti, if one person goes, everybody has to go. It's like family. Guess I better leave." He turned toward the door dramatically, but before he could take one step, the woman said, "We can make arrangements."

So we stayed for breakfast and watched Taylor shake her world-famous torso to the music of a Tahitian guitarist while Burton was cavorting with one of the dancers. What could have been a very snooty affair turned into a fantastic party, and I thought Brando was the coolest guy on the planet.

The next day Dennis stayed in Paris, but the rest of us decided to head to London. We went to the airport, and who do I see at the gate but Marlon Brando. Hell, by now we were practically friends, so we sat next to him on the flight. He was interested in politics and talked about the civil rights movement in America. As we made our descent, I said, "How you getting into town?"

"I don't know. Just take a cab, I guess."

"Why don't you come with us? We've got transportation."

The year 1967 had not been good financially for the Beach Boys, but we still traveled in grand style. We had five Daimler limos waiting for us at the airport in London. On our way to the city, Brando said, "You wanna go to a party?"

"Sure," I said. "But why don't we stop by our hotel and drop our bags off first."

We swung by the Hilton Hotel in London, where we had booked corner suites, one on top of the other, overlooking Hyde Park. We walked into my suite, with a living room, a bedroom, and a balcony, and Brando said, "You cats really know how to travel." We then proceeded to another party.

I got back to my hotel room at some point, and the phone rang. It was Dennis. "You have to come back to Paris," he said.

"Why?"

"Because Maharishi is going to teach us how to meditate."

"You sure?"

"Yeah, I think so."

"Okay, just make sure."

Dennis called back to confirm, and we had our "initiation" set up with Maharishi for the following morning. I never saw Brando again but would always remember his kindness toward me, and the breakfast.

We flew back to Paris early Sunday morning. The taxi driver asked me if I had ever been here. "Yes," I deadpanned. "Yesterday."

Maharishi was staying at the Hôtel de Crillon, and the initiation took place there. The puja, or devotional ritual, required that you bring fruit, flowers, and a clean white cloth, so eight of us—Dennis and Carole, Carl and Annie, Al and Lynda, Suzanne and me—

scrambled to get what we needed. We entered Maharishi's suite for an introductory lecture. The windows were open, and the room was quite cold—we had to keep our coats on. But Maharishi, in his flowing robe, seemed impervious to the chill. I immediately understood why so many were captivated by him. Using a blackboard to illustrate some of his points, he spoke calmly and confidently about TM as a technique that is practical and concrete as well as scientific. Having its origins in the Vedas, the oldest Indian teachings, it is not tied to any one faith or philosophy but is available to anyone. Within each person there exists an unbounded reservoir of energy and intelligence, and—once taught—TM systematically taps into this vast resource as it normalizes the nervous system and takes you on a journey within. Other types of meditation have benefits, but they take place within the conscious level of the mind.

Not TM, which, according to Maharishi, had cumulative benefits. If you meditated regularly over enough years, you could attain "cosmic consciousness," which he defined as "just being yourself, without the stress." He also described the broader implications of TM as a movement to better the world.

"If the forest is to be green," he said, "then each tree must be green."

After a brief rest, Maharishi met with us again as a group and then as couples, where he gave us our mantras, a word or phrase that is repeated to create a meditative state. We then met as a group for our first meditation. No two people have the exact same experience, but in my case, it was intensely visual. Sitting on the floor, the shades drawn, my eyes closed, I saw these molecular structures in multiple colors and felt myself going deeper and deeper within my own self, reversing a thought process from outwardly directed to inwardly directed. I felt my breathing slow and my blood travel to my extremities, and I moved past the individual self toward some uncharted area of life . . . a place that was quiet and safe and beyond the conscious level of the mind. I wasn't dreaming. But the state itself was deeper than the deepest sleep. It was neither dark nor light. It seemed as if I had arrived at a grove where all the laws of nature resided and had found a place of infinite peace, of profound rest.

"Open your eyes," Maharishi said.

We had meditated for about thirty minutes, and I had two thoughts: this is so easy that anyone could do it, and if everyone did it, it would be an entirely different world.

The most important revelation was that it allowed me to relax in a completely natural way. For years, I had been relaxing by drinking beer or vodka or by smoking weed or hash. I stayed away from everything else (notwithstanding my brief foray into mescaline) and was never out of control, but these intoxicants and chemicals were all unnatural ways to unwind, often leaving me bleary-eyed or achy or just lacking in clarity. I also saw what was happening throughout the music industry and knew all too well what had happened to Brian and increasingly to Dennis. It was as if we were all living in this laboratory of self-destruction, and TM offered a healthy escape.

I had also been reading more and more about history, philosophy, and religion. It seemed to me that all faith traditions—Christianity, Judaism, and Islam—offered their people various forms of salvation, atonement, and redemption, and all of it sounded inspiring, but it didn't make any difference. The history of mankind was still a history of bloodshed and treachery. I had been obsessed with this idea since junior high school. It was not our original sin that bothered me but our continuous sin. In his own way, Maharishi recognized that as well, and changing the arc of history was the goal of Transcendental Meditation: using the full potential of the mind to create a better person and ultimately a better world, where the earth would shine not with the fires of war but the light of humanity. Maharishi described his efforts as a "Spiritual Regeneration Movement." I thought it was revolutionary.

In January of 1968, just one month after we met Maharishi in Paris, he was in New York for a lecture at the Plaza Hotel. I flew in to attend and then followed him to Boston, where he spoke at the Harvard Law Forum. I sat in the same section as Mia Farrow, the svelte actress with short red hair who had just completed filming *Rosemary's Baby* (in which Mia discovers that her baby is the spawn of Satan). When Maharishi was introduced, he took one step toward the lectern and paused. Then he took another step and paused. By the third step, everyone stood in unison. I thought people were going to applaud, but instead there was silence. I had witnessed hundreds of standing ovations, but this was the first one I had ever seen in *silence*. There was so much emotion in the room, I got choked up.

After his lecture, I called Maharishi's hotel and asked if I could speak to someone staying with him. The call was put through, and a man picked up.

"Hello," he said. "Who is this?"

"This is Mike Love with the Beach Boys."

"This is Maharishi."

I can't even recall what I wanted to ask him, but he asked me, "Are you coming to India? You should come and bring the rest of the group."

The invitation was to visit Rishikesh. I didn't know who else was going to be there, what the conditions would be like, or even what the trip's exact purpose would be, but I had been meditating for a month, and I wanted more of it.

My cousins seemed to feel the same way, including Brian, who met Maharishi in the states in 1968. After the meeting, which included Dennis and Carl, Brian typed a letter to his parents, informing them of the remarkable encounter. He affirmed the simplicity of Maharishi's "technique" and how much peace and energy it brought him. "It is not a hype or sales job, but a real natural way to get happiness," Brian wrote. He said that TM was much better than drugs, which "wore off," and asked his parents if he and his brothers could talk to them about it.

Alas, Brian's commitment, and that of his brothers, went only so far. After my invitation to Rishikesh, I returned home and asked my cousins if they wanted to go there as well. They all declined, and Suzanne was pregnant with our second child, so she was staying home.

I would make the journey by myself. I still had a front man's mentality, so I went to Profils du Monde in Beverly Hills and bought custom-made cashmere and silk shirts in vibrant colors and Nehru collars, and topped it off with a pith helmet, in mock tribute to the Brits' colonial rule. It was late February, and I booked a flight on Pan Am 1, flying from Los Angeles to New Delhi, with stops in Hawaii, Japan, and Thailand—almost 12,000 miles, which is roughly half the circumference of the globe. But the spiritual distance was even greater.

When I walked off the plane in Delhi, dawn had just broken and the sun was rising, and something felt different. I truly thought that I had entered a holy land. After a night of rest, I hired a taxi and, dodging carts, cows, and even a camel along the way, rode about 140 miles northeast to the foothills of the Himalayas. There stood the ashram, or compound, in Rishikesh, but it was on the other side of the Ganges River, so I enlisted two bearers with a scow to pull me and my trunk across the swift current.

Rishikesh itself had long been an established center of spirituality, with many ashrams, and the Ganges serves as a kind of sacred perimeter, its banks, according to Hindu texts, given "an aura of blessing" by the saints. Maharishi's fifteen-acre ashram was enclosed by a barbed-wire fence, and next to the entrance gates lay a stone wall with the message "Jai Guru Dev" (hail the divine teacher). Inside were about half a dozen cement-and-stone structures, like a motor court, painted white, each one with at least six rooms to provide shared living quarters.

The bungalows faced wooded campgrounds, including benches and tables made for indoor and outdoor eating. Surrounded by jungle, we didn't keep the animals at bay so much as share the space with them. Spiders, stray dogs, and even an occasional tiger roamed the grounds. The night sounds were a shrill chorus of wildlife—peacocks, crows, and parrots. The wails and cackles may have unnerved some, but I felt at peace. In the mornings, with the mist rising from the Ganges, I walked amid the sheesham and teak trees and felt that I was close to something hallowed.

The food was perhaps my biggest adjustment. I was raised on roast beef, lamb, and chicken, but the ashram was strictly vegetarian. Not even fish was served. Breakfast was cereal and toast. Lunch and dinner offered bland soup, rice, and vegetables with no spices. We drank juice, coffee, or tea. Drugs, of course, were forbidden. Someone later wrote that I had brought in hashish, but that wasn't true. I had actually smuggled in something far more subversive—beef jerky.

Our isolation had a purpose, the easier to immerse ourselves more fully in meditation. I meditated for four, six, eight hours at a time, and found myself even more relaxed and more at peace. The ashram's hub was a large lecture hall, with ceiling beams and whitewashed walls. Charcoal fires burned in tin pots. Candles flickered on the armrests of chairs. At one end of the hall was a wooden stage, with an altar adorned with flowers and tinsel.

I didn't even know it until I arrived, but Maharishi had invited about sixty Westerners to be trained as instructors of TM. That was one surprise. The other surprise occurred when I walked in my living quarters, looked up, and saw Paul McCartney. He was staying in the room next to me and was here with John, Ringo, and George.

I had traveled to the other side of the world with the expectation of total seclusion, but here I was, impossibly, in the media spotlight, as reporters from all over were trying to cover the Beatles in Rishikesh. It was hard to fathom. The Beach Boys and the Beatles had been circling each other for the last five years on at least three different continents—a battle of screaming headlines and devoted groupies and demanding egos—and now I ended up with them in a remote compound with scorpions crawling around at night and monkeys sauntering right up to your dining table in search of scraps.

Strange, yes; but not bad. Regardless of the rivalry, I liked all four of them. I had met the Beatles a few years ago, in August 1965, when they were playing at Portland Memorial Coliseum. I flew up there with Carl, who in our group followed the Beatles most closely, and we were introduced backstage before the show. We were all into cars, George Harrison in particular, and I listed those that I owned, proudly noting that I was an anglophile when it came to autos. So too was Carl, who owned a silver Aston Martin. The conversation turned to tonight's performance and the "ooh!" part of "She Loves You."

"My voice won't be great there," John said, "so when we get to that part, let's shake our heads, the girls will scream, and nobody will know the difference."

And he was right.

The following year, in 1966, after we performed at the Illinois State Fair in Springfield, Bruce and I chartered a single-engine plane to Chicago to stay at the glamorous Astor Tower, where the Beatles were staying. In the morning, we went to their comfortable suite for breakfast. Ringo and Paul were in their bathrobes, and with Beatle-bad hair, I called them "the morning mop-tops." Bruce used their in-tune piano to play and sing parts of a new song that had not yet been completed: "Good Vibrations." They seemed to like it.

It was actually George Harrison's wife, Pattie Boyd, who was the catalyst behind the Beatles' interest in TM. Pattie was the first to practice it, and then she encouraged George and his bandmates to attend a lecture by Maharishi in London. George, already immersed in Eastern spirituality—he had taken sitar lessons from Ravi Shankar—embraced Maharishi's message immediately, and he persuaded his three cohorts to come to Rishikesh: John with his wife, Cynthia; Paul with his girlfriend, Jane Asher; and Ringo with his wife, Maureen. The Beatles weren't interested in becoming instructors, but it didn't matter. They were the Beatles. If Maharishi wanted to start a global movement, he had the world's most powerful prophets right there with him.

John and Paul always wore these white cotton kurta pajamas and leather sandals. John also wore a leather talisman around his neck, and in some ways, he was the most intriguing of the four. When all the attendees met at the lecture hall, John asked Maharishi thoughtful, penetrating questions. He was a skeptic about everything, edgy, as if unsettled by something from his past. At these lectures, he wasn't so much rejecting the veracity of Maharishi's statements as he was probing for some deeper truth. I thought the TM experience for him was more intellectual than spiritual, but I also thought he was committed to the same goals—and wasn't surprised that his bestselling song as a solo performer, "Imagine" (1971), echoed Maharishi's ideals of "living life in peace," "sharing all the world," and predicting "the world will live as one."

Paul was easier going. One morning he came out of his bungalow with his acoustic guitar while I was sitting at the breakfast table.

"Listen to what I've been playing, Mike."

He began singing a song that started with a flight in from Miami Beach. I was present at the birth of "Back in the U.S.S.R."

"Wow," I said. "That's pretty cool."

"Yeah," Paul said. "It's sorta Beach Boy style." He laughed.

I thought he was on to something. "You know what you ought to do. In the bridge part, talk about the girls around Russia. The Moscow chicks, the Ukraine girls, and all that."

If it worked for "California Girls," why not for the USSR?

So Paul went back and wrote it:

Well the Ukraine girls really knock me out.
They leave the West behind.
And Moscow girls make me sing and shout.
That Georgia's always on my my my my my my my my my mind!

"Back in the U.S.S.R." was a helluva song, and it's lasted longer than the country.

One night Paul and I were on the roof of our building, with the stars glittering above, and he said to me, "Mike, you really ought to take more care of what you put on your album covers."

He had me on that one. The cover of *Sgt. Pepper's Lonely Hearts Club Band* featured them in Day-Glo military-style uniforms, surrounded by life-size cutouts of famous people (including themselves). A flower arrangement spelled out "The Beatles." The cover brilliantly captured the whole psychedelic era—another reminder, for me, about how much more savvy in marketing and design they were than we were.

Now Paul was making the same point, so I had to say something in our defense. "You're absolutely right about that," I said, "but we always thought what was more important was what we put *inside* the sleeve."

Other celebrities had made it to India. Donovan Leitch was there, though he was just known as Donovan, a twenty-one-year-old Scottish singer and songwriter with thick, dark hair and close ties to the Beatles. He had a unique fingering technique with his guitar, which he taught John Lennon while in Rishikesh. His hit record "Sunshine

Superman" had already brought him international acclaim, but he had a humble, soft-spoken way about him.

Mia Farrow was also there. Her personal life had already been splashed all over the tabloids. In 1966, at age twenty-one, she married Frank Sinatra, who was thirty years her senior. By the time she traveled to Rishikesh, the divorce proceedings had begun. It was actually Mia's younger sister, Prudence, who introduced her to meditation, and Prudence joined her in India. While Mia was a gentle soul who seemed more captivated by the animals—she adopted a stray puppy—Prudence was immersed in meditation entirely, isolating herself for long periods and inspiring John to write "Dear Prudence." The song suggested that Prudence was missing the wonders of life (*The sun is up, the sky is blue/It's beautiful and so are you/Dear Prudence, won't you come out to play*), but that was misleading. TM worked miracles for Prudence, who later described Rishikesh as "a boiling pot of silence" in which "moments were bathed in waves of bliss, drawing me further inward." Through meditation, Prudence forged an identity separate from her famous sister while putting herself on a spiritual and professional path that has included producing films, receiving a doctorate in Sanskrit, and teaching meditation and yoga, including to Mia's children.

Of course the most important figure in Rishikesh was Maharishi, who spoke to us each day and night in the lecture hall. He had studied Sanskrit and learned the scriptures from a well-known Indian sage named Swami Brahmananda Saraswati, who was for Maharishi his Guru Dev, the teacher whose wisdom he hoped to now disseminate and a picture of whom was found on the lecture hall stage.

Sitting on a deerskin, fingering his 108 prayer beads, Maharishi spoke to us from that stage on many subjects: the nature of creativity, the nature of the mind, how to live life to the fullest. He asked us to consider the archer who holds his bow and arrow. If he pulls back on the bow only somewhat, the arrow will still travel, but it will fall far short of its maximum range. In a similar way, most people use only a small percentage of their minds throughout their lives. TM allows a person to begin to use more of his mind, similar to the archer who draws his bowstring farther back in order to reach a greater distance.

Meditation, I discovered, could resolve stress or phobias. I had always had a fear of knives—just an irrational feeling that I would be stabbed. Death by stabbing, I thought, was the absolute worst way to go. One day when I was meditating in my bungalow, I felt this intense pain in my thigh, as if I were being stabbed. I was sure a blade was cutting right through me, and yet I knew that was impossible. So I kept meditating, kept going deeper into myself, kept unraveling some mystery buried in my subconscious—a fear that I didn't even understand, perhaps something from another life, perhaps something from my childhood, who knew?—until finally, slowly, the root of the problem was resolved, the pain left my body, and the fear of blades was gone forever.

My practice of meditation allowed me to bond with George Harrison in a way that I did not connect with the other Beatles. (Ringo and Maureen left after only one week, saying they didn't like the food.) George was into everything Indian—the food, the music, the culture, but most of all the meditation. We would walk the long path to the lecture hall, and George spoke openly about the limits of fame and wealth as a means to happiness, about what being a rock star could or could not buy you, and about meditation as a pathway to a rich inner life. He called it a "vibration" that was on "an astral plane," and it was his way of connecting with God.

Both George and I are Pisces, our birthdays overlapping during our time in Rishikesh. When George turned twenty-five, we sang "Happy Birthday" to him, and Maharishi gave George a birthday cake that included a plastic globe turned upside down. "This is the world," he said. "It needs to be corrected."

When my twenty-seventh birthday arrived, on March 15, John,

Paul, and George, as well as Donovan, wrote a happy birthday song patterned after "Fun, Fun, Fun," playing acoustic guitars and throwing in some Beach Boy harmonies. George also presented me with a painting of Guru Dev.

But even more meaningful that day was the invitation I received from Maharishi.

His bungalow was nestled in a grove of trees, fronted by a manicured lawn graced by small fountains and flowerbeds filled with orange and yellow marigolds. I walked up a stone path, left my sandals on the porch, and entered a small bright meeting room covered in white futons on which visitors could sit. After a while, a brahmachari, or disciple, showed me down to a small room, which was carved out of rock and reminded me of a cave. The quarters were so tight I had to wait on my knees. A photograph of Guru Dev hung on the wall. Several minutes passed, and then Maharishi descended the stairs and graciously offered me a birthday greeting. There was little chitchat. Just as Maharishi had used the puja to initiate me into TM, I would learn the same to become a TM instructor. But whereas before I was part of a public ceremony, with my cousins, Al, and their spouses, now I had a private ceremony. It was all so quiet. Maharishi began by lighting candles, burning incense, and offering rice, flowers, and fruit to Guru Dev. He recited Sanskrit slokas, or stanzas, which venerate the knowledge and power of the masters who have been with us since the dawn of civilization. Maharishi explained that to become an instructor, you must learn these words, for they will raise your consciousness while fully integrating the spiritual world with the material world.

Maharishi continued to make offerings to Guru Dev, and I experienced this intense feeling of devotion to him as well. At the end of the puja, Maharishi bowed toward Guru Dev. I bowed as well. After about a minute, I sensed Maharishi rising, so I lifted myself, except I couldn't. I fell back down, dazed. My heart was overwhelming me.

Maharishi reached over with his left hand and patted me on my neck three times, and I'll never forget what he said.

"You will always be with me."

The puja was over, and exhausted but elated, I returned to my quarters.

Maharishi introduced me to a level of love and commitment that I had never contemplated, embodying the Vedic definition of a man of God: "Softer than the flower, where kindness is concerned; stronger than the thunder, where principles are at stake."

One chilly night I was meditating in my room, and the mantra I was given assumed a little melody. I was sort of singing it to myself, and then suddenly, from some other part of my mind, I thought, Well, I'm in India, and I heard this sitar-ish impulse in the melody. And then I was thinking of an African kind of impulse, with rhythmic drums. And then an up-tempo Latin beat and then a Chinese singsong approach and then an Irish hillbilly jig. All these sounds from all over the world, spinning through my mind, being played with different instruments and voices until the sound built to a blinding cacophony . . . except it was all so clear, and it all made sense. The whole world, in all its diverse expressions, could be in harmony, and once attained, the world could be in harmony with the universe and the cosmos. All these thoughts were careening through my head, all born from that one melody that grew into a symphony of nations.

Before this trip, I had already concluded that meditation was a far better relaxant than alcohol or weed, and I would eliminate those. But now I also wanted my body to be as pure as possible, so I stopped eating meat as well (and even gave up the jerky). I was just at the beginning, really, of integrating Vedic principles of health, nutrition, and spirituality into my life.

I had to leave Rishikesh shortly after my birthday. Maharishi urged me to stay to complete my teacher training, but I had to return to the states for a tour. (I would become a TM instructor in 1972.) While I was sad to leave, I also couldn't believe how much I had learned and how far I had come since my introduction to TM three months ago. It was also my first of numerous spiritual retreats, ranging from two weeks to six months, each one offering an escape, a respite, from a world that I saw as cynical, damaged, or corrupt.

The Beatles were not long for Rishikesh either. Paul left perhaps a month later, followed by John and George. Then came the controversy that overshadowed all else for the Beatles in Rishikesh.

John came to believe that Maharishi had made sexual advances toward one of the women, which—if true—would have been wrong under any circumstance, the more so because Maharishi claimed to be celibate.

While George retained his ties to Maharishi, the other Beatles declared that they were no longer his spiritual disciples, and John wrote a song whose first line was *Maharishi—what have you done? You made a fool of everyone.* George prevailed on him to change "Maharishi" to "Sexy Sadie," and the song appeared on the Beatles' so-called White Album, but the original lyric was known by many.

I was long gone by the time the alleged incident occurred, but I didn't lose faith in Maharishi. I'm not saying he's infallible, but I didn't believe the accusations. Maharishi eagerly wanted the Beatles and the Beach Boys to help him spread the word about his movement. He was also surrounded by female devotees his entire adult life. Yet the *only* time he was ever accused of misconduct was when the Beatles were right there with him? Please. In the years following John Lennon's death in 1980, Paul noted—according to the *New York Times*—that the rumors of Maharishi's misconduct were raised by Alexis Mardas, known as "Magic Alex," a friend of the Beatles who was there in Rishikesh. Pattie Boyd also attributed the claims to

Mardas. (Mardas has denied responsibility.) In the 1990s, both Paul and George were convinced of Maharishi's innocence and apologized to him.

For all the controversy surrounding their departure, the Beatles' time in Rishikesh could not have been more productive. They wrote nearly forty songs, including all thirty that were on the White Album (whose actual title was *The Beatles*). Maharishi was also credited for weaning them from LSD, though not from drugs entirely. Donovan was also productive, writing "Hurdy Gurdy Man" and "Jennifer Juniper" while in Rishikesh.

I didn't write music there, but the experience expanded my musical consciousness. I had written about physical things like surfing and girls and had written introspective songs like "The Warmth of the Sun" and "When I Grow Up (To Be a Man)." But after Rishikesh, I wrote spiritual songs, such as "All This Is That," with Al and Carl. The song's title is an English translation of a line from the Vedas, and the lyrics included words inspired by Robert Frost: *Two ways have I both traveled by/And that makes all the difference to me.* (The two ways being the outer and the inner.) Al and I also wrote, with Brian, "He Come Down," which included the line *All the saints through all creation/Sing the same song of revelation.*

Perhaps the song that meant the most to me, in this vein, was written after George Harrison died of cancer in 2001. It was a terrible loss, and I wanted to pay tribute to him as an artist, a humanitarian (the Concert for Bangladesh), and an exemplar of peace and love. I wrote "Pisces Brothers," which the Beach Boys now perform in concert, combined with video images of those days in Rishikesh. The music is a poignant remembrance and tribute for all those who ever loved George and for anyone who has ever felt true devotion, and when we perform it, it brings the whole audience, myself included, to those holy grounds on the Ganges.

Not for fortune or for more fame,
But for enlightenment we came.
To Maharishi and house sublime,
It was an atmosphere divine.
Such precious moments now in the past,
Music and memories are all that last . . .

And though we'll miss you, now that you're gone.
Your songs of life go on and on.

CHAPTER 11

A VIOLENT AGE

When I left Rishikesh, I told Maharishi that I wanted to visit Russia before returning home. I didn't know anyone in that country, but we had gotten fan letters from there, and I wanted to see it. We were told the Russians were our enemy, but I didn't want to succumb to demonization. Remember, this was 1968, when Americans were in the streets protesting their own government. Maybe our government was bent on war. Maybe the Russian government was bent on war. I didn't like the militarization of either government and thought that the people of the world deserved better.

I told Maharishi that I wanted to fly to Russia for three days, bring a bunch of LPs from the Beatles and the Beach Boys, and give them out at the student union at Moscow State University. Neither group had performed in Russia, but I knew that the kids there loved both bands. If Russia and the United States were ever going to improve relations, I figured that music was a good place to start, and if we were going to have peace on earth, we had to start somewhere.

Maharishi said, "Better not to go to Russia right now."

Well, he didn't say *not* to go, just that it was better not to go. So I intended to follow up on my plan. I went to New Delhi and, with a couple of nights to kill, was invited to dinner at the home of some affluent Indians. I don't know what I ate, but whatever it was, I wasn't ready for it. I'd been eating bland foods for the past two and a half weeks. When I returned to the Oberoi Intercontinental Hotel, I got violently ill and found myself on my bathroom floor. The hotel doctor came by and gave me something to drink, but I was off my feet for three days and had to cancel my flight to Russia.

I was disappointed, but it wouldn't be long before we were playing in a Communist country.

Perhaps the notion that either music or meditation could bring about a more peaceful world was naive, but when I returned to the states in March of 1968, it seemed that madness had become the norm. In Vietnam, where the body bags were mounting, an American official explained that it was necessary to "destroy" a particular village in order to "save" it. At home, the nonviolent counterculture, of peaceniks and poetry, was losing to a more bellicose opposition. Black militants were urging revolution. White reactionaries were demanding crackdowns. Even suburban housewives were taking up arms. That summer, the police would batter protesters at the Democratic National Convention in Chicago; urban riots would kill forty-six people; and a gunman would murder Robert F. Kennedy in Los Angeles. America, according to Daniel Patrick Moynihan, was going through "a nervous breakdown."

Rock fans wanted music that spoke to the times, songs that exalted antiwar protests, free love, and recreational drug use, and they got that with artists such as Country Joe and the Fish, Jefferson Airplane, the Doors, Cream, and Jimi Hendrix.

And the Beach Boys? In 1968, Capitol Records was promoting us as "the nation's number one surf band."

In fairness, we weren't recording commercially successful music at the time, so Capitol didn't have much to work with. We also remained clueless, or at least stuck in the 1950s, in our image. We had finally rid ourselves of the striped shirts but replaced them with all-white suits. Music fans wanted jambalaya; we were selling vanilla ice cream. We sometimes toured with a big band and performed Four Freshmen standards like "Graduation Day," which went over well in 1964 but not for the new FM-radio-centric rock audience. In October of 1968, we played at the Fillmore East in New York, which was known as "the church of rock and roll" (and the counterpart to the more famous Fillmore West in San Francisco). Our appearance caused an outrage. *The Village Voice* said "it was the weekend the Fillmore tried out as a whore," and the *New York Times* said we were overshadowed by Creedence Clearwater Revival, which was the opening act. I took some comfort in knowing that we sold out the place, or so we thought. We accused the club's famous promoter, Bill Graham, of undercounting ticket sales and forced him to do a stub count after the show. Graham swore he would never have us back.

The Fillmore was the culmination of a disastrous concert season, which began in earnest with a major tour in April. We invested about a quarter of a million dollars in a new sound system. We hired eight musicians who would back us up. We used our own money to reserve many of the venues and to underwrite the promotions. It was called the Million Dollar Tour, not because we had that much money at risk, but it just felt that way.

We were to begin in Nashville on April 5 and do thirty-three shows in eighteen days, mostly in the South. We flew out on Thursday, April 4.

At least one member of the group later recalled that we had heard that Martin Luther King Jr. was shot before we took off, and then we were told he had died after we landed—the thirty-nine-year-old civil rights leader, standing on a hotel balcony in Memphis, struck in the cheek by an assassin's bullet. What I remember was standing on the balcony of our Holiday Inn in Nashville and watching the troops massing down in the street. In fact, 4,000 Tennessee National Guardsmen were deployed after the police received reports of looting.

Marches and protests, some violent, broke out all over the country, and over the next several days, more than a hundred cities convulsed in riots while 55,000 troops were summoned to try to restore order.

I felt numb more than anything else. If you lived through President Kennedy's assassination, you can't really be shocked by the mindless killing of another American leader. I also couldn't help but juxtapose my experiences in Rishikesh with what I was witnessing at home. If any country was in need of spiritual regeneration, it was surely ours. This was the second time in five years that the Beach Boys were scheduled to play a concert in the immediate aftermath of an assassination, and just as we did after President Kennedy's death, we intended to perform after Martin Luther King's. That's what we do—play music to bring something positive to people's lives, and when would people ever need something positive more than after a national tragedy?

We went to Nashville Municipal Auditorium, and a good crowd had showed up, but as we were preparing to take the stage, the Guardsmen arrived, asked us to leave the premises, and then ordered the audience home.

Our Million Dollar Tour wasn't worth a plugged nickel, as many of the concerts were either postponed or canceled, and we lost whatever money we had already put down plus another several hundred thousand in forgone revenue.

The following month, we tried something different. I invited Maharishi to join us on a seventeen-date tour in America, specifically to appear on college campuses, in more intimate settings, where I thought his message would resonate. His associate, Jerry Jarvis, had been traveling the college circuit for several years, and it seemed that young people were a natural audience for an Eastern guru who was advocating a new way of thinking about the world. The Beach Boys would play a set, and Maharishi—before or after—would take the stage and share his philosophy. The group would not make any money on the tour but would use the proceeds to cover expenses while donating the rest to Maharishi.

It didn't work. The Beatles' repudiation of Maharishi suddenly cast him in a negative light. For the tour itself, we were unable to book college campuses and ended up in large auditoriums, such as the Washington Coliseum and the Baltimore Civic Center, raising our costs and leaving many seats empty. Technical problems intervened. Maharishi had a soft voice, but he refused to allow anyone to put a microphone on him—he didn't like to be touched. We found special boom mics that had good reach, but Maharishi was still hard to hear. Finally, most of the people who did attend came to see the Beach Boys. We continued on for a couple more days, to New Rochelle and to Philadelphia, but the crowds were no better in size or temperament. Some audience members taunted Maharishi, which ticked me off, but he never lost his cool. At one press conference, he faced a particularly obnoxious reporter, and we were getting ready to throw him out. But Maharishi instructed someone to tell the journalist that he would like to speak with him after the conference, and Maharishi would try to gently enlighten him.

We called off the tour less than a week into it. Like our canceled southern tour, this one was costly financially, and I take responsibility for an idea that didn't work. But I don't regret it. I thought I could do some good for people who were lost, confused, or troubled, particularly those who were young and idealistic but also vulnerable, and I thought that was true for a whole bunch of us.

If our tours were out of step with the times, so too was our new album—*Friends*, featuring mostly serene and spiritually uplifting songs. Dennis contributed two soulful ballads, "Little Bird" and "Be Still," which he cowrote with the poet Stephen Kalinich. But the album bombed. Capitol, in a panic, promptly released an LP of Beach

Boy hits, but included only the instrumentals, as if the lyrics didn't mean anything. That LP, *Stack-o-Tracks*, fared even worse than *Friends*.

Brian was content to let others contribute equally. I knew that this democratic approach, while allowing the rest of us to grow musically, would never replicate our past success. I figured I would have to inspire Brian to do what we had done in the past. One day I got together with a high school friend, Bill Jackson, and we went to our old surf spot at San Onofre. It was one those perfect Southern California days—the sun, the waves, the girls—and it reminded me of how life used to be. I rushed like hell back to Brian's house and literally got him out of bed. Told him about the day and gushed about how great it was and that we ought to write a song about it, and we could call it "Do It Again."

So Brian sat down at the piano, and we did it again. He found the key, and I related the words.

> *It's automatic when I*
> *Talk with old friends.*
> *The conversation turns to*
> *Girls we knew when their*
> *Hair was soft and long and the*
> *Beach was the place to go.*

Brian included a groovin' "Hey now, hey now" chorus that was patterned after the 1950s song "Finger Poppin' Time," and "Do It Again," in its lyrics and melody, very much evoked the music of our early hits. Carl, it should be noted, added the overdubs and actually finished the record. The song was released as a single on July 8, 1968, only a month after Robert Kennedy's assassination and amid the summer turmoil of riots and protests—in other words, a song that was completely out of touch with what was going on in the country and the world. Yet it reached No. 20 in the United States, and it went to No. 1 in the United Kingdom, No. 1 in Australia, No. 3 in Sweden, and No. 5 in Canada and the Netherlands.

The song defied the conventional wisdom that our surf-and-sun harmonies were tied to a more hopeful time in American history, but I thought that people would always want to hear songs that made them feel good. Brian, for his part, said in an interview in 1980 that "Do It Again" was "probably" our best collaboration. It was certainly among them, and it was a reminder that the Wilson-Love tandem hadn't lost its touch with the public. It was also a rare bright spot in a year that brought mayhem to the nation and the devil to the Beach Boys.

CHAPTER 12

DEMONS AMONG US

By June of 1968, Dennis's marriage had broken up, and he was renting an old hunting lodge, once owned by Will Rogers, on Sunset Boulevard. Late one night, he pulled his Ferrari into his driveway and noticed the lights on inside. That wouldn't have surprised him—friends drifted in and out all the time. But after he parked the car, the back door opened, and out walked a small man with long dark hair and a scruffy beard, wearing jeans and a work shirt. Dennis had no idea who this guy was, and something about him was frightening.

"Are you going to hurt me?" Dennis asked.

"Do I look like I'm going to?" the man replied.

The stranger fell to his knees and kissed Dennis's feet.

That was how Dennis met Charles Manson.

Of all the troubling subplots in the history of the Beach Boys, Dennis's relationship with Manson stands alone, and the episode affected all of us for years to come. My cousin's interest in Manson now seems inexplicable, but in reality Manson tapped into parts of Dennis that make it all too explainable.

It starts with the positives about my cousin. To his credit, Dennis was generous to a fault. He really didn't give a damn about cars or clothes or anything of material value, and was glad to give away what he had. We once rented a piano for him, but when it was time to return it, he didn't have it. He had lent it to someone but couldn't recall who. Money? Didn't care about that either. One night he was in a bar in Tulsa, after a concert, and he couldn't get served because he didn't have an ID. He was with our promoter, who was carrying our cash from the box office, and Dennis told him to give the bartender what he had, which could be held as security. The promoter put $10,000 on the counter. In cash. To Dennis, it was only money, and he wanted a drink.

The other thing about Dennis, and this is the negative, was that his appetite for sex was insatiable. I'm hardly one to sit in judgment, but for Dennis, too much was never enough. He once picked up two women that he was going to take to his house, but instead, he stopped at the house of our road manager, who lived on the very same street. When the road manager later asked Dennis why he just didn't go to his own house, Dennis said, "I couldn't wait that long."

Dennis's obsession made its way into our 1969 song "All I Want to Do," which was written by Dennis and mixed at a studio in the Capitol Tower. After the vocal tracks were completed, Dennis wanted to perk up the ending; so according to our sound engineer, Stephen Desper, Dennis walked over to Hollywood Boulevard, found a prostitute, and brought her back to the studio (using a side door to avoid the security guards). Desper had arranged a love nest in the middle of the studio, using a carpeted riser as a bed, some acoustic blankets for cushion, and another upended riser for privacy. Two condenser mics, mounted on long booms, hung over this makeshift cove. With Desper working the controls, Dennis and his partner disrobed, put on headphones, and listened to the song while providing their own lusty bass line. One take provided all the acoustic effects that were needed, but Dennis said he wanted to "overdub" a second pass. So they did it again, the song and the sex, and Desper integrated these carnal flourishes into the track, in stereo.

So it was completely in character for Dennis, in the spring of

1968, to pick up two young women hitchhiking on Sunset Strip and to bring them back to his house. Dennis mentioned his involvement with Maharishi, and the women said they too had a guru, named Charlie. The women didn't know who Dennis was, but when they returned to Manson, he knew exactly who Dennis Wilson was.

Manson was a thirty-three-year-old former convict (armed robbery and car theft) who believed he was a talented singer/songwriter and was just one recording contract away from stardom. He was also a charismatic speaker who, starting in the Haight-Ashbury section of San Francisco during the Summer of Love (1967), reeled into his thrall desperate young women. Manson extolled their beauty, insisting that they submit themselves to him, sleeping with them to demonstrate his love, and exhorting them to surrender their egos. He compared himself to Jesus and used LSD as a perverse sacrament. It was all part of the initiation. These were his disciples, and they were now part of a family, a family that actually cared about them.

Manson and his "girls," as they were called, moved to Los Angeles at the end of 1967, the better for him to fulfill his destiny as a rock star. They lived in communal arrangements and picked up stragglers along the way, including some men, increasing the size of the group to about twenty. But Manson's efforts to break into the music industry foundered, so when two of his girls told him that Dennis Wilson had picked them up and taken them to his house, Manson pounced.

Dennis was the perfect mark—a famous, well-connected entertainer who could help a musical neophyte get discovered. Dennis lived in a luxurious house, on three acres, with a swimming pool and plenty of guest rooms. Guileless about others, indifferent about his own possessions, a rebel in his own right, Dennis was all too happy to allow Manson and his girls to move in, use his charge cards, take his clothes, eat his food, even drive his Mercedes. Manson, after all, had something for Dennis—a stable of young women who catered to his every desire.

Sex, however, wasn't the only appeal. Manson knew how to nurture the grievances of new recruits, telling them that their father caused their problems. This made sense to Dennis, who surely told Manson about the beatings he had received from Murry. Manson's frustrations with the music industry and his diatribes about the injustices of the world dovetailed with Dennis's own disappointments that his music skills were not taken more seriously and that society never really understood him. Manson was a racist, and Dennis, while not outspoken or meanspirited, may have absorbed his father's uncharitable view of black people. Finally, while Dennis had been drinking heavily for a number of years, he had also developed an appetite for drugs, including LSD, and Manson's blending of psychedelics, sexual servants, rock music, and new-age rhetoric was too much for Dennis to resist. In the summer of 1968, Manson and his girls moved into Dennis's house, and Dennis joined the family.

In a few short months, Dennis swerved from Maharishi to Manson, two diminutive but hypnotic figures who promised a better world for their followers. Dennis was looking for answers—no different from the rest of us—except he had no filter to distinguish between the divine and the diabolical. In a 1968 interview with the *Record Mirror*, he said: "I still believe in meditation, and I'm experimenting with tribal living. I live in the woods in California, near Death Valley, with seventeen girls." Referring to the first two girls he met, he said, "I told them about our involvement with the Maharishi, and they told me they too had a guru, a guy named Charlie, who'd recently come out of jail after twelve years. His mother was a hooker, his father was a gangster, he'd drifted into crime; but when I met him I found he had great musical ideas. We're writing together now. He's dumb, in some ways, but I accept his approach and have learned from him." Asked if he was supporting all of these people, Dennis said, "No, if anything, they're supporting me. I had all the rich status symbols—Rolls-Royce, Ferrari, home after home. Then I woke up, gave away fifty to sixty percent of my money. Now I live in one small room, with one candle, and I'm happy, finding myself."

Dennis took Manson out to nightclubs, introduced him to people in the industry, and proselytized to me and the other Beach Boys about his new guru's wisdom and depth as well as his musical talents. Bruce Johnston and I finally drove out to Dennis's house to meet his new roommates over dinner. That itself was interesting. Charlie's girls drove Dennis's Rolls-Royce to a supermarket in Pacific Palisades and scrounged for discarded vegetables, which they brought home and prepared. On some of these trips, they panhandled from people who they thought could afford it, and one can only imagine the person who gave them spare change only to watch them climb back into their Rolls.

My most vivid memory of Manson occurred after dinner. He told us to come into the den, where he turned on a strobe light and revealed all of his girls lying there, naked. He started passing out LSD tabs and orchestrating sex partners. I love the female form, but this was too much even for me. The place was hot and claustrophobic, so I walked out to take a shower. No sooner had I stepped under the showerhead than one of the women walked in with me. It was "Squeaky" Fromme, who years later, dressed in a red nun's habit, tried to assassinate President Ford. (Her handgun didn't go off.) Squeaky thought this would be a fine time to take a shower with me, but before I could tell her to get lost, Manson himself arrived.

He looked up at me with those dark, beady eyes and said, "You can't do that."

"Excuse me?"

"You can't leave the group."

"I'm really sorry, Charlie. But Bruce and I have to get back to the studio."

We got the hell out of there, and as we pulled out of the driveway, I thought, Denny, you've got a real nut case for a roommate now.

Dennis wanted Brother Records to record Manson, bringing him into our offices and hyping his talents. (He gave most people the creeps.) Dennis set up recording sessions for Manson with Stephen Desper in Brian's home studio. The idea was to cut a demo good enough to convince either the Beach Boys or others of Manson's appeal. Manson arrived at Brian's home with several of his girls—they sat on the floor in a daze, apparently stoned, though they also found the bathroom. Marilyn later said she had to disinfect the toilets. Desper thought Manson's songs were okay, perhaps even recordable, and Manson returned on several occasions (Brian stayed in his bedroom). But Manson resisted Desper's instructions, was ill informed about the industry, and was fidgety and impatient. At one point, Manson pulled out a switchblade, supposedly to clean his fingernails but more to intimidate Desper. Our sound engineer, used to the idiosyncrasies of artists, later said it didn't faze him. He finally had to end the sessions, not out of fear but because Manson smelled so bad. The guy was not fond of showers. Desper also couldn't understand why so many young women, eagerly awaiting him at each session, wanted to sleep with him.

Someone at Brother Records checked Manson's background and discovered his criminal past, and our accountants were raising flags about unexplained expenditures on Dennis's charge card. For my cousin, the truth about Manson slowly emerged. Beyond what was spent on his card, Dennis paid the medical costs for the women who were treated for sexually transmitted diseases. His house was ransacked. Furniture, clothes, guitars, stereo equipment, gold records— they took most everything of Dennis's that wasn't nailed down. They also totaled his Mercedes. By summer's end, Dennis figured he had lost about $100,000 to his roommates, and even for him, that was too much.

Though Dennis didn't back down from anyone, he didn't want a confrontation with Manson, who had a penchant for flashing his switchblade and making threats. So instead of demanding that Manson and his girls leave, Dennis just vacated the premises. The house was leased, and when the lease expired, the owner kicked out the squatters. Manson decamped to Spahn Ranch outside of Los Angeles but continued his association with Dennis, whom he still needed to launch his career; and Dennis, through some combination of loyalty and gullibility, continued to visit Manson with producers in tow.

Dennis liked one of Manson's songs, called "Cease to Exist," whose lyrics he tweaked. I didn't think much of it, but the Beach Boys changed the tune some more and recorded it as "Never Learn Not to Love." Dennis took the credit for what was essentially Manson's music and lyrics. Though the song is remembered by few, it did appear on the B side of a 45, and we performed it on *The Mike Douglas Show* in early 1969.

That was the extent of our direct musical involvement with Manson, and Dennis, for his part, slowly recognized Manson's demonic streak. In May of 1969, in an interview with *Rave*, Dennis was asked if he was afraid of anything. "Sometimes the Wizard frightens me— Charlie Manson is another friend of mine who says he is God and the devil! He sings, plays, and writes poetry and may be another artist for Brother Records."

Around that time, Dennis's illusions about Manson finally ended, when he paid a visit to Spahn Ranch. Upon his return, Dennis stopped by Brian's house, where I was working in the studio. Dennis was visibly shaken, and I asked what was wrong.

"I just saw Charlie take his M16 and blow this black cat in half and stuff him down the well," he said, referring to a black man.

Dennis was too frightened to go to the police. I think he was just hoping that Manson and his family would disappear, but his entanglement could not be undone.

Dennis had introduced Manson to Terry Melcher, the former musical partner of Bruce Johnston, who by 1968 had produced the

Byrds' covers of "Mr. Tambourine Man" and "Turn! Turn! Turn!" and had helped Paul Revere and the Raiders become a top-selling rock group. Any artist would love to work with him, and that included Manson, who accompanied Terry and Dennis on several of their club outings. Manson was also in the car one day when Dennis dropped Terry off at his rented home at 10050 Cielo Drive, at the top of a steep hill in the Benedict Canyon area. Terry lived there with his girlfriend, the actress Candice Bergen.

Once Manson realized that Dennis wasn't going to deliver a recording contract, he homed in on Terry, who, like any producer, was always looking for new talent. Perhaps as a favor to Dennis, he went to Spahn Ranch twice in the late spring of 1969 to hear Manson sing. Terry was Manson's last hope, but he was unimpressed and had to tell Manson that he couldn't help him, effectively ending Manson's musical ambitions.

Manson wouldn't stand for it. Consumed by rage and seeking revenge against a corrupt society, he convinced his followers that the apocalypse was coming in a bloody race war, at the end of which he and his disciples would take over. All of this was prophesized, Manson said, in the White Album—in the very songs that were written by the Beatles in Rishikesh. Invoking one of those numbers, Manson called the race war "Helter Skelter."

To get it started, he and his followers had to commit some spectacular murders, and Manson chose to kill the occupants of 10050 Cielo Drive. Terry Melcher, however, had moved out in January of 1969, with Candice Bergen, and was living in a house owned by his mother, Doris Day. The move was no accident. I was good friends with Terry and also got to know Doris well. Terry, Doris's only child, was extremely close to his mom. He had told her about Manson— and about some of his scary antics, his brandishing of knives, his zombie followers—and that Manson had been to the house on Cielo Drive. This petrified Doris, and both Doris and Terry told me that she insisted he move out. A mother's intuition, perhaps, and it may have saved his life.

The next occupants of the house were Roman Polanski, who had just directed the satanic rituals in *Rosemary's Baby*, and his wife, the actress Sharon Tate. Four members of Manson's family—three women and a man—entered the house late at night on August 9. Manson had ordered them to murder all who were there, and they killed five people, including Tate, who was eight months pregnant. (Polanski was out of the country.) Also murdered was Jay Sebring, America's most famous hairdresser. Tate was a beautiful starlet whose death, on its own, would have been headline news, but the slaughter's cold-blooded carnage, its gratuitous brutality, transformed the murders into one of the most sensational crimes of the century. One victim was stabbed fifty-one times; another, twenty-eight times; another was bludgeoned with the butt of a gun; two victims were hanged by a nylon rope over a ceiling beam.

Two more murders were committed the following night, of Leno and Rosemary LaBianca in the Los Feliz section of Los Angeles, and Manson himself participated in these. The slayings were equally gruesome (one of the assailants carved "WAR" in Leno's stomach), but three months passed before the authorities connected the two crimes.

Neither Dennis nor I nor anyone associated with the Beach Boys had any idea that Manson was involved in these murders. Stories were written linking the crimes to drugs and sex rituals and the occult, but no one knew who was responsible, and panic swept the city. Gun sales soared. Security systems were installed. Guard dogs were purchased.

I had my own issues during this period, which were challenging enough but were affected by the Manson craziness.

In 1968, after I had been at a studio session at Western Recorders,

Suzanne met me outside, with Hayleigh in her arms, and there she told me that she wanted to end the marriage. Hayleigh wasn't even two yet, so she didn't understand what was being said, but she knew something was terribly wrong. I'll never forget the look on her face, as if something had crashed all around her. I'm sure my face didn't look much better. I didn't want to split up but also didn't realize how unhappy Suzanne was. Christian was a baby at the time, and I now have a better appreciation for how much stress Suzanne was under. I was traveling constantly, still free to do what I wanted to do, while she was home with two young children. Those roles may have been the norm in that era, but she had every reason to resent how they played out in our marriage.

I was less forgiving about how the actual process of the separation and divorce played out. Suzanne and I were still living together at 1215 Coldwater Canyon when she told me she was having an affair with Dennis. I'd be a hypocrite if I said I was angry over her infidelity. I had had my dalliances as well. But I was outraged that she was sleeping with my cousin. More than outraged, actually. Seething. For Dennis (as he later told me), it was an act of vengeance. I had briefly dated his first wife, Carole, *before* she had met Dennis, and Dennis resented that. It was just part of our insane competition over women. Now Dennis was going to return the favor and sleep with my wife, tit for tat. And Suzanne obliged.

The day Suzanne told me about the affair, I tried to maintain my perspective, but I couldn't, and the more I thought about it, the angrier I got—feelings of disbelief mixed with fury. So angry that I really wanted to kill both of them; so angry that I sat in our den and thought of how I would do it. These were horrible, lethal thoughts. My wife and my cousin, both dead.

The switchblade . . . and the butterfly.

I turned to meditation, and in this room all by myself I shut my eyes and began to cool down. At times the anger resurfaced, but it didn't get the better of me. I kept meditating and concluded that that was them, that's what they wanted to do, but it wasn't me and I didn't want to involve myself with them. I continued to meditate until the anger slowly drained from my body. And finally I was relaxed.

I have a certain amount of empathy for people in prison. I can understand how emotions can get the better of you and lead you into doing something terrible. Without TM, I might have done something terrible.

I moved into my house in Manhattan Beach and was living there when the Tate-LaBianca murders occurred. Around that time I got a phone call. I picked it up and said hello, and a man's voice was on the line.

"Prepare to die, pig."

I didn't know who it was, and I'm sure many people would have just hung up, but that wasn't my style.

"Fuck you!" I said. "Come down to Manhattan Beach, and we'll see who dies!"

No one came to visit, and he didn't call again.

In November, three months after the murders, the case finally broke. Manson family members had been picked up for grand theft auto and began leaking information. The authorities promptly contacted Dennis, and front-page stories soon appeared about the Beach Boys' connection to the crazed cult leader who allegedly masterminded these slayings. Brian and Marilyn, whose home studio was used by Manson, each wrote the police department's phone number on their arm and kept it there for two weeks.

Terry Melcher, who had recently vacated Tate's home and had rejected Manson, had even more reason to be scared. The police recommended that he get some guns and a bodyguard. Terry assumed that Manson had meant to kill him—as revenge—and the lives of five innocents were taken instead. The guilt was devastating. According to Terry, when he went to see a psychiatrist, the doctor said, "I

don't know what to tell you. You're going to be crazy for a while."
Terry went on the lam, and a full year passed before he was told that
he was not Manson's target—Manson knew that Terry had left
10050 Cielo Drive. But that didn't change the fact that Manson
knew of that house only because of Terry, and I know from our con-
versations over the years that Terry was haunted by those murders for
the rest of his life.

At least Terry could testify at Manson's trial in 1971. Dennis,
shaken to the core, couldn't do that. He couldn't talk about it with
anyone—family, friends, the investigators. To my knowledge, he
never told the authorities that he saw Manson murder that "black
cat" at Spahn Ranch, and he certainly couldn't testify in court, where
he would have had to look Manson right in the eye. Dennis never
wanted to face the questions: How could you allow a bunch of future
murderers to be your roommates? How could you even think of
wanting to join such a "family"? How could you befriend its mania-
cal leader? Dennis, I think, just wanted to lock away the whole episode in some deep recess of his soul, but as the years went by and his
troubles with alcohol and drugs deepened, it was one more burden
that he couldn't escape.

After the arrests were made, I realized that my threatening phone
call had come from someone in Manson's group, and it occurred to
me that I was on TV singing a song that Manson had essentially
written. I assumed that his followers would have liked to murder all
the Beach Boys, but at no point was I frightened. I knew what a real
threat looked like—I had been robbed at gunpoint at a gas station
and had had a Luger pointed right in my face in Munich. I went to
school with tough kids who taught me that if you back down, you get
rolled. For better or worse, I don't get intimidated.

The worst part of Suzanne's affair with Dennis wasn't even the
affair. Terry Melcher later told me that after we separated, Suzanne
and Dennis would sometimes go out and leave our two young chil-

dren with a babysitter. On one occasion, the babysitter was Manson disciple Susan Atkins. I never sought confirmation from Suzanne or Dennis, but Terry was one of the most trustworthy people I knew, and he would not have fabricated such a story. During her trial, Atkins testified that she held Sharon Tate—who pleaded with the killers to spare her life and that of her unborn child—while another assailant, Charles "Tex" Watson, stabbed her to death. In a theatrical flourish, Atkins used Sharon Tate's blood to write "PIG" on the outside of the front door. She was convicted of participating in eight murders and was sentenced to death. And she was our babysitter.

CHAPTER 13

EXPORTING THE AMERICAN DREAM

After Suzanne and I divorced, I was determined to maintain custody of our two children. Nowadays, that might not be so unusual; but back then, it was rare for fathers to prevail in such a hearing, and I'm almost certain that no male rock performer had ever been awarded custody. My lawyer told me explicitly that I had no chance. I know that Suzanne loved our kids, and it was true that I still traveled a lot. But I thought I could provide a healthier, more stable home. What's more, I was so rattled that Susan Atkins babysat our children, I just thought they would be safer with me. I felt strongly enough about it that if I had lost custody, I considered moving to London with Hayleigh and Christian.

It didn't come to that. A judge assessed our respective claims and awarded me custody, for which I've always been grateful. (Suzanne had visitation rights, including Christmas and other holidays.) I hired a young woman, Connie Pappas, who had been a receptionist at a recording studio, to be the caretaker for the kids. She did a wonderful job, and she stayed with us until I bought my next property on 101 Mesa Lane in Santa Barbara. Another couple lived on the property, and they would take care of the children when I traveled. The compound itself was far more rustic than any place I had ever lived. It was three and a half acres, which included six redwood structures, the main house a former girls' school with a common kitchen. We had filtered water, landscaped grounds, and organic gardens planted for maximum yield according to the moon cycles from *The Old Farmers' Almanac*, all surrounded by cornstalks and lemon and eucalyptus trees. The house was perched firmly on a cliff that overlooked the Pacific Ocean, and we had a steep, hundred-step staircase that led directly to a nude beach.

It was an idyllic setting, soon equipped with a studio to record music, and in the years ahead, Maharishi himself would pay a timely visit.

B ut I could not escape the present, and the Manson murders had one other ricochet effect on the Beach Boys. The breathless coverage cast Southern California as a breeding ground for sadism, criminality, and freaked-out hippies. This made a mockery of the Southern California we had glorified and reinforced the perception that the Beach Boys were impossibly detached from what was happening in our country and even in our own city. I'm sure that was the thinking of Capitol Records, which didn't believe in the music we were now doing and did not renew our contract in 1969. For the first time in seven years, we didn't have a label. Financially, we had little money coming in, were still reeling from our tour-related losses, and were behind on many of our bills.

In August of 1969, some 200,000 young people descended on muddy farmland in upstate New York for what would be the most significant rock festival in history—Woodstock. The Who played at sunrise and Ravi Shankar performed in the rain. Jimi Hendrix riffed an electrified "The Star-Spangled Banner" that mimicked dropping bombs and machine-gun fire. And the Beach Boys? We weren't invited. It wasn't our time and it wasn't our music, but I can't say I was heartbroken. I thought the atmospherics at these concerts—the drugs, the mayhem, at times the violence—were getting out of hand. On December 6, at the Altamont Speedway in Northern California, another counterculture rock bonanza unfolded, with a lineup that included Jefferson Airplane, the Grateful Dead, and Crosby, Stills, Nash & Young. Violence scarred the event from the beginning, with dozens of fans beaten or maimed. One woman had her skull fractured by a thrown beer can. Two people were killed by a hit-and-run driver; another was drowned; and one fan was stabbed to death by a member of the Hells Angels while the Stones performed "Under My Thumb" onstage.

Our concerts were tame indeed. In fact, we sometimes performed in near-empty halls. On Thanksgiving, we did three shows in one day—two in South Dakota and one in Sioux City, Iowa. I drove one of the station wagons to a place called the Corn Palace, and running late, I think I gunned it at about 100 mph while Bruce ate turkey off the dashboard. We performed in front of about fifty people.

But no matter how meager the crowds, at least someone showed up, and I never lost faith in our talent. We released an album, *20/20*, which included a couple of cuts from the *Smile* era ("Our Prayer" and "Cabin Essence"), two good numbers by Dennis ("Be with Me" and "All I Want to Do"), and Carl's brilliant cover of "I Can Hear Music." That song was released as a single, became a hit in the United Kingdom (while charting at No. 24 in the United States), and demonstrated Carl's growth as producer and arranger. We continued to develop new music, and our fans overseas still believed in us. In June 1969, we toured Europe for a month and, in London and the Netherlands, in Paris and Frankfurt, played before enthusiastic, sold-out crowds. There was nothing unusual about that. What was unusual was that we played in our first Communist country.

Starting in the mid-1950s, the State Department began sending jazz musicians to Soviet bloc countries, turning the likes of Dizzy Gillespie and Duke Ellington into goodwill ambassadors. Music, it seemed, was one of the few things that the two superpowers could agree on, and these cultural exchanges continued. In 1969, Czecho-slovakia was part of an Eastern Europe Rock and Roll Festival, en-dorsed by the Soviets, and the festival's organizers approached the State Department and asked if the Beach Boys would participate. We were supposedly the only rock group in America that was acceptable, all others considered too decadent. I of course had wanted to perform in a Communist country for several years and absolutely agreed that music was one of the best ways to bring people together. We accepted the invitation, and a representative from the State Department flew to Los Angeles and swore us in as official ambassadors. We were given guidelines on how to act, what to say, what to eat, and were told specifically not to have intimate relations with anyone behind the Iron Curtain. We assured them there would be no cross-border liaisons.

It was actually a remarkable time to make the trip, as we flew from Paris to Prague on June 17. The previous summer, in response to reform movements in Czechoslovakia, the Soviets sent in 200,000 troops and 2,000 tanks to occupy the country while arresting the movement's leader, Alexander Dubček. Czech resistance was mostly nonviolent but included two students setting themselves on fire in Prague's Wenceslas Square. I didn't know what to expect, but when we arrived, and with the tanks still in the streets, we were treated like conquering heroes. Kids peppered us with questions about America and asked us for our autographs—some had us sign on their arms.

We got a crash course in the shortcomings of a planned economy. We were paid in the local currency, but it couldn't be exchanged out-side the country—it had no value—so we had to scramble around buying stuff (clothes, dishes, suitcases) before we left.

Prague's roads were bumpy, and the jarring ride over to Lucerna

Hall damaged the batteries that powered our console and Fender amp heads. No batteries, no show. But our sound engineer found replacements that were the size of tank batteries, wheeled in by eight armed guards. We also needed a Hammond organ. Only two were available in the entire country, and the one we got had sticky keys, a missing amplifier tube, and some rogue notes.

In truth, the music hall was so rowdy, it didn't make any difference. We played two shows, and more than 6,000 fans who were unable to get tickets stood outside, forcing the police to bring reinforcements. Inside was hot, stale, and smoky—there was no air conditioning, and supposedly no air conditioning in the country—and with so many people jammed together, the columns were perspiring. One of our keyboardists said the sweat and humidity were so great the piano keys were too wet to play. I had been wearing a white monk's robe, reflective of the spiritual influences in my life, and the room was so stifling that I took it off and performed bare-chested in white pants. But more than anything, it was just deafening—stomping, whistling, screaming—so loud that you had to scream into the microphone if you had any chance of being heard.

Our performances coincided with the release of our album on a Czech label, making it our first record distributed behind the Iron Curtain. Titled *The Beach Boys* and featuring liner notes in the local language, it included "California Girls," "Good Vibrations," and "Fun, Fun, Fun." The Czechs wanted our music, but I don't believe that the music alone was our appeal. In our three days in the country, in Prague and Brno, we were besieged by fans fascinated by the United States. They were desperate for anything Western. In contrast to their own suffocating conditions, the Beach Boys represented sun-kissed beaches and high-powered hot rods. But we also represented freedom, prosperity, and opportunity. The irony: in America itself, we were too closely associated with those values, but abroad, those values made us idols.

All music has a political context, and we performed ours when the Soviets and the Americans were vying for the allegiance of people from across the world, from Europe to Asia to Africa as well as Latin America. Unwittingly, our music exported the American dream in two-minute capsules. I'm not claiming we helped win the Cold War, but I've heard from Russians and Chinese, Cubans and South Africans, East Germans and Vietnamese, who listened to our music on American Forces Network or pirate ships or bootlegged tapes or old-fashioned albums. And they loved our songs, many of which offered a vision of America, and a way of life, that they themselves wanted.

And so on that hot night at Lucerna Hall in Prague, amid the cheers, cries, and applause, I wanted to be heard. We were told that we had a special guest in the audience—the country's ousted leader, Alexander Dubček. I stepped to the mic and, with a song that we had recently recorded, yelled, "We're very happy to be here, all the way from the West Coast of the United States of America! We dedicate this next number, which is called 'Break Away,' to Mr. Dubček, who is also here tonight!"

The place went crazy.

CHAPTER 14

STOLEN LEGACY

B y 1968, the Beach Boys had created a new entity called Brother Publishing, whose intent was to buy other writers' songs and record them ourselves or find other artists to do so. Brother Publishing, along with a company called Filmways, had a joint partnership in a recording studio in Hollywood. Now we intended to partner with Filmways to buy the Sea of Tunes catalog, which held most of our songs. For a group of young guys who lived for the moment, this was a rare time when we tried to plan for the future. As Al Jardine later said, our goal "was to create a musical empire of our own, something we could fall back on when we weren't touring."

Brian and I talked in some detail about the proposed acquisition of the catalog, which would finally resolve my copyright problem. Despite my protests over the years, I still had not received credit on many of my songs. The catalog had between 140 and 150 numbers, and I had cowritten about 80 while receiving credit on only a fraction of them. Brian kept reassuring me that his father had mishandled the paperwork but that he, Brian, controlled the catalog, and that I would recoup my losses eventually. The tone shifted a bit in 1968, when Brian told me that he wasn't getting along very well with his dad, complicating efforts to pressure him. I wasn't on speaking terms with my uncle Murry at the time, but Brian said once we bought the catalog, we would own the publishing rights and could resolve the copyright issues ourselves.

I didn't understand the details and didn't even understand what it meant to own the publishing rights. All I knew was that if I wanted credit and compensation for my songs, we had to buy those rights, and to do that, we had to give my uncle some money.

We were all excited about the impending purchase—not just Brian but Dennis, Carl, and Al as well. This was our music, our legacy, and we didn't want Murry to have anything to do with it. Our business manager, Nick Grillo, was involved in the negotiations. Letters were written. Meetings were held. Updates were given. But months passed, and nothing got finalized. I assumed this was just the way the business works.

I was wrong. On August 20, 1969, Grillo told us that the Sea of Tunes had indeed been sold—but not to the Beach Boys. It had been sold to Almo/Irving, the music-publishing arm of A&M Records. A&M agreed to pay $700,000 for the entire catalog, and the payment was going to Uncle Murry. In cash.

What the fuck!

Dennis and I both wanted to take a swing at someone, but we didn't know whom. None of it made any sense. If Brian controlled the songs, how could his father sell them? And why? They were our songs! Not only did we write and record them, but we had spent years on the road performing them, increasing their value. And now not a penny for our efforts.

I drove to Brian's house in Bel Air to see if he knew what was going on.

At the time, Brian was not in good shape. After he learned to meditate, he stayed away from the drugs for a year, but he didn't stick with it, and in his relapse, he used cocaine for the first time. Brian didn't tell us about it—he disclosed it years later during a court deposition—but what I did know was that he was acting spacey. He was also living in the chauffeur's quarters of his home while Marilyn slept in the master bedroom.

When I reached his house, I stormed into his room and asked what happened with our songs.

"My dad fucked us," he said.

"Yeah, no shit."

Brian appeared angry, but he didn't do anything to try to stop his father. I had no sway with Murry, but I did call Chuck Kaye, the head of Almo/Irving, and cursed him out for being party to such a betrayal. I also told him that Murry was responsible for driving both Brian and Dennis to drugs, and now he had screwed all three of his sons as well as his nephew. "This is the most chickenshit thing he could have done," I said.

"Yeah," Kaye agreed, "we all know Murry is an asshole, and he is hard to deal with. But this is what he wants to do. He sold it to us, and there's nothing you can do."

Actually, there was something. For the deal to go through, the agreement had to be signed by Brian, Dennis, Carl, Al, and me. No signatures, no sale. The Beach Boys, however, had a lawyer, Abe Somer, who told us that it was a done deal and that everything was in order—Murry controlled the catalog and could do with it what he wanted. We had no recourse.

I complained bitterly. I told Somer that many of my songs had not been credited, so what could I do if they were now owned by a third party?

Somer worked for a big Los Angeles law firm, Mitchell, Silberberg & Knupp, and I had no reason to question his judgment. He said I was all confused. He told me that I had to sign the agreement to ensure that I kept my name on the songs that I had already been credited for. If I didn't sign it, I could lose credit for those as well.

Those were my options: If I *signed* the agreement, I would never receive credit for "California Girls," "Help Me, Rhonda," "I Get

Around," "Surfin' USA," and many other songs that I cowrote. But if I *refused* to sign the agreement, I might lose credit for "Good Vibrations," "Surfin' Safari," and "The Warmth of the Sun," among others.

That's one helluva choice. What could I do? I had to sign the agreement to retain what I had. Everyone else signed too, and with that, we lost all that we had created.

I couldn't get any answers, from Somer or anyone else, on how Murry had stolen our songs, sold them, and walked away with $700,000. We were all in the dark. As Al later said, "It was done quite in a cloak-and-dagger kind of way, really. Very mystifying." I don't know if Murry ever shared any of that money with his sons, but I never saw a penny. I suspect that Murry needed a few more dollars for himself. The year before, in 1968, he had moved out of his house in Whittier and bought a second home a mile away—though he and Aunt Audree remained married, he lived in one house, she lived in the other. The arrangement made sense, I guess, because around that time, Murry went to Thailand and brought home a young woman, who moved in with him.

But as I later learned, money wasn't the only consideration in my uncle's decision to sell the catalog. He assumed that by 1969, the Beach Boys were finished. He actually thought we were done long before that. On May 8, 1965, he wrote an angry letter to Brian in which he predicted that the band would soon "finish this short cycle of Beach Boy success" and that "the way things are shaping up now, the Beach Boys cannot go on and on because cycles of music change as well as fads, like the Beatles, the Presleys, etc."

Part of that was wishful thinking—the more we squirmed out from under his control, and especially after we fired him as our manager, the more my uncle wanted us to fail as evidence that he was the mastermind behind the group. He even took over the management of a local band called the Renegades, renamed them the Sunrays, and recast them in the image of the Beach Boys, including the striped shirts. Uncle Murry, like many in his generation, was also rabidly opposed to drugs and told his sons they were doomed if they ever got involved with them. He was furious at the people who sold or gave the drugs to Brian and at Brian himself, and he surely believed the damage to Brian was irreparable. So if the Beach Boys were has-beens and their leader was a druggie, why not cash out when a buyer still existed?

It was, of course, one of the dumbest decisions in music history. The Beach Boys didn't die, and the catalog was a cash machine for decades to come, generating more than a hundred million dollars in publishing royalties, none of which Murry or the Beach Boys ever saw.

Uncle Murry and Aunt Audree continued to live in their separate houses, still married and seeing each other on a regular basis. But Murry suffered chronic stomach pain and became increasingly isolated, rarely seeing even my mom. In May of 1973, she spoke to Murry on the phone; he had recently undergone a serious operation and sounded weak. Seemingly out of the blue, he thanked my mom for sponsoring his first musical (in which young Brian sang my song). Three weeks later, on June 4, 1973, with Aunt Audree in the house, my uncle went into the bathroom and dropped dead of a heart attack. He was fifty-five.

Murry Wilson, to be sure, was a driving force in the Beach Boys' early success, but his greed and vindictiveness deny him any tribute. The most forgiving thing I can say about him is that he was simply an inheritor of his own father's cruelty. My mom, for her part, was always loyal to her brother, as she was grateful for how Murry had protected his siblings against the violence of their father. I wasn't going to sully my mom's devotion to that brother with an explanation of his betrayals against his own family.

I did not attend Uncle Murry's funeral and don't know whether Grandpa Wilson was there to bury his own son. Grandpa Wilson himself did not die until 1981, long after I or anyone in the Love family had anything to do with him.

Aunt Audree, meanwhile, wanted a fresh start after Murry's death. She sold both houses in Whittier and moved back to Los Angeles, where she was closer to her grandchildren.

The sale of the catalog, for me, had a long ripple effect. For years, I'd been expecting a lump sum of money for the lost royalties on my songs, and, once the writing credits were fixed, I assumed I'd be receiving a new flow of income. Now all that money owed would stay with Brian and those future songwriting royalties would also go to Brian. The rest of us would have to make do, and without any new hit records, that meant even greater reliance on touring. It was lose-lose for me and the touring band. Instead of being recognized and promoted as the co-lyricist of our most popular songs (three No. 1s and ten originals that charted in the Top 10), I was simply the perennial front man, and any effort on my part to set the record straight was seen as my vanity run amuck.

In March of 1970, I finally reached my own breaking point. So much had been happening around me—Charles Manson, Susan Atkins, Suzanne's affair with Dennis, the sale of our catalog, family betrayal, financial stress, single parenthood, everything—I wanted to purge all the evil from my system, and I thought I could do that by going on a fast. I had read about the power of fasting in Szekely's *Essene Gospel of Peace*, which said: "For I tell you truly, that Satan and his plagues may only be cast out by fasting and by prayer . . . The living God shall see it and great shall be your reward. And fast till Beelzebub and all his evils depart from you, and all the angels of our Earthly Mother come and serve you."

I'm sure that fasting, in moderation, can be healthy, but moderation has never been my style. For three weeks, all I consumed was juice, tea, and water. Medically, excessive fasting can cause your body to purge toxins (or high levels of ketones), which seemed appropriate—I wanted to free my body of anything pernicious. It was my way to escape. But those toxins, once they enter your bloodstream, can also impair your brain and central nervous system. I didn't realize this, and the longer I fasted, the more light-headed I felt. I recall driving in Hollywood and seeing a flock of birds and sensing that their flight had some profound meaning, and feeling extremely emotional and manic and sensitive to everything around me. I drove through several stoplights, and then a police car pulled me over. I'm vague on the details, but I recall that an officer threw me onto the street, hand-cuffed me, and drove me to a substation. I was put in a cell, and I could hear the cops using nightsticks to beat the living shit out of some guy in another cell. I thought to myself that I may be a smar-tass, but I'm not going to cause any problems.

Nick Grillo bailed me out and took me to my place in Manhattan Beach. The next thing I recall is my dad and my brother Stephen coming to get me. I guess I was a little amped up. I don't remember it but was later told that when they were trying to get me into the car, I bit Stephen, and he yelled, "I thought you were a vegetarian!"

They drove me to Edgemont Hospital in Hollywood, a psychiat-ric facility. I was later told that I had a bad reaction to a drug and was put in a straitjacket. I do recall that I was given some pills (which made me nauseous) and was forced to rest. My physical recovery was not complicated: I started eating again, and I was released after a couple of days. I learned the obvious lesson about the perils of exces-sive fasting and of using such a tactic to escape your problems.

The episode was hard on my parents. I told them about my ex-treme diet. They didn't ask me many questions beyond that, but they knew I had other troubles. Neither they nor I knew how to talk about them, but I knew I had their love and support. As my mom later wrote in her memoir: "I like to think there is a God, a power that will help me in my time of need. I guess the hardest I *ever* prayed was for Michael when he was overworked and unhappy and had a short breakdown. He had a bad reaction to a drug the doctor gave him and went into convulsions. Milt and I thought we were going to lose him . . . I can still see the room. Mike came through it all right and maybe would have anyway, but I like to think my pleading prayer helped."

Reaching my limits forced me to consider what I was doing with my life. At the time, I was fighting for custody of Hayleigh and Christian, and I knew I had to be stronger, and smarter, for them. I had a lot at stake professionally as well. I was angry that our music had been stolen from us and that I had lost a huge part of my own legacy. I realized that the only way I could claim ownership of the songs that I had written, the only way I could stay connected to them, was to be a road dog: to rejoin the guys, get back onstage, and take our music to all four corners of the country and beyond.

That would be my nourishment, and my revenge.

A new decade had begun, and a new era as well. The year 1970 saw the Beatles break up, for the same reasons that virtually all rock bands break up—creative differences, clashing egos, fights over money, the accumulation of grudges, slights, and irritants. The Beach Boys had all those as well, but I assumed we would stay together for years to come. We just had to reconnect with our fans.

Our first album of the decade, *Sunflower*, was one of the best recorded and mixed albums of its day, with an approach to stereo that made even the Beatles' *Abbey Road* sound primitive. Stephen Desper was something of a mad genius, and at the time he was researching the acoustic properties of center channel quadraphonic sound, which offered breathtaking effects on two speakers when decoded by a device he later called a "spatializer," and it was used for two cuts on *Sunflower* ("It's About Time" and "Cool, Cool Water").

The album itself turned out to be a product of desperation and trial and error. *Sunflower* was to be our first LP with our new label, Warner/Reprise, but the record company rejected our first two submissions.* At the same time, we were trying to fulfill our last contractual obligations to Capitol Records, so we took several of the best songs from our last Capitol master reel, including Dennis's "Forever" and "Got to Know the Woman," Bruce's "Deirdre," and "All I Wanna Do" by Brian and me, and we quietly spliced them onto the new *Sunflower* reel. It made a difference. "Forever" was Dennis's most acclaimed ballad, as it captured the raw emotion and bluesy sensibility that he brought to his vocals. Capitol, meanwhile, mixed the tapes from a 1968 concert and released a *Live in London* LP for the United Kingdom, which satisfied the demands of our Capitol contract.

Carl later said that *Sunflower* represented the Beach Boys' "truest group effort," while Bruce said it was his favorite Beach Boys album. I thought it was damn good, and it received excellent reviews and has only grown in critical appreciation over the years. In 2003, it was voted No. 300 for *Rolling Stone*'s 500 Greatest Albums of All Time. I also know that we have fans who cherish that album like none other. But it sold poorly, charting at No. 151, making it our worst-performing album to date (excluding a compilation in 1968).

We were still out of kilter with the times. Our music was viewed as too conventional to reach the FM rock audience, and Warner/Reprise was adrift on how to position *Sunflower*. Its name evoked peace and love, and the cover featured the Beach Boys on a tree-lined

---

* The contract was between Brother Records, which was the Beach Boys' label, and Reprise Records, which was the distribution arm of Warner Records. The imprint on the labels combined the Brother and Reprise logos, so the label was technically "Brother/Reprise," but it's usually referred to as "Warner/Reprise" because Reprise controlled which records were released.

golf course, holding our young children in our laps or on our shoulders. Inside photos showed Bruce sitting on the bumper of a deluxe car, Carl standing next to a horse, Dennis with aviator goggles, Brian with a blue "Good Humor" cap, and me in my long white robe and full beard (a bit like Maharishi's). The images might have worked five years earlier, but *Sunflower* was released in August of 1970, just three months after the Kent State shootings and during a summer of campus protests and street rallies in response to bombing raids in Cambodia. The world was aflame; we were projecting innocence and harmony. We were still doing concerts and television appearances in all-white uniforms, and even our name, the Beach Boys, sounded like we were mementos from a bygone era. We thought about shortening the name to "Beach" but concluded that was even worse.

Our fortunes, however, as well as our image, would soon begin to change.

When *Sunflower* was released, Bruce, Brian, and I did an interview at an alternative station called KPFK Pacifica Radio. The DJ was Jack Rieley, whom Brian already knew; Brian was part owner of a health-food store, and Rieley was an occasional customer. Brian told him and his listeners about our problem. "The first half of our career, the surf thing was projected so much," Brian said. "It was so clean—the sound was so clean, we looked clean, and about 1966, I think people started rejecting that image. We got a little funkier about that time, but they didn't know it . . . I'm proud of the group and the name, but I think the clean American thing has hurt us."

Rieley was a chatty sort who said he had worked in television news, and he saw an opportunity. A week or so after the interview, he sent a memo to Brian and recommended a publicity campaign to make us more contemporary. And he would be our publicity manager.

Rieley's brazenness offended some of our existing managers, but I liked him. The Beach Boys were too disorganized and fragmented to master the publicity and marketing part of the business, so Rieley came on board and began the makeover. We ditched the matching uniforms, Carl and Al grew beards, and we began a promotion campaign that said, "It's okay to listen to the Beach Boys." Another said: "The Beach Boys—They've changed more than you have!"

Carl had assumed Brian's role as our producer, and he and Jack worked to improve our live act, seeking to get the new rock audiences to take our music seriously. That effort took us to the Big Sur Folk Festival in Monterey in October of 1970—the same locale we spurned in 1967, but now we appeared before 6,000 fans with Joan Baez, Kris Kristofferson, and other performers heralded by the intelligentsia as hip or relevant. We also played the debut of "Student Demonstration Time," originally recorded in the 1950s as "Riot in Cell Block No. 9." But I had rewritten it to fit our era, referring to Kent State as well as Jackson State College (where the police killed two students). While it wasn't so much a protest song as a message for kids to stay safe, it was at least connected to the nation's tumult.

Around the same time, a young booking agent in New York, Chip Rachlin, thought the Beach Boys could still attract a big crowd in Manhattan. So too did another young fan, Michael Klenfner, who worked for Bill Graham at the Fillmore East. Graham was still angry about the stub count after our last visit, so when Chip and Michael asked him about the Beach Boys returning, he called us "goyish scumbags." If my Yiddish is correct, that meant no.

Chip and Michael then asked the operators of Carnegie Hall if the Beach Boys could play there, and Carnegie agreed to let us perform two shows on a Monday night in February in 1971. Only then did Chip actually call us; he said the Beach Boys were such a big draw we wouldn't even need an opening act. (In truth, he couldn't afford an opening act.) Chip and Michael gave us a $9,000 guarantee, but they could sell enough tickets for only one show, so they didn't make anything. But we still had our night at Carnegie.

To promote it, Chip spoke to Pete Fornatale, the popular DJ at

WNEW-FM, and asked him if he'd do some ticket giveaways. Forna-tale, a huge Beach Boys fan, agreed but also asked if he could emcee the concert.

"Sure, Pete," Chip said, "but there is one rule. They're not an old-ies act. They're an act with a catalog."

"Of course," Fornatale said. "I love the new music."

On the night of the performance, the lights came down, and For-natale walked onto the stage with a surfboard.

"Do you know," he asked, "how tough it is to get one of these motherfuckers in February?"

After the audience stopped laughing, he continued. "Growing up wouldn't have been half as much fun without these guys. Ladies and gentlemen, the Beach Boys!"

Our appearance at Carnegie was an unexpected success, with stel-lar reviews. Chip joined us full-time and, seeking the "*Rolling Stone* magazine crowd," started booking us on college campuses and in hipster clubs. Even Bill Graham, seeing how well we had been re-ceived at Carnegie, softened his view, and on April 27, 1971, we re-turned to the Fillmore East, where laughing gas was available on the second level, Bob Dylan was in the audience, and the Grateful Dead was the headliner. When the Dead introduced us, the place was si-lent, save for one guy in the back clapping. No one could believe it was actually the Beach Boys, but it was, and it went over so well that we played there two months later on the club's last night before clos-ing. We also performed at the May Day Peace Demonstration at the Washington Monument before tens of thousands of protesters, though I asked that we play first, so we would be gone before any riots broke out.

We played a benefit concert for the defense fund of the Berrigan Brothers, the peace activists, even postponing a show or two to make it happen. We did a couple more concerts with the Dead in the Bay Area and returned to Carnegie as well. *Rolling Stone* put us on the cover. I did an antiwar concert without the Beach Boys, which I would do on occasion. Dylan was one of the headliners, and he asked me to sing "California Girls."

I knew Dylan liked our music, but I didn't know that that was the right song for a crowd of activists.

"Are you sure?" I asked him.

"Yeah, they'll dig it."

So I sang it, and it went over fine.

We were still working on the cheap, maybe clearing $1,000 a show, riding a chartered Trailways bus, and—in one infamous performance—playing at the Paris Cinema in Worcester, Massachusetts, where unknown to us, porno films were shown. But at least we were still in the game.

CHAPTER 15

OUR TOUGHEST COMPETITOR

Transcendental Meditation would continue to be a big part of my life and would lead to my next meaningful relationship.

In July of 1971, I went up to Humboldt College in Arcata, California, where Maharishi was visiting to teach a course on the science of creative intelligence, basically a deeper exploration of human consciousness and how that expands your knowledge. While at a lecture, I saw a young woman with long dark hair, wearing an embroidered shirt from India. I told her how much I liked it. She thanked me and walked off. It was a small campus, and we ran into each other again. Tamara Fitch was a college student at the University of Oklahoma, a vegetarian, an environmentalist, and someone who had embraced meditation.

She wasn't particularly impressed with my credentials. Her first concert, in junior high school, was the Beach Boys (she liked Dennis), and in high school she did pompon routines to our music, but she didn't think we were that popular anymore. Nonetheless, we began seeing each other, and I was touched by her compassion for all living things. When we took our first drive, she saw an ailing deer on the side of the road and tried to convince me to take it to a vet. (Vets don't treat deer.) We had an immediate spiritual connection as well as physical. I knew that I wanted to be with Tamara, but we didn't believe in living together without being married. So six weeks after we met, and after checking with an astrologer for the day and time, we convened at the Malibu house of Charles Lloyd, a jazz flutist and saxophonist who played with us. There we had a midnight marriage ceremony that included Hayleigh and Christian. Three months later, in January of 1972, Tamara and I went to Majorca, Spain, and then to Fiuggi, Italy, to become TM teachers. I briefly considered quitting the Beach Boys to become a full-time instructor, but Maharishi told me I could do more good by spreading positive messages through our music. "Live your own life, but stay in the group," he said.

Tamara moved into my Santa Barbara compound, joining Hayleigh and Christian. For a while we also hosted Maharishi and other members of his organization, who were planning the creation of Maharishi International University. Tamara was pregnant at the time, and our visitors' chanting, singing, and meditating added a spiritual dimension to the pregnancy. Tamara's delivery room was our bedroom, scented by candles and incense. A doctor delivered our baby, and Maharishi gave his blessing to our daughter, Summer Love. (Her middle name, Bhavani, means "Mother Divine," in Sanskrit.)

But I was still too young, too impulsive, to make lifelong decisions. My spiritual connection to Tamara was constant, but that wasn't enough to keep us together. We drifted apart, and as we drifted, I reverted to old habits when I was on the road. I thought that as long as it didn't affect what was happening at home, it would be okay, but that was wrong. Our daughter was barely a year old, and I didn't want the marriage to end, but that wasn't possible. Tamara returned to Oklahoma with Summer, but they came back to the Santa Barbara property when Summer was five. They lived there for a year and then moved to a nearby residence.

I now had five children. I was never going to be the typical nine-to-five dad who drove his kids to soccer practices, and I was never going to spend the volume of time with my children that other parents spent with theirs. But I tried to make up for quantity with quality, finding unusual or special experiences to share. I hired a helicopter and took Melinda and Teresa on a flight around the Statue of Liberty, or I brought the kids with me to Switzerland or Ireland when they were on summer vacation and I was there at meditation courses. It wasn't enough, I know, but these experiences were meaningful and reflected who I was.

The Beach Boys' transformation continued, as the next several albums reflected our efforts, led by Carl, to reach new audiences as a serious album-oriented rock (AOR) FM band. Though the youngest in the group, Carl was well suited to be a leader, not just for his musical instincts but also for his people skills. He was nonjudgmental, shunning confrontation at all cost. He once had to fire one of our agents. When he called him up, he prefaced the bad news by saying, "You're going to experience a period of discomfort."

As a group, we were more aware of image and marketing, as evidenced by the cover of our 1971 *Surf's Up* album. It was based on a painting of a James Earle Fraser sculpture, *The End of the Trail*, of an American Indian on his horse, his head bowed, cradling a spear in his arm. It was both searing and beautiful, and—by slapping it on our cover, with an ominously dark aqua background—it distanced us further from our surfing past.

The album itself reflected Warner/Reprise's desire to have more songs by Brian, which was how the title song came about. "Surf's Up" was from the *Smile* era, though in this incarnation the number was cobbled together from existing tapes by Carl and Stephen Desper and completed by them as well. Brian had little to do with the production; and once it was released, he told reporters that he thought the song was "atrocious." Otherwise, we all contributed to the album: Carl, teaming with Jack Rieley, composed a quasi-gospel number in "Long Promised Road." Bruce wrote the crowd-pleasing nostalgic song "Disney Girls." And Al and I wrote "Don't Go Near the Water," a warning about water pollution.

Surf's Up was our bestselling album in four years, charting at No. 29, while faring even better in the United Kingdom (No. 15).

After that LP, we added two South African performers, drummer Ricky Fataar and guitarist Blondie Chaplin of the group Flame. Carl saw them play in London and produced one of their records. Not only were they good musicians, but their presence was itself a statement. Formerly living under apartheid, they integrated the Beach Boys, bringing us greater diversity in race and sound.

But it wasn't enough for us to take off musically. *Carl and the Passions: So Tough* (1972) was a disjointed rush job, hastily assembled between live gigs, that even Carl admitted was weak overall. We included two quirky Brian rocker songs (produced by Carl), two Blondie and Ricky tunes that didn't sound like the Beach Boys at all, two solemn Dennis songs with full symphony orchestra tracks, and two TM-themed songs by Al and me, with some help from Carl and Brian. More than anything, the album emphasized how confused we were about our brand. Warner/Reprise released it as half of a double LP set, coupled with *Pet Sounds*. The Beach Boys, as part of a settlement with Capitol Records, had the rights to our LPs from after 1965 for ten years, so someone at Warner/Reprise had the bright idea of coupling *Carl and the Passions: So Tough* with *Pet Sounds*, undermining the whole makeover strategy.

Our *Holland* album (1973) is primarily known for the fact that we spent more than six months in the Netherlands recording it, as an add-on to a European tour. It was Jack Rieley's idea, supported by

Carl, who thought a change of scenery would be good for us. It's a scenic country, but the logistics—of moving so many families, finding housing, and transporting so much equipment—were another story. Our new sound engineer, Steve Moffitt, had to build a mixing console in the states, take it apart, ship it piecemeal to Holland, and then reassemble it in a barn in Baambrugge that was converted into a studio. We shipped nearly four tons of stuff. The mooing of the cows in the background complicated our actual recordings, and the crippling costs made the whole endeavor questionable.

The results weren't that great either. Warner/Reprise rejected our first submission, concluding (rightly) that it didn't have any hits. The reality of the recording business hadn't changed: if you want a top-selling album, you needed a hit single that got air time on the radio, and for all our efforts to become more progressive and relevant, we weren't producing hit singles. The *Holland* album was saved by our old friend Van Dyke Parks, who was working for Warner at the time. He prodded Brian to finish "Sail On, Sailor," which he had apparently begun a year or so ago. The song was finished by committee (five people were credited with writing it), and Brian himself wouldn't even attend the recording session, instead offering suggestions by phone while Carl produced the track in a studio in Los Angeles. A bluesy number with seafaring images—and with Blondie singing the lead—it satisfied the label. *Holland* was released, and it charted at No. 36.

If Ricky and Blondie gave us some new blood, we were also missing some of the old. In June of 1971, Dennis, apparently drunk, put his hand through a plate glass window, severing his nerves and tendons and making it impossible for him to play the drums for the next several years. The incident occurred during a stressful time for Dennis anyway. During the recording of *Surf's Up*, he got into an argument with Carl over the sequencing of numbers, and he pulled several of his songs.

Dennis had remarried by now, to a lovely brunette, Barbara Charren, with whom he would have two sons, Carl and Michael. But musically, Dennis found himself in limbo, wanting to create an independent identity from the Beach Boys but, for whatever reason, not quite getting there. His biggest problem, as far as I was concerned, wasn't his lack of talent (of which he had plenty) but his lack of discipline. With his injured hand, he still showed up at Beach Boy concerts, and he would wander around the stage, play some keyboards, maybe sing a little, often under the influence of drugs or alcohol. One time at the C. W. Post Campus of Long Island University, he took an open mic and went on a lengthy rant. Another time, Dennis and Chip Rachlin went to a Queen concert at the Los Angeles Forum, and during a drum solo, Dennis, drunk, tried to climb up onstage. Chip and others had to pull him down before he made a fool of himself before 17,000 people.

As for the Beach Boys, we succeeded in updating our image as well as our music, but when we played live, we discovered that we were competing against someone we had never anticipated. It wasn't the Beatles or the Rolling Stones or the Doors or anyone like that. We were competing against ourselves.

When we played our new stuff at our concerts, it just didn't go over as well as, say, "Barbara Ann" or "Help Me, Rhonda," and we found ourselves at odds with our audience. We once performed at the University of Virginia and were doing our new tracks, and a guy in the audience yelled, "I want to hear the car songs!"

I shouted back, "We'll do that for the encore!"

He blurted, "What encore?"

Again and again, that happened. Over the years, I've been accused of not supporting our new music from this era and of just wanting to play our hits. That's complete bullshit. For one thing, I wrote plenty of the songs from this era. I was also, as the front man, the one promoting these songs onstage and have the scars to show for it. Neal Gabler wrote a story about us for *New Times*, an alternative newspaper, on April 2, 1976, and he recounted a concert that he attended in 1971:

> The audience had come to camp it up and boogie in the aisles to "Surfin' USA," and from the first minutes it was like a showdown. The group's frustration was palpable. "We want to play something from our new album," Mike announced, while the audience squirmed and snarled. "Play 'Rag Doll,'" someone yelled from the balcony, referring to the Four Seasons' falsetto hit. "Go soak yourself," Mike snapped, as the group slid into unfamiliar material. The tensions didn't subside until the Beach Boys came back ripping with the early hits. From its inauspicious beginnings, the concert ended with the entire auditorium on its feet (every concert does).

Tensions within the band continued to simmer. No one admired Brian's music talents more than Bruce Johnston, but Bruce stayed clear of drugs and was increasingly frustrated by their effect on all my cousins. One day, when he was recording at Brian's home studio, Bruce posted a sign on the door: "No Wilsons Allowed." And soon there would be no Johnston either. With the support of Jack Rieley, the Wilsons voted Bruce out of the band in 1972, but it didn't turn out bad for him. Bruce won a Grammy for writing the lyrics and the music for "I Write the Songs," performed by Barry Manilow in 1975. Bruce didn't do it for the Beach Boys, he later said, because he thought it would have been a career killer for us. He rejoined the Beach Boys in 1978 and has been with us ever since. Rieley, meanwhile, never returned from Holland and tried to manage the group from Amsterdam, but that wasn't feasible, and he was let go.

By that time, my brother Stephen had been working with us for a number of years. Stephen had the sharpest business mind in the family, having earned an MBA from USC. He was smart and organized, with a black belt in karate, which meant Dennis couldn't intimidate him. He took over business management responsibilities after Rieley.

There were more changes in the band. Stephen got into a fight with Blondie Chaplin, who then quit; Ricky Fataar left about a year later, after Dennis returned to the drums. Excellent musicians would join us—Billy Hinsche, Carli Muñoz, and Ron Altbach on keyboards, Bobby Figueroa on drums, Ed Carter on guitar. Another important change occurred in 1973 with the addition of Jim Guercio. Best known as a successful producer for the rock band Chicago, Jim had been a guitarist in Frank Zappa's band (Mothers of Invention) and had produced an LP for Blood, Sweat & Tears that had sold more than 4 million copies and had won a Grammy. He now had his own Caribou Records label and management company. He was also friends with Dennis, who visited him at his home in Colorado to lament our sagging fortunes. Jim attended one of our concerts on the West Coast, noticed a half-filled arena, and was surprised that we had compressed our early hits into a fifteen-minute medley. He sat us down and offered some advice: Don't hide from your past. Play your old classics in full while integrating enough of the new songs to satisfy the "artistic crowd." Be the Beach Boys! We took the guidance, and as we moved into 1974, our live act was recognized for its musicianship as well as its slamming encores. What we didn't have was a hit record. But that was about to change.

CHAPTER 16

BRIAN'S BACK

For years our wholesome image had been our albatross, a reminder that we were part of an American era that was now denigrated for its conformity and patriotism. Our music changed and our album covers changed and we changed, but it didn't matter. We were still the Beach Boys. Then, finally, America changed too, and the albatross turned into a pearl.

The early 1970s was defined by disillusionment. Our combat troops finally left Vietnam, though it didn't appear that we won. The Watergate hearings began. An Arab oil embargo led to gas lines; inflation spiraled; the economy sputtered. In August of 1974, a helicopter removed Richard Nixon, one last time, from the lawn of the White House. In April of '75, another helicopter evacuated our marines, for the final time, from our embassy rooftop in Saigon.

The greatest country in the world had lost its way.

Where were you in '62?

That was the tag line for *American Graffiti*, the 1973 film about a group of recent high school graduates who hang out at Mel's Drive-In, cruise the streets with their radio blaring, and sweetly anguish about the future (go to college, don't go to college). All this happens on one languorous summer night in 1962, complemented by a soundtrack of early rock and roll hits. The film's writer and director, George Lucas, drew on his experiences growing up in Modesto, California, capturing a moment of innocence and faith that he clearly relished. Only at the end of the movie, when it's revealed that one character would be killed by a drunk driver and another was missing in Vietnam, does reality intrude.

American Graffiti could have walked right out of the pages of our early songbook. The car in the movie that attracted the most attention is a lemon-yellow little Deuce Coupe, whose radio plays "Surfin' Safari" and whose tomboy passenger, Mackenzie Phillips, believes the "Beach Boys are boss." The movie shows no drugs, no violence, no sex, and when the credits roll, the soundtrack plays "All Summer Long," which Brian and I wrote in 1964.

I thought the movie captured the spirit of our music and the era, and in future concerts, we even used a white T-Bird as a prop onstage—the car that in the film Suzanne Somers drives with seductive élan.

What few people anticipated was the impact of *American Graffiti*.

It was considered a small film, made for $700,000 and before anyone had heard of George Lucas. But it was a blockbuster, winning critical acclaim, earning five Academy Award nominations, including Best Picture (it lost to *The Sting*), and earning more than $200 million in box office sales and rentals. That doesn't even include the LP, which charted at No. 10 and whose forty-one songs included such grand oldies as "Sixteen Candles," "Johnny B. Goode," and "Love Potion No. 9."

The movie triggered a wave of nostalgia. The sitcom *Happy Days*, about preternaturally well-adjusted teens in the trouble-free 1950s, premiered in 1974. *Life* published a hefty "Best of Life" edition in 1973 that prominently featured photographs from the 1930s, '40s, and '50s. Old-time comic books were popular. Restaurants with jukeboxes drew crowds. Kate Smith sang "God Bless America" at hockey games.

Americans, rightfully disillusioned and understandably cynical, found comfort in a less threatening, more carefree time. People just wanted to feel good about something, and anyone who could fill that positive niche would be in business.

Well, the Beach Boys were still in business, though nostalgia alone didn't spur our revival. We had stopped fighting with our audiences and overhauled our live show to showcase our hits. In November of 1973, Warner/Reprise released a *Beach Boys in Concert* album that was heavily weighted toward our early songs ("Surfin' USA," "Fun, Fun, Fun," "California Girls," "Good Vibrations"). It charted at No. 25, making it our bestselling LP since 1967 and our first gold album for the label.

Capitol Records noticed, and it wanted to release another collection of our songs. Labels love compilations, as they don't have to spend money on new music while getting one more shot to cash in on existing recordings. I spoke with the Capitol executives, who said they wanted to once again use the "Best of" construction to name the album. We already had *Best of the Beach Boys, Volumes 1, 2,* and *3,* the latter charting at a miserable No. 53. There had to be something more original. Capitol was going to use our old surfing and hot rod hits, which I thought were timeless, so I suggested that the album be called *Endless Summer.* For a new generation of fans, it would be like a new album instead of a collection of oldies.

Endless Summer was released in June of 1974, with twenty songs exclusively from 1962 to 1965. Fans assumed that Capitol chose those songs to take advantage of the country's pining for those innocent days of the early '60s. In truth, Capitol couldn't use any songs after 1965 because in settling its lawsuit with us, the Beach Boys had exclusive rights to those post-1965 numbers for ten years. (Capitol added "Good Vibrations" to an *Endless Summer* CD in 1987.)

The response to *Endless Summer* was stunning. Four months after hitting the stores, it reached No. 1 and remained on the *Billboard* album chart for a remarkable 155 weeks; more than 3 million copies were sold in the United States. In 1976, the album, with a modified song list and retitled *20 Golden Greats*, was released in the United Kingdom, where it was No. 1 for ten straight weeks and sold an amazing 1 million copies. (The U.K.'s population at the time was only 56 million, a quarter of the U.S. population.)

The album's success, at least in America, was credited to nostalgia, but there were plenty of bands from the 1950s and '60s that did not experience a renaissance. What propelled *Endless Summer*, I believe, was that the Beach Boys were no longer stigmatized. Many fans have told me how in the late '60s or early '70s, they would buy a Beach Boy album and then hide it as they left the record store or conceal it from their friends back home. We were objects of ridicule. Almost overnight, the stigma was gone. I was thirty-three years old, Brian and Al thirty-two. Only Carl, at twenty-eight, had yet to reach thirty. We were *ancient* by pop music standards. But when "Catch a Wave" and "I Get Around" and "Don't Worry Baby" and all those other classic songs were introduced to a new generation of teenagers, they embraced the music just as their predecessors had.

In April 1975, Capitol once again scooped into our early songs (including "Dance, Dance, Dance," "Barbara Ann," and "409") and released *Spirit of America*, and it raced to No. 8. Over the years, the Beach Boys have taken a lot of heat for promoting our old songs at the expense of our new ones, but we couldn't control the marketplace. In this case, we had our past record company (Capitol) competing against our current one (Warner/Reprise), and our past was winning big. So Warner/Reprise went retro as well. In 1975, it released *Good Vibrations, Best of the Beach Boys*, its own collection of oldies, mostly from 1966 to 1968 (including "Surf's Up," "Heroes and Villains," and "God Only Knows"), and that album charted at No. 25. Including *Endless Summer*, we had three albums of past songs competing against one another. In 1976, when Capitol released *Beach Boys '69—Live in London*, we had four.

The release of *Endless Summer* coincided with an eight-city summer tour with Crosby, Stills, Nash & Young. The epitome of countercultural, folk-rock hip, CSN&Y was on a ballyhooed "reunion tour," and the promoter, the omnipresent Bill Graham, prevailed on the group to share the stage with the Beach Boys. Our own concerts had already been on the upswing, moving from college auditoriums and performing arts centers to an occasional stadium, but the pairing with CSN&Y gave us more cachet and put us before even larger crowds (52,000 at County Stadium in Milwaukee, 50,000 at the Astrodome in Houston).

We were the opening act, and even though CSN&Y had a loyal following, it's almost always the case that when we perform with another band, we take the air out of the place, in part because very few bands have our broad catalog of hits. As the *Kansas City Times* wrote about the concert at Royals Stadium on July 19, 1974: "The crowd's biggest reaction was saved for the Beach Boys, stars of the middle 1960s. The group was called back for an encore after performing for an hour and a half. Standing ovations followed each of the group's three encore numbers, including golden oldies 'Surfer Girl' and 'Good Vibrations.'"

Rolling Stone, which hadn't taken us seriously in years, named us Band of the Year in 1974, and the CSN&Y gigs were a prelude to an even more ambitious effort the following year, when we joined Chicago on a twelve-city tour. Known as "the rock band with horns," Chicago was at its commercial peak, in the midst of recording four consecutive No. 1 albums. The "Beachago tour" was put together by Jim Guercio, who rightly assumed it was a can't-fail proposition: the two bands had combined for about thirty-five Top 10 hits. Dennis, Carl, and Al had even contributed to one of Chicago's singles, singing backup on "Wishing You Were Here" in 1974.

I had ideas on how to maximize the shows. Chicago featured many long, jazzy solos, so I thought Chicago should start the concert, then we'd join them and do the rest of the show with the bands integrated. But the bands weren't equals, or at least the Chicago guys didn't think so. They were at the top of the heap, and we were on our "comeback"; they were the headliner, while we were the opening act. We thought they were condescending toward us, so before we took the stage on our first show in Houston, I told Dennis, "We'll do an hour, and we'll kick their fucking ass, and they'll wish they never toured with us."

We performed a solid hour of hits, brought everyone to a frenzy, and left the crowd exhausted. An intermission followed, and then on came Chicago, with their jazzy riffs and extended solos—really good music, but no match for us. As *Rolling Stone* wrote after our show in Kansas City: "Though Chicago headlined . . . the Beach Boys, playing more than 1,000 miles from an ocean, stole the show . . . The crowd, high-spirited and dying for a good time, had sung along with the Beach Boys, but spontaneous clap-alongs for the less catchy Chicago songs soon trailed off into limbo."

The tour was a huge success: we sold out five nights at Chicago Stadium and added a sixth night. We sold out four nights at Madison Square Garden while packing 62,000 into Schaefer Stadium in Foxborough, Massachusetts; it was, at the time, the largest crowd to ever attend a concert in New England. The tour generated more than $7.5 million in revenue and was seen by more than 700,000 people.

Each concert ended with the Beach Boys joining Chicago onstage, and one number was Dennis singing "You Are So Beautiful," written by Billy Preston and Bruce Fisher, though Dennis was an uncredited contributor. It became, for many fans, Dennis's signature song, one that he would perform solo at concerts. He would take the mic, his dark hair falling to his shoulders, his beard closely cropped, his presence still riveting, and sometimes say, "I want to dedicate this song to the girls here tonight. Awwright! Do you mess around?" And the girls would scream as Dennis cupped his ear in solemn appreciation, and then his voice, growing heavier and rougher by the year, would serenade a touching version of "You Are So Beautiful."

Of course, nothing with Dennis was ever simple. By the time we toured with Chicago, he had divorced Barbara and was dating the model Karen Lamm; her former husband was Robert Lamm, a keyboardist, singer, and founding member of Chicago, and it seemed that Dennis was singing "You Are So Beautiful" to Karen. I don't know how that went over with Robert, but as they say, that's rock and roll.

The summer we performed with Chicago we also shared the stage with Elton John, among other rock luminaries, at Wembley Stadium in England. It was an eleven-hour event attended by 75,000 people, including Paul McCartney and Ringo Starr, who sat in the Royal Box area of the stadium. Elton John was the world's biggest-selling rock star, but it didn't matter. According to *Melody Maker*: "Unfortunately for Elton, [who played] endless songs from his new album *Captain Fantastic*, the Beach Boys had already stolen the show hours beforehand as they played their marvelous surfing songs under the blazing sunshine of the longest day." We saw Elton backstage, and he was so distraught over the fans' lukewarm reaction to his new songs, he was in tears. But there was no need. *Captain Fantastic* was a huge seller soon enough, in both the United Kingdom and the United States. It was, however, the last time he ever played with us onstage.

We had risen from the musical dead and, with Dennis, Carl, Al, and a rotating cast of talented sidekicks, we had established ourselves as one of the best live acts in America. Our compilations were also flying out of record store bins. What we weren't doing, however, was recording new songs. We also didn't have Brian.

B rian went to Holland with us in 1972, though that took some doing. Marilyn and their two daughters had gone on ahead of him, and Brian traveled alone. But when his plane landed in Amsterdam, he wasn't on it. He had reached the Los Angeles airport, changed his mind, and returned home. Someone got him on the phone and persuaded him to fly out the next day. Once again his plane landed, and once again he was nowhere to be found. This time, however, he had walked off the plane at the Amsterdam airport and fallen asleep on a couch in the duty-free lounge. He was soon found.

Brian contributed to the *Holland* LP, as he had to all our recent albums, but then our recording of new music essentially stopped. We were all responsible, but Brian's seclusion was a factor. His withdrawal began in 1973, when his father died. For all the traumas he had with his dad, Brian was still staggered by his death. He didn't attend the funeral, and then he retreated into his bedroom in Bel Air and pretty much wanted to stay there, showing little interest in his family or friends, in writing or recording music, in doing much of anything productive.

Brian's lack of self-control had long been a problem. At one concert, he saw a bottle of Carl's cough syrup backstage, and he gulped the whole damn thing because it had codeine. At a hotel in Texas, he once ordered an entire tray of grasshopper shots. He once went to Denny's with some bandmates, one of whom ordered steak and eggs, and Brian scooped up five inches of steak fat from the guy's plate and sucked it down.

When Brian went into hibernation, his compulsive habits intensified and became an unfortunate part of Beach Boys' lore. Brian gave up regular bathing, allowed his hair to grow long and stringy, smoked incessantly, ate indiscriminately, and gained more than a hundred pounds. He lay in bed and watched television for hours, listened to "Be My Baby" over and over, and wandered the house aimlessly in his pajamas and bathrobe. He drank excessively and gulped down amphetamines. He smashed a couple of cars as well.

I saw Brian occasionally but didn't speak to him much. I thought he was so gone mentally there wasn't much that I or anyone in the family could do. Brian should have been with us to enjoy the Beach Boys' "revival," but that wasn't possible.

Marilyn didn't know what to do. She wanted to get Brian professional counseling, but Brian refused. She and my brother Stephen decided to ask for help from my other brother Stan. He was twenty-six, the youngest, biggest, and most athletic of the three Love brothers. At the University of Oregon, he led the Pacific-8 Conference in scoring two straight years, and then he was drafted in the first round by the Baltimore Bullets. He was known as a free spirit whose heart was in California—he'd show up to games in flip-flops, even in the winter. Stan did play briefly for the Los Angeles Lakers, but his luck didn't improve much. Our mom was so upset by his lack of playing time that she wrote a letter to the coach (he didn't respond). After the 1975 season, uncertain about his basketball future (Stan ended the year playing in the ABA), he agreed to help Brian get back on his feet. He had no particular training for Brian's emotional and psychological problems, but he was an athlete who understood discipline, focus, and exercise, all of which Brian desperately needed. And like all my brothers and sisters, he revered Brian as the fun-loving, gentle soul who gave him his singing part at our Christmas parties, and he couldn't stand to see the condition he was now in.

Stan's first job was to find where Brian stashed his drugs and to get rid of them. Then it was compelling Brian to get out of bed, bathe, get dressed, eat right, and move around. He even removed the coffeepot, so Brian couldn't use it for a caffeine high. Stan also favored tough love. He would yell at Brian, and after he caught Brian breaking his diet, he poked him in the chest and called him a "fat rock star." Several months passed, and Brian was making some progress, but then Stan received an offer to play for the Atlanta Hawks and moved on. Marilyn, out of desperation, next reached out to a therapist who was recommended by a friend. His name was Eugene Landy, and he was just unconventional enough that Marilyn thought it might work.

Landy was a self-advertised psychologist to the stars, providing his therapeutic magic to Alice Cooper, Richard Harris, and Rod Steiger. He had thick dark hair, a medium build, and a bulbous nose, and whenever he was in an argument, he believed that whoever yelled the loudest won. (By that measure, he usually won.) His background was nothing if not colorful. Born and raised in Pittsburgh, he overcame dyslexia to earn both a master's in psychology and a doctorate in philosophy. He began his career by treating adolescents and drug addicts; he trained volunteers for the Peace Corps, worked with Vietnam vets, and published a book, *The Underground Dictionary*, that defined hippie slang. He also claimed to be a record-company promoter, having "discovered" fellow Pittsburgh resident George Benson on a city street corner. Benson later said that he severed ties with Landy when Landy sought too much control over his career.

But what Landy was most known for, as a psychologist, was his twenty-four-hour therapy—according to a paper he wrote on the subject, it required "complete patient dependency on the therapist and total control of the patient's life."

At her first meeting with Landy, Marilyn told him that Brian was "very bright and manipulative" and needed someone who could think on his level. Landy said he could do that, but to persuade Brian to submit, they hatched a plan for Landy to come to their house under the ruse that he was there to counsel Marilyn. Brian, feeling left out, would ask for his own time.

That's what happened, and Landy began seeing Brian. He then brought in his three aides, at least one of whom was always at the house. Landy put chains on the refrigerator door, got Brian to walk and jog, kept the drugs and alcohol at bay, soaked him in water when he wouldn't get out of bed, and ensured that he didn't wander off into the street. After five or six months, Marilyn saw progress: Brian began losing significant weight and was more lucid and energetic, though he still smoked constantly. There were also red flags. Landy used another doctor to prescribe—in Marilyn's words—"mind-controlling drugs" for Brian, what we now know were psychotropic drugs such as lithium. Landy had also begun to shut Brian off from his friends and family, blocking visitors and phone calls. Even more disturbing: One of Landy's aides tried to discipline Brian and Marilyn's young daughters, locking one (at age seven) in their sauna for supposedly misbehaving. The sauna wasn't turned on, but it was still upsetting.

Nonetheless, Brian was improving, and as 1976 rolled around, we were under pressure to record a new album for Warner/Reprise. It seemed that Brian was well enough to contribute, not only in the studio but also onstage, which he had not done since 1970. Brian's incapacitation had been covered by the media, so my brother Stephen developed a campaign to reintroduce Brian to the public while giving a boost to our next record and concerts.

The campaign slogan: "Brian's back."

It was pithy and evocative. It raised the hopes of our fans, and did it ever work. Our publicist, Sandy Friedman, held a press junket at the Sheraton Fisherman's Wharf Hotel in San Francisco. The Beach Boys sat in different rooms while members of the media, print, radio, and television, circled through to interview us. That night, we took reporters to the Joffrey Ballet, featuring Twyla Tharp, at San Francisco's War Memorial Opera House, and we convinced the troupe to dance their smooth arabesques to "Little Deuce Coupe" and "Wouldn't It Be Nice." The journalists were blown away, and it didn't hurt that we also took them out for a nice dinner afterward.

We were on the covers of *Rolling Stone, Crawdaddy!,* and *New*

Times and were featured in *TV Guide*, *Time*, and *Newsweek*, whose title for the story was . . . "Brian's Back."

There was only one problem. Brian wasn't back.

It should have been apparent to anyone who bothered reading the stories. In the cover article in *Rolling Stone*, Brian asked the reporter if he could scare up some cocaine or speed, and his request was included in the piece. NBC featured the Beach Boys in a one-hour prime-time special that was produced by Lorne Michaels, creator of *Saturday Night Live*. In one sketch, Dan Aykroyd and John Belushi, dressed as cops, rousted Brian from bed and hauled him to the ocean. There, in his robe and carrying a surfboard, Brian rambled in, was mauled by the waves, and finally mounted his board, unaware that he was riding it backwards.

Carli Muñoz, a jazz musician who played with us for many years, once observed that Brian always had a firewall around him—bodyguards or agents or someone who shielded Brian from others. Landy was now that firewall. When *People* magazine wanted to do a photo shoot of us, Landy wouldn't allow Brian to participate, nor would he allow Brian to leave the house on his own. We couldn't even pick Brian up because one of Landy's minions was always at his house, even overnight. So we were left with one option: we had to kidnap Brian.

Sandy Friedman got a couple of guys to go over to Brian's home in the middle of night. They brought a ladder with them, and one of the guys climbed to the second story and knocked on Brian's window until he woke up. He told Brian that he had to get to a photo shoot, and Brian, half asleep and in his pajamas, made his way down the ladder, got into the car, and was whisked away.

They made it to the photo shoot, and on August 23, 1976, the Beach Boys, all sporting beards, were the first rock band to appear on the cover of *People*. The caption: "Still Riding the Crest 15 Hairy Years Later."

After so many years in the wilderness, we had a chance to record an album when fans were actually demanding to hear our music. We wanted an LP that recognized our fifteenth anniversary and would be released in conjunction with our bicentennial concerts in July.

Landy supported Brian's involvement in the album, but his return was bumpy. One day Al and I were with Brian in a studio, and he was trying out an early version of a new song, "T M." Brian hadn't sung a real lead vocal on a Beach Boy album in years, apart from two brief lines on *Holland*. When he tried singing now, his voice was hoarse and croaky and utterly unlike his once-radiant falsetto. I assumed the cigarettes had damaged his vocal cords, which, to me, was like spray paint defacing a national monument. Al would sing the lead on "T M." Brian sounded better singing lead on a couple of other songs, but many fans were still dismayed by his wavering, off-key vocals.

The dynamics in the band had also changed. Carl had been producing our albums, and both Carl and Dennis had been recording their own stuff, either as potential tracks for the Beach Boys or, in Carl's case, as a producer and arranger for others. But now for this new album, "Brian was back." The fans wanted Brian. The media wanted Brian. The label most definitely wanted Brian. But Brian was in no shape to take charge, his once-flawless tracks marred by idiosyncratic arrangements or weird musical textures, which others had to fix. Carl, justifiably so, felt passed over, and Dennis felt ignored.

The album, *15 Big Ones*, was a hodgepodge of new songs and old, lacking any thematic unity. Both Dennis and Carl took the unusual step of criticizing their own album in the press, saying it was "unfinished" and "rushed," and calling out their older brother. As Dennis told *Newsweek*, "We were heartbroken. People have waited all this time, anticipating a new Beach Boy album, and I hated to give them this. It was a great mistake to put Brian in full control. He was always the absolute producer, but little did he know that in his absence, people grew up." Dennis and Carl criticized Brian as well as Al and me for releasing a record before it was ready. They preferred to take additional time to do an entire album of new songs.

15 Big Ones did indeed have some rough sections, but I disagreed that all we needed was more time. What the press didn't report was that Carl had suffered a debilitating back injury, causing him significant pain. Sometimes he was forced to lie flat on his back in the studio when he was doing some of his guitar parts; other times he would do vocal parts from a wheelchair. He was also self-medicating and drinking, problems that would emerge publicly in a couple of years.

We had been recording music for a decade while the whole concept of the Beach Boys seemed obsolete. We should release *15 Big Ones*, I thought, before we lost the momentum, but even with that momentum, we needed a hit song. When we were in the studio, I reminded Brian of the success we had in tapping into Chuck Berry's "Sweet Little Sixteen" for "Surfin' USA." I told him we should do another Chuck Berry number, and we agreed to cover "Rock and Roll Music." Brian did the track, I did the lead vocals, and it was released on May 24. Honestly, it was barely finished and kind of scratchy—Brian produced a better version for the album—but it still sounded cool and ballsy on highly compressed old AM car radio speakers. I was both relieved and happy that it peaked at No. 5, making it our first Top 10 single since "Good Vibrations" in 1966.

15 Big Ones, released in July, charted at No. 8; excluding our compilations, it was our bestselling album since *Beach Boys' Party!* in 1965. The LP also included "It's OK," an original that Brian and I wrote that I thought was a great summer song. I believe if it had been released as a single at the end of spring—or if it had been the album's lead song—it would have been a hit and gone down as one of our classics. But Warner/Reprise didn't want it to compete with "Rock and Roll Music," so it wasn't available as a single until August 30, and by then it was too late. It only charted at No. 29. A missed opportunity, in my opinion.

Despite its success, the album proved to be one of our most polarizing, its critics seeing it as evidence of putting commerce ahead of art. I saw it as recognition of how the music world operates. We were trying to defy the laws of musical gravity, remaining viable from one decade to the next. That rarely happens for a rock band. So when an opportunity arises, you can't dawdle in search of artistic perfection. Instead, we moved fast, and *15 Big Ones* would be our last Top 10 album until 2012.

Unintentionally, the album's cover said a lot about the band. It was designed by Dean Torrence, who had his own graphic design company. He started it after Jan Berry suffered severe head injuries in a 1966 car accident, leaving him partially paralyzed. The duo would perform again, but Dean began a second career as a designer, specializing in album covers. Nineteen seventy-six was an Olympic year, so for *15 Big Ones*, Dean put the five Olympic rings on the cover, each ring filled with one of our portraits. The images of Brian, Dennis, Carl, Al, and me in five interlocking circles could have been a metaphor for five bandmates united in common purpose, or five guys living in their separate worlds. With us, it was both. What drew the most attention, however, was the photo of Brian, who, with shoulder-length, lacquered hair and heavy jowls, bore no resemblance to his younger self.

The highlight of the Brian's Back campaign was his joining us for two bicentennial concerts, the most memorable one for me at Anaheim Stadium on July 3. Billed as Southern California's Only Bicentennial Rock Event, it drew a sold-out crowd of 55,000. America, one of my favorite bands, opened for us, and we joined them onstage to play "Sister Golden Hair" and "A Horse with No Name." After a short break, we came back alone.

In the weeks leading up to the concerts, I needed to make a change, as I had gained a few pounds and was feeling sluggish. So I entered a program at the Hippocrates Health Institute in Lemon Grove, California, which offered a much safer way to purify the body than what I had tried the last time. The institute believes in the medicinal power of raw, organic foods, particularly wheatgrass, used to create a nutrient juice. You drank it to cleanse your cells and purify your blood, and you had enemas and "wheatgrass implants." You also ate a lot of raw greens, sprouts, and seeds. This wasn't for the weak of heart—I called it the Marine Boot Camp of Purification—but I lost fifteen pounds in about two weeks and was totally reinvigorated.

I also enjoy the costume-design part of rock and roll, the sartorial plumage, and for the concerts I could now wear a tight gold lamé vest, with no shirt, beads, and white bell-bottoms. We had an amazing band, with Billy Hinsche (guitar and keyboards), Ed Carter (bass guitar), Bobby Figueroa (drums), Ron Altbach (keyboards), and Carli Muñoz (keyboards), and I jammed on the stage to "I Get Around," "Be True to Your School," and "Surfin' USA." But the crowd in Anaheim! Sitting on the outfield grass and in the stands, they sang, rocked, and danced, and you could feel their energy. Then the passions ran too high. During "I Get Around," I looked up and saw the upper deck swaying and the banks of lights moving. It was like a low-level rumbling earthquake without the actual earthquake. One fan later swore that the stands were swaying to the beat of the music. We had to halt the concert for a PA announcement, which asked the people in the upper deck to stop jumping up and down because chunks of concrete were breaking off under the grandstands. I was ecstatic that the Beach Boys could still bring down the house, but I was pet-rified that we were going to *actually* bring down the house.

The stadium survived the concert, which was about all we could say for Brian as well.

He began offstage, and then after we had played a couple of num-bers, I spoke to the crowd, offered some introductory chatter, and then said: "By the way, there is someone with us tonight who doesn't go to many places with us lately. He's here tonight. He's responsible for us being here. His name is Brian Wilson! Let's hear it for Brian!"

With Landy coaxing him on, Brian walked onstage and made his way to the keyboard, and the fans went wild, with some waving Bri-an's Back signs.

Even when healthy, Brian hated performing before large crowds. Now he sat on his stool in some medicated haze, rarely singing or playing. There were times when he seemed aware and engaged and could perform; but mostly he drifted and mumbled. At one point, appearing to have a panic attack, he yelled, "Get away from my piano! Get away from me." *Melody Maker* wrote of Brian, "Apparently, per-forming is part of his therapy program. But he should have stayed home." Perhaps, but there was no doubt that the fans loved seeing him, in whatever shape.

For our first encore, Dennis sang "You Are So Beautiful," which as always electrified the crowd, and it was followed by "Rock and Roll Music," "Barbara Ann," and "Fun, Fun, Fun."

The crowd gave us a long, standing ovation—but that wasn't the best part. The best was that my parents attended. They didn't see that many of our shows, as we didn't play that many in Southern California; but they always enjoyed them. Back in the early 1960s, they attended one of our concerts at the Hollywood Bowl. After-ward, the guys and I were taken away in our cars while about a hun-dred kids were trying to get our autographs. One of them noticed my mom and asked her for her autograph, which she proudly gave. That led to requests from a half-dozen other kids, all of whom my mom obliged until my dad pulled her away.

Now in Anaheim, I was really happy that my parents saw a concert that drew such a large, raucous crowd. They were obviously proud of me and their nephews, but I wasn't that good at telling them how meaningful their example was. All I could do onstage was sing and prance. They sat on side stage, wearing earplugs, and when I first saw them during one of our songs, I went over and gave my mom a kiss and my dad a hug. As I returned to center stage, my mom looked out onto the field and saw it packed with kids yelling, some girls on top of their boyfriends' shoulders, everyone with their arms waving.

"This is an example of mass hysteria!" she yelled to my dad.

"Yes," he shouted back, "but good hysteria!"

No "comeback," real or imagined, can last forever, and so it was with Brian's. The most immediate change in his life occurred at the end of 1976 when Stephen and Marilyn fired Landy. Landy was always expensive, but he was now charging $32,000 a month, part of which was being picked up by the Beach Boys. The cost was indefensible while Landy's obsession with control was too much, and he was gone.

But there was a time, early in the campaign, that I hoped Brian really was back, and there were times in the studio or even onstage when Brian would reconnect to the music and his voice would soar and he would hit the high notes as only Brian Wilson could. I would watch in amazement and get so emotional I'd have to choke back the tears. I couldn't tell him how I felt, but I wrote this song instead, called "Brian's Back."

Teenage gambol(ers)
Sittin' in a Rambler

Listenin' to the radio.
And then standing in the grandstand,
Following the game plan,
Watching life's plays unfold.

You fell in love with a pretty cheerleader.
I even married one.
And we once rode a cab outta Salt Lake City
Comin' up with "Fun, Fun, Fun."

They say that Brian is back.
Well I've known him for oh so long.
They say Brian is back.
Well I never knew that he was gone.
Still they say Brian is back.
I know he's had his ups and downs.
Well they say that Brian is back.
But in my heart he's always been around.

I still remember,
You soundin' sweet and tender.
Singin' "Danny Boy" on Grandma's lap.
And those harmony highs
Could bring tears to my eyes.
I guess I'm just a sentimental sap.
"Good Vibrations" caused such a sensation,
Not to mention ol' Pet Sounds.
And we traveled the world,
As the banners unfurled.
I guess you'd have to say we got around.

CHAPTER 17

THE FRACTURING

The Beach Boys were about to enter a new era, what I call the fracturing—fractures in the band, in our families, in our marriages. For a group that often shattered in place, this period had more sharp edges than most.

Our personal lives took the biggest hit. Carl and Annie separated in 1978, in one of the lowest points in Carl's life. Like all broken marriages, this one had a number of issues, but drugs were one of them. Carl had been in a downward spiral, much of it from cocaine, which by the mid-1970s had cut a wide and devastating swath through the entire music industry. Carl was the most stable of the three Wilson brothers, but even he reached a point where he was squandering money on drugs, hallucinating, or acting irrationally. On September 1, 1977, before an afternoon concert in New York City's Central Park, Carl was so dazed that several guys had to put him in a cold shower just to bring him around. He made it onstage but sounded terrible. As Annie later said, "When you're talking to your drug dealer more than your friends, that's a problem."

Dennis, meanwhile, ended up marrying Karen Lamm in 1976, which made both their lives even more combustible. There were the drugs, including Dennis's first use of heroin. There were the fights. And there was recklessness. Karen once shot Dennis's Ferrari with a pistol. Dean Torrence was with Dennis in Hawaii during this period, and as soon as Karen arrived, all hell broke loose. As Dean later said, "To feel loved, Dennis had to be in turmoil." Seven months after Dennis and Karen got married, they divorced. One year later, they remarried; that lasted two weeks before Dennis filed for another divorce.

After Landy was fired, Marilyn rehired my brother Stan to be Brian's bodyguard. Stan was joined by Steve Korthof, Brian's first cousin who had previously worked as a Beach Boy roadie, and by Rushton "Rocky" Pamplin, a friend of Stan's who had tried out for professional football teams but was probably more well known as a model, including a nude centerfold for *Playgirl*. (Rocky also gained notoriety in Beach Boy circles for his affair with Marilyn while he was Brian's bodyguard.) Even with three minders, Brian didn't change, his craving for drugs as great as ever. Stan moved in and resumed his tough love, yelling at Brian about how fat and lazy he was and how he had to get his life in order. But while Stan was in the shower, Brian would sneak out in his robe and hitchhike in search of drugs; one time he was picked up by Merv Griffin and brought home. Marilyn complained, argued, and begged, all of which Brian increasingly hated. They separated in 1978 and later divorced (presided over by Judge Wapner, before his television fame).

Reflecting on these experiences years later, Annie believes that none of us was prepared to handle the pressures and temptations of the era. "It was too much too soon. Success. Conflict. All in intense doses. You're barely a teenager, and you're in another world. I think the drugs were all about escape, to have a different experience, to get away from it. But it's a lie. You can't get away from it."

Annie took drugs with Carl, including LSD once or twice, and considers herself fortunate. "I marvel at anyone from that era who came out of it unscathed," she said.

As for me, drugs had nothing to do with my life, and they had everything to do with it. I saw the wreckage, not only of my cousins but many in the business. Janis Joplin, Jimi Hendrix, and Jim Morrison were among the highest-profile casualties, all dead at twenty-seven. Guitarist Tommy Bolin, Brian Cole (the Association), and Danny Whitten (Crazy Horse) never saw thirty. Elvis was gone by 1977, and neither Keith Moon nor Sid Vicious made it out of the decade.

So I turned inward, isolating myself further from my bandmates while going deeper into Eastern spirituality. After becoming an instructor of TM, I learned more about Ayurveda, which combines the Sanskrit words *ayur* (life) and *veda* (knowledge). It represents a system of ancient Hindu medicine that includes health remedies, astrology, and spiritual ceremonies to bring your life greater balance. That growing awareness led me to attend, in 1977, an advanced training seminar, called the TM-Siddhi program. With Charles Lloyd and others, I spent three months in Vittel, France, and three months in Leysin, Switzerland, changing venues to take advantage of off-season hotel rates. As in Rishikesh, we attended lectures and seminars and also meditated, but it was all done with greater purpose. *Siddhi* means paranormal powers or abilities, and the program's entire thrust was how to use these siddhis to develop human potential. This can be done through the practice of sutras, or aphorisms, compiled around the second or third century CE by Patanjali and now introduced to us. While you are meditating, the sutras develop qualities of the mind and body, honing your intellect, refining your senses, and nurturing your soul. The process is spiritual as well as physiological. It is also aspirational, whether to improve your vision, heighten your intuition, or broaden your sympathies—it's about how to improve yourself and the world around you. What has generated the most attention over the years are the flying sutras, or levitation. Perhaps saints or yogis have defied gravity, but for mortals like me, I can only practice, cultivate these attributes of personal improvement, renew my energies, overcome my fears, push forward, and with the grace of God, *transcend*.

———

If Eastern spirituality set me on a better path in most areas of my life, it did not help in my relationships with women. I knew that the family household my mom had created was something that I wanted, but I continued to plunge headlong into commitments that I hoped would fill gaps in my life but ended badly.

In 1977, I married Sue Oliver, a divorcée whose first husband was wealthy, who had a wide circle of friends (Sammy Davis Jr., Peter Lawford), and who was one of the most socially adept women I'd ever known. I went with Sue to the Kennedy Compound in Hyannis Port, mingled with Prince Bandar of Saudi Arabia in Washington, and met Senator Ted Kennedy's teenage son, Edward M. Kennedy Jr., who lost his right leg due to bone cancer. I had never been part of that world, but I found it fascinating, and I thought Sue could show it to me while providing a home as well. She even traveled to a meditation course on her own. When we got engaged, she asked me for a diamond ring and a fur coat. That should have been a red flag, but I looked past it. Sue was attractive and fun, but I learned that you can't marry someone because you want to improve your social skills, particularly when you place different values on material wealth. The marriage was annulled after six months.

My next relationship couldn't have been more different, in every possible way.

On a swing through Jacksonville, Florida, I visited Dr. Batchelder, the surgeon who had operated on my grandpa years ago, and he introduced me to Patricia DePadua, who came from the Philippines and was part of a family of doctors. Innocent, romantic, and beguiling, still in her early twenties, Trisha played the guitar and loved to sing, and I was swept up again. Her father had died, and she was still mourning his loss when I met her. Her devotion to him was affecting, and I found in Trisha a purity of motives and spirit that was refreshingly at odds with the world in which I lived. We took a romantic vacation to Hawaii, and then Trisha stayed with me for several months in Santa Barbara. When I had to leave for my TM-Siddhi course in France and Switzerland, I sent Trisha back to Jacksonville to live at her home until I returned to the states. Once I was abroad, we spoke on the phone on a regular basis.

Immediately after the course, I was in London for a Beach Boy gig at a CBS convention, as we had just signed a $2 million contract with CBS Records/Caribou. I received a call from Trisha's brother-in-law, who told me that she had been involved in a horrific car accident, in her Volkswagen, on a rain-slick road. She was now on life support. The news just froze me. She wasn't dead. She wasn't alive. She was, for the moment, in some netherworld, and only a miracle could bring her back.

I fulfilled my obligations at the CBS convention, and between concern about Trisha's fate and the effects of my last six months in meditation, I was in a state of extreme sensitivity, all of which came out onstage. Brian was with us, under Stan's care, and he had lost some weight. But when we were onstage, Brian was at the piano, just drifting in and out. *Melody Maker* wrote that Brian "looked totally zomboid and completely unaware of what was happening around him."

I was steamed, and not just at Brian. I really wondered what the hell I was doing up here. For the past six months, I'd been surrounded by people who were determined to increase their knowledge and advance their personal development; and now I was surrounded by people who thought they were hot shit because they could get into a limo and do a lousy show while the only thing they really cared about was their self-indulgent drug habit. So during "Fun, Fun, Fun," I walked over to Brian's piano, lifted up one side, dropped it, pushed it, and knocked over his mic. When the song ended, Brian, horrified, stood up and left the stage.

Trisha died when I was still in London, and I flew to the funeral in Jacksonville with Stan; but I was so distraught that I stayed to my-self as much as possible. I believe my relationship with Trisha would have grown and flourished, and I spent many long nights wondering how things could have been different had I not sent her back home. There are no answers to such questions, no way to heal that wound; all I can do is accept that some things in life cannot be explained or understood.

At least there is music, and I wrote and later recorded the song, "Trisha," with Carl on the backup vocals. The track, which has been available on bootlegs for decades, has a yearning, bittersweet quality throughout.

> *Oh darling, Trisha.*
> *I just love you so*
> *Oh, so much more*
> *Than you'll probably ever know.*

The band's lifestyle divide had been present for years, but now a deeper schism emerged—between the meditators (Al and me) and the partiers (Dennis and Carl). The terms *smokers* and *nonsmokers* were also used. When Bruce Johnston rejoined the band in 1978, he joined our group. He didn't meditate, but he didn't take drugs either. The split was so intense that when we traveled, we chartered two planes, the costs be damned, with the partiers usually including a number of our roadies. When Brian traveled, accompanied by Stan or his other bodyguards, he usually flew on our plane. When we had to take one plane, one camp sat in the front, the other in the back, and the middle was Switzerland. Other issues came to a head over the management of the group, its musical direction, and disputes involv-ing our record labels (we signed the deal with CBS/Caribou while we still owed Warner/Reprise two albums). Our dysfunction could not be concealed. The day after the Central Park concert in 1977, on the tarmac of the Newark airport, a red-faced argument broke out above the din of our idling planes. I was sitting in one of the aircraft, but a *Rolling Stone* reporter who saw the debacle compared it to a scene out of *Casablanca*.

That movie, at least, ended with the beginning of a beautiful friendship. Those kinds of bonds were increasingly rare in the Beach Boys, even among those of us who sat on the same plane. Al and I, for example, were spiritual partners and shared strong interests in the environment. We wrote several songs together, and his soothing, bendable voice was the perfect fit in our harmonic stack. His country rock rendition of "Cotton Fields," an international hit, showcased his talents, and his arrangement of "Come Go with Me," turning a golden oldie into a Beach Boys' special, became a surprise Top 20 hit in 1981.

But Al and I weren't close personally. He was always in an odd position—within the original band, he was the one non–family member. Then he quit the Beach Boys, and when he returned in 1963, my uncle Murry, in retribution, made him a salaried employee. He didn't become a shareholder in Brother Records until 1971. Perhaps he felt he was never given his due, financially or artistically. Whatever the case, he could be prickly and rude, particularly to staffers or subordinates, with a grating sense of entitlement. I'm sure he had his bill of particulars against me as well.

Our next several albums reflected our dismal state. *The Beach Boys Love You* LP (April 1977) was written almost entirely by Brian but was not what his fans were expecting. Sparsely produced and relying heavily on analog synthesizers, it was undeniably original but fragmented and just plain odd. No one knew what to make of it when it came out, and Warner/Reprise did little to promote it.

Our next LP, at Al's and my urging, was recorded at Maharishi

International University in Fairfield, Iowa. By the winter of '77, we had grown increasingly concerned about Carl and believed that a healthier environment might pull him out of his spiral. We thought it'd be good for Dennis as well. If nothing else, we figured there were fewer temptations in the middle of Iowa. But while the meditative life might have once appealed to my cousins, it didn't now. They took the whole experience—living in dorm rooms at a midwestern college in the dead of winter, recording in makeshift facilities on rented gear—as a personal affront, and they came and went with little interest in the music. Brian was with us but miserable throughout. The album bombed.

My guess is that everyone who's ever played in a rock band has wanted to do a solo album. It's only natural to ask—how far can I fly on my own wings? Every Beach Boy has done at least one solo album, and it's not surprising that Dennis, of the original five members, had the first. He wanted it the most. Dennis also had the support of Jim Guercio's Caribou Records, and he had the perfect place to record new songs. In 1973, the Beach Boys purchased a former porn theater on 5th Avenue in Santa Monica and remodeled it into Brother Studio. Dennis and Carl became the co-owners, and it was, for Dennis, a musical haven.

Dennis wrote most of the songs for the album—to be called *Pacific Ocean Blue*—in collaboration with Gregg Jakobson, but he asked me if I would write the title song. I accepted gladly.

Dennis's music was a reflection of his life—the longing, the sadness, the moodiness, all drawn from his own experiences, all evident in his lyrics and melodies. Even his love songs were plaintive, including his most popular number, "Forever." (*So I'm goin' away/but not forever/I'm gonna love you any ol' way.*)

Pacific Ocean Blue's title song was about the environmental threats to this great body of water, a rabid concern that Dennis and I shared.

We grew up on the edge of the Pacific, and we were the ones who went to the ocean as teens to catch the morning swells, so it was part of our history together. Musically, Dennis collaborated far differently than Brian. Brian was interactive: I typically sat with him at the piano as he tinkered with the melodies and chord progressions while I provided the hooks and suggested the rhythms and syllables in the background. The lyrics emerged organically in this process. Dennis, on the other hand, wrote out the music entirely, gave it to me, shared his thoughts about the wording, suggested a few phrases, and then had me write the rest. Brian, I think, enjoyed having company when he worked and was codependent on most of his lyricists. Dennis was the ultimate free spirit.

Either way worked, and I thought "Pacific Ocean Blues," as part of a thematically tight album on the impossibility of love and the transience of friendships, had a poetic, melancholy grace:

We live on the edge of a body of water,
Warmed by the blood of the cold-hearted.
Slaughter of the otter.
Wonder how she feels, mother seal.
It's no wonder, the Pacific Ocean is blue.

The album, released in September of 1977, was cheered by critics as another Wilson brother's finding his voice. It was a tougher sell commercially, charting at only No. 96, but strong enough that Dennis began work on another solo album. I think we were all hopeful that *Pacific Ocean Blue* would open doors for Dennis, musically and personally. A false rumor from this period was that Dennis wanted to promote the album on a solo tour, but I told him that if he did, he couldn't return to the Beach Boys. That was not true. In fact, I was looking forward to writing more songs with Dennis for his solo efforts. We may have had different musical styles and sensibilities, not to mention lifestyles, but our love for the environment bridged that divide and would have allowed us to collaborate for years to come.

Unfortunately, none of it came to pass, not the environmental songs or the second album or the solo career. Even Brother Studio was lost, sold in 1978. It was expensive to maintain, and when Carl decided to sell his stake, Dennis couldn't afford it on his own.

Ever since the mid-1960s, Brian had been surrounded by people who have wanted to help him or, as the case may be, claimed to want help him but have had other agendas. I've usually been able to discern who's had Brian's best interests at heart and who were the frauds. But I never would have anticipated the events that took place in January and February of 1978, when those supposedly closest to Brian led him astray.

We had a three-week tour in Australia and New Zealand, promoted by the English talk-show host David Frost. The tour itself, if it is recalled for anything, is known as the time when a drunken Carl fell on his ass on a stage in Perth, and he apologized on national TV the following day. It was the trip on which Carl, now almost as heavy as Brian, truly bottomed out. An unsteady Brian was with us, along with all three of his bodyguards (Stan, Steve Korthof, and Rocky), and so was Dennis. As a group, we often stumbled through our sets, though that didn't seem to bother the large crowds. Our bigger problems were offstage.

Brian's bodyguards did all they could to keep the drugs away, inspecting his hotel room drawers and closets to intercept any contraband. They were also supposed to keep Brian in sight at all times. But one night in Melbourne, one week into the tour, we were staying at a Hilton, and Brian slipped away and was later found vomiting in his room. When Stan, Steve, and Rocky investigated, they concluded that Carl had purchased $100 of heroin from an employee of David Frost's entertainment company, and that Carl gave the heroin to Dennis as well as to Brian.

Heroin was relatively new to the band. Over New Year's back in the states, Dennis had apparently taken it for the first time with Karen Lamm. As narcotics go, heroin has few equals for its destructiveness, and the rest of the group, including our tour and business managers, were all outraged when we learned that Brian had gotten hold of the stuff, apparently through his brothers. We also had contractual obligations. In our negotiations for the tour, Frost required that Brian be onstage.

After Brian's bodyguards found him in his room sick, they sat down with him and tried to warn him about his brothers.*

> ROCKY: You have to know better next time. There can't be a
> next time on that shit.
> STAN: I can't believe you let your brothers drag you down like
> that . . . They're trying to put you back where you were ten
> years ago.
> STEVE: Here we are trying to treat you like an adult, and this
> blows it apart.

Rocky and Steve also talked about my feelings for Brian, which was something I could never do myself.

> ROCKY: Look how much Mike Love loves you. He can't even
> sleep at night because he thinks they're trying to give you

---

* Stan brought his tape recorder, and his recording was used for this account.

heroin, and he wants to strangle Dennis—that's how much you mean to him. That's love.

STEVE: Do you know that Mike cries when you do a good show?

ROCKY: The more I look at, if your brothers are doing this to you in '78, what have they been doing to you all along—

STEVE:—in '66.

ROCKY: To fuck up your head and get you involved in drugs.

BRIAN: I'm not going to do it again, I'm telling you that. I'll never do it again.

That night onstage, at the Myer Music Bowl in Melbourne, Carl was stoned, and Brian and Dennis disappeared so often that the *Melbourne Herald* noted: "It was like 'Exodus' gone wrong."

Afterward, Frost heard that some of us were talking about sending Dennis home (our contract ensured that Brian stayed), and Frost held an emergency meeting with the group, but excluding Brian and Dennis.

Frost was an elegant Brit who was perhaps at the height of his fame, having just completed his blockbuster interviews with Richard Nixon, and the last thing he wanted was an international drug incident—or for Dennis to leave the tour. It was all about "truth in advertising," Frost told us.* If Dennis wasn't onstage as advertised, the insurance company that underwrote the tour (AGC) would be furious. AGC, Frost explained, wasn't "a textile company or a food company. Their business is based on trust and always delivering what they promise . . . They have $2 billion in assets, and they might sue me, and they would certainly sue you for $50 million."

"So," I told Frost, "you're going to use the threat of a $2 billion company—"

"No, no—"

* Stan taped this meeting as well.

"—which would blow out our brains financially, [so you can] save Dennis Wilson's ass, for doing something unforgivable, in my opinion."

"I appreciate the principle," Frost said, but "we are all on this gloriously successful tour, a marriage that cannot be broken or splintered without terrible consequence to us all."

Frost wanted to pretend that the heroin didn't happen. I had seen this behavior for years—indulge the drug use and sweep it under the rug. The show must go on. I also don't like to be threatened, particularly with $50 million lawsuits, and I didn't like Frost placing his financial interests above all else.

"Maybe I'm emotionally overreacting to this," I told him, "but you're telling me I can't throw someone off the tour, slap his hand, send him home, or something . . . A whole fucking group of drug addicts blowing their fucking brains out . . . I see this as condoning fucking bullshit. We aren't the fucking Rolling Stones!"

I was actually pretty calm compared to Rocky, who had spoken to Frost's employee, a guy named Merton. He had told Rocky that he had bought the heroin for Carl. Now Rocky demanded that Carl admit it, but Carl refused.

"I had nothing to do with it," Carl said.

"Don't lie to me, man!"

"I'm not lying."

"Merton didn't say a word today that wasn't truthful. He gave the smack to you. You gave him a hundred dollars. Don't fuckin' deny it to me, Carl! Don't fucking deny it."

"Butthole—"

Carl said he flushed the heroin down the toilet.

"You didn't flush it down the toilet soon enough," Rocky said, "because Brian and Dennis both did it, and you bought it, Jack! And you own that! You can't be a man, Carl. You're a piece of shit!"

"Don't call me a piece of shit, Rocky, or I'll bury your ass."

I asked Carl why he was "covering Dennis's ass."

"Michael, I know all about drug abuse. I abuse drugs. I do not condone it. I mean, what do you want me to tell you, Michael? I flushed it down the toilet."

Rocky and Carl continued to argue until Carl finally said, "Fuck you!"

Rocky had heard enough. "Fuck me? Yeah?" He walked over to Carl and—*wham!*—struck him with a menacing right uppercut, lifting him off the floor and up against the wall, where he fell to the floor.

Someone yelled, "Look! One of the Beach Boys is on the ground."

Someone else said, "I've never seen anything like that before."

"I don't care," Rocky said. "He doesn't tell me to get fucked."

In about a minute, Carl regained consciousness and tried to say something, but Rocky told him, "The best thing you can do is be quiet."

David Frost, surveying his embattled investment, said, "I believe Rocky owes Carl a vast apology."

At the end of the meeting, Frost proposed that we all "make the necessary moral affidavits" to ensure that these drug incidents not recur. That way, he said, we can continue the tour and "plow on to glory."

I don't know what motivated Dennis and possibly Carl to give heroin to Brian. They both idolized their older brother. Maybe they thought that he would enjoy it, or maybe their judgment was clouded by their own drug use. Stan believed that Carl, frustrated by Brian's endless struggles, wanted Brian off the stage and even out of the band, and figured the heroin would do it. Whatever their motives, the spectacle, for me, was a reminder of how vulnerable Brian was, trusting those around him, even his own brothers, to his detriment.

Dennis remained on the tour, and we finished in Sydney, playing before 35,000 fans and plowing on to glory.

We had less traction in our recording efforts. We had not yet delivered any music to CBS Records and were summoned to Black Rock, the company's headquarters in New York. Joined by our tour manager, Jerry Schilling, we waited in the office of CBS Records president Walter Yetnikoff. When he finally walked in, bearded and rumpled, he leaned against his desk and said, "Gentlemen, I think I've been fucked."

We all looked at Jerry, and he looked at us. Then Brian raised his voice and said, "Mr. Yetnikoff, I've got some ideas for some songs, and I want to do them at the Criteria Studios in Miami."

"Okay," Yetnikoff said. "We'll be down there in two weeks."

Brian defused the crisis, and we traveled to Miami. But when Yetnikoff came down a couple of weeks later, the tracks that we had been working on were unusable. That's when we called back Bruce Johnston, and he ended up producing *L.A. (Light Album)*. It was mainly a collection of solo efforts, including a remake of a disco song, "Here Comes the Night," that Brian and I wrote for *Wild Honey*. As originally recorded, it was two minutes and forty seconds, but now it was nearly eleven minutes. By the time *L.A. (Light Album)* was released in March of 1979, the disco craze was over, and the LP charted at No. 100.

Stan, Rocky, and Steve were all eventually released, but it didn't really matter who was trying to save Brian. He had reached the point where he could no longer function. He was hospitalized on two occasions in 1978, including November, when he was admitted to the psychiatric ward at Brotman Memorial Hospital and diagnosed with schizophrenia and manic-depressive psychosis. He stayed for three months, was released for a month, and then readmitted a third time.

———

Though the Beach Boys were a family band, I made a point never to tell my parents about the chaos among their sons and nephews. They were living quietly in Cypress, attending occasional concerts, and enjoying our music. My mom, however, had complained about back pain for several years, and the doctors didn't know what was wrong. She finally had exploratory surgery, which revealed that cancer had wrapped around her spine. They suspected the cancer had begun in the ovaries. While she was undergoing chemotherapy and perhaps even before the diagnosis, I had encouraged my mom to visit the Hippocrates Health Institute, on the theory that a radical diet might help and certainly couldn't hurt. But that idea didn't have much support in the family. I do know that the cancer had spread too far to be reversed by Western medical science.

I can't say that my mom and I drew any closer over the years. While she took great pride in the Beach Boys, I know she was also disappointed in my personal life. Once my marriages broke up, it was hard for her to accept my children—as if the marriages themselves didn't happen. She shunned anything that violated her own principles or values. That's who she was. My eviction from the house, however, probably served me well by forcing me to become independent and to take my music career seriously. It was also my mom, more than anyone else, who taught me to love music and to use it as an emollient for long-held grudges or as a canopy under which all could stand.

My sister Marjorie cared for our mom in her final months, an enormous burden for someone who had not yet reached twenty. But Marjorie's love and compassion ensured that the end of our mom's life would be filled with peace. Mom died young, at sixty, and I'm sure that part of her regretted that she was not able to pursue her own musical ambitions. Hers was a life of sacrifice, for her husband and her children, and those sacrifices were expected in her era. But she knew that everything was changing. Born one year before American women could vote, she saw the greatest expansion of women's rights in history, and even as someone who was often uncomfortable with social change, she knew that future generations would not be constrained as she was.

"Since 'women's lib,' the young women see a chance to do important things on their own," she wrote in her memoir. "Not just living in the shadow of their husbands whom they feel are doing more worthwhile things than 'just' raising children.

"For me it was right. I have been rewarded many times for the years I spent home with my kids, but each woman should have her choice in a country like this . . . Old customs are hard to change, but thank God we live in a progressive country. Things are looking up for girls here. They can choose a career or marriage or both.

"Lucky girls to be born in this generation."

CHAPTER 18

THE OCEAN BLUE

My personal life remained chaotic, so much so that I have a single file that holds the divorce papers from one marriage and the wedding invitation from the next. (I may need to work on my filing system.)

I was good at falling in love but lousy at being in love.

But there were patterns amid the disarray, as women from different parts of the world or with different ethnicities continued to attract me. That sparked my interest in Sumako, who was of Korean descent and as beautiful as her name. She grew up with her mom in America and never met her dad, so I wrote a melancholy song about a young girl who wants to go with her mother to a place called "Sumahama" in search of her father. I really like the ballad, which appeared on our *L.A. (Light Album)* and included Japanese verses. Sumako and I were briefly engaged but did not marry.

I did, however, marry the next woman I dated seriously. In 1981, I bought a house in Incline Village, Nevada, which is next to Lake Tahoe. There I met Cathy Martinez, who was working at a leather goods store. Even though I was now forty years old, I was still not willing to allow a relationship to grow and develop and was still unwilling to live with a woman with whom I wasn't married. So Cathy and I did marry, and Wolfman Jack, who was now an ordained minister, officiated the wedding. Cathy and I had a son, Mike

Jr., in 1982, but my relationship with Cathy was never strong, and we split up in a couple of years.

The marriages contributed my financial problems in the early 1980s. I had never been good at handling my finances, allowing others to take care of them. That was a mistake, as I never really knew how much money I had coming in or going out, and I would eventually learn that I had a lawyer who was skimming money from me. By the early 1980s, I had taken out significant real estate loans to build out my property in Santa Barbara and to buy the house in Incline Village. I had also borrowed money to buy property in Kauai, Hawaii. The borrowing was excessive under any circumstances, but then I was clobbered when interest rates soared in the late 1970s and early '80s. I was involved in several new entertainment-related businesses, but execution and follow-up have never been my strengths either, and none of these businesses panned out. I lent $50,000 to a friend and never saw that again. The Beach Boys, meanwhile, were experiencing some of their leanest years, so I didn't have the income to cover my debts. I was also involved in several costly lawsuits in which the Beach Boys were aligned against my brother Stephen over various real estate deals. (Stephen was fired from the band in 1979 for unrelated reasons.) The lawsuits dragged on for years and severed my relationship with my brother, who in 1988 was convicted of embezzling more than $900,000 from the band. In 1996, Stephen successfully petitioned the court to have the conviction vacated, a fact I only learned in 2016.

As for me, I owed the IRS money but was in too deep of a hole. In September of 1983, I filed for Chapter 11 bankruptcy protection from my creditors, giving me time to sell some assets, rein in costs, and pay off my loans. It was necessary medicine, but it would take a couple of years before I met the right person who could get my personal life as well as my financial life in order.

In our own ways, all the Beach Boys were trying to put the pieces together. Carl, after the Australia trip, could have been lost for good, but he had never been a chronic drug abuser. He had been surrounded by some bad people in the late 1970s who wanted to take over the management of the band and tried to win Carl's loyalty by giving him cocaine and other goodies. Those guys were finally run off, and Carl, with the help of a few friends, pulled himself together in remarkably short order.

Carl was inscrutable to most of us. We all knew, however, that he took great pride in the music, and I'm certain that when he saw the video of any of his performances in Australia or New Zealand, he was embarrassed. He was also deeply spiritual, always searching for peace and equilibrium. Though he abandoned TM, he began practicing est (Erhard Seminars Training) in the middle of the 1970s and befriended its founder, Werner Erhard. He then discovered John-Roger, who started a new-age movement that held that the individual soul can be liberated through prayer and meditation. Carl started listening to Insight tapes, derived from John-Roger's seminars that tried to guide adherents to a path of joy and love, and Carl meditated to these tapes for two hours at a time and attended the seminars as well. He began going to the gym every day, which he hated, but it helped him with his back pain. He lost weight and in time quit smoking. Carl met his second wife, Gina Martin, daughter of Dean Martin, in the late 1970s (they married in 1987), and that too was a stabilizing force.

While the band might have been stagnating, I had lost none of my ambition for big performances, and I still believed we could rise to the occasion when the lights were brightest. I had an idea in 1980 for a Fourth of July concert on the Washington Mall, though I wanted to do more than just one show in one city. I envisioned a globe-girdling Independence Day bonanza. Start with a morning gig in Paris; then fly to London for another concert; then take the Concorde to Washington for a show on the mall; then fly next to South-

ern California; and finish off the day in Hawaii. I wanted to chase
the sun across the earth, play in five different time zones, and call it
the Endless Summer Celebration.

Chasing the sun . . . how cool would that be? The logistics, however, proved overwhelming, so we settled on one show in one city, on
the Washington Mall, and that was challenge enough. We wanted
the concert to be free, but a free concert isn't really free, as it takes
tens of thousands of dollars for the staging, security, and cleanup. To
help with the costs, we recruited corporate sponsors, which was rare
for music performers in the early 1980s but something we helped
pioneer. We wanted to include different types of bands to reflect the
breadth of American pop music—country-western, rhythm and
blues, soul—and we intended to invite Earth, Wind & Fire. But the
National Park Service told me no because black bands had caused
crowd-control problems in the past. I told the Park Service officials
that the Beach Boys had played with all kinds of bands all over the
world and had never had an incident, but they wouldn't change their
minds.

Our 1980 concert drew more than 500,000 fans, our largest
crowd ever, and we had more than 400,000 the following year at
the same locale. We didn't draw these numbers because we were
at the zenith of our popularity or riding a hit single. We had played
Fourth of July concerts in the past and never had crowds like that.
But there was something about America at this particular time that
made the Beach Boys and the nation's capital a very good fit.

All Americans were jarred in November of 1979, when Iran held
hostage our diplomats and citizens, their captors marching trium-
phantly in the street while calling the United States the Great Satan.
It was a daily humiliation, played out on television, with its own de-
spairing, trademark headline: "America Held Hostage." Oil prices
went through the roof, the Soviets invaded Afghanistan, and the
taunts escalated. We seemed to be powerless. Americans, I think,

wanted a reason to wave the flag and feel patriotic, and for many, celebrating the Fourth of July with the Beach Boys served that purpose. Writing patriotic songs never crossed our minds, but if we wrote songs that made people feel patriotic, or at least made people feel good about America, so much the better.

The Beach Boys had never endorsed a political candidate and had stayed clear of most political issues, and that remains true to this day. In 1979, however, the presidential campaign of George H. W. Bush contacted us about playing a fund raiser. At first our tour manager, Jerry Schilling, said no, because it was something we had never done. But the campaign contacted Jerry again, and this time Jerry came to us. I remembered that Bush had been America's de facto ambassador to China as well as the director of the CIA, and that intrigued me.

I wanted to play in a large Communist country. In 1978, we were supposed to go to the Soviet Union with Joan Baez and Santana and perform in Leningrad's Palace Square. Levi Strauss & Co., working with Bill Graham, had contributed $350,000 for the tour, and CBS was going to film it. We even had a promotional photo taken with Joan Baez and us holding a surfboard, half of it painted as an American flag, half painted as a Soviet flag. But the Soviets, for reasons they never disclosed, canceled the visit.

China fascinated me as well, and one of my best predictions— emboldened by a bit of weed and made to Richard Pryor, of all people—involves that country. Back in the mid-1960s, I used to watch Richard perform brilliantly at a comedy club in West Hollywood. After one show, we were hanging out and somehow got on the subject of China.

"Richard," I said, "in my opinion, one day the Chinese will be drinking Coca-Cola."

"No way, Love. That's the 'yellow peril,' man. They ain't going to be drinking no Coca-Cola in Red China."

"No," I said, "I believe they will someday."

It turned out that carbonation indeed trumps Communism, and the Chinese were drinking Cokes by 1979 (the Russians were drinking Pepsi as well). I lost touch with Richard but saw him backstage at the Academy Awards show in 1983. He was hosting it and had a hundred things to do, but he walked over to me and had something on his mind.

"Love," he said, "you were right about the Chinese and that Coca-Cola."

Damn good memory, I thought.

Well, if the Chinese liked Coke, I figured they would also like the Beach Boys—two of America's finest global brands. But we needed Bush's help if we were going to be the first American rock band to perform there, so I suggested that we meet with him. Bush was campaigning in Salt Lake City in November of 1979, when we had a concert there, so all of the guys got dressed up—even Dennis wore a sports coat—to meet him for brunch at our hotel.

Bush arrived in his sweat suit, having just gone for a jog. The meeting was supposed to last for a half hour, but he stayed for ninety minutes. He was a nice guy, smart, funny, interested in what we did. We asked him about running for president and traveling all over the country. A television was on, and when John Connally, the former Texas governor who was also running for president, appeared, Bush said, "I don't like that guy."

I asked him about China, and Bush thought it was possible. When he asked about our performing at one of his fund raisers, we said we couldn't do anything officially, but we'd be willing to do an event at a small venue that was *not* promoted as a political event; and if he showed up, he could come onstage, and we'd donate the proceeds to his campaign.

I thought this was a good compromise, and if he became president, he could help us get to China.

On March 9, 1980, we appeared at the Sunrise Theatre in Fort

Pierce, Florida. At one point, we told the crowd of about 1,000 people that we had a special guest, George Bush, and he came onstage and sang "Long Tall Texan" with us, and we chipped in our proceeds to his campaign.

George Bush lost, of course, to Ronald Reagan, but he became the vice president, and following the election, Bush contacted us again and invited the Beach Boys to the Inauguration. (We had connections to the Reagans as well, as Dennis had dated their daughter, Patti.) We accepted, played a Concert for Youth attended by 3,000 teens as part of the inaugural festivities, and were listed as honorary chairmen of one of the entertainment committees. All of which was great, but the vice president was unable to open any doors for us to China.

By 1980, Carl was easily the most ambitious and creative of my three cousins, which was seen on our *Keepin' the Summer Alive* album, released in March. Carl had two songs, written with Randy Bachman, that demonstrated his interest in funky R&B rock. The following year, Carl quit the Beach Boys while also releasing his first solo album, and it's often assumed that he left the band to pursue a solo career. But that wasn't the case. Carl wrote and recorded his album, *Carl Wilson*, while he was still with the Beach Boys, and he could have done the same for future recordings. He quit in part because he was fed up with all the drama and the discord and what he considered to be the band's lack of commitment to the music. He had also grown weary of his role as the caretaker of Brian's legacy, and he wanted to break free. As he wrote in the autobiographical song "Right Lane," which appeared on his solo album:

Always believed I could get what I wanted.
Even if it took a little while.

Always believed I could take care of my brother.
Do my thing with style . . .

I've been livin' in the right lane.
Seeing others cruise me by.
I've been tryin' to do the best thing.
Think I'll give the passin' lane a try.

My frustration with the band focused more on the destructive lifestyles, but I never wanted to leave the Beach Boys. I did, however, have the opportunity to branch out. In the late 1970s, seeking to work with performers who preferred meditation to drugs, I formed a band called Celebration. It featured guys who also played for the Beach Boys, including Ron Altbach, who was a superb concert pianist, and Charles Lloyd, the jazz saxophone and flute player.

I once heard him play the most amazing solo in the studio on the song "Feel Flows."

"Hey, Charles," I said. "You may not always be with us to play that. Can you write that down?"

"Shit, Love, you can't write that shit down."

In 1981, I was approached by Neil Bogart, the founder of Casablanca Records who had signed KISS, Donna Summer, and other artists, and he asked if I wanted to do a solo album for his new label, Boardwalk Records. I gave it a shot, recording ten songs, half of which were covers.

Neil, tragically, was diagnosed with lymphoma while we were recording, and he died in May of 1982, at thirty-nine. *Looking Back with Love* was released in October of 1981. I liked some of the songs, and the album might have had a chance commercially, but not with the label reeling from Neil's diagnosis. I also recorded more than a half-dozen songs in the late 1970s, including "Brian's Back" and

"Trisha," but didn't release them. To succeed, they would need to have the right producer or to be part of the right soundtrack, and no matter what I recorded, I would always be competing against my former self. Anything I do that is compared to "Good Vibrations" or "California Girls" will appear second-rate—which, of course, is the same bind the Beach Boys have been in for decades.

Regardless of these solo efforts, I prefer playing in a group, because I like the teamwork of a band. My favorite part of *Looking Back with Love* was that I hired a group of musicians who traveled with me to promote the album. I called the group the Endless Summer Beach Band, and we played cuts from the LP as well as Beach Boy hits.

One of the guys I hired was Jeff Foskett, a twenty-five-year-old singer and guitarist who then joined the Beach Boys when Carl quit. Though we were older, we still played outrageous pranks, and the guys soon pulled one on Jeff. For his birthday, they hired a black prostitute named Chocolate. But the prostitute was a transvestite, which Jeff discovered in due course. The evening came to a quick end, but for some time afterward, the guys asked him, "So, have you heard from Chocolate lately?"

Carl returned to the Beach Boys in May of 1982, just a year after he left. It was all about the music, and Carl could not achieve as a solo artist what he could achieve as part of the group. That was true for all of us. What made the Beach Boys special, in my opinion, were our layered harmonies, which could not be replicated by any individual. Carl returned with conditions, however. Assuming full control as band director, he insisted on more rehearsing and more focus while bringing in some new musicians and dismissing a few others. Even though Jeff Foskett was playing Carl's parts, Jeff stayed in the band because he was so good. Carl also revamped the set list that allowed us to play our favorite songs, including Bruce's "Disney Girls"; for Al, "Runaway" by Del Shannon; and Carl's cover of "I Can Hear Music." The improvement was dramatic.

Not improving, however, was Brian, who after his release from Brotman in 1979 moved into a house in Santa Monica Canyon and received daily assistance from several nurses. He performed with us on occasion, but he was probably at his nadir, often chain-smoking at the keyboard (he went through four packs a day), singing off-key, and mumbling through the lyrics. A couple of times he even gave the crowd the finger. At 310 pounds, he was now morbidly obese, but even that didn't reflect how dire things had become. In March of 1982, Brian was rushed to St. John's Hospital and Health Center in Santa Monica, where he was seen by Dr. Lee Baumel, a psychiatrist who had treated Brian before. In his report (which was part of a future legal proceeding), Dr. Baumel said that Brian had previously been diagnosed with schizophrenia, bipolar affective disorder, and organic brain syndrome. In recent months, however, Brian had suffered from "increasing decompensation marked by massive abuse of Cocaine, marked weight increase, affective lability, threatening harm to others, breaking objects and windows in his home and a man who could be dangerous to himself or others . . . [Brian has] obtained over $20,000 within the past 4 to 6 weeks for purchase of Cocaine. The patient has become threatening and abusive when money is not readily turned over to him for this purpose . . . The patient is not overtly suicidal. However, he dictated a letter to his attorney implying early death."

Brian was released after a few weeks.

Earlier in the year, when we were performing at Harrah's in Lake Tahoe, Brian received an unexpected visitor—Dr. Eugene Landy. They spoke for a while, and then in the summer, Landy called Jerry Schilling with an interesting message.

"I want to finish my painting," he said.

"What do you mean?" Jerry asked.

Landy explained that he wanted to work with Brian again. He met with Jerry and Carl and proposed that he revive his around-the-clock program for Brian—it would last twelve to eighteen months and cost $900,000.

Everyone knew it was a risk. Even though Brian and Marilyn were divorced, Marilyn had worked most closely with Landy the last time, so Jerry and Carl asked her opinion. "I guess he could help Brian again," she said, "if he doesn't get outrageous." They asked my opinion, and while I knew that Landy was unorthodox, egocentric, and a little bit dangerous, I said that he had previously had success with Brian in getting him active and making him more responsible in his dress and social activities.

We believed we had a choice to make: pay Landy the money to take over Brian's life or watch Brian die.

We hired Landy. Brian resisted, so on November 5, 1982, Carl, Al, and I met with Brian, and I handed him a letter and asked him to read it.

It said that the Beach Boys had fired him and that he couldn't be part of the band until he entered treatment with Landy.

Brian was stunned as well as hurt.

"What the fuck? What in the fuck am I going to do for money if you kick me out of the group?"

"Look," I said, "you got to lose weight or you're going to die. You're smoking cigarettes, and you weigh over three hundred pounds."

We argued for a while, but Brian eventually conceded. He knew we weren't changing our minds, and I believe he also recognized that this was the only move left. He was soon off to Hawaii to begin his recovery.

If Landy succeeded with Brian, we discussed possibly hiring him for Dennis, whose condition was of equal concern.

I don't know that Dennis ever recovered fully from the sale of

Brother Studio, which he had to sell when Carl liquidated his stake. It not only complicated Dennis's recording efforts but marked a point at which the two brothers began to diverge. Dennis's public blowouts had also become more conspicuous. In June of 1979, he went on a drinking binge during a week of concerts at the Universal Amphitheatre in Los Angeles. During one show, I was trying to get him to focus on his drums, and he stood on the riser, glared at me, kicked the set over, and jumped me. The brawl didn't last long, as security personnel, roadies, and other band members dragged us offstage and separated us. It would have been embarrassing under any circumstance, but all the more so because Aunt Audree was in the audience. An intermission followed, after which we all returned to the stage, though I stayed as far away from Dennis as possible. Afterward, we told him that he couldn't perform with us anymore until he dried out, and he was gone for the better part of a year. He made few contributions to our next album, *Keepin' Summer Alive* (March 1980).

After his second divorce with Karen Lamm, Dennis moved in with Christine McVie, the keyboard player and singer with Fleetwood Mac. Just a few years after the release of *Rumours*, she was one of the world's most successful recording artists, and she later said of Dennis: "Half of him was like a little boy, and the other half was insane." McVie was also part of a musical group, when it came to drugs, that "made the Rolling Stones look like a Salvation Army band," according to the *Daily Mail* in London. McVie later said she gave up drugs in 1984, but at the time, she and Dennis shared the same zeal for the good life.

Dennis rejoined the Beach Boys for a summer tour in Europe in 1980, and to celebrate the Beach Boys' twentieth anniversary, we were going to have a New Year's concert in Los Angeles. As part of the promotion, the five of us appeared on *Good Morning America* from ABC's studio in Los Angeles. With the camera running, Dennis, either hungover or stoned, slumped over on the couch, and when

Joan Lunden asked him the opening question, he buried his head in his arms and almost fell to the ground. After Carl spoke, and with Dennis lying on his side, Lunden asked, "Dennis, how are you doing? Are we keeping you awake?" And Dennis, after reaching for Carl's mic, mumbled, "Is this ABC?"

Live television with the Beach Boys.

My own skirmishes with Dennis were relatively minor compared to those he had with my brothers, particularly Stan. When Stan was Brian's bodyguard, he was constantly fighting Dennis's effort to give Brian drugs. One day in an elevator, Stan turned to Dennis and said, "Look it, if you keep trying to give Brian cocaine, I'm going to kick your ass."

Dennis put his finger in Stan's face and said, "I swear to God on your mother's grave, I didn't give him cocaine."

Stan was very close to our mom, who had just died, and took exception to the reference. Moreover, Stan's love for Brian is unconditional, and he decided that the next time Dennis gave Brian drugs, he would exact his revenge.

The opportunity came after Dennis had parted ways with McVie in 1981 and was renting a house on Wavecrest Avenue in Venice Beach.

Stan had heard that Dennis had gotten Brian a huge stash of cocaine. Though he was no longer Brian's bodyguard, he thought it was time to teach Dennis a terrible lesson, and who better to join him than Brian's other former bodyguard, Rocky? The two of them went to Dennis's house in Venice and knocked on his front door. When Dennis didn't let them in, they returned, and at about one A.M., knocked the door down. From there, they pursued Dennis through three rooms of the house, dragged him by the hair, pushed him through a glass window, kicked him and punched him in the forehead, and crashed his head into the wooden footboard of the bed. Stan also picked up the telephone and whacked Dennis in the face.

All these years later, Stan says of the incident, "Rocky had to pull me off after a while because he didn't want me to kill him by accident."

Dennis suffered a broken nose, numerous lacerations, and a suspected concussion. He pressed charges against both men, and they were given fines and placed on six months' probation.

Nothing Dennis did deserved such a brutal beatdown; but Stan was convinced that Dennis was trying to destroy Brian, and this was Stan's bare-knuckle message to stop.

The setbacks for Dennis continued. His most prized possession was a sixty-two-foot sailboat that he had bought in 1975. He rebuilt the vessel, which had a golden pelican on the bow, and docked it at Marina del Rey. He called it *Harmony*. Dennis marveled at how the teakwood's true beauty emerged only when it was wet: you could see the grain, but the boat had to be in action to fully appreciate the texture. Dennis could relate. *Harmony* was his escape from his troubles onshore and also a place where he lived for stretches of time. For someone who cared nothing about material possessions, it was the one thing that he truly loved. And then he lost it, in 1981, when he could no longer afford the payments, and a bank auctioned it off for a fraction of its worth.

Over the years, we went to great lengths to try to find Brian proper medical treatment. Dennis's needs may have been even greater. But while Brian was at times a reluctant patient, he was willing to go to the hospital, consult with psychiatrists, and at least make an effort at rehabilitation. Dennis either rejected outreach attempts or, once he did go to a hospital or detox center, never made a serious commitment. Dennis once came to visit his mom, and when he was there he called Jerry Schilling and said he needed to go to the hospital. Jerry picked him up in his Jaguar, and as they were heading to Century City Hospital, Dennis lowered the glove compartment mirror and began snorting heroin.

"I have to do this," Dennis said. "I hope you don't mind."

"Whatever it takes to get you to the hospital," Jerry said.

The benefit of the hospitalization was short-lived.

I once got a call that Dennis was wasted on the streets of Venice. I drove down and found him and brought him to his house. I don't recall much about the conversation, but I know that he made promises about getting help, and before I left, he said, "Let's meditate."

For all of my battles with Dennis, he made the single most important call in my life—from Paris, to tell me that Maharishi wanted to meet us. I was always grateful for that and could only regret that our lives had diverged so dramatically.

"Yes," I told him, "let's meditate."

For a while, Dennis was living with his teenage daughter from his first marriage, Jennifer, and one day she brought home a friend. Her name was Shawn.

Shawn Love.

She told Dennis that I was her father.

In the 1960s, after my divorce from Frannie, I had a brief affair with a young secretary from the Ukraine. Some months after the affair ended, she named me in a paternity suit, even though she was living with a fireman at the time. It occurred to me that I had more income than the fireman, and I was skeptical of the paternity claim. This was before DNA could establish such things, so we went to court and took blood tests and lie-detector exams. The judge ruled that the "plaintiff has not established by a preponderance of the evidence that the defendant is the father of the minor plaintiff." The mother agreed not to appeal in exchange for $9,500, which I paid as a lesson learned, and I assumed that chapter was closed.

But it wasn't. The child used my surname, so she grew up as Shawn Marie Love. I knew nothing of her whereabouts until someone told me that she had moved in with Dennis. Shawn was now seventeen, and Dennis was thirty-six. Their son, Gage, was born in October of 1982, and Shawn and Dennis were married the following July.

While Dennis was always reckless, the damage was usually to himself. This was different. Broke and broken, he was in no position to care for himself or a teenage bride, let alone a newborn. Some believe he slept with Shawn as revenge against me, a final act of sexual conquest with a tinge of incest for good measure. Perhaps Dennis saw it as a defiant stroke against all three Love brothers. Or maybe it was just Dennis being Dennis: he met an attractive teenage girl, and he couldn't help himself.

Shawn and Dennis separated a couple months after they married. I never spoke to Dennis or Shawn about why they got together, nor did I take it personally. We all knew the relationship was doomed, and the one who would pay the steepest price was baby Gage.*

Dennis continued to make occasional appearances with us, including at the Pacific Amphitheatre in Costa Mesa, California, on August 3, 1983. By then, the scruffy, chiseled rock magnet was gone. Dennis had shaved his beard and cut his hair. He was thicker around the middle, his face puffy. He had had two throat surgeries to repair his vocal cords, and his singing voice, which once had a pleasing roughness, was hoarse. But when he stepped from behind the drums, he still loved the moment as he spoke to 15,000 fans.

"Folks," he said, "if you knew what it felt like to be up here singing and playing, you know, in front of you. The joy it brings to us. Thank you so much." He sang "You Are So Beautiful," sweating at the end, and above the cheers, he waved to the crowd and said, "God bless you, the Beach Boys."

In a final effort to get him straightened out, Carl, Al, and I told

---

* Shawn experienced liver failure and died in 2001, and I was never in touch with Gage.

Dennis that he was cut off from all touring revenue until he entered a treatment program. In September, when Brother Records inadvertently sent him a check, our lawyer asked him to return it.

On December 28, just after he turned thirty-nine, Dennis was visiting friends on a boat at Marina del Rey, where the *Harmony* had once docked. Despite his heavy drinking of vodka the night before and that morning, Dennis dove into the fifty-eight-degree waters in search of trinkets or keepsakes. He found a silver frame that once held a wedding photo of him and Karen Lamm, which he had tossed off the *Harmony* after they divorced. On his final dive, he came to within two feet of the surface and then sank back down. His friends, uncertain if Dennis was playing a joke, waited a while longer. When they were about to dive down themselves, they spotted the Harbor Patrol, which searched the waters for about thirty minutes before finding the body. Dennis was pronounced dead three minutes later. The coroner's report said that Dennis was legally drunk, with an alcohol level of .26, and he had traces of Valium and cocaine in his tissues.

When I heard the news, I felt sadness, particularly for his mom, but not surprise. I always thought Dennis had a death wish. Maybe it was frustrated ambition or guilt over Charles Manson or the addictions that he could never shake. Maybe our destinies are set at an early age. In the Wilson household, Brian was the genius, Carl the angel, and Dennis the rebel. And Dennis could never break that mold. Aunt Audree used to say that even as a boy, all "Denny" ever wanted was Murry's attention. Dennis did improve his ties with his father in the last few years of Murry's life, talking with him more on the phone, reliving the old days, and forging some kind of connection.

Gage was Dennis's fifth child, so perhaps there was closure to Dennis's relationship with Murry Gage Wilson.

Dennis's family received permission from President Reagan to bury him at sea, and his short life came full circle. When we were kids and someone was driving us to the beach, Dennis would push his upper body through the window, strain his neck as far as it would go, shade his eyes, and peer westward. He wanted to be first to glimpse the ocean.

Sail on, sailor.

CHAPTER 19

AMERICA'S BAND

To the Beach Boys, Dennis's death was a reminder that we were not indestructible. To many of our fans, he was the performer who embodied the spirit of the band, the one true surfer who could still elicit screams from teenage girls. But we never considered shutting down the act. From our earliest days, we had been a rotating cast of performers. None of us was irreplaceable, and Dennis's involvement had been erratic for years. One of the tragedies of his death was that in his final year, he saw the beginning of another unlikely Beach Boy resurgence but passed away before its fruition.

Back in April of 1983, I was in a hotel room in the small Canadian town of Moncton, fast asleep, when an early-morning call jostled me awake. I picked up the phone, and the guy on the other end introduced himself as a DJ from Cleveland.

"I just wanted to know your reaction to James Watt's comments."

"My reaction? To what?"

The DJ said that Watt, the U.S. secretary of the interior, had decided that the Beach Boys could not perform on the Washington Mall this year on the Fourth of July. The band, Watt claimed, played "hard rock," which "attracted the wrong element," and the nation's capital was not going to "encourage drug abuse and alcoholism as was done in years past."

The DJ wanted to know if I had a comment.

I was still half asleep, but, yes, I had a comment.

I knew about Watt. I knew that he wanted to drill for oil in federal waters off the California coast, including Santa Barbara, and he wanted millions of acres of undeveloped land to be opened for drilling. He was on the cover of *Newsweek* with the headline "Digging Up the Last Frontier?" He was all about drilling, not protecting; I figured he would drill in his grandmother's backyard if he could. I also thought it was idiotic that Watt would associate the Beach Boys with anything un-American. I couldn't resist.

"Someone ought to drill his ass for brains," I told the DJ, who fortunately did not repeat it on air.

The controversy, I thought, would be over by day's end: just another stupid comment by a gaffe-prone cabinet officer. How wrong I was. Moncton is about 260 miles from Bangor, Maine—pretty much in the middle of nowhere—but we found ourselves in a jammed press conference before our performance. Carl tactfully defended the honor of the Beach Boys.

"Beach Boys' music represents joy of life and joy of living," he said. "I don't think [Watt's comment] applies to us."

Phone calls came in from all over the United States and abroad, and after the press conference, I was told that I had one more call. The White House was on the line.

The White House?

I went to a private room and picked up the line.

"Mike, this is Nancy Reagan."

"Hello, Mrs. Reagan."

After Watt's remarks had hit the papers, the president and first lady had brought him into the White House for a scolding, and Watt then told the press that he didn't realize "the Beach Boys were fans of the Reagans."

That prompted the call from Nancy Reagan, whom I had met at the Inauguration, but we weren't exactly on a first-name basis.

"I want to apologize for what James Watt said," she told me.

"What was that?"

"He said that the Beach Boys were fans of the Reagans. No, no, no. I told him, 'Ronnie and I were fans of the Beach Boys.'"

"I appreciate that," I said, "but it's not the first time and won't be the last time that he said something that wasn't quite correct."

"Well, Ronnie and I would like to invite you to the White House."

Publicity is a tricky thing. A rock group can hire the industry's most creative marketing team, spend hundreds of thousands of dollars on a lavish campaign, and end up with nothing. Or a band can spend a whole year on a single album, release it, and see it disappear into the void. At other times, publicity—the good kind—just falls from the heavens. That's what happened to us in 1983. We hadn't had a hit song in seven years, and what little media coverage we did receive usually focused on our status as an "oldies band," the disarray within the group, or Brian's health. But James Watt delivered the Dis Heard 'Round the World, and we were now deluged with support. DJs, editorial writers, music critics, and even politicians rallied to our defense. We received invitations from all over the country to play on the Fourth of July, including one from Senator Robert Dole to perform in his home state of Kansas. "The group seems to be available," he said.

It didn't hurt that our adversary was the most unpopular figure in the Reagan administration, an easily recognizable bureaucrat with a shiny pate and an uncanny ability to offend. He once described Indian reservations as "failures in socialism." *U.S. News and World Report*, marveling at his job security, published the headline: "Watt: A Light That Never Dims."

Trying to make amends, Watt reversed direction and asked the Beach Boys to play on the Mall on the Fourth. But he had already invited Wayne Newton, the dark-haired crooner known as "Mr. Las Vegas" and a heavy contributor to the Republican Party. We declined the offer. As I told reporters, "We're not going to do anything that would upstage another entertainer."

We did, however, accept the invitation to the White House. We were in Washington on June 12 for a previously planned concert at RFK Stadium, so we also performed on the South Lawn of the White House for a fund raiser on behalf of the Special Olympics. President Reagan thanked us with a quip: "We were looking forward to seeing them on the Fourth of July. I'm glad they got here earlier."

We were able to renew our acquaintance with Vice President Bush, who happened to be celebrating his fifty-ninth birthday. He invited us to his residence at the U.S. Naval Observatory, where we had a little party for him in the backyard and sang "Happy Birthday" to him. As a tribute to his wife, he joined us in singing "Barbara Ann," but he kept flubbing the opening lines.

Dennis told him, "Don't give up your day job."

The president owned a ranch in Santa Barbara County, and he did so much work there it became known as the "Western White House." When I chatted with Mrs. Reagan, I told her we were practically neighbors. "Whenever you go to the Western White House, the helicopters go right by my place, so I know when you're shopping." She laughed, I think.

The nice showing at our Fourth of July concert that year in Atlantic City surely benefited from the controversy. An estimated 200,000 people gathered on the beach and packed the Boardwalk; they climbed on the rooftops and sat on windowsills and lounged on a couple of hundred boats just offshore. It rained on Wayne Newton in Washington, and things only got worse for James Watt. In September, in an effort to mock affirmative action, he said of a government panel, "I have a black, a woman, two Jews, and a cripple." He resigned soon after.

In 1984, we were invited back to Washington for the Fourth, and we accepted knowing full well that the brouhaha had turned this into a cause célèbre—what the *Washington Post* would call "the rebirth of rock-and-roll music on the Mall." Fans came from all over the country and began assembling in the predawn hours, and the Monument grounds had so many people that the performers could reach the stage only by chopper; that included the Hawaiian Tropic Girls, who danced onstage as part of a sponsorship with the tanning lotion company.

If everything about the day was improbable, the biggest surprise was Brian. He had played with us last August and a few times since then, so we knew that Landy's extreme therapy in diet and exercise was taking effect. But by July 4, 1984, in the nineteen months that he'd been with Landy, Brian's physical transformation seemed nothing short of a miracle. He had lost about a hundred pounds, his belt size shrinking from a 55 to a 36. His hair and beard were neatly trimmed, and he spoke clearly.

"Brian, you look fantastic," I told him.

"Yeah, Landy's got me swimming a mile a day."

Prior to the performance, we had a media gathering under a tent, and Brian seemed eager to resume his career as a Beach Boy. "We're a very small family, but the family that sings together stays together," he said. "We love each other. We don't see each other very often, but when we do, we really get down and sing good . . . It's a time where we need to be strong and face up to our responsibilities, and come through. We started out as babies and grew up to be the Beach Boys. It's a very dramatic story, you know?"

It was sunny, hot, and hazy, and helicopters from various news stations circled above. We were able to recruit some of the world's top headliners, and I invited the entertainers who reflected my original goal of representing the broad sweep of pop music. (My pitch: first I teased them that they needed to get off their lazy asses, then I said the event would be all about celebrating our country's values of freedom and liberty.) The opening act, America, had both the iconic songs ("Ventura Highway," "A Horse with No Name") and the very *name* to begin the day. Next came the R&B group the O'Jays—to hell with any possible prohibitions on black artists. Dressed in white pants and white shirts, they sang "For the Love of Money," spinning and grooving across the stage. They were followed by country-western star Hank Williams Jr., wearing an unbuttoned red, white, and blue shirt, who took center stage and announced, "I just got back from Japan, and I don't want Japan to outsing the biggest crowd in musical history!" (Hank's time onstage was productive; he met a Hawaiian Tropic Girl whom he would later marry.)

Wolfman Jack was the emcee. His paeans to rock music, in that distinctive gravelly voice, had made him the most famous DJ in America, enhanced all the more by his star turn in *American Graffiti*, in which he played, flawlessly, himself. His introduction of us boomed out over the masses. "Ladies and gentlemen!" he cried. "What you've been waiting for! The legendary Beach Boys!"

Brian, waving to the crowd, a completely new man, wore a white short-sleeve shirt and white shorts. Al, who seemingly hadn't aged, wore a short-sleeve orange shirt and bright yellow pants. Bruce—tan, lean, and crisp—wore a blue shirt and very short white shorts. And then there was Carl, who always took pride in his well-groomed beard and professional attire. Despite the heat, he wore a long blue suit with a white dress shirt, the collar buttoned. I was clean shaven, having gotten rid of my beard two years ago, and opted for a patriotic ensemble—a red, white, and blue button-up shirt, white pants, and a blue beret. We were not exactly color coordinated, but for a group of guys ranging in age from forty-three (me) to thirty-seven (Carl), we appeared more physically fit than we had in years.

We walked on the stage, and more than half a million people, across this long, triangular expanse of land, stood and began cheering. (It's always nice to get a standing ovation before you play a single note.) American flags waved. A few beach balls were batted in the air.

A "Surfin' USA" sign was held aloft. It was a blur of jubilant humanity. We always wanted our concerts to be celebrations, but this was completely different—gleeful defiance of James Watt, yes, but also an expression of gratitude for what the Beach Boys had meant to the country.

I stepped to the microphone: "Thank you, all you undesirable elements!"

We played our set list, including "California Girls," "Help Me, Rhonda," and "Little Deuce Coupe." I was dripping with sweat by the second song but had never felt more energized, and was thrilled to see Brian pounding the keys of a white piano, in sync with everyone else. Landy, on the other hand, was an awkward presence, standing on the side of the stage, wearing an orange shirt emblazoned with the phrase "The Perfect Nut."

We needed an exquisite "surfer girl," and I believe we found one in La Toya Jackson, who had distinguished herself separate and apart from her famous brothers. I introduced La Toya as a "member of the first family of music," and she was radiant in a white jumpsuit, gold belt, and gold necklace. I then brought out Julio Iglesias, the Spanish heartthrob who was at the height of his American popularity and had flown all night on his private jet from South Shore Lake Tahoe to join us onstage. The Beach Boys had a good thing going with Julio. He had invited us to sing background on "The Air that I Breathe," which was included on his 1984 album *1100 Bel Air Place*, and that record had put him on the map in English-speaking markets. (Julio gave each Beach Boy a Patek Philippe luxury watch as a token of his appreciation.)

Now on this steamy Independence Day, Julio was joining us onstage. He hadn't quite mastered the words to "Surfer Girl"—the lyrics were on a crumpled piece of paper that he held in his hand—but it didn't matter. He had his left arm around La Toya, and his was the sexiest version of that song I've ever heard.

Other headliners included Three Dog Night and the Moody

Blues, but the biggest name was Ringo Starr. The irony of a Brit helping America celebrate the Fourth was not lost on Ringo. "Everyone say, 'Happy Birthday,'" he told a reporter backstage. "Sorry we lost." He came out onstage to a raucous ovation, now a middle-aged mop-top with a shaggy beard and shades, and took his place behind the drums. Some of our speakers temporarily went down, so the crowd could hear our instruments but not our voices. We had to play something, and with Ringo sitting there holding his sticks, Carl asked the band, "Do you know any Beatle songs?"

They did. They played "Day Tripper," which the crowd loved, even without the vocals. When the speakers were revived, Ringo played twenty minutes with us, including "Back in the U.S.S.R."

Toward the end, Carl took the mic: "We'd like to dedicate this next song from all of us to all of you, and today, I want to include my brother Dennis. Dennis Wilson just really was a great guy, and we think about him a lot these days." And above the cheers, we launched into the mystical opening of "Good Vibrations."

Our return to the Washington Mall had been a triumph, and we could have returned to our hotel rooms, enjoyed the fireworks, and called it a day. But why do one show in one day if two shows were possible? We took a chopper over to National Airport, piled into a Boeing 727 jet (which Braniff chartered for us), and headed for Miami.

Not everyone could join us. The three singers from America (Dewey Bunnell, Dan Peek, and Gerry Beckley) had already agreed to play in Casper, Wyoming, so I suggested that they do what I was still hoping the Beach Boys would do: follow the sun. After their thirty-minute set on the Mall, they took a chopper to National Airport, flew 1,800 miles to Casper, and performed again at nine P.M. Beckley then flew 1,000 miles from Casper to Van Nuys, California, got a ride to his home in Sherman Oaks, and was in bed before midnight. "How was your day?" his wife asked.

Most of us went to Miami, including Ringo and his wife, the actress Barbara Bach. The flight was uneventful, except for the end. As we began our descent, Ringo was in the cockpit doing a live radio interview. Our concert would be on Miami Beach, and the pilot somehow got approval to fly very low right over the crowd—I mean, very low. We could practically see the coolers, and Ringo, doing the interview, spoke to the fans directly (at least to those with radios). By the time we landed, we were running late, so we got into a bus and were led down a highway by a phalanx of police motorcycles while patrol cars barricaded highway exits. Once we reached Lummus Park on the beach, we were escorted by a dozen tow trucks, whose job was to remove the many parked cars in our path. It was like something out of sci-fi movie. We reached the stage, only forty minutes past our scheduled nine P.M. start time, and did our entire concert again before more than 100,000 fans.

We made news everywhere. That evening, *Nightline* did a story on our Washington concert, interviewing fans who had traveled from St. Paul, Minnesota; Davenport, Iowa; and Houston. Ted Koppel introduced the segment by saying that "thousands of people showed up on Washington's Mall for the re-emergence of the Beach Boys." (The official estimate was actually 565,000, but who's counting?) Film footage was used for a TV special titled *D.C. Beach Party*, and an album was recorded called *Fourth of July: A Rockin' Celebration of America*.

The whole experience, one of the great publicity coups in the history of rock music, cemented our reputation as "America's Band."

The day's events, however, still raised some concerns, for we knew that despite the outward signs of good health, Brian wasn't entirely right. Wherever he walked, he was surrounded by Landy's handlers, and if anyone got too close to him, they intervened. We knew he was receiving medication, but at times he seemed completely detached. We wanted to keep the band intact the entire day, but instead of flying with us to Miami, Brian took another plane to London, with Landy, so they could do studio work on what would become the

Beach Boys' next album. It appeared that Landy was not just Brian's therapist but also his business and recording partner. This was not what he was getting paid to do. With Brian's apparent improvement, I thought we might get together to write music again, and I assumed it was just a matter of time before Landy moved on. But that wasn't happening. Landy had already extended his time beyond the agreed-upon eighteen months, and now no one was sure what his intentions were.

The success of the Fourth led us to an even larger effort the following year, in which we did Independence Day concerts in Philadelphia and Washington, joined by the likes of Jimmy Page, Christopher Cross, Joan Jett, the Oak Ridge Boys, and the histrionic television personality Mr. T, who played the drums for us. The day began at Washington's Union Station, where the band rode a train up to Philadelphia. It was hot in the cars, and Mr. T was so rambunctious that he knocked out a window. After our performance in Philadelphia, we boarded a jet back to Washington, and Mr. T wouldn't stop talking. Finally, Carl—who never raised his voice—turned to him and said, "Shut the fuck up." The concerts themselves made it into the Guinness World Records for the most people that a single band had ever played for in one day—an estimated 1 million in Philadelphia and 750,000 in Washington. Of course, if Guinness kept such records, the Beach Boys might also be recognized for performing in front of the fewest number of people in one day. A long career keeps you grounded.

We may have been America's band, but that didn't mean fans were rushing out to buy our records, and we weren't producing many new ones to begin with. In May of 1985, CBS Records released *The*

Beach Boys, which included "Getcha Back," written by Terry Melcher and me. Released as a single, it recaptured the traditional Beach Boy harmonies, including Brian's falsetto, and was supported by a campy video of an earnest but awkward young man trying to win the love of his childhood sweetheart. The song charted at No. 26, which was lower than I was hoping for but it did reach No. 1 on the adult contemporary charts and stayed there for a solid month. *The Beach Boys*, produced by Steve Levine (who'd produced hits by Culture Club), relied heavily on digital recording and included covers of Boy George and Stevie Wonder; it stalled out at No. 52. (It would be our last album for CBS.)

The LP was another example of our group competing against our former selves—our records, regardless of quality, did not meet the expectations or interests of our fans. Just three months before the release of *The Beach Boys*, David Lee Roth covered "California Girls," now twenty years old, in conjunction with a wildly bizarre but entertaining video. (Imagine *The Twilight Zone* entering the Playboy mansion, with David Lee Roth as tour guide.) Carl as well as Christopher Cross provided prominent backup vocals, making it sound like the Beach Boys were on the recording. It reached No. 3 (just like the original), while the video became a cult classic.

With little success in the recording studio, we had to redouble our efforts as a touring band. Even when we were at our peak in the 1960s, I believed in doing smaller markets to maximize revenues, regardless of the long bus rides in the middle of the night. But by the 1980s, I started working with our managers (including Elliott Lott, Tom Hulett, and John Meglen) to do "doubleheaders"—two shows in two different cities in one day. We had done that over the years on the Fourth, but those were special events. I wanted to do them on a more regular basis. It was all about scheduling and routing.

On one summer day, we woke up in Los Angeles and flew to Chico, California, in the northern part of the state, and did a show.

Then we got on a plane and flew to Park City, Utah, for a second show, and then we boarded our flight again and went to Denver, where we would perform the next day. Four cities in one day. Not exactly chasing the sun, but I liked the tempo.

At other times, we combined humanitarian needs with patriotism. On the morning of July 4, 1986, we performed at Farm Aid II in Austin, Texas, to raise money for family farmers. We then flew a commercial flight 1,500 miles—coach—to New York City, where we were picked up by a bus and hustled to the New York Harbor. It was all part of Liberty Weekend, in which the Statue of Liberty, under restoration for two years, was unveiled by President Reagan. Some of the country's top entertainers performed over three days, and we had the honor of doing a show at night on board the battleship USS *Iowa*, where a stage had been built on top of the gun turrets. Al's song, "Lady Lynda," which was based on a Bach melody and composed for his first wife, was rewritten as "Lady Liberty." Throughout our performance on the ship, we pointed our speakers toward the adjacent USS *John F. Kennedy* and, as the saying goes, blew 'em out of the water. We didn't realize that President Reagan was giving a speech on that ship at that very moment. The Secret Service called our ship and asked us to stop, which of course we did, and when the president concluded his remarks, we finished our concert.

Even before our designation as "America's Band," we had corporate sponsorships. Companies assumed that we weren't going to embarrass them onstage with profanity or stupidity, and the sponsorships gave us another revenue stream. But I wanted to go beyond the typical relationship, in which a company wires you a check and then slaps its logo on the stage. I thought a sponsorship could work both ways—the company gets exposure, but so does the band. So in 1978, we had an agreement with Sunkist Orange Soda, in which the company paid us $1.5 million to use "Good Vibrations" in its commercials and to put the phrase on its packaging and in-store displays. While I loved the campaign, I didn't necessarily love the product. After our last concert in which we were promoting Sunkist, we had a reception, and a company executive approached me.

"Well, Mike," he said. "I have to know. Do you drink Sunkist?"

I'm not one to filter my thoughts. "If I was driving my Range Rover through the Mojave Desert and it broke down, I would first drain my radiator fluid and drink that before I had a Sunkist."

That pretty much ended the conversation, but the company had no complaints. The "Good Vibrations" campaign helped launch the brand, and it became America's No. 1 orange soda in 1980.

We also had a productive relationship with Chevrolet, which, among other deals, sponsored the Heartbeat of America Beach Boy Tour in 1988. At the time, we were grossing about $75,000 a show. Chevrolet guaranteed us $100,000. Anything over $100,000, Chevrolet kept. Anything under, it lost. Each side promoted the tour, and both brands reinforced the other. I don't know what the ultimate financials were, but I think Chevrolet was happy, and so were we. As part of the deal, the company gave each of the guys a free Corvette.

In a perfect world, our music alone would have carried the day, but we were a group of middle-aged white guys trying to survive in a young man's game. So we performed after college football games or Major League Baseball games. We invited cheerleaders from local colleges to join us onstage. We used props, including cars, surfboards, yacht flags, and palm trees. We had beach parties. We tried to make each concert not just a show but an event. Carl and Al didn't favor all of these efforts, but they understood we had to broaden our appeal and reach new fans.

Perhaps the biggest boon was our three cameos on *Full House* in the late 1980s, invited by Uncle Jesse himself, John Stamos. John grew up in Orange County, not far from my parents, and he used to ride his bike past their house, catching a glimpse of the gold and platinum records on the wall. He met Jeff Foskett in the early 1980s, and Jeff introduced him to us. By then John had already appeared in *General Hospital*, but he could also play the drums, so we asked him to play at some of our gigs, including the Fourth of July concerts in 1985. And why not? He was young, popular, good-looking—kind of like us twenty years before. He was also a damn good drummer (and he told Jimmy Page in what key to play "Barbara Ann").

More than anything, John was a fan of the Beach Boys. He wanted to introduce our music to kids of the day, and the best way to do that was through television. So in 1986, even before *Full House*, John invited us to appear on the show *You Again?* with John and Jack Klugman. Not long after that came the cameos on *Full House*, which was a Top 10 show, and when the sweet Olsen girls appeared on *The Arsenio Hall Show* and were asked who their favorite music group was, they of course said the Beach Boys. In one of our *Full House* episodes, John's character sang "Forever," a great way to revive Dennis's best song, and John performed it as well on our album *Summer in Paradise* in 1992.

I became good friends with the creator of *Full House*, Jeff Franklin, who over the years has invited the Beach Boys to perform at his house for charity events and has had me stay over as a guest. What's interesting is that Jeff bought the very lot on Cielo Drive where the Manson murders occurred. Jeff's current home is magnificent, and he uses it to raise money for the needy, to host music jams, and to bring together friends and family. A great city is always reinventing itself, and in this case, thanks to Jeff, a site that was once associated with infamy is now a place of splendor, warmth, and life.

At any rate, *Full House* may have seemed trivial in the moment, but its impact on our legacy cannot be overstated. Not only was it popular at the time, but it's popular to this day, living on through cable TV and DVDs. I'm amazed how often young people come up to me and say they first saw the Beach Boys when they bought the *Full House* box set (all 192 episodes).

The Beach Boys have long had two groups of fans: the music aficionados, who favored our more progressive work from the mid-1960s on, and the masses, who favored our hits. The aficionados ripped the Beach Boys for all these sponsorship and marketing efforts. Overt commercial initiatives, according to this critique, diluted the artistic integrity of our music. Actually, we were just ahead of our time, as the ties between performing artists and corporate sponsors have grown far beyond anything I ever imagined. Just visit South by Southwest in Austin, Texas, the world's largest music festival, and you'll see a long list of major companies, from Mazda to McDonald's, underwriting the event as a whole or artists individually. This too may disappoint the purists, but singers and songwriters have never had it easy, and they are grateful for any support that comes their way. Even Bob Dylan did a Super Bowl commercial for Chrysler. I hope they gave him a new car.

CHAPTER 20

MY HOUSE IN ORDER

On March 15, 1987, my forty-sixth birthday, I was invited to be a celebrity judge for a bikini contest in Waikiki, where they take their bikini contests seriously. Television crews and photographers from Australia, Japan, and beyond were on hand, and about eighty contestants gave them plenty to shoot. We had a chance to interview the young ladies, and I was impressed by a striking dark-haired woman who was not only beautiful but exceptionally articulate. Her name was Jacquelyne, from Chicago, where she was a registered nurse, currently working for an immunologist. She was in Waikiki on vacation and was a bit embarrassed by the contest: she was just taking it easy on the beach, and the organizers approached her and persuaded her to enter, though she didn't realize it'd be such a media circus. She didn't know who I was or what I did. I was just another judge.

I couldn't blame the organizers for their interest in Jacquelyne, who turned plenty of heads and was clearly the smartest. The contest, however, was rigged so a local girl would win, and Jacquelyne was knocked out at No. 4. Afterward, I had my picture taken with the winner, but it was Jacquelyne I wanted to see. When I caught her attention (she was now dressed), she came over. With her fiancé. They were on this trip attempting to rekindle their relationship after canceling their wedding. Her boyfriend, Gary, knew who I was, and he said the next time I was in Chicago, they'd be glad to show me around.

He seemed like a nice guy, but, truth be told, I really didn't want to hang out with Gary. When he left to use the restroom, I told Jacquelyne, "I'd love to connect with you when I come to Chicago."

"Oh, sure," she said. "Give Gary and me a call."

"I was kind of hoping it'd just be you."

Jacquelyne said that she was flattered but she was still "technically" engaged and didn't know where the relationship was going.

Gary returned and told Jacquelyne to give me their phone number. Jacquelyne had recently moved out of their place, and the only number she had was her work phone, so she gave me her office number. *Excellent!*

Just a few weeks later, I had to go to Chicago for a promotional event, so I called Jacquelyne before I got on my flight. She told me that her relationship had ended with Gary, but she was working twelve hours that day and couldn't commit to seeing me. I told her that I'd call her later in the day, and when I did, I asked her if she wanted to come by my hotel for a drink.

"If your intentions are to get me into your hotel room," she said, "save me the trip, because it's not going to happen. But if you want to have a pleasant conversation in the lobby, then maybe I can come by and have a glass of wine."

"I can live with that," I said.

So we had that drink, and then I walked her to her car and asked her to call me when she got home so I knew she was safe. She did, and we talked until four A.M.

I had spent time with plenty of women, but I knew Jacquelyne was different—a combination of intelligence and spirituality as well as beauty, and a life story that made her sensitive to those around her. The product of a biracial marriage, she had experienced racism while never quite fitting in with any particular group. Her Italian father was a good man but a heavy drinker, and when Jacquelyne was young and attending a Catholic elementary school, her mother had some health issues. So Jacquelyne lived with two nuns at a convent, sleeping on a thin mattress and covered by a wool blanket, but feeling safe and protected. In the summer the family would go to Mississippi, where her mother was from, and attend a Baptist church. That was a different type of religiosity, but also quite powerful. Jacquelyne recognized her spiritual core at a young age: she was the first altar girl in Chicago, she considered becoming a nun, and she knew that her love of God was part of her nature.

For someone like myself, who found Eastern spirituality as an anchor, I found her devotion inspiring. I also believe she understood my own unorthodox life because hers followed no convention as well. She helped pay her own way through college with various management jobs and pursued a career in health care and administration but was equally skilled in design and choreography. Over the years, she had held positions in retail sales and management, as a fashion consultant, and as a Chicago Bears cheerleader for one season.

She was also sassy. When we were vacationing in Maui, a friend who came to visit asked her, "What island are you from?"

"Chicago," she said.

We carried on a long-distance relationship for a number of months, in which Jacquelyne would leave work at noon on Saturday, rush to the airport, fly to whatever city we were in, then fly back Monday for her job at noon. Between my previous wives and girlfriends, she was hardly the first woman to join me on the road, and because of that, most everyone in the group kept their distance from Jacquelyne—except for one person, Aunt Audree, who was traveling with us. She made Jacquelyne feel part of the family immediately, asking about her background, telling her about the history of the Beach Boys, and swapping stories about friends and travel.

Jacquelyne had been on tour with us for several weekends and had observed the rather itinerant and lonely experience of a traveling rock band when she said to me, "Everyone's unhappy." I asked her why she thought so. "They're all away from their family," she said.

I knew, from the earliest days, that I was happy with Jacquelyne and that the connection, both spiritual and intellectual, would be lasting. Whether it was with friends, girlfriends, or even wives, I had encouraged others to try to meditate. Many did, but few stuck with it. So I decided I would stop asking and just let others do their own thing while I did my thing. That meant, for me, meditating twice a day for one hour at a time, but Jacquelyne came to resent that I would not share this part of my life with her. So I talked about meditation from a scientific perspective—what the research had told us about the positive impact on the brain—and that immediately appealed to someone whose career was in the sciences. She said she wanted to learn TM, not as a way to connect with me but to understand the phenomenon. I offered to pay for it, but she refused—this was going to be hers, not mine.

We were together for about six months when Jacquelyne was initiated. She was in her twenties, and TM did not contradict her own faith but reinforced it. She had less time for church. She didn't visit the nuns anymore. She realized that the demands of adulthood had distanced herself from her spiritual core, but TM allowed her to reconnect to it.

It was a strong foundation for our relationship, and it has grown over time, as Jacquelyne has embraced Catholic and Hindu traditions equally. "I don't think there has to be some sort of title to your particular form of spirituality," she later said. "There is a unity of consciousness, and I find there is something in most religions to embrace, respect, and love."

In September of 1987, I asked Jacquelyne to live with me in Los Angeles, which would mean leaving her family, friends, and job in Chicago. I knew that Jacquelyne liked to organize and manage and was not a sit-at-home type of person. I had started a nonprofit foundation and asked if she would manage it. She said she knew nothing about nonprofits but was willing to learn, so she quit her job, packed up, and moved west.

By now, I was living in a four-bedroom house in Pacific Palisades while still owning the Santa Barbara compound, the home in Incline Village, and properties in Maui and Kauai. I owned a lot of houses, but they were more like expensive shelters than actual homes. I was single and nomadic and didn't give my living quarters much attention. In Pacific Palisades, I didn't have a refrigerator or a bedroom set and was basically living out of suitcases. One of the first things Jacquelyne did was drive my Jaguar to a home supply store, fill it with pots and pans, and start equipping my kitchen.

Getting my houses in running order wasn't my biggest problem. My finances were still in shambles. I was always about the big picture, not the details, and just as I let others handle the business side of the Beach Boys, I did the same with my own finances, entrusting lawyers, accountants, and others to take care of things. I was responsible for the homes and cars, but my biggest sin had more to do with neglect than profligacy. I couldn't tell you what I had in assets, liabilities, or income, didn't know what interest rates I was paying, and was unaware of how much I owed the IRS. Jacquelyne, on the other hand, loved numbers and had managed medical offices, so she knew her way around a balance sheet. She began inspecting mine, started asking questions, and realized I had no system for paying bills, monitoring my loans, or tracking my investments and income. Far worse, over time she discovered that I had representatives who were skimming money off my earnings from the Beach Boys. It's the same story you hear all the time about artists, athletes, and celebrities. We live in our little bubbles, easy targets, blissfully unaware of the world around us. Most of us don't like confrontation until we have no other choice. In my case, I fired those who were stealing from me, but I was as angry at myself as with them. I got a new team of lawyers, accountants, and advisors and set up automatic payment and savings plans and set up my first retirement account. I emerged from bankruptcy proceedings in 1988, but in truth I was still not receiving what I was owed. That would take a few more years.

What I wanted in my personal life was what I had as a child—the family experience, the togetherness of the holidays. The Loves were an imperfect family, but the emotions were perfect. Now in my forties, I had a family that was fragmented. I had six children from four different wives who didn't know each other, and while I tried to spend quality time with each of my kids and supported them financially, I was not a significant figure in any of their lives. I wasn't good at birthday cards or Christmas gifts or phone calls. Summer later said that when she was growing up, it was tough walking through the mall and hearing a Beach Boy song. She heard me more there than in person.

Jacquelyne was very close to her family, and I knew that family— her family, my family, whatever family she was part of—was always going to be her first priority. That meant bringing my kids together, and I saw this in our first year, in December, when we were on tour in Asia. Jacquelyne came with us, and by then she had met my kids, and as Christmas neared and we were winding down the tour in Japan, Jacquelyne started asking me when we were going to get them gifts. We'd have to do it here, and now, because there wouldn't be enough time when we got back home.

One morning in our hotel room, frustrated by my procrastination, Jacquelyne flung a pillow at me. "This is our last day!" she scolded. "We won't have time to shop when we get home." So off we went to the stores, which were well stocked for most of our needs, except for Christian's gift. He had become an avid surfer, so we had to order him a surfboard by phone.

I don't think he was expecting anything. "Whoa, Dad," he said when he received it. "What's wrong with you? Have you lost your mind?"

I assured him I hadn't.

A round the same time, a very different family matter, something far more traumatic, brought Jacquelyne and me closer together.

After Jacquelyne had moved to Los Angeles, her younger brother Christopher, just twenty-one years old, was diagnosed with a brain tumor. Jacquelyne flew home to visit and found him in his childhood bedroom, sleeping peacefully. Christopher loved soft fur—when he was a kid, his mom had given him a pelt, which he slept with—so Jacquelyne took off a fur coat I had given her and draped it over her brother and kissed him. He awoke. "Sissy, I was just having a dream about you," he whispered. "You were pregnant and were going to have this golden-haired baby, and you were going to nickname him Lovey."

Jacquelyne assumed he was taking some really good meds, because she was not trying to get pregnant.

Jacquelyne had two other younger siblings, and the house was under great stress. Their father had lost his job, their mother was getting laid off, and creditors were calling. But Christopher assured Jacquelyne that he would be okay.

Shortly thereafter, we went to Asia, and when we returned in December, we flew to Chicago and saw Christopher in the hospital a couple days before his surgery. He was in remarkable spirits. He had a cherubic face, with brown curly hair and long eyelashes, and when he smiled, his large amber eyes smiled also.

He told me he wanted to be a pilot and had applied to aviation school. Then he said, "I always wanted to play the saxophone. Do you play?"

"Yeah," I said. "I don't know if you'd call it playing, but I play it."

"When do you think I should start?"

"Start now," I told him. "I'll buy you a saxophone for Christmas."

I left before the surgery, but Jacquelyne stayed and was with her brother when he awoke from the operation. He was alert and funny, and a full recovery was expected. Jacquelyne had to return home but assured him she'd be back soon.

"Go on, Sissy, you have to live your life," he said.

Back in Pacific Palisades, we were hosting friends who had come in for a Ravi Shankar performance. The morning after and with a houseful of guests, Jacquelyne received a call from her family. Christopher had gone into a coma.

While I tended to our visitors, Jacquelyne stayed in the bedroom and called Deepak Chopra, whom she had met through me when she moved to Los Angeles. Deepak, trained as a medical doctor, is now one of the world's most famous spiritual advisors and an advocate of alternative medicine as a path toward personal transformation. When Jacquelyne met him, he was relatively unknown but was a leading spokesman for TM and, at the time, was working closely with Maharishi to expand Ayurvedic health practices in America. Deepak and Jacquelyne became friends quickly—she appeared in one of his promotional videos—and he was, for her, a source of strength and wisdom.

Deepak told her that Christopher's first seventy-two hours in a coma would be his most important, but, he said, "You have to prepare for the fact that this might be the time that your brother makes his transition, and perhaps his job here is done."

Jacquelyne flew to Chicago and saw Christopher in the hospital, but he was almost another person, pale and greenish. She called

Deepak, who reminded her that we are all here in a dance with one another. "One dance might end and another one might begin," he said, "but we're all here, and once our dance card is full, we go on to a different kind of dance."

Jacquelyne asked him if she could tell Christopher her mantra, and Deepak said yes. "Whisper it to him and hold his hand," he said, "and he can hear you. He's very aware that you are there. He's more concerned for you than you are for him."

"That's impossible."

"It is possible," he said. "The spirit cares for those that it leaves behind."

After about a week, Jacquelyne flew to Washington to meet me at a meditation course with Deepak. This was our first Christmas together, and I knew how much she loved the season, so I had someone bring a Christmas tree to our hotel room. She had a sleepless night on December 23, and then the following morning, the morning of Christmas Eve, her dad called and said that Christopher's heart had given out an hour ago.

"I already knew that," Jacquelyne told him.

Christopher had been in a coma for twelve days, and during that time, his prophecy came true: Jacquelyne learned that she was pregnant.

With so much trauma, we were worried about Jacquelyne's two other siblings, Steven, eighteen, and Raven, nine. Their mother was so distraught that she continued washing Christopher's clothes and laying them out on his bed. Raven was calling Jacquelyne every day, shaken and desperate. Finally I said, "Send them out here."

"Here" was in New York, where on January 20, 1988, the Beach Boys were going to be inducted into the Rock and Roll Hall of Fame at a dinner at the Waldorf Astoria. Jacquelyne's aunt took the kids to the airport and put them on a plane, and they stayed with us in New York in the days leading up to the event. They didn't have enough winter clothes, so we took them shopping, showed them the sights, and invited them to a special dinner with a living legend.

I had first met Muhammad Ali back in the 1960s when he was still Cassius Clay, and I had always admired him, particularly his stance against the Vietnam War. I was friends with Ali's business manager, Gene Kilroy, who told me a story about Ali that I never forgot. Back in the sixties, Gene was with Ali when they were to meet Martin Luther King Jr., but King's entourage told Gene he couldn't enter the room because he's white.

Ali told them, "Then I'm leaving too."

Gene was admitted.

Through Gene I was able to reconnect with Ali, and I asked him to sit at our table for the Hall of Fame ceremony. A few nights before, Jacquelyne and I, with Steven and Raven, met Ali at an Indian restaurant with his wife, Yolanda, and Muhammad's children.

The former heavyweight champion, now forty-six, sat with Raven on his lap, pulling quarters out of her ear. Steven took a shine to one of his daughters. He wanted to ask her out but, raised in a traditional household, knew he had to ask her father's permission. He approached Ali cautiously.

"Sir, may I ask a question?"

Ali growled at him.

Steven tried again. "I don't want to disturb your dinner, sir, but I just have one question."

Ali pushed back from the table and barked, "What you got to ask me!"

Steven seemed to shrink in front of us. "I was just hoping to take your daughter to the movies tomorrow night."

Ali sneered, then relaxed, smiled, and replied sweetly, "Okay, what time you gettin' her and what time you comin' back?"

The next night, I met Ali with a couple friends at a sports bar. We were just hanging out when I looked up at a TV screen and saw, incredibly, a replay of one of the classic Ali-Frazier fights from the 1970s.

"Hey," I said. "What do you think of that?"

Ali looked at the screen for a long moment.

"Well, Mike, look at that guy dancing. I wonder what it's like to be him."

I smiled and gave him a tap on the arm. "You're still the greatest, champ."

I thought it made perfect sense to have Ali sit with us at the Hall of Fame ceremony, which in my view was a tribute to the era in which we were all young and making our mark. That Ali was a Black Muslim also gave the crowd some much-needed diversity. His presence was one of the highlights of a night that didn't go as I expected.

Elton John introduced Brian, Carl, Al, and me to receive the award. Brian, reading off a sheet of paper, spoke of our early days and our love of music, and Carl thanked everyone on behalf of Dennis. Then I spoke. I had something specific in mind. I thought that the music industry, instead of coming together at a spiffy hotel to give its members prestigious awards, would do better if it had a concert for a charity. There were plenty of examples—Live Aid for the Ethiopian famine, Farm Aid, the Concert for Bangladesh. If the Rock and Roll Hall of Fame meant anything, I thought, it should mean pooling our abilities and doing something positive.

I got off on the right foot. "You heard from my cousin Brian the reason we started making music, and the reason that keeps us going. And it sounds corny, but you can hear it in the harmonies . . . and the reason that people like the Beach Boys is that we love harmony . . . and we love all people too."

I tried to challenge the audience. "What I want to see is that this one room recognizes that there is one earth here, and I want us to do something fantastic with all this talent, and all this wonderful spirit and soul . . ."

But I got offtrack and began to ramble, and sounded angry, which I probably was. (I didn't have time to meditate that day, so I was even more on edge.) I had been in the business for twenty-seven years, and in that room, I knew, were any number of agents, lawyers, and record company executives who were more intent on dividing artists than supporting them. A united music industry could accomplish a great deal, but we couldn't even be united on our Hall of Fame night. The Beatles were inducted as well, but Paul McCartney didn't attend because of his conflicts with his former bandmates and with Yoko as well. I called them out by name. I also mentioned Diana Ross as a star who didn't show up. I had also wanted to challenge the Rolling Stones to a Battle of the Bands competition by satellite on two different continents. I thought it would be a great fund raiser. But I admit, I too closely associated the Stones with the drugs and all that represents, and sometimes I have a hard time keeping my emotions in check. I botched my line and said Mick Jagger "has always been chickenshit to get onstage with the Beach Boys."

The switchblade . . . and the butterfly.

The ballroom band started to play, and I was escorted offstage as reporters raced for the exits to call in my remarks. You don't take a shot at the rock and roll aristocracy with impunity. My comments were reckless, but my biggest regret was that my appeal for collective action was poorly expressed and then buried under an avalanche of criticism.

Nonetheless, I kept the evening in perspective. Steven and Raven were with us, and they traveled with Jacquelyne and me to Los Angeles and then to Hawaii and stayed with us for another month, and in light of the pain that they had been through, and because I knew that there is life and there is death and there was a Christmas saxophone that I was never able to deliver, it was easy enough for me to dismiss my misguided remarks.

My trip to Rishikesh, India, in 1968, deepened my connections to Maharishi.

By 1970, we had all grown musically (Carl and Dennis standing, Al and Bruce in back).

Throughout the years, I've sported many different looks
reflective of the changing times.

Ricky Fataar, far left, and Blondie Chaplin, both from South Africa,
added diversity to the group in the early 1970s.

My brother Stan, whose
loyalty to Brian has always
been unconditional, was
Brian's bodyguard for several
years in the 1970s.

When it comes to cars, I'm an unabashed Anglophile.
Here I am with my 1948 MG TC.

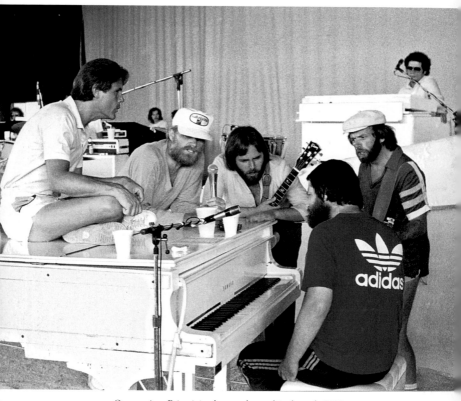

On occasion, Brian joined us on the road in the early 1980s.

Eugene Landy was reenlisted to treat Brian; the results were mixed.

Though I'm an introvert, performing on stage allowed me to develop different aspects of my personality.

In 1984, our Fourth of July concert on the Washington Mall culminated one of the greatest publicity coups in music history.

In 1983, after James Watt said the Beach Boys attracted "the wrong element," President and Nancy Reagan invited us to the White House for a few laughs and, more important, to honor the Special Olympics.

My friendship with President Bush led to the creation of STARServ, a
nonprofit inspiring students K–12 to engage in community service.

We received this award for "Kokomo," which was No. 1 in 1988, twenty-two years after "Good Vibrations," the longest interim between two No. 1 songs by the same group.

At the Hall of Fame induction ceremony in 1988, I had a chance to hang out with heroes and friends alike, in this case Little Richard, Bob Dylan, and George Harrison.

Jacquelyne and I met in 1987 and married in 1994, and she brought love and stability into my life.

Ambha showed her musical talents at a young age.

I named baby Brian after his famous second cousin, and my son also dazzled on stage.

The fiftieth anniversary tour had plenty of stress, but when it was just the Beach Boys themselves—Al, Brian, David Marks, me, and Bruce Johnston—we had a blast.

Five decades later, the Beach Boys are playing more concerts than ever before, here with band director Scott Totten, left, and old-friend John Stamos, who sometimes joins us.

I learned TM in 1967, and Eastern spirituality has been a big part of my life ever since.

This meditative gathering included my lawyer Mike Flynn, front left, who won my copyright suit against Brian

Here's a sweet moment backstage with Mike Jr. and me in 1987.

My two oldest daughters, Teresa and Melinda, as beautiful young women.

My other three daughters, Hayleigh, Ambha, and Summer, artistically gifted in distinctive ways.

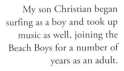

My family and I learned about the miracle of
the monarch on this trip to Mexico, and when
a butterfly fell with frozen wings, Ambha
picked it up and breathed life into it.

My son Christian began
surfing as a boy and took up
music as well, joining the
Beach Boys for a number of
years as an adult.

From my house in Incline Village, the serenity of dawn across Lake Tahoe.

I actually saw Mick Jagger backstage at the Hall of Fame ceremony, and I told him the reason I said what I said was that I thought a fund-raising competition between the two bands via satellite would raise a helluva lot of money.

He thought about it for a moment. "That's good," he said.

Several months after the Hall of Fame dinner, Terry Melcher asked me to come to his studio in Santa Monica and help him on a song that would be used for a movie. I always thought Terry was one of the industry's better producers, and at the studio, he played me a verse that had been written by John Phillips, of the Mamas and the Papas, and Scott McKenzie, who wrote "San Francisco (Be Sure to Wear Flowers in Your Hair)." I thought the verse had a nice melody but lacked a groove. Terry told me the movie was about a bartender who quits his job in New York and moves to Jamaica, where he meets his love interest. It didn't sound like *Gone with the Wind*, but there was enough story for a good pop song.

I wrote the lyrics at the studio. To complement the breezy melody, I thought the chorus needed a good hook and the same R&B feel that was in "Smokey Joe's Café," and Jamaica allowed me to use the same travelogue approach that I employed for "Surfin' Safari," "Surfin' USA," and "California Girls."

Aruba, Jamaica, oh I want to take ya.
Bermuda, Bahama, come on, pretty mama.
Key Largo, Montego, baby why don't we go, Jamaica

Al Jardine hated "pretty mama," but lyrics work best, in my view, when they resonate with the largest number of people, and that was more likely when the words had several meanings. "Come on, pretty mama," could be a child tugging at his mom or an old geezer with his wife getting into their Winnebago for the winter. I liked the first verse by Phillips and McKenzie, but one of their lines was:

Off the Florida Keys, there's a place called Kokomo.
That's where you used to go, to get away from it all.

I thought the past tense (*used to go*) sounded like a guy lamenting his misspent youth, so I changed it to:

That's where ya want to go.

The second verse was Chuck Berry–esque in its rhyme and alliteration.

We'll put out to sea, and we'll perfect our chemistry.
And by and by we'll defy a little bit of gravity.
Afternoon delight, cocktails and moonlit nights.
That dreamy look in your eye, give me a tropical contact high.
Way down in Kokomo.

"Contact high" was slang that described someone who inhaled marijuana smoke passively, but it could also mean making contact romantically—another double entendre. When the Muppets covered the song in 1993, Kermit sang "tropical island sky," puppet frogs being averse to suggestive lyrics.

Some days after I wrote the words, I got a message that Terry needed to speak with me, so I called him from a pay phone. He was recording the demo, but he didn't have the paper on which I wrote the lyrics. So there on the phone, with cars passing by, I started singing, "Aruba, Jamaica, oh I want to take ya . . ."

For the actual recording, Van Dyke Parks, the lyricist from the *Smile* era, played the accordion, and Carl's voice—*Ooh, I wanna take you down to Kokomo!*—evoked the lush tone he used in "Good Vibrations." I never had a booming voice, but in recent years, it had become thinner, noticeable toward the end of long concerts. But in "Kokomo," Terry used a wide-open mic and an ambient reverb to give my voice a breathy effect that fit the romantic mood of the track.

We did a video, performed outside the Grand Floridian Resort at Walt Disney World in Florida, with John Stamos on congas and me "playing" the saxophone. (It was actually my friend Joel Peskin who played the part, nailing it in one or two takes.) The song was written for the movie *Cocktail*, starring Tom Cruise and Elisabeth Shue, and when the director, Roger Donaldson, first heard "Kokomo," he told us, "This is your best song since 'Good Vibrations.'"

Really?

"Kokomo" would be on the album *Cocktail*, an eclectic group of numbers that included Bobby McFerrin's "Don't Worry, Be Happy" and Little Richard's "Tutti-Frutti." But Elektra Records released "Kokomo" two weeks before the album. The label didn't do much to promote it, so we hired our own promoters and tried to get it airplay, first on adult contemporary stations and then contemporary hit radio. And it caught on. It was just one of those catchy songs that when people heard it, they wanted to hear it again, and it got exposure from some unlikely places. Some of our fans recall that we performed it on *Full House*, at the halftime in a college football game at the Los Angeles Coliseum. Less well remembered, but still raising the song's visibility, was a performance on the daytime soap opera *One Life to Live*, in which we played "Kokomo" as part of a story line about a high school reunion. Then there was the movie *Cocktail*, which became an unexpected hit.

We thought Brian would be joining us on the vocals, but when Terry made the request through Landy, Landy said that Brian would come down to the studio only if he, Landy, were an executive producer on the song. Terry said no. Landy was supposed to be Brian's therapist, not his producer; and the last thing Terry needed was some cloying musical wannabe coproducing our song. Landy later told Brian that the Beach Boys had maneuvered to keep him off the song. Brian believed this fabrication for years and said, in a 1998 deposition, how badly "hurt" he was by our snub.

We hadn't snubbed anyone—Brian was victimized by his own therapist turned producer—but I'm sure that part of his "hurt" stemmed from what happened with the song.

"Kokomo" climbed the charts to No. 1, twenty-two years after "Good Vibrations," the longest interim between two No. 1 songs by the same group. "Kokomo" became the most successful song in the history of the Beach Boys, selling a remarkable 7 million records at a time when 45s had already begun their slide into oblivion. The "Kokomo" video was also No. 1 on VH1. But it was the other stuff that got to me. We started receiving bags of mail from schoolchildren and teachers describing how the song spurred their interest in geography, with some students even poring over maps in search of this enchanted island.

Far be it from me to tell them it didn't exist. I was invited to Newark to speak to the Boys and Girls Club, and the kids sang an absolutely beautiful version of the song.

If they believed in a place called Kokomo, then so did I.

CHAPTER 21

THE GLUE THAT
BINDS US

rian's absence from "Kokomo" alarmed those who had propa-
gated the myth that the Beach Boys were a one-man band, the
rest of us sticking around to fill in the harmonies. Those claims
drove Carl nuts. "We're not just a pimple on Brian's ass," he would say.
"Kokomo" did have the classic Beach Boy sound (the vocal arrangement, the harmonies, the bass line), and I give Terry the credit, as
he gave "Kokomo" those Brian-like touches, which made all the difference.

And where was Brian? Neither his brothers nor his mother nor I
nor most anyone else could reach him. Landy controlled all access
and appeared to control Brian's career as well. Brian's self-appointed
savior had given interviews in which he discussed his work with Brian
on his first solo album, to be released one month before "Kokomo."
Landy was credited on six songs, and he suggested that if the album
were a hit, it would launch Brian's solo career, which would mean the
demise of the Beach Boys. Why would anyone bother with us, his
thinking apparently went, when the only Beach Boy who mattered
was recording and performing on his own?

I finally saw Landy for what he was. His goal was not to drive a wedge between Brian and us. It was to destroy us. Then he would be the sole custodian of Brian's career and legacy.

Brian's solo album cost $1 million to produce and received a great deal of publicity, including a lengthy profile in *Rolling Stone* about Brian's "long journey back from madness." It was the Brian's Back campaign but with a different name. (Curiously, in the *Rolling Stone* issue with Brian, the cover featured Tom Cruise promoting his new movie, *Cocktail*.) But Brian's album plateaued at No. 54, and after "Kokomo" became a hit, Landy claimed that the Beach Boys had prevented Brian from being part of the recording. Actually, we wanted Brian to be part of the group, and the funny thing is, Brian wanted that as well.

While the Beach Boys had long been divided, as a corporate entity we have always been connected. After Dennis died, we had four partners and board members—Brian, Carl, Al, and me. Our corporate name remained Brother Records, which owns our masters, the trademark name "The Beach Boys," and the catalogs of two music publishing companies that hold much of the music we created after the Sea of Tunes was sold. The board was never efficient, but at least we tried to meet on a regular basis. That ended after Landy assumed control of Brian's life. On August 8, 1988, however, just after the release of Brian's solo album but prior to "Kokomo," a board meeting was called at the Ritz-Carlton in Chicago. (We were on a tour of the Midwest.) We had not met in nineteen months. All directors were present as well as our business manager and lawyers.

I had other things on my mind. Two days earlier, Jacquelyne had given birth, and we had an agreement regarding the name: If the baby was a girl, Jacquelyne would name her, but I had the honors if the baby were a boy. Just as Christopher had predicted, the newborn was a golden-haired boy, so the responsibility was mine. I couldn't decide, and Jacquelyne, two days after the fact, needed to call him *something.*

Now I was in Chicago, at a board meeting, and I had to focus on the agenda, which included an urgent request from Landy. Despite his apparent desire to see the Beach Boys implode, he very much needed our help.

In February, California's attorney general had filed charges against him for gross negligence in his dual role as Brian's therapist and business partner. He was also charged with prescribing drugs for Brian, which he was not licensed to do because he was not an MD. Separately, Landy was charged with prescribing drugs for a female patient and forcing her to have sex with him. His career was on the line, despite his role in saving Brian.

"Brian was pretty fucked up," Landy told us as we sat around a conference table. "He was almost dead. Now, he's alive, and he's well, and he is functioning, and it appears to be that way because of Dr. Landy."*

Yes, that's Landy referring to himself in the third person.

Brian, who at 180 pounds looked as good as I'd see him in years, agreed. "A miracle has occurred obviously, because I used to look really a little puffed out of shape. My head didn't work. I was flipping the bone to the audience. I was crazy. I was a crazy person. I was poisoned. I was sick."

Rolling Stone quoted Brian saying that he suspected his family— his mother, Carl, and me—of filing the charges against Landy. Now at the meeting, Carl and I told them that we had nothing to do with the inquiry. Al, however, had answered questions from the AG's office, which Landy found "astounding." In his eyes, Al was a traitor.

Landy said we could all remedy this injustice against him if we wrote a letter to the AG attesting to Brian's recovery. "That is a

---

* All quotes are from a transcript of the meeting.

very simple statement," he said, "and you don't need a special meeting to do it."

Landy left the room so Brian was allowed to speak freely. In *Rolling Stone*, the psychiatrist who dispensed Brian his lithium, his sedatives, and his antidepressants said of Brian: "He's become, shall we say, a well-adjusted adolescent."

But not much was adolescent about Brian at the meeting in Chicago. He was alert, clear, and ambitious, and he began by talking about the future of the band.

"I don't think there is any glue that you can see that bonds us all together," he said. "You know, there is no real glue between us except through music or spiritual things. That is the only real sense of being together as one thing, but there is no real glue." The music, however, was still powerful. Wondering aloud about what were life's "magical connections," he said, "It's music obviously, you know, and sex, of course, but I choose music over sex because I was born that way."

Brian looked at me as he discussed what came next for the Beach Boys. "Now where we go from here depends on myself as a leader and, of course, Michael's ego and talent and abilities to create things. The greatest things we ever did was when I worked with Michael on something . . . I mean, it boils down to do we want to go for the gusto and do something really heavy, or do we want to kind of slide and do a new wave kind of thing? It's all up to us. It's in our hands."

Brian said he wanted to "shake off the past," both musically and personally, and acknowledged the difficulty in that. "But one of my secrets is that I am able to do that and live in the now, and I am glad to say that I have got [my solo album] happening on the charts, and who knows, it might even go to No. 1, but that is a shot in the arm for the Beach Boys too."

Brian reiterated his goal: "Like I said, when Mike and I work, and we don't work too often, and we don't talk too often, but when we do work, something magical occurs."

He said the disappointment of our last album in 1985 should not deter us. "We worked very hard on it, and nothing came about. Easy enough to turn to the past and say, 'Well, fuck it, the other one didn't go, why fuckin' try again.' That is easy to say. Too easy to be negative, you know. When I say we can look forward with courage, we record something that could be a milestone or a good memory for everybody, you know, put it in a memory bank, a subconscious winner or a hit, you know what I mean?"

We were all a little bit stunned. For the past three years, my lawyer had been exchanging letters with Brian's lawyer and with Landy to establish an agreement for Brian and me to write songs together. Nothing ever happened (though we later discovered that Landy thwarted all agreements). Now Brian appeared to be telling us that he wanted to rejoin the band.

"It would be great," Carl said.

"That is great," I echoed.

Brian said there really was a glue: "an invisible glue, or, the sound of our voices or the music that we make is what glues it all together, and nobody should be afraid of that. No one should fear the creative process. It's awesome, yes, but nobody should be afraid of it. And I want to do my job as a producer and an artist too."

He wanted to start immediately. "Don't fear the future," he said, "because the future is really now."

There were questions about studio time and producers and other logistics, and Brian had a realization.

"You know, Murry Wilson would have been great about this time," he said. "That's what we need. 'Get in the fuckin' studio, and get your asses in there.'"

It was clear who was serving that role today.

I said to Brian, "Gene is kind of like Murry Wilson to you, isn't he?"

"He is a spark plug, yes he is."

"He makes you do things that sometimes you wouldn't ordinarily do, like lose a hundred pounds."

"He did it to me, all right," Brian said. "Well, you know, he had no choice. He was saving my life. He was very uptight. He was very nervous and generally grumpy for a couple years, because he was working with a blob like me—do you know what poison means?"

"Yes."

"Have you ever heard of poisoned blood?" Brian asked. "That is what we are all made of."

I thought to myself, That's a problem. We're not all made of "poisoned blood," but Landy had convinced Brian of that, and Brian believed that the only way to purify himself was through his attachment to Landy. That bond had catapulted Landy's role in Brian's life into something big and smarmy. In *Rolling Stone*, Landy referred to himself as "Eugene Wilson Landy," while claiming that Brian identified himself as "Brian Landy Wilson."

Al asked Brian if he saw a distinction between Landy as his doctor and Landy as his producer.

"I can't," Brian said. "It's real tough for me. It's hard . . . Something very substantial has happened since I went with Gene . . . I don't think I would be able to swing anything without [him]. I mean, I could. I mean, I could force myself to get back into the old mode of thinking and get the production ego going and the juices flowing like that, but I can't concede to that. I mean, I don't see the possibility."

Both Al and Carl explicitly rejected Landy's qualifications as a producer, while Carl added that Landy was "abusive and unkind to people."

"To who?" Brian asked.

"To us," Carl said. "He has been very cruel to your family."

"To you?"

"Yes. He has shut us off for five years."

"What do you mean, 'shut you off'? How do you figure?"

"What do you mean, Brian? Long time, no see. No communication."

"You mean, shut me off from you?"

"Yes. It's very cruel, Brian."

Brian was living in a cocoon but barely seemed to know it. Al told him he didn't even have Brian's own phone number.

"What do you mean?" Brian asked. "I have a phone number."

"It was Dr. Landy's exchange. I have never been given a number, and I have never been offered a number."

"Are you kidding?" Brian asked in amazement. "All you have to do is call his office."

Al rolled his eyes. "Wonderful feeling."

Brian complained that we all had the "the negative shining on me through Gene."

"No," Carl said. "On Gene, not on you."

"On Gene through me."

"No, no, no," Carl insisted. "We all love you very much. We are very proud of you. Extremely so, and I say that our so-called estrangement . . . is completely contrived. It's not our choosing whatsoever, but it is Eugene Landy's choosing."

I redirected the conversation to writing music with Brian. I was open to Gene being part of the process, because he gave Brian structure, but I did not want him rewriting my lyrics. I told Brian it was obvious he was capable of going into a studio and producing, but referring to his solo album, I said, "I think I could have done a better job with you than Gene or anybody else on concepts and lyrics, because that is where I relate, and that is how I think."

Brian: "Why not give Dr. Landy the option to re-fine-tune the lyrics?"

"Fuck that."

I told Brian that there was no reason for someone else to intervene in our work. "If you and I left this room and went up to the piano," I said, "I could make two or three hits with you if we had the desire and wanted to, because I have a few ideas fermenting up here."

"Your attitude is right on!"

The conversation continued, and we made some headway, as we agreed that the group, with Landy, would go on a retreat, with a counselor, and work through these personal issues. We told Brian that some "healing" was needed because of Landy's comments in the press that if his album was successful, it could destroy the Beach Boys. Brian, who never read newspapers or magazines, said he was unaware of those statements. We also said we would consider writing a letter on Landy's behalf. I thought Landy's medical treatment had had clear benefits, though Carl said he could not "in good conscience" support Landy.

Landy returned to the room, and Al told him how well Brian was doing. Landy was magnanimous. "From this point on," Landy said, "I would like to go forward with the idea we are a group. We have got a whole human, a real person, who is able to do his thing. It should be all together. We have fought for four years. I would like to not fight. I would like us to be total. It is my personal desire that we all work together toward something. You, we, have got a great thing going. We would like to join you. We would like you to join us, and we would like to join together."

I didn't know if we were truly going to see a "new Landy," but I thought I had seen a new Brian—someone who was recovering physically and mentally, someone who would reconnect with the group, and someone who would sit at the piano, like he and I did in the old days, when the magic occurred. Maybe it was a miracle.

A couple of nights later, it was well past midnight when I called Jacquelyne on the phone, and I was emotional.

"I have our baby's name," I told her. "It's Brian."

CHAPTER 22

A SPECIAL PLACE IN HELL

Around others, we called our son "Baby Brian" or "Little Brian," hopeful that he would acquire the best personal traits of his famous second cousin and believing that Brian Wilson would once again be part of all of our lives. I even had reason to believe that the injustices committed long ago against both of us, by my uncle Murry, would be reversed.

Tom Hulett, our manager, would have drinks with Landy as a way to keep the door open with my cousin, and in 1986, Landy told Tom that Brian was going to sue Irving Music, the parent of A&M Records, whose Almo/Irving publishing arm bought the Sea of Tunes catalog in 1969 for $700,000. According to Landy, Brian was going to try to win back his publishing rights, and he, Landy, was driving the case.

One of Brian's representatives called me to discuss the suit, and on December 5, 1986, my lawyer, Robert Kory, and I met with Brian's attorneys, John Mason and Jim Tierney. They said they believed they could reverse the 1969 sale. Even though it had occurred seventeen years earlier, they said mental incompetency could overturn the statute of limitations, and they were going to argue that Brian was mentally incompetent at the time. My testimony, Tierney said, would be critical in explaining the early days of the Beach Boys and how Murry interacted with Brian. He asked me some questions about Sea of Tunes, and I told him I really didn't know anything about it, beyond what Brian had told me, which was that he controlled it while his father administered the songs.

I told them I was still unhappy about the many songs that I had coauthored but had never been given credit on nor compensated—I had been cheated, and no one had been held accountable. Tierney said if they won the suit, they would get the songs back so that we could correct the copyright issues. He also told me that they would give me a third of whatever they won in the case. We talked as well about my writing with Brian again, without any interference from Landy.

All of that sounded good to me, incredibly good, as I had given up hope that I would ever regain the copyright of my songs. I assumed that even if I had a valid legal claim, the statute of limitations had expired. That occurred to me when David Lee Roth's cover of "California Girls" had become a sensation. Even if I told people that I had written the lyrics, who'd believe me? I reached the point that whenever someone asked me what I did for the Beach Boys, I just said I was the lead singer and didn't mention that I was a lyricist.

On December 22, 1986, just a few weeks after we had met with Brian's lawyers, they sent me a letter confirming what we had discussed, including that I would receive a third of any proceeds from their suit. That was fine, but what I most wanted was to set the record straight on my songs and to once again work with Brian.

The problem was Landy, who was never going to cede control of the person who was making him rich (Brian was paying him about $300,000 a year) and famous (Landy was profiled on TV and in magazines as the man who saved Brian Wilson). Landy was negotiating with Warner Brothers about a movie on the Brian Wilson/Gene Landy story. The relationship was naked exploitation, and creepy. Landy and Brian once went to a costume party together—Landy dressed as a doctor, Brian as a skeleton. Landy created a company called Brains and Genius, for "Brian and Gene," a partnership that allowed Landy to pursue his songwriting ambitions while Brian was attempting his comeback as a solo artist. Even after our board meeting in August of 1988, when Landy vowed to reconnect Brian to the group, the "firewall" remained. Landy's pledge was a ruse to get us to write a letter in his defense against the California authorities.

We never wrote the letter, and Brian's public behavior continued to unsettle. In 1989, at the end of an interview with Howard Stern, Brian said that appearing on the show was "like taking two amphetamines!"

While the California AG's office investigated Landy, my brother Stan was not waiting around. He saw a television news report about a lawyer named Tom Monson who had just won a large judgment against a psychiatrist. Stan wrote Monson a letter explaining Landy's control of Brian and asked Monson if he could help him remove Brian from Landy's grip. Monson recommended filing a petition for conservatorship, which, if successful, meant that a court-appointed lawyer, or conservator, would be responsible for Brian's financial affairs and medical decisions.

I contributed money to get the ball rolling, and Stan garnered the necessary support from Brian's children, Wendy and Carnie; from Brian's mom; from Carl; and from Marilyn, who in a deposition accused Landy flat-out of "brainwashing" Brian. Aunt Audree said the same thing.

As Stan was laying the groundwork, the AG's investigation of Landy finally yielded results. In 1989, Landy signed a settlement with state authorities over charges of professional misconduct, including having sex with a female patient. Landy was forced to surrender his license to practice in California, and he agreed not to petition for reinstatement for two years.

The walls were closing in, as Landy's principal—maybe only—source of income was now Brian, not as a patient but as a business partner. It was all the more reason for Landy to lead the charge against Irving Music. That suit, filed in September of 1989, sought

$50 million in lost publishing royalties and $50 million in punitive damages, while the catalog itself, if reclaimed, was thought to be worth much more. Landy was to receive 15 percent of all proceeds.

In December of 1989, my attorney and I met with Brian and his lawyers as well as Landy to review my involvement in the case. I told them that I had drawn up a list of songs that I had cowritten but not been credited on, including "California Girls" as well as "I Get Around," "Help Me, Rhonda," "Catch a Wave," and "Be True to Your School"—several dozen in all, which was only a partial list of the songs that I had written with Brian. I told them that I wanted credit for my songs.

Landy jumped off the sofa, yelled that I had no talent, and asked, "How dare you make this claim now?"

Landy understood that if I were given credit, the songwriter royalties that had been flowing to Brian as the sole author would now be divided with me, which would mean less money for Brian and less for his business partner, Eugene Landy. But I didn't budge from my demand, and we secured the promises from Brian's lawyers: if they prevailed, I would receive credit on those songs while also collecting 30 percent of the lawsuit's proceeds, or a minimum of $2 million.

It was a strange time, in so many ways, as I was involved in two simultaneous legal proceedings with Brian—one allied with him and Landy in their claims against Irving Music, and one trying to drive them apart.

In May of 1990, as *Wilson v. Irving* began making its way through the courts, Tom Monson filed the petition requesting the conservatorship, and the filing prompted one of the most bizarre press conferences that anyone had ever seen. (The Beach Boys were touring and did not attend.) At the Los Angeles Press Club, Stan was at the lectern, explaining why Brian needed to separate from his "former psychologist," when he looked up and stopped short. In strode his cousin.

"Why, we can ask Brian," Stan said in amazement. "He's here. I haven't seen him in five years, and he just walked through the door."

I'll say this much for Landy—he was clever. When he got word of Stan's press conference, which was held on a Monday, he sent Brian up to San Carlos, California, that weekend, and there he joined the Beach Boys, unannounced, onstage. He hadn't performed with us, I believe, in three years, and we didn't know why he appeared.

Immediately after the concert, Landy sent Brian back to Los Angeles, moving him like a pawn on a chessboard, and had Brian show up at Stan's press conference. Wearing a tan sports coat and a black button-up shirt, Brian looked to be in good shape. Stan gave him the microphone, and Brian read from a piece of paper: "I have heard of the charges made by Stan Love, and I think they are outrageous, which means they are out of the ballpark . . . I feel great."

Brian's lawyer also disputed the claim that Landy had kept him estranged from the Beach Boys. Why, Brian had just performed with the group that weekend!

But Brian clearly wasn't great. He slurred some of the words, appeared medicated, and was surrounded by bodyguards. Monson had had a difficult time serving him with his summons, so he ran out to his car, grabbed it, and pressed it against Brian's chest on his way out.

News reports struggled to make sense of a story of one cousin trying to save another cousin against the wishes of that cousin.

The coverage, however, was seen by a former employee of Landy's, and she gave us our first real glimpse into what was actually happening behind closed doors. We knew we were right in our efforts to free Brian, but it was far worse than any of us imagined.

Kay Gilmer, a twenty-seven-year-old music publicist, interviewed with Landy in March of 1990. She applied for the job because she loved Brian's music—so much that she was not deterred by Landy's offensive questions.

"Do you have a boyfriend?"

"Do you have a girlfriend?"

"Do you have both?"

"Do you give head?"

When Landy asked her what she thought about psychiatry, Kay said, "I think it's for people who are too lazy or too scared to dig down deep and work hard to find solutions for their own problems."

"My," Landy said, "you're a feisty one, aren't you? Can you start tomorrow?"

She worked at Brian's studio on Pico Boulevard, and the office assistant, Caroline Henning, took her into her confidence and explained how the office worked. Brian was not to receive any phone calls or mail from his family, and he specifically was not to accept any calls from Gary Usher, one of Brian's early lyricists. Gary was dying of cancer, and all he wanted to do was say good-bye to Brian, but Landy didn't like him and would not allow it.

Extreme measures were also taken to isolate Brian from loved ones: Brian's daughters had formed a singing group, and their first album was out, but any story about them in any of the trade magazines had to be ripped out before Brian could see it.

Even more alarming, to Kay, was how heavily medicated Brian was. Unable to prescribe meds himself, Landy called Dr. Solon Samuels, an eighty-two-year-old psychiatrist who ordered whatever Landy requested, and a pharmacy in Beverly Hills made the delivery. One of Landy's aides, known as the "surf Nazi," followed Brian around with a bag of pill bottles, and whenever Brian twitched or lashed out, the aide gave Brian pills to calm him. At times he swallowed eight or nine, of all different colors. Once, after Brian punched a hole in the wall, the aides sat him down, put an IV in his arm, and told him he was receiving a vitamin B_{12} drip. They would do it again, telling Brian that it was "time for your B_{12} drip." Kay didn't know what was in the solution, but she did recognize the name of one of the drugs dropped off by the pharmacy—amyl nitrates, or "poppers," used to enhance a man's sexual experience. Landy received boxes of them. Another time, Kay went into Landy's office and saw twenty-five different bottles of drugs prescribed to Brian over a three-month period.

Landy frequently told Brian that Carl, Bruce, Al, and I were all "money grubbers" who were jealous of him and were trying to keep him down, and that only he, Landy, had his best interests at heart. This echoed what Brian had heard in the 1960s from his father as well as from some of the hipsters who told Brian that the Beach Boys were dragging him down. Landy seemed to enjoy humiliating Brian: when he had to sign a document, Landy made him get on his hands and knees. Landy or one of his surrogates kept Brian under constant watch, including in his social life. According to Kay, Caroline told her that Landy set up Brian with Melinda Ledbetter, and they double-dated with Landy and his girlfriend. Other accounts have Brian meeting Melinda randomly in a car dealership and dating under the supervision of Landy's aides.

What was most disturbing was that Landy did not discard long-expired drugs but kept many half-filled bottles on the top floor of the office building. Some dated back to the 1970s, with the names of his famous patients still attached—Alice Cooper or Rod Steiger.

Though Kay had been there a short time, it was no secret that Brian was depressed and lonely. He once said to her, "You know, Kay, do you ever think about looking out into the ocean and swimming and swimming." Landy's actions made no sense: why keep these expired drugs within arm's reach of a despondent, isolated man? She told Landy, "This stuff is dangerous. Shouldn't you dispose of it?"

"No," Landy said. "You keep it exactly where it is." Stranger still were bottles of liquid adrenaline, with syringes, that were kept in a studio desk. When Kay asked about them, Landy said, "Don't you touch that."

"Brian can get it."

"It's none of your business."

The final straw came when Kay was sent to Landy's house to pick up an envelope. She looked inside and saw a revised will and testament for Brian, drafted by John Mason, which left 80 percent of Brian's assets to Landy and his girlfriend, the rest to Carl and to Brian's daughters. The document had not been signed.

Was this scenario, Kay thought, really possible? Convince Brian to change his will, and then leave out toxic drugs so that Brian might decide, what the fuck, it's time to end it all?

The sequence had an altogether perverse logic: Kay heard Landy talk about how much money they were going to collect in the Irving Music lawsuit. Landy had saved Brian's life when that life generated steady income, but now that Brian stood to collect millions of dollars, that same life, with a revised will, might be worth more dead than alive.

I had long thought Landy to be a greedy bastard and a megalomaniac, but Kay came to a different conclusion: he was pure evil.

She believed that if she stayed any longer, she'd be complicit in Landy's designs against Brian, but before she left, she searched the office Rolodex and found Gary Usher's number. She called him to explain why his messages had not been returned. Gary warned her: "If Landy knows that you're calling me, he'd kill you. He'd literally kill you."

Two months later, on May 25, 1990, Gary died of cancer at his home in Los Angeles.

Kay left her job after three weeks but took with her some of the expired drug bottles as well as names, phone numbers, and bank account information, all of which she turned over to the California Board of Medical Quality Assurance. When a representative of the agency asked her what she thought of Dr. Landy, Kay said, "If I was assured that he would burn in hell, it would be too good for him."

Kay also shared her information with Tom Monson, who used it as part of the conservatorship proceedings. Four months after she stopped working for Landy, Kay began getting late night calls. She recognized the voice as someone who worked with Landy. "We know where you are," he said. "You've been a bad girl." Kay moved to Colorado and never heard from Landy or his enforcers again.

Brian's memoir was published in 1991, and to promote it, he and Landy were interviewed in October on *Primetime Live*. Most of Diane Sawyer's questions, however, centered on Landy's misconduct. Compared to just three years ago, Brian looked miserable, his eyes unable to make contact with Sawyer, his face contorted, his answers jumbled. Landy was defiant, but his reign was almost over. As Landy's cash machine, Brian was sputtering. His solo career had not taken off, his lawsuit had yet to produce anything, and Brian, inconveniently, was still alive, so his new will (now signed) did not yield benefits to anyone.

Carl and his own lawyer had taken over the conservatorship efforts, after Stan ran low on money. Carl's style was to avoid confrontation at all cost, particularly in family matters (he was known by some as the "ostrich"), but he recognized Brian's dire condition. His lawyer filed a new petition in 1991, which included Carl's name, as well as Stan's and mine. With Brian's entire family unified, and with the evidence against Landy mounting, Brian's lawyer knew he could never win a trial. In December of 1991, a settlement was reached between Carl's lawyer and Brian's lawyer that formally severed Landy's ties to Brian while allowing a Superior Court judge to appoint a conservator. It would still take months for that transition to occur. Landy, however, had minimal contact with Brian thereafter, but the psychotropic drugs may have caused Brian greater neurological damage than the illegal drugs. Brian struggled for the next several years with shakiness, slurred speech, and mini-seizures.

Dr. Eugene Landy had achieved the near impossible: he saved Brian's life but left him in worse shape than when he found him.

CHAPTER 23

UNIVERSAL TRUTH

I f the legal proceedings against Landy had a satisfactory end, those against Irving Music did not. I was utterly blindsided.

In October of 1991, my lawyer told me that Brian had decided to settle with Irving Music, and the proposed settlement was $10 million for all claims—a fraction of what Brian's lawyers thought they could win. In a phone call, my attorney told me that I would not receive any of those proceeds, nor would I receive credit on any of the songs that I wrote. The case would soon be over, and there wasn't anything I could do about it.

After hanging up, I paced back and forth across the house, not so much in rage but in disbelief, asking myself over and over again, *What the fuck just happened?* I had been deposed for two full days for this lawsuit, and I had helped them get $10 million, and now, no money, no song credits, nothing. This was the *third* time I had been screwed. First when Murry didn't give me credit. Then when Murry sold the catalog. And now this time.

We needed to get away, and in December, Jacquelyne and I took our son, Brian, now three, to the Maharishi Ayurveda Health Center in Lancaster, Massachusetts. We went for *panchakarma*, or "five actions," in which herbal products, oil massages, and other treatments are used to purify the body. The center was run by Deepak Chopra.

Just as Jacquelyne spoke to him in her time of need, I sat down with Deepak and told him what happened with the lawsuit. Deepak told me I had to meet a lawyer who had represented him and was at the center right now. His name was Mike Flynn, and he might be able to help.

Mike joined Jacquelyne and me for dinner. He was lean, with straight dark hair and sharp angular features. Even at a health spa, he didn't seem like the relaxing type, and the more I told him about what happened, the more interested he became. He preferred cases that involved "huge injustices"—right versus wrong, underdog versus top dog, good versus evil. "When I'm looking into the eyes of the jury," he later said, "I want to be wearing the white hat."

Mike Flynn had spent eight years fighting the Church of Scientology and had helped put three of its leaders in prison. He liked high-profile cases as well, representing Joan Kennedy and, later, Monica Lewinsky, though he turned down Michael Jackson.

Our spiritual faith created a common bond—Mike Flynn had practiced TM since 1974—but it was his legal faith that separated him from all others. Dating back to the 1960s, every lawyer I had spoken to about my music-related legal problems had told me the same thing: yes, I'd been cheated, but there was nothing I could do.

Lost causes, combined with huge injustices, were the very causes that Mike Flynn embraced.

His willingness to help me was a revelation, but we still needed to do our astrological vetting. Jacquelyne asked Mike over dinner what his birth date was and what time he was born. He excused himself to call his mother and returned with the information. Then Jacquelyne left the table and returned with our astrologer's planetary assessment of Mike: "In the twelfth House of Justice, he has an exalted Jupiter."

That was good enough for Jacquelyne. "Hire him," she said.

Mike Flynn, who had offices in San Diego County, began his work, and it included filing a suit against HarperCollins for defamation in Brian's memoir. The book itself cast Gene Landy as Brian's savior (Landy also collected a third of the $250,000 advance), while depicting me and the other members of the band as shameless malefactors who exploited Brian. Over the years, I've told many people, including reporters, that *Wouldn't It Be Nice* is "my favorite book that I've never read," because HarperCollins settled the suit for a good deal of money. But that flippant remark deflected my true feelings. I read as much of Brian's book as I could stomach and was stung by the false attacks against me, some of which were recycled from the 1970s. Describing me as "smarmy," "creepy," and "flashing an evil grin," the memoir falsely claimed that I "hated everything" about *Pet Sounds*, alleged that I had cost Brother Records "millions of dollars in lost royalties" in bad business decisions, and blamed me for Brian's descent into "booze, drugs, and food." Writing songs with cousin Mike, Brian wrote, "had nearly killed me several times over."

What was most irritating was Brian's disparagement of me and virtually everyone in the Beach Boys as musical incompetents. "The proper thing," Brian wrote, "would've been to remind Mike that if not for me, he'd still be pumping gas, Al that he'd be a medical supply salesman, and Carl that he'd be running errands for me."

HarperCollins also settled defamation lawsuits from Carl and Brother Records.

In his depositions, Brian said he had only skimmed the manuscript and couldn't account for the falsehoods. "I don't recall nothing," he said. We assumed that Landy wrote the actual lies, but as far as I'm concerned, that doesn't exonerate Brian. It's his book, and if you buy it online or find it at a used bookstore, it doesn't come with a cover sticker that reads: "Warning: False and Defamatory Statements Included."

The most despicable section was the attack on the person who loved Brian the most—his mother. According to the book, Brian often saw his mom "pour a drink in the afternoon and continue sipping through the evening," a bystander to Murry's abuse. She once "looked on as [my dad] tied me to a tree as punishment," and after Murry caught Brian masturbating in his bedroom, Murry demanded that Audree deny their son dinner for two nights.

"My mom complied," Brian wrote.

Aunt Audree sued HarperCollins, but the judge threw out that case. I don't know if Brian ever apologized to his mom.

My suit against HarperCollins allowed Mike Flynn to gain access to the transcripts of Brian's interviews with his collaborator, Todd Gold. Those interviews affirmed—according to Brian—that I had been the inspiration of the group and that I had written many of the songs that were now in dispute.

All of that was a cornerstone for Mike's investigation into what happened in Brian's case against Irving Music. Brian's $10 million settlement had been finalized in May of 1992, which Brian split with his lawyers (who received 40 percent). Around that time, Mike called me at our house in Incline Village and asked to come up. He had some important information.

I knew that over the past three decades, plenty of things had happened to the Beach Boys that I either didn't understand or had neglected, but when Mike sat down with us in our living room, he came with piles of documentary evidence that he and his law firm had collected and analyzed, documents that I had never seen before, some dating all the way back to the inception of the group. He had copyright applications for songs, minutes from Brother Records board meetings, incorporation papers from Beach Boy–related companies, and letters. I then received a history lesson in deception, greed, and misplaced loyalty.

For one thing, Brian's lawyers misled me from the beginning about the grounds on which they were going to overturn the sale of the catalog. It wasn't only that Brian was mentally incompetent. It was also that our lawyer at the time of the sale, Abe Somer, was representing both sides of the transaction. He was the Beach Boys' attorney, but he was also the lawyer for Irving Music and its subsidiary, A&M Records. In addition, Somer was on the board of directors for both Irving Music and A&M Records, and he assisted Irving in the transaction. He never disclosed his dual representation to me or, as far as I knew, to anyone in the Beach Boys. It was a clear conflict of interest, and it was used in Brian's case against Irving Music to try to overturn the catalog's sale.

That was a shot to the gut. The guy we had entrusted to protect our songs was a snake, and as Mike Flynn explained it, the lies continued to this day. Brian's current lawyers had to know that if I was aware of the Somer conflict, I would have wanted to join the case against Irving Music. But if I joined Brian's case, we would have to split the proceeds and take money out of their pockets and Landy's. These lawyers concealed the Somer conflict from me, even though some of them knew it as early as 1986. Mike explained that because Brian and I had been music and business partners since the inception of the band, Brian and his lawyers had a fiduciary obligation to share that information with me. Instead, they concealed it, and I testified in their case, in exchange for promises of money and credit—promises, of course, that were never kept.

That was sleazy, but I wasn't surprised. I knew about Landy, and I'd been dealing with corrupt lawyers for decades. But Mike Flynn said I hadn't heard the worst of it. He grabbed another folder and said that the actual sale of the catalog in 1969 was the product of an elaborate scam to defraud me and was the culmination of years of deception.

I was listening.

It started with the Sea of Tunes. When it was formed in 1961, it was a sole proprietorship, and Uncle Murry and Brian each had a 50 percent stake, though Brian gave his half away the following year.

Throughout the 1960s, Brian told me that he controlled the Sea of Tunes, which reassured me that I needn't worry about my song credits. But according to a 1965 letter from Brian, Uncle Murry controlled the catalog.

The actual scam began in 1967, when Abe Somer began representing the Beach Boys. Mike told me that Somer had engaged in these kinds of deals in the past, so he knew what he was doing, and once he and my uncle formed an alliance, he could move the pieces into place.

Their goal was to sell the catalog and pocket the cash, but when Somer investigated the actual songs, he encountered a major problem. When you write a song, you're supposed to assign the copyright to a publisher, through a copyright registration and a songwriter's agreement, and the publisher distributes songwriter royalties from record sales and other publishing fees. For the Beach Boys, Uncle Murry and Brian tried to assign the copyrights to the Sea of Tunes, but when Somer searched for those assignments, he discovered a mess. The wrong songwriter forms had been used, while other forms were incomplete, dated incorrectly, or appeared to have been forged (which was later confirmed). Others were simply missing. Under the laws at the time, if a copyright was not assigned, then it remained with the songwriter, and any alleged copyright holder—in this case, Murry—lost it.

No one would buy the publishing rights to our songs unless they could also buy the copyrights, but in terms of copyrights, the Sea of Tunes was an empty vessel.

Fixing the problem required even more chicanery. It involved the incorporation of Brother Records and the Sea of Tunes catalog, which masked the defects in the assignments and limited the liability for the buyer. Even those secret moves weren't enough to ensure the acquisition. I still owned the copyright to all my songs, and I could assert those rights regardless of who owned the catalog. To get the copyrights assigned to the catalog, Somer could have come to me with a stack of songwriter agreements and asked me to sign them, but I might have asked questions or smelled something rotten. So Somer had to trick me.

After Murry found a buyer for the catalog, Somer drafted the letter that all the Beach Boys were told to sign. Dated August 20, 1969, and addressed to Irving Music, it said that the songs "authored by [the Beach Boys] have been assigned to Sea of Tunes in accordance with normal practice in the publishing business . . . [and] we acknowledge that we have executed songwriters' agreements whereby all of our rights in and to the foregoing musical compositions have been assigned to Sea of Tunes."

I had no idea what the hell that meant. So I asked my lawyer—Abe Somer! He told me there was nothing I could do. He didn't tell me that he had secretly planned this transaction for two years and that he represented Irving Music. It was premeditated, cunning, and diabolical. And in signing the letter, I gave away my songs.

What Mike Flynn told me deepened my contempt for Uncle Murry. I knew he wanted to keep the Beach Boys a family band, but I didn't realize that in his eyes, I was never part of the family. When I later told my dad what happened, he said he wasn't surprised. "I knew he was a crook," he said. "He was always a crook. But he didn't have it out for you. He had it out for me." I'm sure he was right. Jealous of my dad, Murry wasn't going to let the entitled son of his rich brother-in-law receive the credit, the due, that he deserved. My uncle wanted the glory for his sons, and through his duplicity he got it.

Mike told me there was another part of the story. Recall, he said, that Brian had signed the letter of August 20, 1969, that paved the way for the catalog's sale. But I needed to read another document, which said that on December 28, 1967, Somer incorporated the catalog into the Sea of Tunes Publishing Company. Mike then pulled out another file and showed me the minutes of a board meeting, apparently the only one ever held by the Sea of Tunes Publishing Company, and the meeting resolved that "the liquidation and the distribution of [the company's] assets be commenced as soon as practicable."

It was a resolution to sell the catalog.

Mike told me to look at the signatures.

It was signed by the company's sole shareholder and director, Murry Wilson, and by the directors, Audree Wilson and Brian Wilson.

Mike told me to look at the date.

It was July 21, 1969, a full month before we signed the letter to Irving Music. Brian had told me that his father had fucked us when the catalog was sold, but Brian had signed the document to commence the sale a full month before it actually happened. He knew his father was trying to sell the catalog, and he approved it.

Mike also said that in Brian's own suit against Irving Music, his lawyers argued that Brian and Murry each had a 50 percent stake in Sea of Tunes even before its incorporation in 1967, and Brian was now bound by that. In other words, if Brian were a full partner with his father, then all the fraud and deceit surrounding the catalog must also be attributable to Brian. He could not escape responsibility.

"Brian is just as culpable as Murry," Mike said.

I put my head down in my hands.

Mike Flynn said that he needed to pursue Brian in order to subpoena additional documents and to depose Brian and his lawyers, but he thought he knew the outlines of his case—that Brian lied to me from the very beginning about the Sea of Tunes; that he bore responsibility for blocking credit on my songs; that he worked with his father in the fraudulent sale of the catalog; and that he and his lawyers have been concealing information from me for years.

My lawyer was telling me that my cousin was my adversary.

I rubbed my eyes, looked up, and took a deep breath: "Okay," I said. "Go for it."

didn't want to sue Brian, but I knew a resolution was long overdue. I assumed that, in the 1960s, Brian had not credited me on our songs because he wanted to avoid fighting his father. But Murry died in 1973, and even though Irving Music owned the catalog, Brian faced no legal or industry barrier from simply adding my name as a lyricist. But he never did that. Even when I was in bankruptcy proceedings, Brian kept cashing the royalty checks, year after year.

Actually, I thought the suit would be settled quickly. Brian had just wrapped up a three-year legal battle against Irving Music, and the two-year effort to establish a conservatorship had recently been made final. The last thing he wanted was a courtroom bloodletting that reopened old family wounds. Brian also knew the truth.

On August 27, 1992, one month after my suit against Brian was filed, the Beach Boys were playing in New Jersey, and Jacquelyne and I were staying at the Rihga Royal Hotel in New York. She was in the room when Brian called and said he needed to speak with me. Jacquelyne told him I was doing an interview with the Associated Press. Brian called back several more times before I had time to reach him. He quickly got to the point.

"You were right to sue me," he said. "I owe you money. I want to pay you."

I told him that I was sure the lawyers could reach a settlement and that I was less interested in the money than in getting credit on our songs, mainly "California Girls."

He said he knew that. He also told me that he had been working on a new arrangement of "Proud Mary," and he wanted to do it with the group.

I told him I couldn't wait to hear it, and we said good-bye. If Brian agreed that I was right to sue him, what was there to argue about? Or so I thought. The settlement talks, however, quickly broke down between Mike Flynn and Brian's conservator, Jerome Billet, who was appointed by a judge. Billet's job was to protect Brian's assets, and I guess Billet thought he could do a better job of that by going to trial.

What a blunder. I knew that regardless of the outcome, Brian was going to pay a price by exposing himself to a history that he had tried to bury and forget. During a deposition on November 3, 1993, while acknowledging that he owed me money, the lawyers were aghast at what they saw: Brian was hurting himself. His lawyer, Jim Tierney, said, "I want the record to reflect that Brian is digging his fingernails into his arm, and the sores are opening up and bleeding." Tierney urged him to cease.

I knew the lawsuit was also going to be one of the most stressful experiences of my life, but I had found new ways of coping.

One day in the early 1980s, I was driving from my house in Santa Barbara to Los Angeles, a drive I often made, but now I pulled off in Calabasas, inland from Malibu, and saw in the rolling hills a Hindu temple. I didn't know anything about it but decided to check it out. Entering the front door, I took off my shoes, walked through the main temple, and soon found my way into the inner sanctum. There the priest was doing an *aarti*, or a blessing, with a lighted camphor, which emitted a sharp but pleasing aroma. I stood silently as the priest chanted invocations, and then out of the blue, he turned to me.

"Your life is going to get better," he said.

"Excuse me?"

"Your life is going to get better very soon."

"Are you sure?"

"Yes."

I can't recall how it got better at the time, but I do know that the exchange marked the beginning of my friendship with Narasimha Bhattar, a sturdy, dark-haired Brahmin priest whose job was to interpret the cosmos. He explained how the relationship among the planets can influence your daily life and how your birth chart can predict your relationship with others or foretell the success of a new job or even a marriage. His philosophy, his way of looking at things, appealed to my desire for esoteric knowledge. It was an alternative but orderly framework to understand a chaotic world.

On my second visit, Narasimha told me that I should come with him to India to visit the Hindu temples, each one with a presiding deity whose forefather had been a priest there five hundred years ago. I joined him on several pilgrimages to the southern part of that country, to visit these architectural splendors, some of which had been there a thousand years ago. Vedic rituals seemed to recognize the need for physical as well as spiritual engagement; and for someone like me who was easily distracted, these rituals intrigued me because they were active, experiential, and tactile. The supplicants did not have to sit back and await their fate. They could tilt the odds in their favor.

I wanted to do just that for the trial. Our chances of prevailing were not high, given that so much time had passed—more than thirty years—since the initial wrongs were committed. I knew the facts were on my side, but I wanted cosmic insurance.

So with Narasimha joining us, Jacquelyne and I took little Brian, now four and a half, to India. I had been traveling to India for several decades, but this was the first time I could integrate that part of my spiritual life with my family life. We rode the elephants together and explored the sights but were there mainly to visit the temples, and I took great pride that I could share this ancient knowledge with my young son. Vedic priests performed different *yagnas*, or fire sacrifices, in which offerings are made to different deities to achieve results in various parts of your life, including health, career, finances, and personal relationships. Then there are sacrifices for Ganesha, who is the remover of obstacles and whose image—the head of an elephant—is one of the most recognized in the Hindu pantheon.

I needed some legal obstacles removed. Inside one of the temples, I stood next to a small fire, and with hundreds of priests chanting, I threw into the blaze almonds, chili peppers, and food grains. The goal is not to harm any of your adversaries but to evolve them to a more enlightened state, and it seemed fitting that the temple was equipped with its own choral effects. I loved the sound of the crackling flames, the chants, the invocations, the chorus of drums, bells, and gongs. These were harmonies of the spirit.

On another occasion, back in the states, Mike Flynn and I visited the temple in Calabasas when he was taking depositions and had hit some roadblock. We asked Narasimha to chant the thousand names of Ganesha, the linking of the names expressing the belief in the glory of the deity. Narasimha did all the work. Mike and I just sat back and listened until the sounds washed over us. When we got back to our car and drove down the highway, it felt like we were floating.

The pretrial skirmishing dragged on for many months, in part because Brian's lawyers delayed or blocked access to documents. In February of 1994, Judge William J. Rea reopened discovery when Mike Flynn convinced him that documents had been suppressed. The judge also removed Brian's two lawyers, J. J. Little and Jim Tierney, for conflicts of interest, as their misconduct, acting on Brian's behalf, was part of the case. I didn't have the money to cover Mike's expenses, which included hiring a forensics expert to comb through Brian's computer, and Mike would ultimately spend about $200,000 of his own cash just to keep the case going.

If I rushed into my other marriages, I compensated by taking a long time with Jacquelyne. To be honest, there almost wasn't a marriage. Not long after Brian was born, Jacquelyne and I separated, for no good reason except my own fears and insecurities about being a father again and making a commitment to a family. That was my pattern. But this time was different. We had some friends—Terry Melcher in particular—who made sure Jacquelyne and I continued to communicate, and they prodded me to open up in a way that I've never done before. Jacquelyne and I were back together soon enough, as a couple and a family, on a path I had not taken before.

Jacquelyne insisted that it was either all or nothing—either we stay together as a family, including every tour and road trip, or we split up. Tours aren't easy for adults, let along small children, but Jacquelyne said she would handle the logistics. Off we went, and little Brian had a truly unique childhood. By the time he was three, he had exhausted his passport and had to get a new one. In India, he wanted to wear the same kind of dhoti that I wore. Once on a bus in Germany, our tour manager handed him the public address mic and asked, "Brian, what city are we in now?"

"Dusseldorf!" he cried.

Before he was in kindergarten, he had seen more parts of America than most people see in their lives. When we performed at festivals or amusement parks, I took him on rides in between concerts. When he was old enough for school, we hired a tutor and homeschooled him. Before going onstage, I'd put him on my shoulders, and he'd yell, "Let's knock out this show!" Then he'd come onstage with us, but he wasn't a prop. He attacked the tambourine viciously, like his dad, and he could sing! He put his heart into it, and when he was five or six, Carl gave him the last falsetto part on "Fun, Fun, Fun."

It was the first time I'd done the things you're supposed to do as a dad. I regret how much I missed with my other children but savored every moment this time around.

For Jacquelyne and me, those years traveling together went a long way toward building trust and reassuring both of us that this relationship was going to work. Hell, our courtship—seven years—had lasted longer than several of my marriages combined, but we finally knew the time was right to get married.

Jacquelyne had a bridal shower, and Aunt Audree attended and gave her a risqué nightgown. But she told Jacquelyne she couldn't come to the wedding because of the litigation with Brian.

"I don't think it would be the right thing to do," she told her, "but I know you'll be a beautiful bride, and you have my blessing."

A few days before the wedding, Audree called Jacquelyne. "Guess what," she said. "We're coming."

My aunt was always a class act, and I believe she was also instrumental in getting another guest to attend—Brian.

The wedding itself, on April 24, 1994, was at a lakeside mansion in Tahoe. Carl sang "God Only Knows," and my sister Marjorie and her husband, Joe, sang "When I Fall in Love" and "Ave Maria." Mike Flynn was my best man. He had recently deposed Brian for seventeen days, two hours a day, during which time Brian had admitted—to the dismay of his lawyers—that I had contributed lyrics to thirty-five contested songs. (We initially identified seventy-nine, but that number was too unwieldy.) Professional ethics prevented Mike Flynn from speaking to Brian at the wedding, but in his lengthy and very funny toast, he integrated lyrics from all thirty-five songs. Brian sat and listened to it in good humor and later told Carl how much he liked it.

The trial finally began on October 4, 1994, in United States District Court in Los Angeles, and what occurred over the next two months was the most comprehensive history of the Beach Boys ever assembled, in several thousand pages of testimony (including pretrial depositions) and documents (hearings, rulings, motions, contracts, exhibits, letters, interview transcripts, medical reports, boardroom minutes, and more). The jurors heard from Brian and me as well as Al, Bruce, David Marks, Marilyn, and various promoters, record company executives, lawyers, managers, and medical experts. Carl refused to appear in court, but he was deposed at length, and his testimony was read to the jurors.

I was on the stand for all or parts of six days. I knew that, when provoked, I could lose my temper, so I consulted a Vedic astrologer, and she told me I could cultivate "sweet speech" by eating "white candies." On the days that I testified, I either drank vanilla milk shakes or ate divinity fudge. It worked, for the most part, though I may have been too irreverent—when I first took the stand, Mike Flynn asked what my occupation was, and I said, "Hard-core unemployable." (I then noted I played in a rock and roll band.)

Much of my testimony focused on the thirty-five songs. Every Beach Boy, including Brian, acknowledged my contributions, but Brian's lawyers tried to minimize them. Another issue was whether Brian and I were actually "partners." Legally, if we were true business partners, then Brian or his representatives had certain fiduciary obligations to me. But if we weren't partners, then no such obligations existed.

This was no mere legal point. It cut to the heart of the Beach Boys. Were we really a group in which all members contributed, or was this Brian's band, with the rest of us just along for the ride? If the latter was true, I had no case.

All I could do was describe how I worked with Brian to create our music, and the jurors would decide.

When Mike Flynn asked me about "Surfin' USA," I said that Brian borrowed the melody from Chuck Berry's "Sweet Little Sixteen."

"Brian did the arrangement," I explained, "and I took all the disparate words and assembled them in a coherent way so that they would rhyme and you could sing them. There were different surfing spots that were recommended by different neighbors, and I just took the words, wrote them all down, and put them into something that you could sing that rhymed . . . There is part of the song that says, 'Haggerty's and Swami's,' but I ran it together like [singing] 'At Haggerty's-and-Swami's-Pacific-Palisades, San-Onofre-and-Sunset, Redondo-Beach-L.A.' It is like running the lines together in syncopation with the track. So I had to do that because I was singing the lead, and it is an up-tempo song and you just can't go like 'At Haggerty's and Swami's' while the track is pumping. So I remember very clearly tailoring the melody and tailoring the lyrics to fit the track."

"The song," I added, "is credited to Chuck Berry, which is all well and good, but Chuck didn't surf."

"Did you get any credit?"

"No."

Then Mike flipped on a CD player and—*If everybody had an ocean . . ."*—the jurors listened to the song.

Hour after hour, I walked the jurors through the process of how I came up with the words for "California Girls" and "I Get Around" and "Be True to Your School" and all the rest, and then I'd sing a few lines and then sometimes Mike Flynn would play the tune, all of which, I believe, left little doubt that I was either the author or coauthor of these songs.

When Al Jardine took the stand, Mike Flynn asked him what happened when he gave Brian "Sloop John B." "I arranged it in a fashion that I thought Brian would appreciate [and] that we could possibly have as a Beach Boy song," Al said. "I wrote it out for him and played it for him."

Al testified that to his surprise, Brian completed the song on his own, and it became a hit in America and around the world.

"Did you get credit?" Mike Flynn asked.

"No, I didn't," Al said. "No."

Brian, in his testimony, denied that Al helped him, but Al had no reason to perjure himself: he wasn't a plaintiff in the case, he had nothing to gain financially, and the song itself wasn't even being contested. But a pattern of behavior was established.

Beyond disparaging me, the defense centered on showcasing Brian as mentally incompetent from the late 1960s to the current day. It was a dark spectacle. One psychiatrist said that Brian had the mentality of a six-year-old. Another said he had an "organic personality disorder." His conservator said he would not allow Brian to drive because he might hear a voice tell him to turn left when he wasn't supposed to turn left. His current psychiatrist said Brian suffered a "mini-breakdown" as a result of the trial, compromising his ability to testify.

On the stand, Brian told jurors that he took lithium, Zoloft, Klonopin, clozapine, and Benadryl, four times a day, "to keep my head on an even keel."

His bloodstream was a flowing pharmacopoeia—Mike Flynn accused the defense of ramping up his meds to debilitate him for the trial—but the strategy was to generate sympathy for Brian while using his mental health issues to exculpate him.

I attended every day of the proceeding, and Jacquelyne most of the days, and we sat a row behind Mike Flynn and his co-counsel, Philip Stillman. Jacquelyne had to buy me several new suits, as I rarely dressed up, and one night at dinner, our son said, "I want to go to the place where you wear the suits." My general feeling is that the less exposure you have to our legal system, the better, but if little Brian really wanted to join us, I didn't see a problem.

Our son inherited the Loves' blond hair (curly) and blue eyes, and he was in a phase where he wanted to wear the same thing I was wearing. So when I wore a gray suit to the courthouse, Jacquelyne bought him a gray suit, and the three of us journeyed to court one morning.

Cousin Brian was on the stand that day.

We settled in behind our lawyers and watched one of Brian's attorneys, Douglas Day, ask about "California Girls."

Brian acknowledged that I wrote it, though he couldn't remember which parts specifically, and blamed his father for not giving me credit. He was asked about other songs—"Wouldn't It Be Nice," "Be True to Your School," "Catch a Wave," "When I Grow Up (To Be a Man)"—and he said he thought we both wrote some parts of them; others, only he; others, he wasn't sure. And there was "Dance, Dance, Dance" ("Mike and Carl wrote it") and "In the Back of My Mind" ("I don't know").

Little Brian fell asleep between Jacquelyne and me as the testimony droned on, and then the lawyer asked about "I Get Around."

"Do you recall when that song was written?" Day asked.

"Sometime in 1964," Brian said.

"And do you recall who wrote the music for the song 'I Get Around'?"

"I did, with the exception of a possible—possibility that Mike wrote the intro, the 'round 'round.' If you get an instrument, I would be able to demonstrate it."

"Let me ask you, Mr. Wilson, with regard to the writing process, can you explain how you wrote the song 'I Get Around'?"

"No, I can't."

"Can you explain it in words?"

"No, I can't."

Day asked for a keyboard, which was at the ready, so Brian could demonstrate. The instrument was wheeled out, and when Brian sat down at it, he perked up noticeably.

"The dispute," he said, "is over who wrote the introduction patter, the vocal patter, like a riff. And I personally can't remember if I had written that, and it had come up previous times that Mr. Love had said that he had written some of the introduction to 'I Get Around.' So explaining what an introduction is versus what a song is, I explain this in these terms."

Brian then pounded the keys and broke out in song: "'Round 'round get around, I get around!" The chords and his voice were loud and bracing and startled the courtroom.

Brian explained that the song started with one note, and then he played and sang it again: "'Round 'round I get around!"

With that, little Brian woke up, looked around, and blurted, "That's my daddy's song!"

The jurors looked at this moppet in a gray suit. The courtroom fell silent.

It was an unusually bitter trial, a war within a family and a band, with lawyers thundering at one another at every turn. At one point, Judge Rea, who'd been on the bench for twenty-six years, said he had never had a trial in which the attorneys voiced—or yelled—so many objections. And now, out of nowhere, the voice of a child pierced the ramblings of his medicated namesake. I suddenly got emotional and started to well up. I headed for the exit, and Jacquelyne, lifting Brian, followed me to the door.

Brian Wilson, continuing with his testimony, said, "It does sort of sound like a Mike Love–type of riff."

In addition to all the testimony, the paper trail told a clear story of deception and complicity. Thanks to the forensic analysis of Brian's computer, Mike Flynn had supplemented the documents from the 1960s with Brian's diary entries from the late 1980s, and they contradicted the depiction of a mental incompetent. Rather, they showed that Brian was intimately involved in his case against Irving Music, following the direction of his counsel and seeking to maximize his financial gain. Noting the guidance that he had received from his lawyers, Brian wrote:

These kinds of questions were leading to the fact that if I was caught saying that I remember when I was told about Sea of Tunes, the statute of limitation would have started instantly. Anyway J.J. assured me that we couldn't get shafted if I answered the questions that J.J. and Jim had been teaching me . . . We are not talking about two million dollars. We are talking about forty million dollars.

In other examples, Brian's own words undermined his credibility. When he was on the stand, Mike Flynn read for him an interview he did with Todd Gold, his collaborator on his memoir, regarding "California Girls." Brian said that he and I wrote the song but I never received credit.

> **GOLD:** Why? Whose fault was that?
> **BRIAN:** That was my fault.
> **GOLD:** Why didn't you give him credit?
> **BRIAN:** Because I forgot that he wrote it with me.
> **GOLD:** Did you ever regret forgetting to give him credit?
> **BRIAN:** Very much so, yes.

Gold asked why he hadn't given me credit since then.

> **BRIAN:** I don't know. I keep fucking up. I keep forgetting to do it.

He kept forgetting? If "California Girls" had been an obscure song, that might have been believable. But Brian himself described it as the Beach Boys' "anthem." Every time he heard it, played it, sang it, or saw the record itself, he was reminded that this was fraud on vinyl.

There were songwriter agreements in which my name had been

forged, and there were hidden letters and financial arrangements among the lawyers. There was a lot of talk about suppression of evidence and promissory fraud and breaches of contract, but ultimately, after twenty-four days of testimony, the jurors had to decide if Brian Wilson victimized me or was himself a victim of his own frailties.

In his closing argument, Brian's attorney, Michael Crowe, asked jurors for sympathy. Brian, he said, suffers from a "long-term mental disability . . . So unlike you and hopefully me, who every day can wake up and perhaps with some difficulty go to work and conduct our lives, Brian Wilson can't do that. Brian Wilson can't do that today, he couldn't do it yesterday, and sadly enough, he won't be able to do it tomorrow."

Crowe also seemed intent on erasing me from Beach Boy history entirely, as he not only rejected my claim for songwriting credit but said I didn't deserve my name on my existing songs: "If you look at the songwriting credit Mike Love received on the songs that he has received credit on, it is mostly 50 percent. We would submit to you that almost all of that was at recording sessions where he didn't deserve credit."

Crowe suggested that Brian was the real artist; I, a mere handyman: "The artist who creates the music, who is the inventor, gets the credit. You may adjust the frame, but the Picasso doesn't change."

Mike Flynn, in his closing argument, was equally unsparing toward Brian: "The guy who wrote the songs"—me—"helps his cousin for thirty years, supports him during that whole period of time while at least a good percentage of that money that Mr. Love is earning both from touring revenues and songwriter royalties . . . a good portion of that money is being used for drugs by Brian Wilson while Mr. Love is out working. And then they get his cooperation in Wilson vs. A&M, and then they turn around after they get the cooperation and use it against him . . . I submit to you, ladies and gentlemen, when you think of what has happened here, it is simply outrageous."

After a lengthy summary of the misrepresentations and betrayals, Mike Flynn concluded: "It has been a long two months . . . The guy who did all the work and wrote the songs hasn't got anything . . . So after you deliberate and consider all these items, all this evidence, all this testimony, I am going to ask you to return a verdict for this man because he deserves it. He wrote the songs."

To reach a verdict, Brian's lawyers requested that jurors fill out a twenty-five-page questionnaire—a typical request from a defendant. The more that jurors have to consider, or the more deeply they plunge into every piece of evidence, the greater the possibility that doubt will creep in. (Plaintiffs prefer three-line verdicts.) To Mike Flynn's dismay, I told him to accept those instructions. I wanted jurors to consider all aspects of this case. I wanted a long verdict as a document on the history of the Beach Boys.

The jurors began their deliberations on December 2. Though we all knew what was at stake, I didn't feel nervous. I very much believe in karma, which is a doctrine of universal truth. It basically states that notwithstanding the machinations of man—and regardless of the good or evil in the world—if you follow your conscience, the universe will support the truth. Mike Flynn and I talked about this at length. He knows a lot more about the legal system than I do, so he was worried about how the jurors were reacting to various arguments and rulings. At the same time, I was taking hits in the press for my attempted "money grab." But I remained confident that if you follow what is true, the universe will support it. I was at peace.

After ten days of deliberation, the jury returned with its "special verdict," and Judge Rea, who at seventy-four was himself showing the stress of a long trial, looked right at Mike and me with a worn smile. Page by page, he read the verdict. The jurors ruled that I deserved credit on all thirty-five songs; that Brian and I were partners; that Brian or his agents concealed material facts with the intent to defraud me; that they engaged in promissory fraud regarding songwriting credits and royalties; and on and on it went.

It was a clean-sweep victory. I hugged Jacquelyne and Mike, but there was no celebration, no cheering. I was vindicated but subdued. I was thinking about what came next. When I left the courthouse and faced the television cameras, I said that I hoped this case would allow Brian and me to put the past behind us so that we could write music again.

The case wasn't over yet. The trial established Brian's liability, but a second trial would determine damages. The enduring popularity of the songs, which included seven Top 10 hits, left Brian badly exposed. To determine lost royalties or compensatory damages, Mike Flynn analyzed the past financial records of Capitol Records and Irving Music and estimated I had lost between $18 million and $22 million. To determine the value of the actual copyright, Mike was going to have experts testify that it was worth between $40 million and $100 million. And because Brian was guilty on multiple counts of fraud, Mike was going to ask for punitive damages, which—if awarded—would have been ten times the compensatory damages.

Brian was facing potential damages of between $58 million and $342 million—almost certainly the largest case of fraud in music history. Brian's lawyers and friends understood his exposure, and some of them called Mike Flynn, reminding him of Brian's financial commitments to his children and to Marilyn and the costs of his own medical care. They asked him to convince me to settle, but Mike didn't need to. I had no interest in crushing my cousin, and it wasn't about the money anyway. It was about getting credit for my songs. Brian had settled his suit with Irving Music for $10 million, so I proposed that he give me $5 million and we move on.

Brian agreed.

By accepting a fraction of what I could have collected, I cost Mike

Flynn millions of dollars in contingency fees, every penny of which he earned. But he never pushed me to get more money, nor did he ever waver in a case that became a three-year crusade. With all due respect to Bobby Hatfield and Bill Medley, Mike Flynn is the ultimate Righteous Brother.

Frankly, I had no idea how much money I was being ripped off each year. Before the trial, I was receiving about $75,000 a year in songwriter royalties. After the trial, the amount jumped to over $1 million a year. Even that doesn't reflect what I'm owed. I never received credit for "Surfin' USA," the most popular surfing number in history, as it was never part of Sea of Tunes. It was published instead by Arc Music, Chuck Berry's publisher. This apparently stemmed from Chuck's lawsuit against Brian and Capitol, which resulted in Chuck receiving the songwriting credit. I don't know how much money "Surfin' USA" has generated in songwriter royalties over the past fifty-three years, but if I'm going to lose out on millions, it might as well be to Chuck.

The trial set the record straight, but it didn't affect Brian's reputation. By now, the myth was too strong, the legend too great. Brian was the tormented genius who suffered to deliver us his music—the forever victim, as his lawyer said, or as Brian himself suggested in his beautiful ballad "Till I Die":

I'm a cork on the ocean/Floating on the raging sea . . .
I'm on rock in a landslide/Rolling over the mountainside . . .
I'm a leaf on a windy day/Pretty soon I'll be blown away . . .

To Brian's fans, he was beyond accountability. According to the *Houston Press*, "Wilson suffered the indignity of paying $5 million to Beach Boys singer Mike Love, who sued for co-authorship of 35 songs previously credited solely to Wilson." Yes, the indignity. Peter Ames Carlin, in *Catch a Wave: The Rise, Fall & Redemption of the*

Beach Boys' Brian Wilson, wrote: "Mike had taken particular interest in his cousin's lawsuit against A&M's publishing company. And when Brian took home a $10 million settlement in 1992, Mike got in on the celebration by filing a $3 million lawsuit claiming that he had been uncredited for work on [thirty-five] of the songs in question. And if some of Mike's claims were legit . . . others were less convincing." He never mentioned the outcome.

What the trial did not address was Brian's motives in joining with his father to sell the Sea of Tunes in 1969. At that point, the publishing rights were his, so why sell them—and in the process, sell out the Beach Boys? There are possible explanations. I'll never believe that Brian was "mentally incompetent," but it's possible that the drugs and alcohol, combined with mental illness, made him susceptible to his father's demands or prevented him from fully understanding what he was doing. It's possible that his father agreed to give him part of the $700,000. Asked in a deposition if he received any of that money, Brian said he didn't recall.

It's also possible that Brian agreed with his father and with the consensus in the industry—that the Beach Boys were through. All signs pointed to it in 1969. In March, we had sued Capitol Records for over $2 million in unpaid royalties and production fees. The suit ended our relationship with Capitol, with the label deleting our catalog and refusing to ship past albums to music stores. You couldn't even find *Friends*, which had been released in June of 1968. This was temporary but squeezed us further financially. In the studio, meanwhile, Brian struggled to finish songs. He began "This Whole World" and "All I Want to Do," but Carl completed them. Brian's gloom was evident in the lyrics to a song he wrote in 1969— "Till I Die."

Brian stunned all of us on May 27 of that year when he called an impromptu press conference—Brian hated press conferences, yet he would do this one by himself. He told reporters that the Beach Boys were nearly broke. "If we don't watch it and do something drastic in a few months, we won't have a penny in the bank," he said.

Our finances weren't that bad, and we were just about to launch a successful European tour (though Brian, back home, would have been unaware of its success). Brian told reporters that he was placing his hopes on a new single, "Break Away," that he had written with his dad. How fitting, I suppose, that a collaboration between Uncle Murry and Brian would rescue the Beach Boys from our imminent demise. But it didn't happen.

Released on June 16, "Break Away" only charted at No. 63, making it our worst-performing single since our debut recording.

On July 21, Murry and Brian signed the papers to commence the liquidation of the Sea of Tunes Corporation.

And on August 20, the catalog was gone.

Now it's probably worth more than $100 million. I've never asked Brian why he did what he did. Some doors are better left shut.

The experience confirmed everything I knew about the music industry. Recall David Anderle, the "mayor of hip" who presented himself to the writer David Leaf as the defender of artistic integrity during the *Smile* era. Serving as Leaf's "chief guide," Anderle skewered the Beach Boys for our supposed resistance to Brian's creativity and spent years blaming me for Brian's collapse. The author Steven Gaines later reported that it was Anderle who hired Abe Somer as the Beach Boys' lawyer. I don't know what Anderle knew about Somer, but I do know that in 1970, Anderle formed a production company whose main job was sending artists to Irving Music's A&M Records. The label was probably a nice fit for Anderle, as he went to high school with its founders, Herb Alpert and Jerry Moss. In 1973, with Abe Somer still on its board, A&M Records hired Anderle to be its director of talent development.

So in summary . . . the Beach Boy lawyer who engineered the fraudulent sale of our catalog was introduced to us by a man who ended up working at the very company that bought the catalog—a scam that enriched that company mightily and, indirectly, all of its employees, including David Anderle, who, everyone agreed, had a smashing twenty-six-year career at A&M Records.

What a town.

CHAPTER 24

MY GREATEST TEACHERS

In the summer of 1989, Bruce Johnston and I attended an event at the White House in which President George H. W. Bush announced the creation of the Points of Light Foundation, a nonprofit dedicated to volunteerism and community service. The foundation's name came from the "thousand points of light" phrase that the president used in his nomination address. He was the foundation's honorary chairman, and his call for action was moving. I spoke to a friend of mine in Washington, Rick Fowler, who as a publicist helped us immensely with our Fourth of July concerts. I told Rick that given the president's words, I wanted to do something that would involve schools in motivating students to participate in community service.

I thought about the music business. Why does someone want to become a singer or songwriter? Because that person wants to be a star. So let's use that idea as the basis for how we motivate kids to contribute to their community: *You can be a star through service to others.* That became the slogan for our new nonprofit, which we called STARServ.

To make it work, Rick, in consultation with the White House, reached out to education organizations around the country and sought their support in developing a community-service curriculum. He faced resistance because the education establishment tends to be liberal, and it didn't want to work with a Republican in the White

House. But everyone saw the virtue in this effort and set aside their differences. Thirteen different organizations designed the curriculum (in English and Spanish), which included specific ideas on service projects by age. We received generous funding from the Kraft General Foods Foundation and support from the United Way. We had a raft of celebrity endorsements (Gloria Estefan, Larry Bird, LeVar Burton, MC Hammer, the cast of *Beverly Hills, 90210*) and a distinguished advisory committee. In our first year, in 1990, STARServ sent out materials to 107,000 schools, K–12, and the three-year program ultimately involved 750,000 students.

Our association with the Reagans and the Bushes has fueled the perception that the Beach Boys are Republican, me in particular. Given the GOP's penchant for more overt displays of patriotism, perhaps any group that is considered "America's band" would be so designated. It is certainly true that several Republican presidents have been fans of the Beach Boys, but we would gladly play for any Democratic president as well. It's also true that most people don't know anything about my politics. Our music has almost always been apolitical, and the issues that I care most deeply about—the environment and greater cultural exchanges among nations—are anything but conservative causes.

Some of our music, of course, did reflect these concerns, conveying our own growth in the process. "Summer in Paradise," written by Terry Melcher and me in 1992 (and serving as the title song to our album), included these lyrics.

Way back when our master plan,
Was havin' fun, fun, fun as America's band.
Well, we came out rockin' with Rhonda and Barbara Ann,
Singin' of surf and sand . . .

They chop down the forests,
And in their haste leave a trail of destruction.
And toxic waste is leavin' no one safe.
In their home or their habitat.
Can't let it go like that.

Working on that song put me in the frame of mind to travel to Rio de Janeiro in 1992, with the other Beach Boys, for the Earth Summit, a two-week event sponsored by the United Nations. Its goal was to draw attention to the environment by convening heads of state from around the world, including kings, presidents, and dictators. Next to the Earth Summit was a parallel meeting, the Global Forum, involving nongovernmental organizations and attracting 17,000 people. Our group (which included our wives but not Brian) went there as attendees, but we did meet the U.N. secretary general of the conference, Maurice Strong of Canada. He was a fan of ours, but he realized that our commitment to the cause was real. At a Global Forum meeting, he brought me onstage and had me talk briefly about my lifelong concern for the planet. We had our picture taken with Al Gore, and we marched near the front of a parade through the streets of Rio (Pelé led us). But we weren't there for photo ops. We were impressed with the pioneering work of the NGOs, so the Beach Boys donated $100,000 for a project called Eyewitness for the Earth, which gave video cameras to environmental groups around the world so they could document deforestation, threatened habitat for endangered species, and other risks.

All these years later, we have consensus that climate change is real, but I've also learned that progress is slow and that sometimes what's important is not the progress you achieve but the effort you make. That was certainly true when Jacquelyne and I went to President Bush's White House to try to stop the most important decision of his presidency.

In January of 1991, we were in Holland at a TM meeting with Maharishi at the very time that President Bush was preparing to lead coalition forces on an invasion of Kuwait to drive out Saddam Hussein's Iraqi Army. Maharishi asked Jacquelyne and me to deliver a letter to the president, urging him to forestall the invasion. Maharishi believed the conflict could be resolved peacefully, a view shared by many Americans. (The U.S. Senate approved the authorization of force by a narrow 52–47 vote.) I called the White House from Holland, spoke to one of the president's secretaries, and asked if we could hand-deliver the letter. We were told yes, so we flew to Washington and arrived at the White House on January 16. The place was quiet and foreboding. We were told that President Bush couldn't see us because he was meeting with his generals. I dropped off the letter, and we returned to the hotel.

That night, Operation Desert Storm was launched, and the following day we watched the air strikes on TV.

The letter was only one piece of a broad effort involving many people to delay the invasion, and I believe those efforts were noble. Though the invasion was deemed a success—Saddam was driven out of Kuwait—Maharishi believed that could have been achieved without going to war and that the United States would pay the price in the future.

If my political views were often misunderstood, so too was my relationship with Brian. It was thought that the copyright lawsuit drove a wedge between us and that Brian didn't want to work with the Beach Boys anymore. None of that was true.

In February of 1995, less than two months after we had reached a settlement, I invited Brian to our house in Incline Village, and we sat at the piano and worked on new songs for the first time in maybe two decades. We then went to a studio in Glendale, California, and began laying down the tracks. The song was called "Baywatch Nights," to be used for a *Baywatch* spin-off series by that name, and the backing track and chord progressions captured the classic Beach Boy sound.

But for some reason the song was never completed, and professionally we entered a period of fits and starts. Brian had been developing new music for several years now, working with the songwriter Andy Paley on a new album specifically for the Beach Boys. In September of 1995, Carl, Al, Bruce, and I came into the studio and started laying down the vocals, but that album too was never finished.

Brian's personal life, meanwhile, entered a new phase in 1995, when he married Melinda, whom he met when he was with Landy. (Jacquelyne and I attended the wedding.) Melinda also became Brian's conservator and was an aggressive advocate. On November 9, her lawyer sent Mike Flynn a letter that outlined a list of financial demands that would need to be met "in order [for Brian] to go forward with the Beach Boys." Among them: that Brother Records reimburse Brian $250,000 in legal fees that he spent in the HarperCollins litigation. Brother Records rejected that demand, but the company excluded Brian from having to pay any of the settlement costs. (As a partner at Brother Records and as the author of the book, Brian was technically both a plaintiff and a defendant in the same lawsuit.)

Nonetheless, there were still a lot of good vibes going around. In June of 1996, the Beach Boys, including Brian, went to Nashville to record a collection of our hits with country-western stars. Our daughter, Ambha, was born on January 4 of that year. We took her with us, and Melinda bought her some baby cowgirl boots. The idea for the country album was that of Joe Thomas, a producer who was working with Brian. The sessions actually began in late 1995 at Willie Nelson's studio outside of Austin, Texas, and we completed them in

Nashville. Brian and I hung out there, joked around during interviews, and enjoyed our time working with the likes of Kathy Troccoli, James House, and Doug Supernaw.

We also had fun in the studio. The sultry Lorrie Morgan, putting her bare feet up on a chair, said that she was nervous being around the Beach Boys.

"Well," I said, "I can suck your toes if it will make you feel any better."

"You'll have to get in line," she said.

Perfect! And we backed her up on a nice version of "Don't Worry Baby."

Tammy Wynette joined us as well. She was only fifty-four but quite frail. Singing "In My Room," she struggled at first—the song is far more complex than it appears—but then Brian took over the session and gave Tammy direction with such empathy and compassion. He explained to her the pain and loneliness that he was feeling when he wrote the song many years ago, and given the obvious discomfort that Tammy was in—she had to sit while singing—her response was quite affecting, even inspiring. The song was held back for a planned second country album by the Beach Boys, which never happened. Tammy died in 1998, and the album *Tammy Wynette Remembered*, released five months after her passing, included her version of "In My Room." I believe it was her last recording session.

As for the Beach Boys, the goodwill we fostered in Nashville didn't last that long. We talked about resurrecting the *Smile* tracks and finishing that album. Melinda was a strong proponent, but Carl rejected the idea. He remembered what happened to Brian the last time he worked on *Smile* and feared a repeat. The possibility that *Smile* was going to be completed made its way into the press, and when it didn't happen, some of Brian's fans blamed me, even though I had nothing to do with it. I wouldn't have cared, except we received a bomb threat at our home in Santa Barbara. We notified the authorities, who found the suspect in Hong Kong, but we still had them inspect our packages. It was the start of periodic death threats that I receive to this day. Sometimes the would-be assassins identify the specific concerts in which I'll be taken out. Though the threats upset Jacquelyne, I've never given them much thought. I spend so much of my life onstage that if I ever let those things bother me, I'd be through.

Meanwhile, Brian wanted to focus on his solo career, and he and Melinda would get a house in the Chicago area to be near Joe Thomas and work on projects there with him. Nothing had really changed. The Beach Boys would continue on without Brian.

When Carl was on the road, he and his wife, Gina, used duct tape on the window shades to ensure that no light entered so they could sleep peacefully in the morning hours. It was the perfect metaphor for a man who tenaciously guarded his privacy and sought spiritual calm in all corners of his life. Carl and I remained very close musical and touring partners. In constructing the set list, we'd go over which songs he used a six-string guitar, and which ones he used a twelve-string, and I'd group the numbers accordingly. Carl always protected the band's image, always demanded musical precision. He was righteous in his own way: when he disagreed with you, he'd roll his eyes and drawl, "Blow me." But even when he and I disagreed, we resolved those differences because we each wanted what was best for the Beach Boys.

Carl and Brian maintained their brotherly love, but often at a distance. Despite Carl's role in ousting Landy, Carl and Brian went through long periods during which they rarely spoke, and the rift predated Landy's arrival and extended beyond his dismissal. Like the rest of us, Carl was frustrated by the people who interposed themselves between Brian and his family, but it went beyond that. Musically, Carl was effectively in control of the Beach Boys by the end of the 1960s, and I don't believe the two brothers ever reconciled that transition.

Carl often played the diplomat within the band, at times defusing tense situations. These came up on occasion with Al, whose great voice continued to deliver some memorable performances, such as in our 1986 black-and-white video of "California Dreamin'." But in one instance, we were including professional dancers in the show, with Jacquelyne working as the producer. The band was in Atlanta, and after a long day of rehearsal with the dancers, Al approached Jacquelyne and began chastising her. Al was angry because a dancer who'd been released was also working as Al's nanny, and now Al would have to pay her travel expenses if she continued to work in that capacity.

I had to leave early that day, and the hostilities continued. Jacquelyne, who also had little Brian nearby crying and with our nanny visibly upset, had had enough. She reached into a wardrobe case, pulled out an iron, and swung back to clobber Al.

Carl grabbed her. "You don't want to do that," he said.

"Yes, I do."

"No, you don't."

Jacquelyne put down the iron, and Carl turned to Al and said, "Shame on you." (Al called Jacquelyne that night and apologized.)

When we gathered in Nashville in the summer of 1996, we were all asked to do extended interviews for a video. Carl probably preferred a root canal without anesthesia to a video interview, and in Nashville he didn't even want to be filmed doing studio sessions. He had put on some weight recently and was apparently self-conscious about his appearance. But he did sit down for a lengthy interview and was willing to explore more spiritual or even esoteric elements of the music. With his lilting voice, his wavy dark hair swept back, and his thick beard now flecked with gray, he looked like a Greek deity before the camera.

"The music does have a spiritual quality to it," Carl said. "Small wonder everybody connects to it so well. It so enriches our lives, and it's soothing and healing and it can bring us up, and we can hear something sad and it's a real safe place to experience some of our sadness and get it out."

He continued: "I asked Brian one time—we were just having a long conversation about life and some of the stuff we'd gone through—'Why do you think we succeeded in such a big way?' and he said, 'I think the music celebrated the joy of life in a real simple way.'"

Carl concluded: "Well, you know, everything's perfect, and we're all here to make each other crazy. But I do think my partners are my greatest teachers."

In retrospect, I wonder if Carl had some premonition about his own life, or even if he had medical news that he wasn't sharing. About six months later, in early 1997, he disclosed that he had lung cancer, though he revealed little about his prognosis. Like everyone else in the group, I was stunned because Carl had been the steady hand on the tiller for so long, and of the three Wilson brothers, he was always the healthiest, most stable, and most reliable. Carl said that he was confident he would beat the cancer and that he would continue to tour. We had, as always, a busy summer schedule, and Carl was with us, but his strength was ebbing rapidly. He used a wheelchair to get through airports. He and Gina rode alone, in a separate bus, because the chemo had compromised his immune system. He traveled with pain medication and an oxygen tank, which was kept side stage, and when he performed, he usually sat on a stool. The steroids he was taking had caused his weight to balloon ever further. His doctors traveled with us and attended the shows, and sometimes Carl invited them onstage to jam with him.

Carl was heroic, but if he was going to survive, he wasn't going to do it by trooping through airports and riding buses. Toward the end of the summer, a blood clot developed in his leg, and I finally told him, "You need to devote all your attention to healing."

"Yes," he said, "but I've been the backbone of this group onstage."

"That's true," I said, "but that backbone may need a chiropractor."

He nodded with a grin.

The summer tour ended with six days in Atlantic City. Jacquelyne and I were there with little Brian and Ambha. Carl was a terrific father to his sons, Justyn and Jonah, but he always doted on my kids as well. When we were in the dressing room at the Resorts Casino, Carl was sitting at the piano when he saw my son.

"Come sit with me," he said.

Brian, nine years old, sat next to him, and Carl said, "Show me what you got."

Brian started playing, and Carl looked at him and smiled.

Then Carl picked up Ambha, eighteen months old, who was wearing a furry leopard jacket given to her by Carl and Gina, and he sat her in his lap and told her to play. Ambha banged the keys, and Carl said, "Brian, you're going to have some competition!" And he kissed her and called her "little Jackie."

We knew he was leaving the tour after this performance, to recuperate back home in Colorado, and we didn't really know what the future held. But that final night, on August 29, he came onstage in a wheelchair and sat on a stool while playing his guitar, and when the opening chords were played for "God Only Knows," Carl closed his eyes and sang with raw, undaunted emotion. The guys in the crew were crying. So were friends and family standing side stage.

Afterward, as we were preparing to leave, Carl came out of his dressing room in his wheelchair and rolled down the hallway. He passed each of our rooms, with our names on the door, and then he stopped, wheeled around, and gazed. "I just have to hold on to this memory," he said.

Even as Carl's health was declining, his mother had been ill for some time, and she too took a turn for the worse. The two were emotionally inseparable. To Aunt Audree, Carl was the favorite son and the light of her life. She endured Murry because that was the role she believed she was supposed to play. (Once asked why she didn't divorce him, she said, "That's not what women did back then.") She was often estranged from Brian, supportive of him at every step but hurt by his many years of isolation. She loved Dennis but couldn't control him and despaired at his early and unnecessary death. And then there was Carl. When she joined us on tour, he had a special chair for her on side stage, and at the end of each concert, Carl walked over to his mom and helped her off.

It made 1997 all the more poignant and even otherworldly: devoted mother and beloved son, dying in lockstep.

I believe Aunt Audree knew that Carl was ill but did not know the severity of his illness. I also believe that Carl was determined not to die until after his mother had passed. To spare her that agony would be his final gesture of gratitude.

Audree died of heart and kidney failure on December 1, 1997. She was eighty years old. Her contributions to the Beach Boys have rarely been acknowledged, perhaps because music historians and journalists, most of whom are men, could not imagine that a housewife could play a significant role in a patriarchal family and business. She was tough and protective and even in her twilight years didn't think twice about letting fly the occasional swear word. Her own musical gifts, passed down to her sons, were extraordinary, but her greatest gift was her support for the band, for all of us, and it was unconditional. In those early years, she was often with us in the studio during those marathon sessions, and no matter how our careers were faring—good, not so good, or off the radar—she always made it safe for us to be a Beach Boy. We were all her family.

Two months later, on February 6, 1998, Carl died. He was fifty-one, and his passing shook the music industry and many of our fans.

It was tough for all of us. I called David Marks with the news and had to apologize for being so emotional.

For many years, Carl had a routine before each concert, in which he played a cassette tape from Steve Miller. The singer-songwriter recorded himself chanting a series of notes—a bunch of *la la*s—and Carl would warm up by singing those notes. Miller also sang a line: "It's a beautiful day." And Carl would intone that line again and again, and everyone knew that line was Carl's thing. His mantra, if you will.

At Carl's wake, Gerry Beckley delivered one of the eulogies, and at the end, he pulled out a cassette and said he wanted everyone to listen: it was Steve Miller singing, "It's a beautiful day," and the words seemed to drift over us, heaven-sent.

CHAPTER 25

MY RADIO IS ON

Without Carl, Dennis, or Brian, who in 1998 was working on a solo album, it was assumed that the Beach Boys were through. We hadn't had a hit record in a decade, and Carl was our band director, our lead guitarist, and the lead vocalist on many songs. No more Wilson brothers, no more Beach Boys.

I was nearing sixty, I had a young family, and I could have retired or at least scaled back dramatically. But I wasn't about to do that. For one, I'd go crazy sitting around. I also rejected that our music was too closely connected to a long-gone Camelot era or the Reagan era or any era. Good music always has a time and a place, and I wanted to continue to play ours.

Brother Records owned the touring license, and I was one of four shareholders in the company. The other three were Brian, Al, and Carl's heirs (Justyn and Jonah). Brother Records offered licenses to tour as the Beach Boys to Al, Brian, and me. Brian declined it. Al and I each received a separate license, and we would each have our own Beach Boys' band. Al and I had been touring together for thirty-seven years. Very few groups survive that long, so maybe a divorce was inevitable. But in Al's case, an incident surrounding Carl's death ensured that we would not tour together again.

After Carl left the tour in August of 1997, his lung cancer metastasized to his brain, and we all knew he wasn't going to make it. In

December, a promoter called me and asked if the Beach Boys would be interested in doing a tour with symphonies around the country. In light of Carl's condition, I told him no. The promoter then went to Al and made the same proposal. Al was all for it, figuring he would just get replacements for Carl and me. I got wind of this in early February, and when I called our manager, Elliott Lott, I told him rather heatedly that I wasn't going to do any symphonic tour while Carl was ailing.

Carl died that night. The symphonic tour never happened. And I decided that my touring days with Al were over.

Al and I both assumed a Beach Boy touring license and took to the road, but after a few months, Al's band kept generating demands for refunds. Brother Records sued Al for payment and compliance issues, and Al lost the license (it's been reported that I sued Al over the license, but that's false). Brother Records in turn offered me an exclusive license to tour as the Beach Boys, and a vote was taken by the board. I abstained. Al voted no, but Brian and Carl's heirs voted yes, so by a 2-1-1 vote (Carl's heirs got one vote between them), I received the exclusive license.

But it still didn't mean the Beach Boys would survive. As part of the agreement, I had to pay Brother Records 17.5 percent of all touring revenue (after expenses for lights and sound); that money would flow directly to the shareholders, including Al. I also paid the usual 10 percent in management and agent fees, so 27.5 percent of all touring revenues—before salaries, travel, insurance, and all the other expenses—came right off the top. To make the tours work financially, we'd have to be a lot smarter and a lot more efficient.

Though he wasn't on the board, Bruce Johnston could be classified as the "original non-original" Beach Boy. Over the years, he's played a significant role as an ambassador for our songs—it was Bruce who traveled to London to promote *Pet Sounds*—and his musicianship was as high as anyone's in the group. He once stated that his goal was to win an Oscar for a film score, and if he had gone down that path, he might have done so. Fortunately, his passion for Beach Boys' music ran deep, and he brought energy and enthusiasm to the stage every night, imploring audiences to clap, dance, and sing. So in 1999, Bruce and I went back on the road with one of the best groups of musicians in the business, and that included David Marks.

After leaving the Beach Boys, David had his own band for a while, studied jazz and classical guitar at Berklee College of Music and the New England Conservatory of Music, and he continued playing and recording. I always liked David and had stayed in touch with him, and I knew that he too had been cheated by my uncle Murry. In the late 1970s, David performed with my other group, the Endless Summer Beach Band, and after Carl became ill, I asked David to rejoin the Beach Boys, which he did. Unfortunately, David had severe drug and alcohol abuse problems, which he had struggled with for years and which now led to erratic behavior on and off the stage. I told him that he needed to straighten out or that he'd end up like Dennis. I feared the worst.

David stayed with the band until July of 1999, when he grew tired of us insisting that he sober up. Then in December, he was diagnosed with hepatitis C, a viral infection of the liver; the disease can be contracted by intravenous drug use, which may have happened to David. He received experimental treatments and was told that he had to give up drinking. He did and made a remarkable recovery, and he would play with us again.

I had been arranging tours since the 1960s and knew how to do them. We were not looking to play in football stadiums, where promoters can lose millions of dollars. Do that once, and no one wants to work with you again. We wanted smaller venues, including festivals and fairs, where refreshments were affordable and families could enjoy our concert as part of the entrance fee. We played at performing arts centers and amphitheaters that could easily accommodate intermissions and where the acoustics were often superior. We played at casinos so couples could see a show as part of their evening at the tables. I still believed, as I did in the 1960s, that it wasn't enough to play in the biggest cities but that we should also perform in the smaller markets that are often passed over, in Cheyenne or Wichita or Scottsdale, where fans were so obviously appreciative. We traveled as well to the United Kingdom, Japan, Australia, or anywhere else that presented an opportunity. We played privately for companies or sponsors while also appearing in select arenas that held 20,000. I wanted to play as many shows in as many venues as humanly possible. The guys in the band teased me that I want to schedule the "no más tour": keep playing until they scream, "No más!"

The challenge, however, was to create a show that was vibrant onstage but efficient offstage so we could meet our obligations to Brother Records. I could handle the onstage part, but I'm not a business manager and don't really like telling other people what to do. I asked Jacquelyne to review our operations, and that led to some draconian changes. We were spending thousands of dollars a day on catering while giving employees per diems for food. Our liquor bill was out of control, with Jack Daniel's, tequila, beer, and wine backstage at every show. We were taking our own limousines to and from the airport. Every band member had his own six-foot-tall, heavy wardrobe case with built-in drawers, and that required an employee to set it up and break it down at each stop. Moving these cases around the country cost over $100,000 a year, but as Jacquelyne said to me, "No one sees a Beach Boy concert for the wardrobes."

All of the unnecessary amenities were either curtailed or eliminated. Nowadays, as far as food is concerned, I request gluten-free and vegetarian, and to ensure that my shirts look nice, an iron is supplied. We have ownership in NetJets that was purchased many years ago, but we use private aircraft strategically. We don't have anyone on payroll who is not essential, and we don't squander money on garish stage props or fireworks or overblown production. It's less about conjuring the atmospherics and more about replicating the harmonies.

In 2003, Capitol wanted to release another best-of album. Our music had been sliced, diced, and repackaged in various ways dating all the way back to 1966, when the first *Best of the Beach Boys* was released. Our box set from the *Pet Sounds* sessions in 1997 was a tribute to the original album, but most of our compilations were just that—the compiling of songs on one LP. These made economic sense for the label, and by 2003, about thirty compilation albums had been released. But since the 1960s, only *Endless Summer* and *Spirit of America* had become Top 20 records.

For the 2003 effort, I was able to offer some recommendations to Capitol, starting with the title. I suggested *Sounds of Summer,* as a continuation of our seasonal motif. Capitol wanted to use our biggest hits, but it didn't understand how the sequence creates an overall tempo and vibe—the same effect you create with your set list in a concert—and Capitol got the order all wrong. You don't put "Little Deuce Coup" next to "God Only Knows." So I rearranged the sequence, beginning with "California Girls" and grouping the fast-paced surf and car songs at the beginning, dialing it back with the ballads, and then picking up steam in the last third and ending with "Good Vibrations."

Sounds of Summer included thirty songs, the largest collection of our music ever issued. The cover was a shimmering sunset over the ocean, and the album charted at No. 16 while selling more than 3 million copies—a complete surprise. I think the title, the cover, and the large number of songs all helped, but more than anything it was just a new generation of Americans discovering the Beach Boys.

In the late 1970s, Brian wanted to work with me on some new songs, but I was on a retreat in another country. So Brian wrote a short note and gave it to my brother Stan, who was working for him at the time. The message was addressed to Maharishi and read, "Please send Mike home." Stan had no way of getting the note to Maharishi, so he kept it. Now it stands as a reminder of my partnership with Brian and how much he valued our relationship. I was always confident that if Brian and I ever sat down at the piano, we could be successful again and try for another No. 1 record, but it was never that easy.

In the early 2000s, I saw Brian during one of the settlement hearings between Brother Records and Al Jardine (numerous lawsuits were filed between the company and Al over use of the Beach Boys' license). Brian walked right up to me in the courthouse and said, "Mike, I really want to work with you. I've got all these ideas, but Melinda says it's not time yet."

Years passed. Brian and I continued to communicate, and in March of 2011, he and Melinda joined Jacquelyne and me and most of my children for my birthday dinner in Los Angeles. After dinner, we attended a Lakers game to watch my nephew Kevin Love (Stan's son), who was a star with the Minnesota Timberwolves, and we met with him on the floor after the game. The following month, Jacquelyne and I had dinner with Brian and Melinda in Palm Springs, and the waiter asked us if we wanted anything to drink.

"Do you want to share a beer?" Brian asked me.

"I think we can afford two," I said.

In May, Brian called me about doing a rock and roll album, and we spoke of some hits that we wanted to cover. I was all for it. We'd had success with past covers ("Rock and Roll Music," "Barbara Ann," "Sloop John B," "Why Do Fools Fall in Love"); the music was already written; Brian could do new arrangements; I could sing in my bass voice, my "Kokomo" voice, my "Surfin' USA" voice, whatever voice; and it would be a way to get the partnership going again.

We discussed the album as part of a larger effort involving the Beach Boys' fiftieth anniversary—a tour as well as a new album. Brian and I had our own bands and our own representatives, so a lot of time was spent hammering out a collaboration agreement, or partnership, that would rightfully honor fifty years of the Beach Boys. The crux of the partnership, according to Joe Thomas, Brian's producer, was that Brian would be "king of the studio" (for the new album), while I would be "king of the road" (for the tour). We knew our fans would love the idea—all of the "original" living Beach Boys (Brian, Al, David, Bruce, and me) would be on tour—and I believe Brian was as excited as I was about writing new songs together.

"We still got it, Mike," he told me. "We still got it."

Capitol Records, however, wasn't interested in an album of rock and roll covers, and that was the least of my problems. Melinda and Joe Thomas, who had produced Brian's *Imagination* album (1998), went to Capitol with songs that Brian had left over from his solo efforts, and Capitol gave us a contract that would require using those numbers. Even though Brian and I had a partnership agreement, I was never consulted on the record contract and hadn't even heard any of the tracks.

In the summer of 2011, I went to the Ocean Way Recording studio in Hollywood to work on the new album but quickly discovered I had little to do. Most of the songs were completed. I was given some lines to write on a couple of tracks, but I felt that was just to placate me. The result was comical. One person wrote *War and Peace* (1,225 pages), but it took five people, me included, to write "Isn't It Time" (twenty-five lines).

What I came to do—what Brian and I had agreed on—was to collaborate on new material, but that never happened. I didn't ask Brian because I knew he wasn't in control. I did ask Melinda about my agreement, and she told me, "Brian doesn't write that way anymore."

Actually, he does write that way, if he is given the chance, but there was no point in arguing.

Though I was nominally the album's "executive producer," *That's Why God Made the Radio* was delivered to Capitol in 2012 without my approval or without my even listening to the final cut. It was a "Brian Wilson and the Beach Boys" album, even though it was not advertised as such. I had one song on it, "Daybreak over the Ocean," which I had recorded many years ago for a solo LP but never released. I played it for Brian in the studio, and he said it was his favorite song on the new album. To promote it, we appeared on QVC, the home shopping network, and Capitol front-loaded the sale orders, so the record reached No. 3. But it had no hits and quickly dropped from the charts.

The anniversary tour was even more difficult, and it was almost killed before it began.

I knew the logistics would be tricky, as Brian's own band had been performing for a number of years, so we'd have to integrate his group with the Beach Boys. I consulted with Brian on the anniversary set list—he didn't want the lead on "Sloop John B" because he didn't want to sing about fighting—and I drew up the songs that would work for the integrated band. I assumed everything was in place. But when I arrived at our first rehearsal, Melinda was already there, and incredibly, she had changed the set list. She had also ordered five Auto-Tune devices, to correct off-key vocals, and attached them to the mics used by Brian, Al, Bruce, David, and me. But no one used the device except Brian, no one else wanted to use it, and they shouldn't have been purchased and installed without approval.

I'd had enough. I told Melinda that she wasn't where she was supposed to be and reminded her that I was in charge of the tour.

"You know what's wrong with you, Mike Love," she said. "You've got a fucking chip on your shoulder."

"Really? Well, me and my fucking chip are out of here. Enjoy the tour." And I walked out.

Joe Thomas and John Branca, who was one of Brian's former lawyers and was now serving as a co-consultant on the fiftieth anniversary efforts, called me to try to mend the fences, and I told them I would return only if Melinda was banned from rehearsals until the final day, when the press arrived. They agreed, and we continued on.

The tour began on April 24—the five principals, plus a ten-member band, and we sang backup on videos of Carl singing "God Only Knows" and Dennis singing "Forever." Brian had appeared with us onstage in the mid-1990s, but he hadn't really toured with the Beach Boys since the early 1980s. I wasn't sure what to expect, but I assumed that our fans would love it, and they did. We generated more media attention than we had in years, including a performance of "Good Vibrations" on the Grammy Awards show.

Traveling with Brian was both hopeful and sobering. There were times when I'd see the Brian of old. During one sound check, our band director, Scott Totten, asked Brian if he'd like to perform "It's OK," which Brian and I wrote in 1976, but it'd probably been years since Brian had played it or even thought about it. Brian said, "Yeah, great!" He turned to his keyboard and said, "This is what we gotta do!" He then began assigning everyone his part as if we had written the song yesterday.

His memory and his wit could both be sharp. The Beach Boys' drummer, John Cowsill, used to play in his own family band in the late 1960s and '70s. (The Cowsills were the inspiration for the TV series *The Partridge Family*.) One of their hit songs, "Indian Lake," included a war whoop. Way back in 1978, John was performing at a club in Los Angeles, and in the middle of the set, some bearded guy in the audience started banging his hand yelling, "Indian Lake! Indian Lake!" It was Brian, and he wanted to hear the song.

Now on the fiftieth tour, Brian often relaxed in the dressing room, his eyes closed, and one time John walked by, and Brian suddenly yelled out the war whoop from "Indian Lake"—as if to say to John, *I know you're there, and I remember when I tried to get you to play that song long ago.*

Brian even made light of his physical aches and pains. During one rehearsal, his back was hurting, and he had to lie down to relieve the pressure. We didn't know where he was. John Stamos was with us, and after a while, Brian saw John and said, "Hey, Stamos! Could you tell them I'm not dead." John called out the news.

But Brian's discomfort with live shows was still apparent. When we were at the Beacon Theatre in New York, the fans were close to the stage, and when they started cheering for Brian, he became agitated, and Jeff Foskett walked over, put his arm around him, and said, "Hey, man, they love you." Brian used a monitor onstage, not only for the lyrics but even to remind him when to say, "Thank you, ladies and gentlemen." Sometimes during the finale, "Fun, Fun, Fun," Brian's hands dropped to his side, and he wouldn't play or sing.

Interviews were often an ordeal. We did a group interview at Google's headquarters, and Brian was practically inert; when he did speak, he couldn't remember to lift his microphone. At one point, David had to raise Brian's elbow to get the mic near his mouth. There were times in the dressing room when Brian needed help. Jeff Foskett had joined Brian's band years ago and was now authorized to give Brian his medication as part of his duties as caretaker, and when Brian got too excited, Jeff would give Brian a white envelope with his prescription meds.* I had no objections to Brian's medical care, but for those of us who knew Brian in his glory, when his eyes were on

---

* Jeff Foskett left Brian's band in 2014 and rejoined the Beach Boys.

fire and his emotive swings were part of his improvisational genius, it was a bit sad to witness.

For all the success we had onstage, the tour was one of the most stressful things that I or anyone in my band had ever been through. Combining the two groups was like merging two corporations with radically different cultures. Mine was a seven-piece band with five crewmen; we were doing 120 shows a year, and we were light and nimble and knew how to do a great show while staying on budget and making our financial goals. Now we were part of a fifteen-piece band with twenty-five crew members and a revolving door of special guests, and we traveled with far more elaborate lighting, sound systems, and staging equipment.

Brian and I never had a cross word, but those looking out for us did. I always rode in the same bus as the rest of the band, but Brian had his own bus, the expense of which would come out of all of our pockets. Jacquelyne was overseeing my side of the budget, so she had to negotiate with Melinda and Joe Thomas that Brian reimburse the tour for his bus. The disagreements and bruises accumulated. We once had to fly from Florida to New York, but Melinda planned to have the tour buses drive from Florida to New York and sit idle for several days, until the engagement was over. This extravagance the tour didn't need, so we nixed that idea.

We were only a month into the tour when we had a concert in San Diego, near a part-time residence of ours in Rancho Santa Fe and where our daughter, Ambha, was attending high school. Now sixteen years old, Ambha had been singing and dancing with us onstage since she could walk, and she has the voice of a songbird. Whenever we played in San Diego, her second home, she would dance with me on "Surfer Girl" and sing either "Darlin'" or "Sail On, Sailor," and she always brought the crowd to its feet. I asked Brian if Ambha could sing "Sail On, Sailor," which was one of his leads, for this one concert on the tour. He said yes. During sound check, Ambha asked

Brian as well. He agreed but was skeptical that a girl so young could actually do it. Then the band played the song, and Ambha was awesome.

"Wow," Brian said, "you did it better than me."

We were good to go, but then backstage, Melinda, their son Dylan in tow, stormed up to Jacquelyne and contended that Ambha should be singing one of my leads, not one of Brian's. She asked how I would feel if Dylan sang "California Girls."

Jacquelyn said that I would have no problem with that as long as Dylan could sing it well.

The argument got more heated, the two women standing toe-to-toe and Scott Totten having to redirect Ambha to a dressing room. Finally, Jacquelyne told Melinda, "Mike already discussed the matter with his partner, Brian."

Melinda's face reddened. "Mike's not his fucking partner," she said. "I'm his fucking partner."

Well, I didn't sign up for that. You can mess with me, but you can't disrespect my family. The confrontation prompted me to call Branca and Thomas and let them know that the Hollywood Bowl would be my last show. As far as I was concerned, they could go on without me. I really didn't care. Branca, however, told me that my pulling out would be extremely disruptive to the whole enterprise. I figured it was in everyone's interest to finish, so I stayed on.

This crisis actually had a happy ending. Ambha sang "Sail On, Sailor" and got a standing ovation. Brian, speaking into the mic, congratulated her, and Ambha walked over and gave him a big hug. Brian had spent little time with Ambha over the years, but this moment opened the door to a warm friendship between the two for the duration of the tour.

But those bright spots were few. There were endless negotiations and often disputes over sponsorships, endorsements, marketing campaigns, artwork, merchandise, master videotapes, and the tour dates themselves. Vendors weren't paid. Budgets were ignored. Bridges were burned. The tour, in fact, lost money in North America and only finished in the black because of our concerts in Asia—but at the expense of our promoters there, who lost money. So too did our promoters in Spain, and it would take several years to reestablish those markets.

But I will say this—we kicked butt onstage. The tour that was originally planned for fifty dates in fifty major markets was extended to seventy-three concerts in fourteen countries—a five-month whirlwind that ended on September 28, in London. The audience response didn't surprise me, but that we made it to the end was a miracle.

Everyone should have gone home happy, but that would have been too easy. On June 1, we received an email from Melinda that said, in response to a lucrative offer for the reunion band to perform in Israel, "no more shows for Wilson." With the end in sight, the Beach Boys—the non-reunion version of the band—began accepting invitations for when the fiftieth tour was over. (Our license in fact obligates us to continue touring to maintain the revenue flow to Brother Records.) On June 25, Melinda sent another email asking us to disregard her previous message. But by then it was too late. We had booked other concerts, and promoters had begun selling tickets. Besides, the reunion tour was never meant to be permanent—it wasn't feasible logistically or economically. The band was too big to play in smaller markets, but playing those markets is how we've maintained a loyal fan base and kept the catalog alive all these years. And the longer the reunion tour lasted, the more confusion we'd be creating once my band returned to the road.

I had wanted to send out a joint press release, between Brian and me, formally announcing the end of the reunion tour on September 28. But I couldn't get Brian's management team on board (Brian himself doesn't make those kinds of decisions). Everything came to a head in the middle of September, when Brian's lawyer accused me of using Brian's likeness on the Beach Boys' website to promote future concerts that did not include Brian. That violated my license for the Beach Boys. But the website was controlled by Capitol/UMG. Regardless, the lawyer told me that to maintain the license and to eliminate the confusion, I needed to announce the end of the reunion tour.

We still couldn't get Brian's signature on the release, so I had to send it out by myself. The media backlash was swift and devastating: I had fired Brian Wilson from the Beach Boys. This triggered more death threats, by mail and phone, which we had to take to the authorities.

Over the years, I've rarely responded to personal attacks, and I don't believe I have ever defended myself in writing. But this time I wrote an op-ed for the *Los Angeles Times*, explaining that I couldn't fire Brian even if I wanted to, that the tour was always meant to be a limited run, that smaller markets wouldn't support the reunion band, and that now Brian and I—as agreed upon—were returning to our separate groups.

Brian responded with his own op-ed, titled "It Kinda Feels Like Getting Fired."

I'm not sure if Brian, or whoever wrote the column for him, appreciated the irony of his statement. For much of the history of the Beach Boys, Brian and the people around him have tried to distance him from the group so he could shed his surf-pop image and take his place in the critics' pantheon. Me fire Brian? From what? If Brian had wanted any part of the Beach Boys, it would have been quite easy after Carl's death. He could have accepted a Beach Boys license for himself, when it was offered, but he didn't. His new album had just come out. His solo career needed to be nurtured—a career that did not require him to distribute 17.5 percent of all revenues to Brother

Records. Brian's managers and advisors surely told him that he had better opportunities on his own.

And the Beach Boys? Brian gave me the torch, which I've proudly carried since the day we began.

Brian's true feelings came out on the tour. As anyone who was on it will attest, he loved the camaraderie of the guys, he loved the music, and he loved being a Beach Boy again. He wanted the tour to continue, and he said so loudly and often, but you can't change the melody once the score's been written.

And after the tour was over, Brian often told reporters that he still wanted to do that album of rock and roll covers.

The whole experience was bittersweet for me. The concerts were amazing, and I was grateful to play again with all the living Beach Boys. I didn't care for the vilification at the end, though I'm used to it. For those who believe that Brian walks on water, I will always be the Antichrist.

In 1972, Brian wrote "Mount Vernon and Fairway," the corner of my childhood home. It wasn't really a song but a twelve-minute fairy tale, or allegory, about a young Prince (me) whose special bedroom window (like mine) "looked down into a deep, deep forest [and glimpsed] distant lights from other castles in the kingdom." A Pied Piper (Brian) brings magical music to the Prince through a glowing transistor radio (like the one we listened to as kids). The Piper tells the Prince that if he leaves the transistor radio on after midnight, the Piper will bring more magic music to him. In days ahead, the Prince does that, but "he heard nothing like the music of that magic night . . . there's nothing but Bach on this radio." The Prince stops believing in the Piper and disregards the transistor until he hears a mysterious sound one night.

Could it be the Pied Piper himself,
Coming out of the magic transistor radio?
Or was it just the wind whistling by the castle window.

No one knows, but the tale concludes:

If you have a transistor radio and the lights are all out some
night,
Don't be very surprised if [the radio] turns to light green.
And the whirling magic sound of the Pied Piper comes to visit
you.
I'm the Pied Piper
In the radio.

I remember Carl's remark to Brian many years ago that his estrangement from his family was "contrived," engineered by others. It's still contrived. I haven't seen Brian since the reunion tour, and there comes a point where you become conditioned to doing certain things or not doing certain things. I don't know if Brian and I will ever write another song together, or share a meal together, or even have a conversation.

But my radio is on.

CHASING THE SUN

In the early 1980s, my childhood friend Tom Emmel came to a concert, and he told me that the afternoons we had spent chasing monarch butterflies in my backyard had been well spent. Tom was a zoologist who had become one of the nation's leading experts on the monarchs. At his invitation, I accompanied him on a trip to the Trans-Mexican Volcanic Belt of Mexico, where the government had created a world biosphere reserve to protect the monarch. As I learned there, this butterfly was far more miraculous than I ever imagined, and I wanted my family to not only understand that miracle but experience it.

In March of 2000, Jacquelyne and I and all of my children (except Melinda, who had other commitments) flew to Mexico City and rode a bus about ninety miles west to the mountainous forest reserve, which is part of Michoacán. It was our first family vacation that did not center on a holiday, and the conditions were fairly primitive. We packed a "survival kit" for each child (food, supplies, clothes) and stayed in adobe huts; only cold water was available, and we brought space heaters to stay warm at night.

With Tom as our leader, we awoke before dawn and hiked for about an hour, until we reached the edge of the El Rosario colony, at about 11,000 feet. There we looked up and saw hundreds of thousands of monarchs, dark and motionless, clustering on the pine and oyamel fir trees. The sun was still low, but once the shafts of light peeked through, the warmth stirred the butterflies. They twitched, quivered, and opened their brilliant orange-and-black wings, creating iridescent curtains that covered the branches and trunks. Then the monarchs took flight, a few at first, then more, and then by the tens of thousands, drifting sixty feet above us like snowflakes, some fluttering right onto our shoulders or hands, at once fearless and peaceful—representing, to some of the faithful in Mexico, the souls of the departed, but to me, the glories of the present. The butterflies would seek out water from a stream or nectar from a plant, then return to their cluster on the tree. But some fell to the cold ground— too cold for them to move, and unless they warmed up, they would die, literally freezing to death. So Ambha, now four, picked one up, cupped it in her hands, and gently blew on it until it shuddered, warmed up, and flew away. One after the next, she gave them life.

. . . and the butterfly.

The trip taught the kids something about the beauty and fragility of our ecosystem, and it connected them to my youth, conveying something in action—my love of nature, my reverence for the planet, my desire to bring together family—that I was not so great at conveying in words.

Besides, these monarchs had a lot more to teach us.

They would soon fly north, perhaps 1,500 miles, to Texas, where they would mate, lay their eggs, and die. Those larvae would emerge as butterflies and continue their trek north. They would live for thirty days at most, and they too would reproduce before dying. That life cycle, of propagating and dying, would be repeated twice more until the third generation of monarchs reached the northern United States or southern Canada. Those butterflies, instead of expiring quickly, would reverse the itinerary and migrate south through the United States and down the Central Mexican Plateau, then veer west to the forests of Michoacán. It would be an unerring flight of some 2,500 miles—all cued by the sun. Arriving in November and needing to survive the winter, the monarchs would have hundreds of peaks from which to choose and would need to select the one that gave them the most protection.

For such a vulnerable creature, this migration seemed quite peril-ous, but according to Tom, it has occurred each year for the past 1.75 million years.

To identify the right trees across thousands of acres of forest, the monarchs would settle on the branches and trunks occupied the pre-vious spring by their ancestors, whose lingering scent was the gift of life to their great-grandchildren.

I tried to keep my promise to Grandpa Love, to look after Grandma, staying in regular communication with her and making sure she was always part of my life. She was as resilient as her husband was tough. When Brian was born, she gave him a velvet bag of silver dol-lars that she had collected over the years. Not your typical baby gift, but it was perfect from a woman who opened my eyes to that which was unconventional, exotic, and valuable. According to the Vedas, when coins are gifted to a newborn, it is a marked sign of a high birth. I don't believe Grandma Love knew that, but I do believe that she saw something mystical in those silver dollars. She died two years later, in 1990, at age ninety-one.

A recurring theme in my life has been who is and who isn't family, a question that has played out for me in stark and at time painful ways.

In 1993, Jacquelyne and I decided to set up trust funds for my seven children as well as health care trusts. In such a trust, blood samples are collected and preserved for future medical needs. When those tests were completed for my kids, the lab notified me that I was not the biological father of my second youngest child, Mike Jr. (Ambha had not yet been born). It was news that caused us much despair. His mother, Cathy Martinez, was pregnant before we married in 1981, but I had no reason to believe the child wasn't mine. Mike Jr., who was born on April 24, 1982, sometimes asked me why he didn't look like his other brothers and sisters, but I never gave that question much thought. He grew up with his mom in Las Vegas and his maternal grandmother in the San Fernando Valley. I always had a sweet relationship with him, as did Jacquelyne. We saw him as much as we could, and my child support payments ensured that he went to private school.

After we received the lab results, Cathy wanted Mike Jr. to be retested. He was, and it confirmed the initial assessment. I continued paying child support and did not want to lose contact with Mike Jr., but Cathy and I got into a war of words over what happened in the past and what should happen in the future. We ended up in court, and the judge ruled that Cathy had engaged in fraud of paternity and was assessed a fine (which we never tried to collect). The judge also ruled that I was to sever all communications with Mike Jr., but the judge told me, through my lawyer, "Don't worry, someday he will seek you out."

Jacquelyne and I wanted to maintain the relationship, so we set up a series of counseling sessions in Las Vegas with Mike Jr. and his mom, to work through what had obviously been a traumatic turn of events for a boy just starting his teenage years. But Cathy canceled at the last minute, and I was prevented from seeing or talking to Mike Jr. Several years passed, and I didn't know if or when I'd see him again.

Then in 1999, we were playing in Las Vegas, and when I was onstage, I looked to the side and saw Jacquelyne hugging a strapping young man. I walked over between songs, and it was Mike Jr., who had presented his driver's license—Michael Edward Love Jr.—to the security guard.

It took some time and healing to bring us all together again, but the judge was right. Mike Jr. did seek us out, and he is part of our family—one of eight children—that I hold dear.

I never lost my connection to Maharishi, whom I continued to see at World Peace Assemblies, and at one of them, he said something quite curious. "The world plan is accomplished." If the world plan involved peace, health, and a higher consciousness, it didn't seem like we had gotten there. He believed, however, that once his ideas had been set in motion, they would take root, change people's lives, and make the world a better place.

It's what I'd always hoped for.

In 1975, after our last personnel left Saigon, I flew to Washington and asked to meet with a senator who had oversight responsibilities for the Department of Veterans Affairs. I wanted the VA to offer Transcendental Meditation to our guys who fought in Vietnam. I met with a staffer on a subcommittee—himself a disabled vet who had lost both legs and his right forearm in Vietnam—and he told me that the VA dealt only with serious medical issues. He summarily dismissed me.

No one in 1975 had heard of post-traumatic stress disorder, and the VA offered no alternative therapies. But those days are over. The VA now offers meditation, yoga, mindfulness training, and other alternative therapies derived from Eastern practices. Their benefits for pain relief as well as relaxation are recognized fully, and not just by the government. "Mindful work," or meditation, is now offered at many of America's largest companies, including Google, Ford, and Aetna. Meditation or yoga classes are being offered at public libraries, on college campuses, and at health clubs. Mindfulness even has a coloring book (volumes one and two).

These alternative therapies all share common traits with TM. They are being used by celebrities, athletes, and journalists, and their popularity will grow as they receive greater exposure. Interestingly, the Senate staff member with whom I met in 1975 was Max Cleland, who would become a U.S. senator from Georgia as well as a personal friend. When we reminisce about our first meeting, he tells me, "I thought you were a Hollywood flake, but your real problem was that you were forty years ahead of your time."

Maharishi died in 2008, at age ninety—he wasn't ahead of his time, I don't believe. He was just setting a path that others have followed.

You never know how things are going to change. My childhood house on Mount Vernon and Fairway is still standing, but its windows now have iron bars. Charles Manson is incarcerated in California State Prison, Corcoran, where he may have bumped into Phil Spector, who was sent there in 2009 after he was convicted of murdering the actress Lana Clarkson. And the passage of time brings inevitable sorrows. In late May of 2016, a friend called me and said he had someone to speak with me. It was Muhammad Ali, at a lakeside residence in Scottsdale, Arizona.

I said to him, "I love you, Muhammad. We love you. Do you know that?"

He responded faintly, "Yeah."

I never thought that the next news I would hear was that Ali was in a hospital and that he was not expected to live. He died at age seventy-four, but I'm glad I was able to tell him personally my message of love, which turned out to be farewell.

Perhaps my most avid supporter over the many years has been my sister Stephanie, who would be outraged by the attacks against me and would go into the Internet chat rooms and flame the anonymous blowhards who were spreading lies. She was also a wonderful wife, mother, and aunt who gave my kids creative gifts (a clock shaped like a Hawaiian shirt) and brought her own bread maker to our house to help us prepare holiday meals. It was all the more heartbreaking when she developed cancer, apparently the same type that had stricken our mom, in the early 2000s. Toward the very end, Stephanie was hospitalized in the Bay Area, and we went to see her, bringing my dad as well as Ambha.

When we walked in, Stephanie said, "Hey, Daddyo." Ambha gave her a stuffed animal and told her how good she looked, and Stephanie put her emaciated arm around her and gave her a hug. We brought in food and made conversation, but it was too much for my dad. Stephanie was connected to various machines, bags, tubes, and a morphine drip. My dad started to shake, and we all had to step outside for a moment.

"I just hate seeing one of my kids that way," he said.

Ambha, eight years old, spoke up. "Just look in her eyes, Grandpa. It's still her."

That really got to me. From the mouth of babes.

Stephanie died, way too young, in 2005.

It really is about the kids.

In addition to my son Brian, I've been fortunate to share the stage with a couple of my other children. Christian, a guitarist and singer, performed with the Beach Boys for several years, and it was good to have a real surfer in the band again. Ambha has her own dreams of being a performing artist, and it's something to hear my youngest daughter bring new life to songs I wrote decades ago. She also inherited her father's sense of mischief: she likes to walk around the house wearing a Rolling Stones T-shirt, just to piss me off.

The funny thing is, fifty-five years after the fact, the Beach Boys in the broadest sense—I'll call it the extended family—have never been closer. This was driven home to me in February of 2014 when I had the great honor of receiving the Ella Award, named after Ella Fitzgerald and given to a singer or songwriter for his or her lifetime achievements. (Natalie Cole, Elton John, and Frank Sinatra, among others, have been awarded.) John Stamos emceed, and we had performances from so many luminaries, including Dean Torrence, Gerry Beckley, Dewey Bunnell, Micky Dolenz, Peter Noone, and jazz saxophonist Dave Koz. Bill Medley and Jeff Foskett sang "You've Lost That Lovin' Feeling," and Rita Wilson sang "The Warmth of the Sun," while husband Tom Hanks danced in the aisle during "Fun, Fun, Fun."

It wasn't all about the legends—young stars like Jessica Sanchez and Erika Jayne added their soaring vocals—but the night was really an extended tribute to the Beach Boys and all that we accomplished together. And we were together: Al Jardine, whose voice is timeless, assumed the lead on "Help Me, Rhonda"; David Marks played his licks for "Little Deuce Coupe"; Bruce Johnston played the keyboard on "Kokomo"; David Lee Roth joined me on "California Girls."

Brian, who lives ten minutes away, didn't attend.

No matter. His daughters, Carnie and Wendy, were there. So were the children of Dennis and Carl. Seven of my eight children attended; so too did my sister Maureen and many close friends. We heard from California Saga, a band comprised of ten of the Beach Boys' children. That included Ambha performing "Darlin'," which I cowrote in 1967, a song that I would sing as a lullaby to Ambha as a young girl.

I hold you in my heart.
As life's most precious part.
Oh darlin'.
I dream about you often, my pretty darlin'.

For all the strife and turmoil, the music has bonded us together—the Wilson and the Love families, across three generations and counting. Those bonds, I believe, like the music, will endure.

I was honored with members of the Waters family (Julia, Maxine, Luther, and Oren), R&B vocalists whose career as "backup singers" could not conceal their brilliance. Not only was I thrilled to be on-stage with them, but they agreed to join me in singing "Unleash the Love," which I've written and recorded but not yet released.

For most of the show, however, I sat at my table, holding a mic. I was a member of the audience, there to enjoy the music, but I just felt that I had to be part of it. It meant too much to me. I sang the bass part from my seat.

And the Beach Boys play on, having just completed our greatest touring year in history. In 2015, we had 175 concerts—our most ever in a single year—and played in eight countries, including two sold-out shows at Royal Albert Hall in London. I'm more determined than ever to take our music where it's never been. In November, after concerts in Australia and New Zealand, I flew back to the United States to have Thanksgiving dinner with my family in Incline Village. I was home for one day, and then Jacquelyne dropped me off at the Reno airport for a midnight flight to New York, where I caught another flight to Frankfurt, Germany, and then caught yet another flight to Innsbruck, Austria. There we met up with the band and took a two-hour bus ride to Ischgl, a breathtaking resort town in the Austrian Alps. We arrived midday, which gave us time for some interviews and a long gondola ride, with an ascent of more than 4,000 snow-covered feet. (We took a surfboard for press photos.) The outdoor concert began at six P.M., and bundled in our coats and hats, we took the stage, which was adorned with palm trees and space heaters. It gets a bit brisk during ski season in the Alps, and my hands nearly froze holding the mic, while the guitar strings felt like sharp blades. But my bandmates never complained. We did our entire one hundred-minute show (adding "Cotton Fields," which was a big hit in Europe), and a crowd of 15,000 fans, wearing their parkas, hats, and mittens and standing near the moonlit pistes, danced to "Catch a Wave." What a sight! We briefly attended an after-concert party, went to bed, and were awakened at three A.M. Our bus steered out of town and headed for Munich for a flight to Amsterdam, where we took another bus to Rotterdam for a rehearsal for the Night of the Proms.

I achieved one of my goals in 2013, when we traveled to China and played in Shanghai and Macau. We did so without special intervention from any political leaders, which I count as progress between the two countries. I think that Richard Pryor, who died in 2005, would have been delighted as well. We also performed in Hong Kong, where we played at halftime for the Hong Kong Sevens, one of the world's largest international rugby events. We still haven't made it to Russia, but in 2016 we made our first appearance in South Korea.

Our hard work has benefited everyone. Since 1999, when I assumed the exclusive touring license, the Beach Boys have paid Brother Records $23.8 million, split among Brian, Al, Carl's sons, and me.

The band has never been in greater demand—for each invitation we accept, we turn down two to three. Sometimes as I walk off the stage, the promoter commits to booking us back for the following year.

Why all the love? Because the shows have never been better. I'm surrounded by an exceptional crew and staff, and the performers—Bruce Johnston as well as guitarists Scott Totten, Jeff Foskett, and Brian Eichenberger; keyboardist Tim Bonhomme, and drummer John Cowsill—are extraordinary talents and completely dedicated to the music. But there's more to it than that.

Scott is also our music director, and in the past several years, he has drilled down into our original recordings with the hope of reproducing those exact sounds onstage. Brian's arrangements were so complex and drew upon so many instruments (including the harpsichord, accordion, bass harmonica, theremin, bass saxophone, and alto flute) that the Beach Boys could never replicate those instruments onstage unless we expanded the size of the band, which creates other problems. But dramatic advances in music technology have now allowed the keyboard to reproduce the sounds of real instruments via "samples," in which we record every note in an instrument's range and articulation and trigger it through the keyboard controller. We can also split the keyboard into different zones, where one zone plays one instrument and another zone a second instrument. Thus, on "God Only Knows," Tim plays the piano and French horn in the beginning, later adds the strings, and ends with a flute.

It's taken five decades, but we now have the technology to bring our original sound to the live stage. Improved video has also made a difference. Ten years ago, the video equipment was too bulky to transport, but now a laptop computer does the trick. As we're playing onstage, the big screen behind us not only includes the halcyon images of California back in the day, but also features appearances of Carl singing "God Only Knows" and of Dennis pounding the drums while belting out "Do You Wanna Dance." They both still got it.

While our concerts put an emphasis on the hits, we try to promote all parts of the catalog. In 2015, the Beach Boys performed "Surf's Up" on video with the Fendertones—and YouTube now has this gorgeous version of Brian's masterpiece.

I turned seventy-five in 2016, and over the past fifty-five years, I have performed in more than 5,600 concerts in twenty-six countries. I poke fun at my grandpa image. During concerts, I ask audience members to wave the flashlight on their smartphone for "Surfer Girl," but a roadie has to come onstage to turn mine on. Who can keep up?

But I'm doing my best. In the late 1990s, I was all too often experiencing congestion, so I eliminated my beloved coffee ice cream and my Tillamook sharp cheddar cheese, which I've enjoyed all my life.

Since becoming almost vegan, my vocal capacity has improved immensely.

Nonetheless, I am often asked, "Why do you keep doing it?" Or as one person said, "How many more times can you sing 'Little Deuce Coupe'?"

Fair questions, but the only times I've ever given serious thought to quitting were when I've been frustrated by people in the business. The music itself never gets old. From our earliest days, it had variety in moods, tempos, instrumentation, subject matter, and melodies, and the rotating leads added a pleasing but unpredictable variance and texture. The music is now part of our country's DNA—heard in airports and bowling alleys, supermarkets and restaurants, dental offices and health clubs, and of course on the radio—and if anything, I'm more in awe of it now than ever. In 2015, we performed in San Diego and were joined onstage by a sweet ninety-year-old lady who told us she was having the best time of her life. She was followed onstage by a nine-year-old girl who was wearing Beach Boys attire from head to toe. I asked her what her favorite song was.

"Four-oh-nine!" she exclaimed.

Wow! That's the B side of a 1962 single, and kids still enjoy it. Sometimes four generations of the same family will attend our shows. Older fans sometimes approach the stage with tears in their eyes, and they explain that the music has rekindled memories of a loved one who's no longer with us. Our music reaches people in ways we never imagined—our fans who have autism, for example. Something about our harmonies is soothing, and I see these fans at our concerts, seemingly in their own world but rocking back and forth to the beat. A doctor once wrote me that his autistic son constantly listened to our songs, and these recordings gave him a way of communicating to his parents. We've played at mental health hospitals and assisted living centers and rehab clinics, and the stories I've heard remind me that it's all been worth it. Years ago, a Vietnam vet told me that he listened to our music when he was in the Central Highlands, and he explained how much those songs meant to him in getting through the days and nights. He gave me his bronze bangle, and I wear it to this day.

The Beach Boys have survived every musical trend, from punk and disco to hip-hop and rave. We've lived through vinyl LPs and 45s, 8-tracks followed by cassettes and then CDs, and now downloads and streaming. I know that each generation of fans has very different tastes and sensibilities, and I can't even imagine how consumers will buy and listen to music in the future. But after all these decades, I'm convinced that the Beach Boys' appeal has no demographic boundaries, no technological limits, no expiration date. The world has never been without heartbreak or despair; never without war, terror, hunger, or loneliness. That being the case, I believe there will always be a need for a sonic oasis, or music that offers, however briefly, harmony in word, harmony in spirit.

My father was a survivor. After my mom died in 1979, my dad remarried in three or four months to a woman who was also recently widowed and someone he had known for years. Pat was actually a few years older than my dad. "You really screwed up," I told him. "You're supposed to marry someone twenty or thirty years younger, so she can drive you to your doctors' appointments."

They moved to the Portland area, where both Maureen and Stan lived, and little Brian and I would visit him and walk with him up to Starbucks for his hot chocolate. My dad and I both became better at expressing ourselves and in giving each other hugs. He told me stories that I had never heard before. When I was eight years old, we took a fishing trip on the Truckee River, and he couldn't find me and thought for sure I was lost or drowned. I had just wandered off, but he had lived with that moment of panic, of vulnerability, for the rest of his life, and sharing it with me was meaningful.

We'd invite my dad to visit us in Los Angeles, sometimes for his birthday, and take him to El Cholo, a Mexican restaurant on Western Avenue that was one of our favorites growing up. My dad loved to recount the story (forgotten by me) of our family going there around the time we were starting the Beach Boys.

The restaurant owner asked me, "What are you going to do with the rest of your life?"

"I'm starting a singing group," I said.

The owner roared with laughter. "I feel sorry for you!" he said. In other accounts by my dad, the owner said, "I feel sorry for your father!"

Either way, the owner was skeptical of my chances, but I'm glad to report that during our fiftieth anniversary tour, his family—three generations—came to one of our concerts.

I also called my dad more often from the road.

"Where you been, Mike?"

"Trying to make a living, Dad."

I know he regretted not spending more time with my kids back in the 1960s and '70s, and he even apologized to Frannie, but he got better over the years. Melinda and Teresa both became flight attendants, and they would visit with him on stopovers in Portland. He celebrated each Christmas with us at our family get-togethers in Incline Village, and he would join my other kids in Reno each August, when we'd celebrate little Brian's birthday. The Beach Boys would perform at Hot August Nights in Reno.

After Pat passed away and my dad could no longer take care of himself, we moved him to an assisted living facility in Solana Beach, California, near our place in Rancho Santa Fe. We wanted him to live with us, but he was too proud to give up his independence. It was 2013 when he became bedridden. No disease or trauma was going to kill him. He was too strong for that, too stubborn. His systems just began to shut down. In time, he could no longer talk. His eyes closed.

But he could still hear us, and we brought in a guitarist who played spiritual songs, and we lit candles and said prayers and told him that we loved him, and surrounded by family, he took his final breath. He lived a remarkable ninety-five years.

The greatest gift my parents gave me were our family Christmases, when music and food and goodwill triumphed over all. It's a gift that Jacquelyne and I try to give our children. In 2015, as in every year, the preparations began early, around Thanksgiving, when we set up Christmas villages in our interior koi pond at the base of our stairs. Outside, we hung big wreaths at the gate and posted a sign that said North Pole, pointing to the house. In the yard we had animated deer, a hot-air balloon with reindeer, and Santa on a zip line. Inside the house we draped illuminated garland on the staircases, set up a nativity scene in the great room, and brought in a fifteen-foot noble fir tree. Taking turns on the ladder, we decorated it with harps, violins, gold and burgundy ribbons, lights, and, to considerable applause, an angel on top.

We have some permanent fixtures. On our front door is the carved head of an elephant, to represent Ganesha, who stands vigil every day. In the great room stands a Lyon & Healy harp, just like the kind we had growing up, and it's heard whenever Maureen or any other harpist comes to visit. We also have the very same Steinway grand piano that stood in our living room on Mount Vernon and Fairway. My mom gave it to me, and we had it restored. If we bought a Hammond organ, then we'd have all the instruments of my childhood.

On Christmas Eve, we had about thirty-five people, including children, grandchildren, in-laws, and friends, and before dinner we stood in a circle and held hands. Each year we try to discuss the deeper meaning of the holiday. This year Jacquelyne asked the kids why we celebrated Christmas. They were ready for that one—to celebrate the birth of Jesus—but when she asked why the three wise men brought gifts to baby Jesus, they weren't as sure.

"Jesus was a gift himself," Jacquelyne said, "and during the course of his life, he gave selflessly and performed miracles for all whom he encountered . . . We celebrate the birth of baby Jesus because he brought to this world the promise that walking in lockstep with love and kindness is possible, and with that we know there are endless possibilities for all humanity. So hold on to what is in your heart and spread it where you may go . . . Let us say a prayer tonight and remember that love brings the promise of what that birth meant, to kingdom come, and for that we are eternally grateful."

We said a prayer and then sat down to a feast, prepared by Chef Joaquin and Jacquelyne, with family members contributing their signature dishes—our table included king crab legs, turkey, cranberry sauce, green beans, risotto, and stuffing (gluten free). We filled our champagne glasses and turned up the music and later danced in the kitchen, and those family members who were leaving that evening opened their gifts. Mike Jr. and his fiancée, Liz, handed Jacquelyne and me a red envelope. Inside was a sonogram. Jacquelyne roared and cried at the same time. It will be my fourth grandchild, a very special Love.

Jacquelyne and I woke up early on Christmas morning, before any of the children, so we could stuff twenty stockings. From our tour in Germany we brought back gingerbread cookies, and we put one in each stocking, along with a pair of pajamas, and hung them on the fireplace mantel.

Dawn soon broke, and from our kitchen I looked out the window and watched the first rays of light slanting across Lake Tahoe.

It was going to be a busy day and even busier year.

I'm still chasing the sun.

ACKNOWLEDGMENTS

My family had encouraged me for years to write a memoir and to finally tell my story. I found that prospect daunting but knew that if I was going to do it, I had to find the right team. I am blessed to have done just that.

Blue Rider Press has been an outstanding partner in every possible way. David Rosenthal offered wise and patient counsel to a first-time author. Brant Rumble's care for language and storytelling, as well as his love for music, ensured that this narrative hit all the right notes. Aileen Boyle and Linda Cowen also helped make *Good Vibrations* a reality. My agent, Todd Shuster, provided expert advice on how to navigate the publishing world and was a trusted friend throughout the process. John Koch was with me from the first step of this project, offering his insights and judgments to make sure that it all came together. Elliott Lott's knowledge of the history of the Beach Boys has few equals—he has lived most of it—and his contributions to this book were indispensable. I also want to thank John Stamos, whose unwavering friendship means so much to me and who generously gives his time to the Beach Boys' music, for graciously lending his voice to this book. My collaborator, Jim Hirsch, encouraged me to share my story in ways that I never have before, and I very much appreciate that he was with me on this journey.

This book would have never been written without the love, support, and understanding of Jacquelyne, and my story, and life, has been enriched beyond words by Melinda, Teresa, Summer, Hayleigh, Christian, Mike Jr., Brian, and Ambha. To my wife and children, I offer my deepest thanks and my enduring love.

I'm grateful as well to my sisters Maureen and Marjorie and to my brother Stan, who've always been there for me.

I am where I am today because of a lifetime of kindnesses from family, friends, spiritual mentors, colleagues, kindred spirits, and loyal fans. Dozens had a direct hand in the creation of this memoir. Hundreds more have made lasting contributions to my life. All deserve to be acknowledged, but the list would never be complete. So I will leave the stage now, with a prayer, a grateful bow, and a message from the heart.

Thank you, and God bless.

INDEX

CREDITS